THE GODDESS AND THE BELL CAPTAIN

A Tale of Murder and Injustice
The Biggest Mob Murder Cover-up by the State of Nevada in its History

FRANK LAPENA

ABOUT THE AUTHOR

Frank LaPena lives in Las Vegas with his wife Betty LaPena, his dog Samson, his cat Sheba (rest in peace), and his grandson Hunter Pearce. Frank has an incredible love for animals, and he has big plans in the future to help as many animals as possible in need that he can. Frank has teamed up with multiple animal foundations to donate various items to the animals, and also he has helped get forever homes to many homeless animals in Las Vegas shelters. You can find Frank working at the MOB Museum where he tells the incredible stories of his life to every person that enters the museum. Frank is a consistent fighter of adversity, and he has a big brave heart to show for it. Frank has worked over three years on this book, and he cannot wait to share the truth of the "Biggest Mob Murder Cover-Up by the State of Nevada in its History" with the world!

DEDICATION

TO THE LOVE OF MY LIFE, BETTY, THANK YOU SO
MUCH FOR ALWAYS BEING THERE FOR ME DURING
THE GOOD TIMES AND THE BAD TIMES!

I LOVE YOU TODAY, ALWAYS, AND FOREVER!

After seventeen beautiful years with my precious little angel Sheba by my side, I had to say goodbye. My precious angel went to heaven February 10, 2022. God blessed me for seventeen years, and even though I do know that she is in heaven, restored again to perfection, and being young, my heart is broken for this loss. Although my heart is broken beyond words, she was incredibly beautiful and gentle, as you can see in her picture, and knowing she is in heaven looking down on me puts my heart at ease. I know I will see my beautiful little angel, Sheba again one day. She is now playing with Hope, and Star who love her dearly along with protecting her, and I know she is waiting for me as the others are. I can't wait!

I love you, Sheba!

CONTENTS

ACKNOWLEDGMENTS

This story you are about to read has been a collaborative effort of myself and three other very special amazing women: Laurie Kassel, Linda Concetta Razziano and Zoe McGough. I knew Zoe before I met Laurie and Linda at the Mob Museum who volunteered there. These three beautiful lady friends of mine I love dearly. They are real friends who truly care about me and witnessed my depressions as I was at times reliving my nightmares all over again when I tried to block them out. I will say this, "You can leave the prison but after so many agonizing years of pain and suffering the prison does not leave you."

I've had people tell me I should write a book about my life that encompassed over 40 years of fighting the State of Nevada and how did I survive it, "Naw!" "I wouldn't know how or where to start." "Frank you're a living legend no one has ever done what you have accomplished in the legal system". "No! No, I'm not, according to the news media I'm a cold-blooded killer, who has fought the State every step of the way to prove them wrong."

I recall one day at work at The MOB Museum, Laurie asked me if I was going to vote for who I wanted to be president of the United States. I told Laurie, "I don't vote". She in a surprised tone of voice said, "Everybody votes." "I don't". She was unaware I could not vote being an ex-felon with a homicide conviction. Being very curious, she decided on her own to investigate me, though I did not let her know my last name. When she found out my last name, she became so scared of me she almost quit being a volunteer. So, one day she got up the nerve to come in and confront me. Her first words were, "I know who you are I read up about you." "It's all bull-shit lies" I responded. She believed me and I let her read some of my legal work that convinced her even more. "Frank your life story is amazing; you must tell it". It was then that Laurie decided to set the wheels in motion to help me get my story started. She then began to nickname me, "Spats" from the movie, Some Like It Hot, with her favorite Mob Guy, George Raft. L0L!

Laurie was determined that if there was anything, she could do to help me she would do so to the very best of her abilities. Laurie, in the beginning, became the strong voice in helping me   adjust to what I was about to endeavor. She started out as my "research workhorse" regarding how to make the Goddess and the Bell Captain become a hard or soft cover reality for me, her faith, strength, tenacity, and perseverance was instrumental in her quest to help me get me this book started.

Linda came on board at a later date and took over what was the most intricate assignment of all...that of making all the thoughts, ideas, points of view and expression present in the words of the story have comprehensive and cohesive meaning to those who may come to read my life story in the future. Linda worked tireless hours helping me to try and put this book to its conclusion but unfortunately, she suffered a terrible shoulder injury requiring surgery. My friend Zoe took over to help me finish my book. I'm blessed.

My wife, Betty "the love of my life" is the person who would be deserving of the credit for the receiving of any acknowledgments of this work as an energetic, intriguing, fascinating, compelling, entertaining human-interest story. Betty is a pillar of strength who has kept my head on straight for 14 years. This beautiful woman has stood her ground along side of me suffering what I suffered trying to keep our heads above water when I was being denied work (outside of law firms) until Oscar Goodman helped me attain work on April 15, 2016, at the Mob Museum. God blessed me when he brought Betty into my life. I love you!

For over four years I had family members at the Mob Museum come into my life: CEO Jonathan Ullman, Mark A., Ashley M., Geoff S, Felicia L, Bebe Andrews, Jodi B. Sara L. Jacob, Melissa, Alice, Stephanie, Celia, Linda S, Ronnie, Kevin, Lovie, Anton, Jenny, Liz, Kristen, Krystal, Demaris, Greg Lamb, James Allen, Tina, Deana, Dawn, Christi S, Christi T, Megan, Lisa Belair, and many more. I hope you find "The Goddess and the Bell Captain a very intriguing and compelling story as you read it now.

My grandson, Hunter Pearce, has been a huge help with this book. Thank you, Hunter, for all of your hard work getting the pictures together for my book, and for helping piece everything together for me! I love you!

Lastly, I would like to thank my granddaughter, Cassondra Keven. Thank you, Cassy, for all of your hard work with getting my book finished and self-published! I love you!

i

Zoe McGough

Laurie Kassel

Linda Concetta Razziano

Hunter Pearce

Cassondra Keven

INTRODUCTION

The year was 1974. The town...Las Vegas. Organized crime still dominated the Strip. Caesar's Palace, built in 1966 with a 10-million-dollar loan from the mob-linked Teamsters fund, was a huge hot spot. Mobsters ran the most happening casinos, from Irving "Ash" Resnick to Frank "Lefty" Rosenthal (and his enforcer, Tony "the Ant" Spilotro at the Stardust and the Hacienda).

The Mafia had found a river of money flowing through that parched desert valley and it kept it fed by selling the illusion of jackpots hiding behind the next bet. It was a place of wealth and glamour, but also of desperation, greed, and of violence. This Las Vegas of 1974 is perhaps the only fitting backdrop for a case as wild as Frank LaPena's.

To hear the State the State tell it, Frank is a contract killer, his crime the union of a sordid love triangle and a get rich quick scheme gone south. Frank, you see, was a handsome young bell captain at the Hacienda, out to make a fast buck. His girl, Rosalie was a beautiful cocktail waitress at Caesars. But Rosalie was two-timing Frank with a married man: Marvin Krause, a middle-aged slot manager at Caesars. In Rosalie's mind, Marvin was her "live one," but Frank her "true love." Marvin would shower Rosalie with cash and gifts, but there was a limit to his largesse: his wife, Hilda, had all the money. So, Frank and Rosalie hatched a plan. They would hire their pal Weakland to off Marvin's wife (and make it look like a robbery). With Hilda out of the picture, the Hilda fortune would pass through Marvin and straight to Rosalie-with Frank, her true love, waiting in the wings to share it.

At least, that's what the cops got Weakland to say, after he confessed to slitting Hilda's throat and after the prosecutors offered him a sweetheart deal that got him singing. Only one problem. Weakland didn't kill Hilda...but if Weakland didn't kill her, whodunit? (Jeremy Baron, Federal Public Defender for Frank LaPena).

What your about to read contains an unbelievable agonizing sequence of events that propelled me into an environment filled with injustice, deceit and corruption that defies description where the State and its governmental agents intentionally tried to execute me via the Gas Chamber for a heinous crime, they personally knew was committed by someone else, and it wasn't the guy who confessed to it. Here, I was about to undergo and learn a lesson on how the cruelest lies are often told in silence by criminals who wore badges and some judges without honor. This is my story as only I can tell it and expose its corruption.

Now, in my own words: THE GODDESS AND THE BELL CAPTAIN.

1

I CAN'T BELIEVE AND YOU WON'T BELIEVE THIS HAPPENED TO ME!

"So…how'd you do it? I couldn't do it man…how'd you do it?" You have no idea how much over the years I've gotten pretty sick and tired of being asked that question. Sometimes, when I think I wanna toy with the person asking me this, the first thing I'd say is "I didn't do it." That throws 'em off for a minute because they're asking me how I managed to endure the years of crap the State of Nevada justice system put me through. Then, if I feel their inquiry is sincere, I give them a Reader's Digest condensed version of the info, providing them an answer.

My name's Frank…Frank LaPena, some of you may know a little bit about me if you're familiar with some of the history of Sin City. Mine is a story you'd think was created by some author like Mario Puzo. Yeah…a tale originating here in Las Vegas and would be so perfect for Hollywood. The Shawshank Redemption has nothing on my incredible story.

It has all the drama and intrigue one would expect. A love triangle involving a beautiful, already married "goddess" of a woman (you'll catch that frame of reference later), her handsome (if you'll forgive my lack of modesty) love interest, and a Vegas Casino Executive. It's a first class who dunnit murder mystery, with tons of skullduggery by various perpetrators, law enforcement personnel and persons who are officers of the court(s).

It also reveals how the State of Nevada decided to cover up, or omit information and/or evidence which, if known at the time, could have resulted in a very different outcome for me, as I tried to navigate the seas of injustices into which I was tossed.

Like Puzo's novels, my story is based on fact too. Unlike Mr. Puzo's work, my story is based on the personal experiences that I gained as I lived a nightmare of injustice. I'm bringing the story to light in my own words, and it's about my desire to get the truth out, once and for all. It's about telling you of the ordeal I've gone through, and the years I know I'll never get back.

It's widely known, "What happens in Vegas, stays in Vegas." Well…not on my watch.

You're going to learn exactly what happened to me. I lived it…I survived it…and now I'm exposing it.

There have been many miscarriages of justice, but none as serious, as poignant, and outrageous as this one. I was the victim of the rankest form of malicious, selective prosecutorial misconduct in this State's history. I was framed for a contract murder the State of Nevada knew was actually committed by someone else. It's taken years, while doing my own research and conducting investigations, to learn that one of the major players in this tale of intrigue was associated with a number of figures involved in organized crime.

In 1974, I was arrested and charged with the contract murder of Hilda Krause, the wife of Caesars' Palace Casino executive, Marvin Krause. How I found myself in this situation was the culmination of a series of events in my earlier life history. Events I should (or might) have known (had I taken time to recognize the environment(s) I was operating in) would end up placing me in the atmosphere of Vegas casino / mob / murder / corruption and political intrigue existing in Las Vegas back in the 60's, 70's, and perhaps into the 80's.

A few people have written of my case in newspaper articles, and it's been referred to in a couple of books. However, none of them have been able to tell my story as I'm able to tell it because let's face it…I'm the guy who experienced it firsthand!

The more detailed story constitutes a tale of "Murder and Injustice…the biggest mob murder cover-up in Nevada history!" by the State itself. It's the costliest murder case (back in 1989, the figure surpassed 8 million dollars) participated in by both the Nevada State Courts and the Federal Courts. It featured the longest preliminary hearing in 1974, one of the longest murder trials in 1977, the longest evidentiary hearing in 1995 and to date the longest DNA evidentiary hearing from 2011 to 2017.

Sure, this could simply be a typical "who dunnit," but the world's full of run-of-the-mill murder mysteries. Most of them make for intriguing, entertaining reading…particularly the ones that are true, but a lot of them are fiction. During the course of your reading here, you will find yourself attempting to discover who committed the crime and you'll be taking a journey with me through a maze of corruption and deceit.

What happened to me was all too real and gives a black eye to a number of cops, prosecutors, and other officials in governing entities. My contention is that there were people involved in my case who knew I was not the perpetrator of this deed and worked to conceal the identity of the true killer(s).

The path which led me there was a unique one…I was at many times the guy who was in

4

an opportune place, at the opportune time. The incidental path crossings I had with some of the "who's who" of both Hollywood and Vegas in those early days is the stuff of fascinating storytelling. Going down memory lane has not been easy to do, but at the urging of Oscar Goodman, who told me - your story needs to be told, don't lose your history, explore it for what it was – you're a big part of Nevada history.

I've told you a little about the crime...now I want to tell you a little about me. Long before I ever met Rosalie Maxwell or experienced any of the events that would be part of my future, I had been a guy who during my childhood dealt with life challenges that helped build my character. I developed a very tough "never give up" attitude (inherited from my mother), and a strength and resilience that to this day remains unequaled by many, in my humble opinion. That along with my strong faith in the Lord saw me through the numerous ordeals that you're going to read about now!

I was born March 25, 1938, in Manhattan, New York, to Sicilian, Katherine Schillace and Joseph LaPena (probably an alien from another planet). Anyway, I was born 3 months premature, and had to be placed in an incubator, I fought to simply exist from the very start. At 18 months, my belly button burst open (I don't remember the details). I was later told the quick actions of my grandmother saved my life at that time by rushing me to a hospital. At the age of 2 we moved to California where I was run over by a car when I ran out into the street and once again managed to survive. Now, you would think I had endured enough drama in my early life, right? Forgetaboutit!

I was just 3 years old when I was caught up in California's polio epidemic. I had infantile paralysis and not expected to live. Even though I was just a toddler, I can still see myself being put in a crib laying on my back looking at the ceiling. Doctors just gave me penicillin shots from what I remember…I was a pin cushion. Never will I forget hearing other kids crying, they were frightened, bewildered and scared to death and sad to say many did die. Such a horrific disease.

I eventually was placed in an iron lung for an extended long time which I believe was for about one and a half years. I couldn't move my body, so I developed "mind fights." Me, I was going to lick this paralysis. I was determined to walk again. During the early part of my treatment, the doctors told my mother that it was unlikely that I would ever walk, and another believed I wouldn't live since this disease was deadly. My mother sternly said to them, "You don't know my son. He will walk again, he's a fighter, never quits."

Arguing with these doctors over my treatment caused my mother to become disgusted by the doctors' inability to deal with my polio over time. She decided to do something about it and somehow contacted the Sister Kenny Clinic which I believe was in El Monte, CA.

Sister Kenny was a noted Australian nurse who came to the U.S in 1940. (Note: The designation "Sister" is not a religious affiliated term. In commonwealth nations like Australia, the designation is given to "senior qualified nurses." Sister Kenny had developed a "non-conventional" treatment that was initially met with skepticism by the medical community. Her findings ran counter to conventional medical wisdom - they demonstrated the need to exercise muscles affected by polio instead of immobilizing them. Sister Kenny's principles of muscle rehabilitation became the foundation of physical therapy or physiotherapy. Some of her noted patients included singer Dinah Shore and actors Alan Alda and Martin Sheen.

Without a doubt, Sister Kenny was the foremost authority on proper treatment for polio as I was personally to learn. Her success was far greater than any practicing doctor in the entire United States. It was at this clinic I remember the first year that I was able to move my toe. My mother had come to see me, and I was excited to tell her! I was about 5 years old when this happened.

I remained quiet each time I was undergoing treatments, but I was very concerned inwardly as to what was happening to my body. The one thing that stays in my mind is the treatment that she gave instead of the regular shot in the ass of penicillin by my prior doctors. You know, I can still see and visualize it today. With sister Kenny's treatments, they would come to my "crib" room with a roller tub with steaming hot water that had a wringer. They would dip the blankets into the water and then wring them out and then put plastic over my body and put the blanket on my body and let the heat seep in. Then they would exercise my hands and legs. I also remember being taken to a whirlpool where they would exercise me in the warm heat. As a result of that I became partial to warm weather. After years of undergoing the Sister Kenny treatments, I was able to walk again. At the time I didn't know where I got the strength, but it was there, nonetheless. As I got older, I came to realize it was the Lord who was in control. Breathe deep, take ahold of everything that comes your way, don't look over the horizon, that's the Lord's business. And I've done that all my life. Like I said before I was not expected to live, but God had other plans in store for me as you will later learn.

Unfortunately, once I was released from the Sister Kenny Clinic and brought home, I experienced a horrible home life. For reasons I didn't know why, my father became a mean alcoholic and violent person and put my mother, my sister and myself through a series of domestic violence incidents that involved beatings. One of these beatings broke my mother's jaw which landed me back in the hospital for trying to protect my mother, as if I needed that. Yeah, during one of his drunken episodes, that POS actually poured whiskey down my throat forcing me to drink with him. That coward never attempted to hurt my mom when my grandfather Marchello Schillaci was alive. My grandpa who in Sicily was a member of the Black Hand Society had threatened that POS before he married my mother, telling him if he ever hurt his daughter, he would kill my dad mafia style. My mother had a picture of grandpa on his horse and wearing his Black Hand uniform and Blume hat. Anyway, when I was about 14 and my sister was 7, my dad (the alien) POS just decided to take off without notice and left us. Hooray! Good riddance!

I was raised in my early years in Garfield, New Jersey, known as the "hood" and Guinea Heights with street gangs. When you lived in the hood amongst street gangs, you better learn to be tough, which I was. I never became a part of the street gangs nor did they ever bother me, as they knew me as one who would never back down.

One day I was approached by a Wise Guy named (Babe) who owned I believe Kulike's Bowling Alley. Babe knew me from the neighborhood and said to me, "Hey kid, we know your old man split and left you and your family, so you need to make a living for your family. I'm gonna get you a work permit and you're gonna work for me. I'm gonna teach you how to set up pins in my bowling alley and learn how to pump gas at my gas station." This encounter was known as the Mob Code which is to take care of your neighborhood. My whole area was mob infested. We lived in a place known as the "Bookie Joint" run by a crime family downstairs from our apartment. The front was a bar-restaurant, and the back was the bookie joint. I worked evenings at the bowling alley. Babe always made sure I was fed at work and told me I was to bring my homework and finish it after work and he wanted good school grades from me.

I can still see it today when Babe gave me my first paycheck that was not a real paycheck but a sealed envelope. Babe held it in front of me and said, "Kid (he always called me kid), this is your first week's earnings, and you are going to take this envelope and give it to you mother and I better not find out she didn't get it. You capisce?" "Yes sir, I understand." During all my years with Babe, I never opened those envelopes. I just gave them to my mom, and I have no idea how much was in them. Had I opened the envelope I would have disrespected Babe's trust in me.

When Mom found out I was going to work for the wise guys in their legitimate businesses she firmly told me, "Never get curious and ask them about their business, keep to

7

yourself and learn, you understand and show lots of respect you're going to get a great education being around them." If they want to tell you something, just listen, you capisce?" Look Mom, "I'm street wise, I know when and how to keep my mouth shut and see nothing, know nothing, mind my own business, don't worry Ok".

I believe Babe took a special liking to me for several reasons. I didn't talk like a street thug even though I was street smart. He knew I didn't belong to a street gang. Burglaries, robberies muggings were not my thing and he knew my mother's side of her family was connected in Sicily. Furthermore, it was no secret the Mob knew about my Polio challenges as it was written many times in the sports section of the newspapers and, the Mob guys I believe respected my toughness in playing sports that was very hard on me physically. Yeah! As I look upon it today no question Babe became my mentor and treated me like his son.

I'm doing okay...the kid who'd never walk again, now, besides working, is also playing football, basketball, baseball and running track. Started playing football in the 7th grade P.A.L (Police Athletic League). By the 8th grade, we were 18 and O. I had scored 42 touchdowns. In my 1st year of high school, I made the varsity football team as a quarterback and punter. God gave me a gift. I could punt a football 60 yards in the air and could out punt most NFL punters. I was fast as lighting and nobody could catch me from behind especially in the open field. I had dreams of possibly playing in the college and pro levels as most guys do at one time or another. But I still suffered from the aftereffects of my polio with muscle spasms in my body. The pain I was feeling from my head to my toe was absolutely excruciating, but I kept saying through it all, "So what!" I had made up my mind that there was nothing that was going to stop me from playing football!

As I grew older, my education with Babe became more serious as he provided me with some of his life knowledge and experience. He took me aside one day and set me down and advised me, "Kid, I'm going to give you some advice about life experience so heed my words. Don't ever tell anyone what you have done or plan to do. Keep your mouth shut that way no one will ever know anything about you and never let anyone know what's in your head or what you are thinking, and don't ever use a name that could get you killed. Most importantly, you're just seventeen years old now, when you get older, don't commit the ultimate sin, never ever mess with another guy's wife, mistress, girlfriend, or daughter… That will get you killed! You got that?" I responded, "Yes I do Babe, thank you." We will learn more about Babe later.

During these growing up years I also did a little amateur boxing and martial arts. Then one day it just came upon me I needed to have a serious talk with both my mother and Babe that I wanted to join the military. They both supported my wish. I have always been a patriot and decided to serve my country. I served in the Infantry at Ft. Benning, Georgia. I was 20 years old when I got out of the Army with an Honorable Discharge and went home to reconnect with my family. Not much was going on in New Jersey, so I decided to visit my father's brother, Nino, who was in Miami, Florida, and my life took on a new direction.

2

NEW ADVENTURES-FAMILY TIES
MY FIRST TIME

When I arrived in Miami, I went to a place called the Thunderbird Hotel. Prior to arriving there I had been told by my mother that my Uncle "Nino" had a dance studio which he operated with a partner. Nino was a professional dancer, and he taught a lot of movie stars and other notables. Some years prior, Nino and a guy named Steven Peck were a nightclub act in Havana, Cuba, called, "A Night in Havana".

Now, Steven Peck (who is Italian), later went on to have an acting career and played the bad guy in Frank Sinatra's movie "Some Came Running" where he kills Shirley MacLaine. He also played Sylvester Stallone's father in "Rhinestone Cowboy" with Dolly Parton.

So anyway, I walk into the lobby and I said to the front desk clerk, "I'm looking for my Uncle Nino." Before I said his last name, the clerk says, "Your uncle is upstairs where he has his studio." I asked the clerk if it was okay if I could go up to see him, because I wanted to surprise him and myself because I did not remember what he looked like.

The clerk said, "He's teaching a class right now with his partner, Laurie." So, I grab a seat in the lobby for a while, figuring that I'll be able to see Nino after a few minutes. Then I hear this woman as she is walking down the stairs say, "Oh, Nino that was just wonderful!" Then, she trips down the bottom of the stairs! I rushed over to aid her as did Nino. She was okay. Then the clerk called out to Nino, "Hey, Nino, that young man beside you helping that woman, is your nephew."

Well...there we were staring at each other, and I'm guessing that Nino's is so surprised it took him a minute to adjust his thinking, then he said "Frank?" "Yeah, that's me." By the way Nino's first name is Frank. As I looked closer at Nino, I realized he was the "living spitting image" of the legendary movie star "Rudolph Valentino." No wonder I later learned women went head over heels crazy for him in the day, and not much had changed with his impact on the ladies at the dance studio and beyond it.

Anyway, after his initial shock he grabs me as tight as he can, because the last time he saw me, I was fighting for my life from the Polio trauma. Now, to me the funny part comes when he looks me over and says, "Okay we'll go to my barber we have to do something with your hairstyle, and your clothes need a new makeover and your eastern accent needs working on. My partner Laurie used to be a school teacher; she'll help you. Is that okay with you?" What? Wait a minute, I just got here, he and I have not laid eyes on one another in years, and the first thing Nino wants to do is give me some sort of complete makeover? What the hell? How about maybe a "How the hell are you Frank? How's the family, what are you doing in Miami?" I gotta admit, I was looking for something like that. The only thing he later asked me to do was to drop the "Uncle", and just call him Nino. Sounds reasonable, so I followed that request from that point on. Now don't laugh, I suddenly became his younger brother. That cracked me up, especially with the ladies. Sounds reasonable, don't you think?

Aww! now I meet his partner Laurie for the first time. Saying a simple "wow" is an understatement. She is breathtaking, tall (Nino loved tall women), with long brunette hair, long legs, great figure, absolutely beautiful, and had a smile that would melt your heart! I missed nothing guys (Hmm! wonder if I take after my uncle?) So now my education was to begin, and what an education it was.

Laurie spent lots of time with me teaching me proper etiquette, improved speaking skills (pronunciation etc.), the use of utensils (I mean, I knew how to use a knife and fork...c'mon), and most important, being a proper gentleman, especially around women! I had noticed Nino always showed respect to women. My mother had taught me a lot about that last subject when I was a youngster, but the refresher course didn't hurt as I was putty in her hands and loved it.

This "crash course" in becoming a "proper gentleman" brought back a nice memory that proved to be quite an experience for me. It was during the time I was working at Kulik's Bowling Alley for wise guy Babe and growing into a young man. Babe and I were having a conversation one day, and he rather unexpectedly and bluntly asked me if I had a girlfriend that I had become intimate with.

When I said, "No," he laughed and said, "Kid it's time for you to reach your manhood." I was about 17 at the time. Being a street kid, I kind of knew where he was going with this, so I wasn't surprised to learn the wise guys operated a prostitution house. Like mom told me, just listen and you will learn a great deal.

Anyway...Babe took me to this "house." He without question had a big "presence" if you know what I mean and introduced me to the madam of the establishment. He explicitly

11

told her to have one of the girls "go easy on me." Was I nervous? You're damn right! Was I excited...what do you think? If my memory serves me right, I believe her name was Carol.

Well...Carol looked me up and down, then decided to take me under her wing. She asked Babe if he wanted to wait and if not, she would have one of the girls bring me back to his place. Babe left, and soon I'm all alone with Carol. She sat me down and talked to me for a while. As best as I can remember she was a very attractive woman, elegant, classy, terrific body and yes...she gave me quite an education.

Carol really taught me "what a woman wants with a partner, how to please a woman, and that a woman's body is beautiful and is to be treasured!" Wow...I guarantee you...it turned out to be an incredible "rite of passage" for me, as Carol was quite the teacher. I must admit...I loved it, what 17-year-old guy wouldn't?

After several sessions with that magnificent woman, I was confident, ready and eager to apply my "newly acquired skills in the art of lovemaking" on a number of women that I had my eye on. I don't mind telling you that I was made aware that they were rather surprised and pleased regarding my educational experience. I will say this, I'll always be indebted to Carol, and the lovely Laurie. The former "transitioned me from a boy to a man...the latter then turned the man into a gentleman!"

Now...where was I? Oh yeah...Nino got me a job as a bellman at the Carillon Hotel in Miami Beach. But some of my best moments were when I would watch Nino and Laurie give a sold-out performance of Afro-Cuban/Latin dances to the music of Tito Puente and his Orchestra. Their performances were incredible.

My Miami stay didn't last very long, about a year and a half. Nino and I went back East. Me to New Jersey to spend time with mom and sis and Nino to New York. Before he left Miami, Nino had three successful dance studios in the Thunderbird, the Lido and Momarte. He gave all three to Laurie when he left. Nino later on suddenly showed up at mom's place and asked me if I would like to go to Hollywood with him. Hey! why not, sounds reasonable so off we went to Hollywood, California.

3

<u>HOLLYWOOD</u>

Hollywood, we have arrived. Yep! fantasy land, studio moguls, millionaires, high society, the rich and famous. "Alright Everyone, Quiet on the Set" ""Lights, Camera's Roll'em Action," "Cut," "That's A Wrap."

I got lucky when we settled down in Hollywood and I got a job as a parking attendant working for System Auto Parks at the Doheny Towers in Beverly Hills, for a $1.25 an hour, but believe me...the tips were fantastic.

Over the course of that experience, I met a ton of famous names, actors John Ireland, Brian Keith, comedian Red Buttons, creator of Woody Woodpecker, Walter Lantz (and his wife who used to cook for me when I got off work) and many more. I was making good money and pretty satisfied with my life at this point.

After a period of time, Nino and one of his friends became Hollywood agents. I'm not really sure how that actually happened, and I didn't ask for details. I just started hanging out with him, his friends and clients when I had time, and things got pretty good for me. I eventually left the Doheny Towers and opened up my own parking concession at the Yankee Peddler Inn in Toluca Lake.

My star path crossings saw a significant increase in occurrences as I ran into such luminaries as Fred Astaire, Gene Kelly, Suzanne Pleshette, Don Knotts, Andy Griffith and Clint Eastwood (who at the time drove a nice-looking white Jaguar). Actor Jack Elan was a guy I met who always played bad guys in films but was a huge sweetheart of a guy when you interacted with him.

Mary Tyler Moore and her husband, Grant Tinker, would pull up to the Yankee Peddler in their gold speckled Cadillac when they decided to enjoy a meal there. Both of them were so very nice and pleasant whenever I would see them.

Speaking of celebrities and their favorite dining haunts, Robert Stack and Paul Picerne of "Untouchables" fame could often be seen catching a bite at Lucy's. Both of these guys were real gentlemen when I would do the parking of Stack's car.

New Year's Eve, 1960, a phone message from Nino said, "Let's get together…." I called him at 11:30 p.m., and his answering service said, "He's on Harold Way in Hollywood Hills." I hopped into my 53TD MG Roadster (yeah, I'm a boss!) and headed up this mountain road where I came upon a humongous house. Biggest house I'd ever seen. There were limos, Mercedes, Rolls Royces parked everywhere, but I didn't see my uncle's car! I drove back down the hill and called the answering service again.

Answering service said, "I forgot to tell you, he went in his partner's car." Back up the hill I went. As I approached, I heard a band playing and the sounds of people having a good time. I walked down a huge hallway with red velvet cove red walls and unbelievably rich looking carpeting. This place was definitely plush! I was ready to join this party for sure. All of a sudden, I was stunned to see Troy Donahue dancing with a guy, Tab Hunter dancing with a guy, and Rock Hudson, dancing with a guy too! Holy S***! What the hell did I walk into?

Then, from behind me, I got a tap on my shoulder. I turned around and a guy said, "Hi, I'm Lee (as in Liberace) what's your name?" Right away I heard my uncle's voice say, "Lee, this is my nephew, Frank, and he is straight. The place was full of starlets too-Mari Blanchard was among the group of women hanging around Liberace most of the night. He was definitely a favorite among male and female alike.

While I did see a number of straight people there, it was the sight of seeing all of these reputedly tough guys dancing as gay couples that knocking me for a loop to say the least. Later I learned from Nino, that when columnist Louella Parsons learned that Rock Hudson was gay, the studios wanted to cover it up because it would hurt his career.

They made a deal with her giving her exclusive access to one of their hottest rising stars to write about. A real good-looking guy named Rory Calhoun. All was until later on it was revealed that as a young kid, Rory had been arrested for some sort of indiscretion. Bam…so ended his leading man grooming, and he was relegated. to starring in "B" movies. He had a good comeback and is pretty much remembered as a cowboy. Rory was smart. He had a news article published about his crimes which actually helped his career (ladies who like bad boys).

A couple of weeks after the New Year's bash, I was introduced by Liberace to a real beauty. British actress, Diana Dors. She had been referred to as the British Marilyn Monroe by the press in those days. She and I did hit it off, and I dated her for a brief time.

Back when I was working at Doheny Towers, I remember a resident by the name of Mr. Armstrong who was a big-time agent. He said I had the looks to become a movie star. He could "…guarantee me a 5-year contract with Warner Bros." I turned it down because it just wasn't my thing being around them. I later turned down a big-time modeling job from the William Morris Agency in Beverly Hills, California, again because it wasn't my thing.

One afternoon, I was taking it easy as it was my day off, and Nino came over to me. "What are you doing Frank?", he asked. "I have a day off," I told him. "Can you do me a favor?", he asked. I said, "What kind of favor?" He said, "Look, I got this old broad, I call her Diamond Lil, and I need to introduce you to her." I said, "What for?" He said, "Well, she is taking care of me?" What...so now I'm learning that my uncle is some sort of gigolo. I was really curious, so I asked him, "Why do you want me to go with you?" He said, "I told her I raised you as a kid, and I'm sending you to UCLA to be a doctor." I was stunned and said to him, "Are you kidding me-how old is she?" He said, "80." I said to him again, "You got to be kidding me, and I'm going to school to be a doctor?" She'll be asking me all kinds of medical questions that I won't be able to answer." "Don't worry," Nino said, "I'll distract her if she does."

His story got even more ridiculous. He told her that he found me on a doorstep and raised me and educated me. Unbelievable! Who in their right mind would believe that? What's even more unbelievable at this point is that I actually went with him to meet her. We got to her mansion in Santa Monica. We pulled up and he rang the doorbell. When she was opening the door, I almost lost it. There was this woman, cigarette dangling from her lower lip, wearing a leg cast with a bell on her foot! She greeted us with "Oh Nino, how are you? Oh, is this your son?"

I tried to keep a straight face, but I was laughing so hard on the inside. We're in her place and she asked if I wanted a drink. She had white label scotch, and I learned that this woman could drink. "What college are you going to," she asked me. I remembered that Nino told her UCLA, and just at the same time that I said "UCLA," I heard Nino say, "USC." I looked at him in disbelief, and he tried to clean it up by saying, "I'm always changing colleges on him!"

We decided to go out and get some drinks at the Outrigger, a Hawaiian place. We were seated and a nice young lady came over and asked what we'd like to drink. I ordered a drink (I don't remember what), but apparently the waitress didn't think that was the drink to have. She said to me, "Why don't you have a Hawaiian drink?" I asked, "What is that?" She said, "Order a Mai Tai." Fine...so we ordered a Mai Tai. When it came, Lil proceeded to sling down that thing like it was scotch and immediately ordered another one.

With Nino and me still on our first drink, Lil slammed down her second, and ordered her third right away! The waitress at this point reminded her that the limit was three and you're supposed to drink them a bit slower. Lil paid no attention to the suggestion and threw down drink number three in a heartbeat.

I guess Lil's behavior may have caused our waitress some concern, and if by any chance there was going to be a need to impose the restaurant's three drink limit rule, she wanted to be careful regarding whom she might be dealing with.

She returned to our table and asked us, "Are you in the mafia?" I said, "Now, why would you ask that? She responded, "You look like someone in the mafia." I guess that made sense because I had to admit that appearing as I did, dressed in a pin-striped suit and wearing a mob looking hat, I may have certainly given that impression. I said, "No, I am not." That was that.

I learned later that our waitress was Leticia, an extra on the TV show, "Adventures in Paradise." Lil got up to go to the bathroom and lost her balance (big surprise!) and fell. In spite of her declarations that she was fine, everyone was concerned for her because of her age. I told Nino, "You go back with her, I have action here."

Leticia and I dated for a while, and the whole time we saw one another, no matter how many times I told her no, she continued to believe that I was in the mafia. I don't remember exactly how long we dated, and I don't remember what happed at the end. Too bad, she was a very beautiful young woman.

What's really crazy here is that I can't tell you the rest of the Diamond Lil story because I don't know what happened to Nino and Lil the rest of that night. He and I never touched based regarding it, and I imagine that their relationship went on for some time beyond that evening.

I went into a partnership with a buddy of mine, Danny LaMere and opened up a parking concession business. We had about 20 of them, and I used to handle the scheduling of all the guys working for us. One of the concessions was located at Pucci's Restaurant in the valley. Big Ed Pucci was Frank Sinatra's bodyguard. A 350-pound giant of a man who was connected with the wise guys. One of the stars that I met at Pucci's was the Duke, John Wayne. I don't recall much of that meeting, but, c'mon, it was the Duke! You might not remember what may have been said, but you'd never forget being in his presence.

Anyway, one day Ed said to me, "Frank, why don't you audition for a movie? It's called, "Come Blow Your Horn." "I don't do things like that," I said to him. "I'm not a trained actor." He said, "You're perfect for it. Take it." I again said, "No." "You're Sicilian" he said (he's just not giving up). One last time I said, "No, I'm happy doing what I'm doing."

We were going' back and forth on this for a good while when thankfully I guess Ed finally took no for an answer. I was very glad he did because I don't know why he was so insistent that I try out for that role, and how much longer I would've been able to try to convince him that I wanted no part in the movie business. Just for the record, actor Tony Bill ended up in the role of Sinatra's younger brother in the movie.

So, Nino informed me that he had to go out of town for a bit, and he wanted me to look after his apartment while he was gone. I said, "Okay." I got to his place, and the first day I moved in, there was a knock on the door. I opened the door and there were detectives standing there, and they wanted to know if I could do them a favor. "Like what?" I asked them. They told me that they wanted to use the balcony to set up a stake out on a guy that committed a robbery. I told them, "I'm getting ready to go to work." They asked if they could come in. "Yeah," I said.

So, these guys were in there and I told them, "I think you have to go, because I have to go to work and can't leave you here." Just then, one of the cops said, "Oh look what I found. I found some seeds." "Seeds?" I said. He said, "Marijuana seeds" and they arrested me right then and there. Seconds later, they went to the balcony and jumped, and arrested that guy too. What the hell just happened?

I can't remember how long I was in there, but Nino found me and bailed me out. I was so mad that I couldn't see straight. I asked Nino if he knew the guy the cops were after, and he said, "Yeah, I knew him." "Well, you got me in a fine mess here," I said to him. He replied with, "I got a great attorney." Right then that was not making me feel confident one bit.

At the first hearing, the prosecutor came in with guns, clothes and jewelry and placed them on the evidence table. I saw all of this and I thought holy shit! My defense attorney said, "Don't worry, I'm getting it thrown out." "How?" I asked. He said, "It's illegal search and seizure because they had no probable cause that you did anything, and they used you to get to the other guy!"

The judge saw it the way my attorney did, and after administering a real reaming out to the cops, he threw out the case. That was the end of my infatuation with Hollywood if I were to ever consider that I had one.

I have to tell you about an incident that occurred in 1962 that made me (once again) feel that I shouldn't be alive today. You'd think that battling polio as a kid would've been the biggest battle one should face in life. Well, one day Danny and I had met with the owners of the Four Trees restaurant on Sunset Blvd. in Hollywood.

While crossing the street, coming out of that meeting, I was hit and run over by some kid driving a pickup truck. I remembered nothing other than waking up in a hospital after having had brain surgery. I was later to learn that when a neurosurgeon was not available to perform the operation, a Greek intern by the name of Siropopolous (I hope that is the correct spelling), was the guy who stepped in when told that it was crucial to get the swelling of my brain to subside. By the grace of God, and the wonderful medical skill of this intern, my life was saved.

I suffered a loss of memory for a time after that and didn't recognize Nino and Danny when they'd visit. Then (as luck would have it…big shock), I got involved with a shyster, ambulance chasing lawyer who (of course) was diligently working on my behalf to secure compensation for my injuries from the driver's insurance company. Yeah, right. I don't know how this guy came to handle my case as I don't recall signing a contract with him. However, I will tell you that this sleaze bag attorney ended up with nearly all of the insurance money from the case. Big surprise, huh?

4

<u>VEGAS</u>

I came to Vegas in 1964, at the age of twenty-six. Drove into town and checked in at the Flamingo Capri. Not to be confused with Bugsy Siegel's Flamingo Hotel and Casino. The Flamingo Capri was a smaller establishment just north of Bugsy's Flamingo. The Flamingo Capri was owned by Bill Capri and George E. Goldberg. Capri had been an employee of Bugsy's Flamingo before opening his hotel with Goldberg.

During check in, I asked the bellman if there was any work, seeing as how I'd been a bell man in Florida and had experience. He told me to go to the culinary union and sign up. I drove over, signed up and registered, but there was nothing immediately available. The guy I signed up with said, "If you want to work, go upstairs and you can work as a bar back. They need people all the time"

I went up and was told, "Yeah, you can work tonight at the Dunes Hotel in the gold room." "What time?" I asked. "Twelve hundred" was the answer I got. I went to the Dunes and met the bartender and got everything set up. "So, what's going on tonight?" He told me, "It's a private party for Claudine Longet. It's a party." Wow... I found myself in my mid-twenties, working at a party for Claudine Longet, with all the Vegas showgirls in town coming in, only a few feet from me. I was in heaven!

As the evening shows ended on the strip, the partiers started dropping in. Back then most of the showgirls were foreigners. They were sitting at the bar and talking all sorts of different languages. I finally said, "Hey, doesn't anyone here speak English?" One girl answered, "I do." She was from Australia. Her name was Mavis Callier, and she asked me, "Would you like to play silly buggas with me"? I said, "What? I'll play anything with you." She said, "When you get off, we're going to the Guys and Dolls across the street." I told her, "Okay."

As soon as I got off, I headed across the street. Mavis' Australian accent was really sexy as she was explaining she was an adagio dancer at the Tropicana. She also told me she wasn't twenty-one yet...Whoa. I was looking for a place to live, and she told me about where she was staying over in Harmon Court. I went there and there were over 100 girls and 4 guys living there, so I ended up moving in with Mavis and two of her girlfriends.

Two weeks later, I landed a job at the El Cortez Hotel as a bell man. Mavis' visa ran out, and she informed me she was joining another dance troupe and was going to Trinidad. She wanted me to come with her there, and then move back to Australia with her. We were together for seven months and she treated me like a king. She'd gone to New Jersey and met my mother because I was bringing mom out to Vegas. She called me from some other country sometime later, and we talked for a while, but that was it. We drifted apart. She was an unbelievably beautiful, sweet and classy girl.

One of the pit bosses at the El Cortez was a Sicilian guy named Al Facinto. Everyone called him Mokie. Mokie and another guy named Joey Boston, a known bookmaker, decided they were going to leave the El Cortez, and work at Caesars Palace. Al came up to me and said, "If you want a bell man job at Caesars, just go up there, and I'll take care of it." I took him up on it and went to Caesars where I met a guy named John Segota.

After a brief interview I got hired as one of the original bell men to open Caesars. It was August 5, 1966. The very first opening weekend I worked there, I made $1800.

In 1966, my mother was living with me in a rented house, my sister was pregnant and moved to Vegas later, and had her little boy, my nephew Scott. The bell staff at Caesars back then consisted mostly of Italians, but also had a few Irishmen and one Black. I met Benny Caldero there and learned he'd been "juiced" into the job through his uncle. The "juice" in the scenario had come from New York crime boss, Gerardo "Jerry" Cantena, who'd made a phone call sealing the deal for Benny.

Prior to Caesars Palace opening day on August 5th, 1966, the Mob executives had all employees do practice runs to make sure all departments were on track in their performances before we officially opened up. Holy cow did I ever love it as I was in awe at all the beautiful, sexy cocktail servers doing their practice runs. Once we opened, I began to get acquainted with some of the lovely ladies.

Here's a bit of history on Caesars for those of you perhaps not familiar with it. In 1962, developer, hotelier, casino owner, Jay Sarno, got a 10.6-million-dollar loan from the Teamsters Central State Pension Fund. It was rumored certain underworld figures as Raymond Patriarca, Tony Accardo (aka Big Tuna), Sam Giancana, Jerry Cantena, Jimmy Vincent (aka Jimmy Blue Eyes, an associate of Meyer Lansky), all had a piece of Caesars. The casino credit manager at the time was Jerome Zarowitz (Mr. Z), he was the boss of bosses at Caesars. I used to pick up his clothes each day. He wanted his sleeves rolled, and he would leave me a sawbuck ($10.00) on the top of the clothes when I picked them up, then give me another one when I returned them to his suite.

In 1969, a Federal Organized Crime Task Force accused him of having ties to crime figures in New York and New England. Zarowitz had done time in 1947-48, but it hadn't hindered Caesars from getting a gaming license from the Nevada State Gaming Commission. Some other flare-up occurred about a meeting Zarowitz supposedly attended in Palm Springs with a guy named Ruby Lazarus regarding how the ownership of Caesars was to be divided. Lazarus went to jail for not disclosing the purpose of the meeting to the Feds, and that was the last of that incident. To my knowledge, nothing was ever discussed about Mr. Z's associations from that point.

I ran into a lot of stars while at Caesars, I remember Juliette Prowse, she starred in Sweet Charity there. What a classy doll! Omar Sharif, and Telly Savalas proved to be class acts and quite the tippers as well. I had picked both of them up at the airport, took them to their suites and both gave me a $100.00 tip.

I guess it was a good thing I didn't meet Andy Williams, because I remember a story about him from when he was the opening headliner for Caesars. As the story went, the guy did not like to tip. One day, one of our guys, Dominic Baldasaro, was asked to pick up Williams and escort him to his room. Dominic followed his instructions and spent three hours with the guy, from the airport, to the hotel, to his room, after which Mr. Williams gave him $1.00. Dominic came downstairs fuming! He was so pissed, he was going to complain to the union, but was told he'd probably make up the loss by taking care of some other people.

The next day, Williams came down and asked somebody to drive him around town. Another bell man was asked to get the company car and do the honors. Our guy spent hours driving this star around town, and you guessed it...for his labors, Andy gave that guy $1.00 too. That did it...every time we saw Williams coming, we all split and started hiding so the only guy left at the bell desk was the bell captain. We all let him deal with Mr. Williams.

A couple of days after Caesars opened, I remember the bell captain telling me to get the station wagon. I got the car, and out came Xavier Cugat, Charo, and Caesars' entertainment director. Charo sat next to me (looking stunning I might add), in a white mini dress. Cugat was next to her, and the director guy was in the back seat. I said, "So, where to?" and they told me, the County Courthouse. They got a marriage license and we headed back to Caesars where they became the first couple to be married in the newly opened casino.

In 1967, I was standing out front at the steps of Caesars when a stretch limo pulled up to the entrance. Two women emerged from the car, and me being the gentleman that I was, I extended my hand to the first one. She was young and beautiful, and I had the sense she might've been a bit of a snob. Then out stepped the second one…wow! This woman was stunning, elegant, and just oozed class. Without a doubt, she was high society. The woman looked me dead in the eye, and with a voice one would expect to hear from such a person of her class, she asked, "Could you please get our baggage from the trunk, and bring it inside?" "It would be my pleasure," I responded.

The young one walked off, headed inside the hotel, however the classy lady whose name I didn't know while attending to her, waited for me to get a bell man's cart, which I promptly did. Holy crap, you talk about expensive luggage. I'd never seen anything like it before. It was Velvet, with designs I never saw on any other pieces like that…and these bags were huge.

Anyway, she stood watching my every move, and while doing so, she asked my name. After I told her, she said nothing, and she and I entered the hotel lobby. Let me tell you, as we walked in, I saw all of the big bosses waiting to greet her like royalty…which is exactly what they did. There they were big smiles, warm hugs and handshakes were the order of the day for this lovely lady. I still didn't know her name at this point, but obviously she was somebody of note. Was she a Mob Queen…perhaps a wife or daughter of some high-ranking wise guy?

The Hotel Manager greeted her and handed her both of the keys to her suites, then called out to one of the other bell men to take her luggage. The lady was having none of that…she told the Manager, "Thank you, but Frank will take us to our rooms, if that's okay with you!"

I don't recall the exact words the Manager said, but he immediately handed me the keys, and off we went. I walked, thinking to myself, "I'll take the younger one to her suite first," and the lovely lady was thinking the same thing inasmuch as she said words to that effect. "Frank, we'll take (I don't remember the younger one's name, and it's just as well. She never uttered a word to me from the moment she got out of the car) to her room first, okay?" I was only too pleased to respond, "Sounds reasonable."

After taking the younger woman to her suite, the lady and I headed to hers which was much larger. They gave my mystery woman a suite obviously befitting her status in their realm. While placing her luggage on the baggage chair, she and I engaged in pleasant chit-chat. She wanted to know about me and what I did when I wasn't at work.

I told her I had a boat, and spent a lot of time on Lake Mead, waterskiing and just relaxing on my days off. When I was done checking her in, and I went back to the bell desk, I was a bit surprised to see the bosses still mingling around the lobby. A short time passed, and here came the lovely lady, she walked past the pit area, and headed directly toward the bosses…they were once more, just full of smiles.

Although I was standing off to the side, I couldn't help overhearing how there was a special party being planned in this lady's honor. Who is this woman? I was going nuts because nobody told me who she was, and believe me, they didn't treat everybody who came into the building the way they treated her!

During the conversation, one of the bosses told the lady they'd arranged an escort for her, a doctor of stature whose name I can't recall now. I was completely stunned when I heard the lady say, "Thank you for being so gracious in arranging that, but I'd prefer to have Frank escort me to my party." Holy shit! I nearly fell over.

I didn't know whether to run and hide, or smile, or what to do at that moment. Was I in big trouble or what? Mr. Z started to laugh, so did Mokie along with Ash Resnick. The lovely lady had just taken command of the whole situation, and they had simply bowed to her wishes…amazing.

By this time my curiosity had completely gotten the best of me. I couldn't believe all of this was happening to me regarding this mysterious woman who was receiving so much incredibly accommodating treatment. I just had to in a 'round-about way, find out who she really is. Now you've got to be asking, Frank, why didn't you ask the lady when you first engaged her early on, or why didn't you ask one of the bosses?

I don't have an answer for that. Maybe, I was intimidated by witnessing the initial interactions between the lady and the bosses, I really don't know. However, I was about to escort the lady to her party, so I was going to find out who the hell I was dealing with, and that was that! And get this, she wasn't registered as being in the hotel???

I somehow found the courage to ask my mysterious lady her name, and I was simply astonished at what I had heard. Her name was Virginia Hill…Virginia Hill? Yeah, you read it right. I was going to escort Ms. Virginia Hill to a bash being given in her honor. Was I in disbelief? You're damn right I was. Her name was indeed the same as Bugsy Siegel's famous girlfriend.

When she saw the look on my face, she very graciously put me at ease, making a point to let me know she wasn't who I assumed she was. She went on to say, "I'm not the real

Virginia Hill. She was my mother, and only certain people know who I am." My mind was reeling, and I was so pleased with myself to have exhibited the presence of mind to not start acting like a star struck idiot by asking her a ton of sensitive questions. I think back in the day, her mom wasn't in a position to be able to raise her, so she made sure her daughter was raised by a very affluent family. Virginia stated she was from San Francisco, CA.

Make no mistake about it…from the moment she stepped out of the limo the day she arrived, to the day she left, she was regarded as royalty. Well of course, after learning her identity, all of the things I'd seen made perfect sense.

In case you're curious as to how the gala evening went, who attended the affair, what happened and so on, I will only say this much. I was so honored to be Virginia's escort, and so aware I was totally out of my realm the entire evening, I came to the realization one thing is true. When in the presence of royalty, it's best to be quite reserved, speak only when spoken to, and seen only when required to be seen. Ms. Hill was one of the most gracious people I've ever had the pleasure to meet, and to me she will always be remembered as indeed, a very lovely lady.

A couple of the other famous folks I met were the incredible Ms. Eartha Kitt, and one of my childhood idols, the former heavyweight boxing champion of the world, Rocky Marciano. This was very special to me because I met Mr. Marciano many years earlier when I was a kid attending grammar school in New Jersey.

At that time, I was assigned to be a safety patrol person, helping kids and adults safely cross the street. I looked at one of the corners one day, and holy mackerel, guess who was standing on the corner waiting to cross the street: My idol himself, Rocky Marciano. I shot my hand out to shake his hand and was thrilled to death when he extended his hand to meet mine. Are you kidding me? His hands were huge, and you could feel the power in them even though his handshake was quite gentle.

Get this…in 1969 I checked both he and his wife Barbara in at the Sands Hotel and Casino. When I told him, I had met him when I was just a kid in either the 7th or 8th grade, he gave me a big smile and shook my hand once again. Tears filled my eyes when I heard he died in a plane crash in August that year. Meeting him was one of the highlights of my life.

I checked in Sonny and Cher, very quiet couple and really nice. Milton Berle, "Uncle Miltie…Mr. Television", a real potty mouth of a guy, good lord. There was the day I saw John Derek and Linda Evans in the elevator going to their room. Oh my God, talk about a beautiful couple. The famous people I ran into day after day were just amazing to me. Don Rickles,

Don Knotts, James Garner, represented another day at the office for me.

Man, Garner asked me one time if I knew a place where he could do some running. I told him I did a lot of running on a horse trail where the sandy ground wouldn't hurt your feet. Well, guess what…he and I, when I got off work, would go to the horse trail and we became pretty solid running partners. Garner was true class, very intelligent and we had some great times putting' in the miles.

Evel Knievel pulled up in his Bentley one day. I checked him in, along with his wife Linda and son Rob. He too was a really classy guy. I watched him on December 31, 1967 along with a cast of thousands, when he attempted to jump the fountains. That didn't end so well. He crashed and broke his pelvic bone. Years later, I watched Robbie Knievel perform the same jump his dad tried, and he succeeded.

Sad to say another of my star sightings that left me less than enthused was the time I saw Lucille Ball. She was having a pretty rough day as she was screaming a lot of profanities at her kids. Her hubby at that time, Gary Morton, came over to me and apologized, saying she's had a really bad day. He was super nice, and I told him, "It was fine, but it was sad to see her acting that way."

I picked up Paul Anka, at his residence at the Desert Inn Estates, and drove him to Caesars…very personable guy. Ms. Dionne Warwick was absolutely beautiful inside and out. We had some really nice times talking to each other.

Another guy with a terrific personality was Englebert Humperdinck. I didn't meet him at Caesars, but rather at the Riviera. We got along nicely, and I'd been invited to his home once.

I'm at work one day and Mr. Z came over to me and tells me, Frank, I want you to go to the Sands and pick up Sinatra. Frank Sinatra? "Yes, he's moving over here." Wow! That's a surprise, I never thought he would ever leave the Sands. "He had an incident over there. Now he belongs to us. Take the station wagon and go pick him up". "Yes sir."

I went to his suite and knocked on the door. When he opened the door, I said, "Mr. Sinatra I've come to get you and your wife's belongings." He said, "Come on in our things are over here." He was both pleasant and easygoing. He said, "What's your name?" and I said "Frank." I could tell he liked that from the look on his face. As I was grabbing belongings, he was looking at me and asked, "are you Persian Frank?" "No, I'm Sicilian; my family being from Sicily I have the same bloodline as you." Needless to say, he liked that. After gathering all their clothes and putting them in their luggage, we left for Caesars Palace. Let me tell you, the Frank Sinatra Suite was gigantic. I spent a lot of time putting everything away for him. You know, he was a helluva nice guy. He asked me where I was from and I told him I was born in New York but raised in New Jersey. That was the start of a good friendship as he took a liking to me.

Every now and then I would do errands for him and he took good care of me and one day he invites me to his home in Palm Springs. That was a real nice surprise. So, we set up a time and place where he would send a friend of his to pick me up. His friend's name was Tommy Tomatoes and was he ever funny. Sinatra gave him that nickname because he made the best pasta!

Over time I'd gotten some pretty nice gifts from a few famous people that I'd been able to form friendships. Liberace once gave me a cigarette lighter, all in diamonds, with a candelabra design. The cops stole that too.

When I first met Joanne White at Caesars, I didn't date her. She was dating Frank's bodyguard, Jilly Rizzo. She used to take care of the people Sinatra came into contact with, and she would give out the tips.

During my time at Caesars, I did meet and date a number of cocktail waitresses. One in particular was memorable. Her name was Barbara Melon, and she was absolutely stunning. I messed that one up really bad. I cheated on her with another cocktail waitress after dating her for a time. I was out of line as she was a beautiful person inside and out. I think I kind of broke her heart. She eventually ended up marrying one of the owners of Caesars.

Another that I had my eye on was a French breathtaking beauty named Danielle. She was so beautiful she intimidated me, so I never asked her out for a date even though she was always friendly with me when we talked and teased me with her sultry voice by calling me "Franciscus." Her French accent and sensuous lips made my knees buckle and she knew it. Danielle, I believe, was the first cocktail waitress at Caesars Palace to earn a million dollars. I believe she was a few years younger than I, yet classy and elegant. Never felt Danielle would actually go on a date with me as I definitely was not in her class. So, guys how do ya figure out a woman? Little did I know she liked me enough to say YES! You will later learn what a sap and idiot I became when she did say yes.

Then there was Rosalie Maxwell. Rosalie was a "Raven Haired Beauty" I had come to know very well who worked the pits at Caesars, and I assumed a friend of Danielle as they both worked the 21 tables and lounge. I didn't know Rosalie was ever interested in me beyond our co-working friendship, and for two years I was at Caesars from '66 to '68, we always would just hang out from time to time when our work schedules allowed it and, she had dated a guy I knew. Things between Rosalie and I would get much more intense later on but that would be a couple of years down the road as you will learn.

I left Caesars Palace in late 1968 and went back to California for a short time because (and I'll bet this'll throw ya), I wanted to study opera. That didn't last long at all. While I was studying opera though, I got a parking concession called the Villa Capri. It was owned by Sinatra and Patsy D'Amore.

5

BACK TO VEGAS BABY

The whole California thing wasn't really working for me, so I made it back to Vegas in '69 and got a job at the Sands as a bell man. Here's what happened during the application process. There was a question that asked, "Have you ever been arrested for a crime?" I answered no, not thinking of the case a few years earlier where the judge threw out my marijuana arrest due to the cops performing an illegal search and seizure. Anyway, by not revealing that incident, I was committing a misdemeanor under Nevada law!

I'm working at the Sands and I meet Danny Thomas. When I check him in, I learn that he was going to open at the Landmark Hotel. Steve Lawrence and Eydie Gorme were headlining here (Sands), and I was asked by the bell captain to take them to catch the opening of the Landmark. I'm backstage while they're onstage, and they were funny as s***!

We had a great conversation while driving over. I talked to them just like anybody. There are spotlights out front and Eydie says, "Will you come in with me?" She is Jewish, and Thomas is Armenian (his parents changed his name as a youth), and she didn't like him, and didn't want to stay. She wanted to make her presence known and then leave.

I walked in with her, made a brief appearance, and then took them back to the Sands. Steve says, "You wanna catch the show?" "Yeah, I wanna bring my mom and sister." Steve says, "Okay." My mother and sister love the show, and afterwards, Steve and my mom start talking in Italian back and forth. It was a great evening for her!

I met Sammy Davis, Jr., one time very briefly, when I check him in. A real gentleman. He gave me a $100 bill, and we couldn't have interacted more than a few minutes.

I checked in a couple one day, and they got robbed that night. I think the next day, I'm out doing something, and my mom gets a phone call from a detective. So, I make a call to the sheriff's department (the Las Vegas Metropolitan Police Department doesn't exist until 1973), and they ask to come out to see me.

Some rookie with a buzz cut comes out and asks if I mind if they search the house, and if I remembered checking in the couple. He goes on to tell me that the couple was burglarized. I don't remember the couple's names, and I ask, "What does it have to do with me?" The rookie sheriff got my name mixed up with Frank Cazari, a guy who had been busted years earlier for a burglary. "Are you Cazari?" he asks. "No, I'm LaPena."

He then had his partner run my name in police computer and found that I had a previous arrest. So, then he said to me, "You committed a crime by falsifying your work application." He arrested me. I bailed out and went into work the next day and was terminated from the Sands.

After I bailed out, I advised Al Bramlet, the Secretary Treasurer of the culinary union what had happened. He challenged it in the local court and won! As a result of my case, the State of Nevada established a new law requiring that changed the question on a work application to say, "Have you ever been *convicted* of a crime?" Al and I did it, and it felt good! However, it did not help me get reinstated at the Sands.

After that, I landed a job at the Bonanza Hotel, and that place was a dump, they closed down after a short while. In 1970, I headed up to Lake Tahoe where The King's Castle was opening. I was working there as a bellman, when one night Izzy Marian, who I had known from Caesars Palace in 1966, was with a wise guy from St. Louis, and Izzy asked me if I could drive him and his friends around the lake. "Sure," I said. I was working graveyard, so I got the car and drove them around the lake. When we got back, the wise guy handed me $500.00. The next day Izzy and his friend came by the bell desk and asked me, "Hey Frank, do you know of a good place where we could have a late dinner?" I said, "Yes, I know of a place where the food is excellent, and they have a band that plays popular music." Izzy asked, "Can you take us there Frank, and you're invited to eat with us and take off your bellman's uniform." After, I changed clothes, I got the casino station wagon, and I took them to a place across from the Cal-Neva. As we were all sitting down at a long dinner table and who walked in - Lana Turner, one of the most beautiful women in the world, with an escort, and sat in a nice booth.

The head wise guy saw her and was like "OMG...I've been in love with her since I was a kid." Izzy Marian said to him, "Why don't you go over there and talk to her?" The wise guy replied, "I wouldn't know what to say to her." Izzy turned to me and told me to go talk to her and so I walked over to Lana like I knew her, and said, "Hey Lana, it's me Frank, would you like to dance?" The wise guy was totally bewildered, and Izzy said to him, "Frank doesn't fear anything." While dancing with Lana, I knew that she liked wise guys because she used to date the mobster, Johnny Stompanato. I said to her, "There are a couple of wise guys over there who would like to have the honor of having you at their table." She agreed to join us and sat next to the wise guy, and he experienced the best night of his life. As for Lana's escort, I also invited him to join our table which he did.

Three, maybe four hours later when we got back to the hotel, he gave me a $3500.00 toke. (Note: a "toke" is sometimes how tips were referred to in those days. Don't want you to think the guy gave me a token). Turned out to be a really good night.

Remember when I told you I broke a girl's heart? Well, it was during the stint at Lake Tahoe that I went astray. I was up there and ran into Joanne White. I first met Joanne when I was working at Caesars. At that time, she was dating Frank Sinatra's bodyguard, Jilly Rizzo. She used to take care of the people Sinatra came into contact with. When I saw her at Lake Tahoe, she jumped all over me (I guessed she was no longer with Rizzo). When my girlfriend at the time, Barbara Melon learned about that encounter, it spelled the end for us. I started dating Joanne and discovered over time, she was a crazy woman.

Joanne wanted to visit her uncle in Boston for his birthday. When we did go to visit him, I had no idea at that time her uncle was the head of the New England MOB, Raymond Patriarca. When Joanne introduced me to him, he asked us, "Would you kids like to have breakfast with me?" I said, "Okay." When his crew arrived, I was a little surprised because they were four cars deep, thinking to myself that we were going to an Italian restaurant, instead we went to a nice looking Chinese restaurant.

Okay, so we're seated at this big, long table, and I learned I happened to be sitting next to the Chinese tongs. Whoa…time for me to be the quiet kid who knew when to keep his mouth shut. During the meal there were conversations going when suddenly there was a knock at the restaurant rear door. Some guys had delivered a truckload of lobster and delivered them to that location. The guys were paid off, and all of the lobsters were brought in. The meal then continued as if nothing happened. Are you kidding me?

I decided Joanne was nuts and I needed to get away from her. I went back to Vegas and got a job at the Hilton Hotel as a bellman. That's where I met the King himself…Elvis Presley and Priscilla Presley. While I didn't interact with Mrs. Presley that much, Elvis and I really hit it off. One of his bodyguards was a guy I knew named Red West.

Many folks didn't know Red's full name (Robert Gene West), and he was a close friend of Elvis' since high school. As such, he was a bona fide member of Elvis' inner circle, a group of folks who came to be known as the Memphis Mafia. The guy was well known in Hollywood as an actor/stuntman, and also was a songwriter of note.

Elvis, Red and I spent time talking about our mutual interests in the martial arts. At other times, Elvis and I would share our thoughts about our mothers, and our love and admiration of them. Then too, we'd talk about our deep faith in the Lord. While the public knew that Elvis was a man possessed of strong faith, the conversations I shared with him were so much more revealing of the intensity of his relationship with God. I felt most privileged to come to know those facets of the man.

I ran into other notables there of course…Ann-Margret, Raquel Welch, Diahann Carroll to name more of the beautiful stars that crossed my path on an average work day. I would see Liberace there, and Red Skelton would say hello now and then too.

Ike and Tina Turner were a very nice, laid back couple. I had the pleasure of seeing comedian Redd Foxx for the second time when I checked him in. I reminded Redd that I had been a guest of his at his home in Hollywood (or was it in the valley) one evening with Nino. Redd was quite the host then, and while at the Hilton he was again quite cordial to me.

6

GODDESS IN NAME ONLY

ROSALIE AND I

I'll clarify things a bit like this…the term goddess is what the cocktail waitresses were called at Caesars as a reference to the themed association with ancient Rome that the hotel presented to its patrons. Interestingly enough, I wonder (now) if the guys who worked there were ever referred to as gods…I don't think I ever heard it. I saw a few soldiers and gladiators here and there, and occasionally one would see the Emperor himself roaming about the place.

Anyway…I had gained somewhat of a reputation at Caesars for dating a few of the goddesses, if you know what I mean. At that time, depending on whom you'd ask, the goddesses at Caesars were considered to be some of the most beautiful women in Las Vegas. Now…again, you'd probably get the same opinion if you asked the question in all of the other hotels and casinos in the city. I mean, who's not going to say they're in the midst of the most gorgeous women if the question is put to them? You name a place…Aladdin, Flamingo, Sands, Hilton…no doubt about it, the town was overflowing with beautiful women.

They came to Vegas from not only all over the U.S., but all over the world. It was a tremendously advantageous asset to the hotel as guests would be served, pampered and entertained while enjoying the company of the gorgeous ladies of Caesars. I never dreamed there could be so many beautiful women in one place outside of Hollywood.

In my honest opinion, had some of the starlets of tinsel town found themselves spending time in Caesars on any given weekend, they would've had a tough time holding the attention of a gentleman in their exquisite company. They would've discovered themselves to be in quite an aesthetically competitive environment for sure.

I felt like a kid in a candy store….and the store was very well stocked. I never thought anyone would ever blame me for trying to live the life of a pseudo-Hugh Hefner…what a life, if I do say so myself. Captivating women like Barbara Mellon, and Joanne White (who I've mentioned earlier in the story) were joined by sirens like Geneva "Genie" Blue and so many more whose names I can't recall right now.

Rosalie Maxwell was one of the many alluring beauties who could be found among the halls of the palace. I'll give her credit, she held her own in the beauty department, and was every bit worthy of the title goddess, as were all the others. Unfortunately for me, that would be where any illusion to an ancient deity would end.

One particular evening, I found myself thinking about the lovely Danielle (yeah, I hadn't forgotten her from our time together at Caesars), and I decided to drive over to Caesars on my day off, around 10:00 P.M.…maybe it was 11:00 P.M. My intent was to touch base with her again and ask her out. It was a bit of a nice reunion as I also saw Rosalie there, and we caught up on some old times. Yeah guys, I was feeling brave, so I asked Danielle if she'd like to go out and she said yes. We set a dinner date for that evening when her shift would end at 4:00 A.M.

Rosalie was aware of this dinner plan since she was there when we set up the date. Her own shift was going to end a couple of hours earlier at 2:00 A.M, and apparently, she had something else in mind for how I was going to spend my evening. I had no idea at the time Rosalie was such a cunning, conniving, untrustworthy piece of feminine humanity.

I was in Caesars and I got paged over their speaker system there was a phone call for me. Huh? Who'd be calling for me here at this time? I got to the phone, and it was Rosalie. She said, "Hey Frank, why don't you stop by my place for a quick drink before your date with Danielle?" I thought, sure why not, we're all friends, and it'll beat sitting around here for the next couple of hours. I told Rosalie "Okay, I'll be there in a bit."

When I arrived at Rosalie's place, she greeted me at the door in a killer black dress and she looked amazing. I tried to maintain my composure, because while Rosalie was indeed alluring, I was really interested in establishing a nice relationship with Danielle. Hey, a guy can only resist so much, and Rosalie literally attacked me for cryin' out loud. The little bit of a fight I put up was totally futile, believe me.

It was 7:00 A.M. when I left Rosalie's place, and needless to say, I had completely blown the earlier plan with Danielle to oblivion. I felt really, really terrible and I'm not proud of the fact I even asked Rosalie if she would apologize to Danielle for me. Yeah…I was a total jerk.

I learned Danielle was pretty upset about being stood up, of course. Rosalie had the balls to admit to her she had invited me over to her place, and then seduced me. I never touched base with Danielle again and it truly bothered me that I had behaved that way.

So began my dating relationship with Rosalie. It was late 1970, early 1971. Rosalie and I were quite the item.

Rosalie had a good side to her, and we thoroughly enjoyed each other's company. We liked to go dancing at the Sky Room at the Mint Hotel and Casino in downtown Las Vegas on Fremont Street. They had a terrific band that played music to your ears. As always, we dressed up; Rosalie in a provocative gown, which she had many, and me with a suit and hat and go bowling. To my surprise, Rosalie was an ok bowler; although at this time I cannot recall her normal average; however once in a while she would beat me fairly good. I learned not to take her lightly as I became aware, she was very athletic and my scores over hers were actually close.

Now, when it came to water skiing, that was by far our favorite sport and time together. We bought a 25-foot Chrysler twin engine at 220 horsepower. Rosalie was a really good slalom skier; me I used trick skis and loved to jump as high as I could. The Chrysler Clipper slept six people and had a Bar-B-Q in the rear by the motors. We have volleyballs and nets to play in the sand areas. The lake was so clean to the naked eye you could see everything below you almost. Lots of times, Rosalie and I would spend the night out there. Well, let me tell you Lake Mead was my Paradise; 500 miles of shoreline and I knew the Lake like the back of my hand. Skied everywhere and into the Arizona side too. I eventually knew every nook and cranny of that Lake, and like I said before, I took special clients to places no one would find them but me.

I believe the year was 1972, Rosalie bought a new Cadillac, paid cash and wanted to go for a long drive. So, we decided to go to both the San Diego Zoo and Disneyland then to Tijuana, Mexico to shop. If I recall, we both had a week of vacation time so off we went. It's been too long for me to remember how much time we spent at Disneyland but compared to today it was a lot smaller. Anyway, we had lots of fun at the Zoo. Rosalie had never been to a zoo, so she was quite excited about going there. Her favorite was watching the penguins especially the small ones. We spend the whole day there and had lots of fun.

We also liked to go to the drive-in movies and get this actually see the movie!

75 SHADES OF GRAY

Now, you may be wondering what does a guy do with a woman that enjoys 5-8 hours of continuous lovemaking? What specifically did Carol teach me on how to please a woman? Well, first thing first, she told and taught me never and I mean NEVER hurry a woman. I became a quick learner as this experience was right up my alley as I had always loved being around women and fascinated by their sensuality. Carol told me that most guys especially the young ones merely wanted to satisfy themselves as fast as they could. Not me; the longer the better.

Kissing sensuously is an art, and women loved to be kissed. Foreplay, as I was taught by Carol, is also part of the kissing act. I always start by kissing a woman's beautiful mouth and Rosalie loved to be kissed sensuously, and it more than pleased her when I kissed her eyelids, around her ears and slowly down her neck with the slightest touch of my tongue and nibbling on her sensuous areas and listen to her make little sounds of enjoyment.

Rosalie was a provocative dresser when she was in the mood to be…She liked to wear very sexy black, bras, garter belts and silk stockings as well as white laced ones. She had a tiny waist that really showed off her lingerie. Oh, yeah, she had a ceiling mirror over her bed and loved to watch me take her in all kinds of positions. Her moans were so loud I had to close her upper windows by the bed or the whole neighborhood would have heard her. Anyway, simply put, we had great sex! But, one thing must be said, neither one of us was in love with each other.

THE TRUE INSIGHT INTO ROSALIE'S CHARACTER

During the time that we were dating, I was working at the Hilton Hotel & Casino as a bellman. I don't recall the exact moment I found out she wasn't the person I believed she was. Some of the things which took place I'll take responsibility for because I should've known better and walked away from the beginning.

Speaking of walking away, how about I tell you just how I discovered she was a married woman. My unplanned, untimely introduction to hubby happened in a way that would've been a great (or possibly comedic) scene from a Hollywood movie! One particular day, I'm coming down the stairs of her place, heading for the front door. Before I get to the door, the door opens, and a man comes in. I believe we were startled as he asked me, *"Who are you?"* and I replied with a *"Who are you?"* of my own. When he said, *"I'm Rosalie's husband"*.

I said, *"I'm the plumber…just fixed your corroded pipes"* and walked straight out the front door without looking back.

Needless to say, I was upset with Rosalie for keeping such a secret from me. I didn't contact her for several months. I don't remember specifically how we made contact again with one another, but I do recall she wasn't fazed by the occurrence.

A number of months later (yeah…I continued the relationship even though I knew about hubby now…don't ask me why), it finally dawned on me the relationship was going nowhere, as she told me she wouldn't divorce her husband, now get this… because she received great benefits because he worked at the Nevada Test Site. Bingo, the light came on at last for me. I started dating other women. Despite her two-timing me…no wait, I guess it was three timing me, my new free-to-date status didn't sit well with her because one time she came at me with a knife when she saw me with another woman. She declared that she would get even with me and she did.

As an aside to all this that was going on, and while I am thinking about it, in 1974, it was brought to my attention by my friend, Lynn Brady, that Rosalie believed Geneva Blue, (who was living in my house during this time, taking care of it and my little dog B.J.), and I were having an affair…which on my mother's grave, I never did. Yeah, I would guess looking at it today, Rosalie felt she'd been a woman scorned, and we all know, hell hath no fury. Are you kidding me? If anybody should have felt scorned, it was me.

Gotta tell you more about Geneva Blue since I just mentioned her. Years later in my story, when she visited me at the city jail, she told me that my fence needed repair, and asked me to give "power of attorney" so she could use my name to get a loan. Little did I know or suspect that Ms. Blue's true intention was to sell my house, my '64 Corvette Stingray, and my 25-foot Chrysler Clipper boat…each of which she did! I just couldn't catch a break.

One day, I was working my shift when I was approached by Hilton Security's Sgt. Walker. He said, "Frank, we need to talk." I went to his office, wondering what the hell this could possibly be about. "Do you know you're in the Black Book as an International Slot Cheat, with known associates around the world? You need to get your name out of that book Frank." "What?" I was puzzled. How the hell did I end up in that category?

Turned out I'd been banned from going into Caesars based on my appearing in that publication. I couldn't fathom how that could happen, but I knew I'd better get to the bottom

36

of it right away. Hell, I had already lost one job because of some bullshit mistake made by law enforcement some time ago. I damn sure wasn't going to let it happen again.

Sgt. Walker went on to say, "There's a young attorney in town these days. His name is Oscar Goodman. I'll get his number for you." Now let me back up a bit. Most of the security guys around town had at one point or another worked with each other in different casinos at different times. That community was pretty small, and of course word often got around regarding who's hot and who's not as far as folks they need to be wary of going' in and out of the hotels at all times.

The word on my status had also reached Bill Underwood from Caesars and the Chief of Security, Jack Manes. Manes asked Bill to make me aware I'd been banned. So, again I was told about the situation by Bill Underwood.

Who the hell was behind this? Why was it done, and how do I get this straightened out? I anticipated a possible lengthy, drawn-out investigation into this matter, and it was going to be a pain in my ass for quite some time.

So, I hired Oscar Goodman to solve my being placed in the "book." His investigation found out that someone gave my name and my picture to Griffith Detective Agency who placed unsavory character's names into the local hotels and casinos black book which banned them from entering the Vegas casino properties. Oscar worked it out so that my name and picture was removed from the book. After that, I was able to go to any casino properties that I wanted.

Apparently, at the same time that I was in a relationship with Rosalie, she had been having an affair with Caesars Palace Executive, Marvin Krause. And as I explained previously, Rosalie was also married. Since her husband worked at the Nevada Test Site, he would be gone for weeks at a time, and this allowed Rosalie to live life to the fullest, with suitors galore, never any of them to meet. I don't know if her husband ever knew about her lovers, or whether he knew and just didn't care. Who knows, maybe he had something going on around the test site.

It turns out that Marvin Krause is the one that had a private investigator place me in the Hotel and Casino Black Book. Rosalie even knew that Marvin had Caesars Palace Chief Security Boss, Jack McManus 86 me there, so I couldn't see her at work.

Some of this information was only ever discovered years later during the criminal investigation and when my attorney at the time, Oscar Goodman, had the chance to question Rosalie during one of the hearings but outside the courtroom. She said that one day Marvin was at her house and happened to see a photo of me that she had displayed out in the open on some shelf or something. According to Rosalie, Krause became incensed, and he threw the photo against a wall and declared, "This is Frank? I'll get that fucking guinea if it's the last thing I do."

On another occasion, Marvin bought Rosalie tickets to go to Hawaii, but told her I wasn't allowed to go with her. She took the trip without me. When she returned from Hawaii, she didn't immediately touch base with Krause, and he couldn't locate her. I had nothing to do with any of that, and don't know the reason they couldn't connect…but I didn't care. Get this…years later Krause told cop Beecher Avants of his dislike for me saying Rosalie was probably *"…shacked up with that pimp, Frank."*

What the hell was I thinking during this relationship, when so much writing was on the wall indicating Rosalie was a self-serving, cunning individual, with no conscience at all? This became quite evident later on when at my 1977, murder trial Rosalie, refused to testify on my behalf, taking the 5th Amendment against self-incrimination. I couldn't believe this.

This crushed me… want to know why? A fact which would've come out (had she testified truthfully) was she was the only one who ever knew I didn't know nor had ever met Marvin and Hilda Krause. I couldn't believe the evilness she displayed towards me, knowing full well I never knew the Krauses. Her testimony was so crucial and could well have tipped the scale in my favor.

When Rosalie had another opportunity to aid me in my quest, I thought for the first time, it'd be put on record I'd never known either of the Krauses. Yet…she threw me under the bus again. But she did say, "I believe he is innocent."

Now that you have learned a lot about the "character" of the woman who was discovered to be "a goddess in name only", among the biggest surprise during my relationship with Rosalie came when I introduced her to my sister Candi.

After their initial meeting, perhaps it was woman's intuition, Candi told me that she felt Rosalie was a person not to be trusted. My sister believed and felt Rosalie had an "evil" spirit. Maybe I should have listened to her and given more thought to what she suspected. I was sadly reluctant when I had to admit that Candi had been right. She nailed it right on the head.

Rosalie and I were having some sort of discussion one day and a shock came over me when she told me she was an "Atheist." That threw me for a loop! The specific subject of our religious beliefs or spirituality had never come up. I guess I pretty much always assumed that Rosalie was a woman with some sort of faith-based doctrines by which she lived.

So, inasmuch as I was (and still am) a person of deep faith, it makes for an intriguing thought on how Rosalie found it so easy to do some of the things I've described. In complete contrast to that, I have to add that I had on my occasions (believe it or not) seen Rosalie display a good deal of kindness. Maybe it was a "speck of a conscience" that made her do those nice acts.

It's certainly only right that I tell you that Rosalie shared my love of animals, both cats and dogs. She had two cats, "Sam and Freckles". She cried when "Freckles", our tiny cat died of parvo. When I had to post bail, she put up her house as collateral to get me out. Yes…it is crazy, isn't it? When I got out after posting bail, Rosalie found me a rescue dog that I named Solomon.

Rosalie also paid Lynn Brady's mortgage payments when Lynn had become so sick that she could not work. So… who is she? Who really was this woman who was able to profess a disbelief in a higher power who was unfaithful to three different men in her life…who put up her own home to bail me out of jail, then refused to testify on my behalf?

One would not be quick to describe her as a woman who had faith in any religious sense. But, if you determine that she possessed total confidence or "faith" in her own ability to interact with others in a way that would serve to guarantee her a personal benefit, then Rosalie had plenty of faith…most of it self-based or self-focused.

Did Rosalie have a "character" …I guess that even though many would not operate the way she did, she did exhibit glimpses of personal empathy, compassion and I guess her own version of "strength" that made her do things that would ensure her survival in the "human jungle" in which most of us struggle to endure from day to day. Rosalie Maxwell was most definitely an enigmatic persona…one about whom any debate regarding concepts of "faith and character" would be without a doubt both intriguing and spirited.

COCKTAILS, TEA . . .OR ME?

Yeah, I know…the saying goes "Coffee, Tea, or Me", and we're not talking about flight attendants, I get that! However, there were a number of things she did that would earn her the descriptor of "she devil." However, I feel it only fair to give you a more comprehensive understanding of the "universe" in which she found herself existing on a daily basis during the "Vegas era" in which all of this saga took place!

The gaming / hospitality / casino community being as close knit as it was back then (as it still is today actually), there were a number of us who worked together at one time or another in most of the establishments both on "the Strip", or downtown. Rosalie and I had lots of friends who were bellmen, cocktail waitresses, dealers, pit workers, parking valets and the like. I would have occasions to talk with lots of the really interesting guys, and incredibly lovely women throughout that "small community."

Tremendously close, lifelong friendships would develop as a result of us learning so much about one another, and discovering that regardless of our very different backgrounds, there were some experiences that were universal for all of us as we found ourselves working to survive in "Sin City"

I remember the story told to me by one of my dearest friends, about what she experienced when she first came here. When she gave me, her take on her becoming a Cocktail Waitress and what she was subjected to for that position, I was not surprised as it was amazingly similar to the stories of so many other women here in Vegas at that time! This is her story:

"When I arrived in Las Vegas in 1969, I was just "a small-town country girl" quite naïve and gullible. I was divorced and had 6 children to raise! I was told by my ex-husband to become a cocktail waitress. I had no idea what was going to happen to my life next. While trying to find out exactly how I could become a cocktail waitress, I learned that you must join the Culinary Union, and then wait to be called. Lucky for me, my ex-mother-in-law was very influential in the community, and with her assistance, I was introduced to the Secretary Treasurer of the Culinary Union (Big Boss) who had the power to place me in one of the top casinos on the Strip!

I was absolutely stunned when my "interview" took place, as it was a very shameful embarrassing experience. I had to show my legs, my boobs, and be a size 6-8. I

40

felt so much shame! At age 27, I started working at the well-known Strip Hotel and Casino and was told that I would work the pit area (21 tables) juiced in. My first introduction to cocktail waitressing was a nightmare! Apparently that area was very "cut-throat" as I discovered that they (the other more tenured waitresses) wanted no part of me, "an outsider", working their pit tables.

They told the bartenders to mess my drinks up, so everyone would complain. They took my extra shoes, combs and lipstick(s)…whatever they could do to make my life miserable, and they did just that! I would go home every night crying. I hated it there. They were rude, mean, unkind and jealous! During that time in history, you were as they thought, "everyone's property…to touch, sometimes fondle…and be spoken to in the most disrespectful ways!"

Now, remember, to keep your job you smiled, and went about serving drinks, and I followed the rules of the game (as it was) because I had children to feed! Well, to my surprise I started to change over the years, I could feel myself becoming pretty hard inside. I found I had very little feeling, as you can only cry and be gullible for so long. Life was now just a game you play…there was no more "nice girl." I had learned that it was "dog eat dog," and you might say that in order to survive…the "bitch" came out! Yeah…I learned the game and how to play it…and I don't mind telling you that I became a master at it!

Life became very different…a lot of parties, drinking, and so on… before long and in spite of my desire not to, I became one of them…I had successfully become (numb). The "Head Cocktail Waitress" would arrange for girls to escort "high rollers" for dinner, gambling and whatever! We had a union, but you only complained once as there would be consequences if you were one of those who they would identify as a" troublemaker or repeat complainer." You learned fast…or else.

I now was living a double life…shame! Don't get me wrong, not all Cocktail Waitresses were mean or rude…just the pit girls. The word "Pit" says it all…and make no mistake…to me, it was hell working there. I did 19 years in that hell, then retired. I stopped drinking, and I became a better person…The young lady was back!"

I also had a chance to talk to another woman who worked in one of the casinos located on the "Strip," a number of years later (she was there during the late '90s…some 20 plus years after all of this) and was not surprised when she so pointedly said to me that nothing changed in the "universe of the women of Vegas" in all that time! I was totally intrigued as this lovely woman told me her story:

"I was hired in 1998 to work in one of the casino's guests' clubs signing customers up to receive player's cards. This is one way the casinos track the gambling habits and patterns of their clientele as they play the slot machines and the table games. In return, the customers receive points they can redeem for minimal perks like mediocre buffets, second rate comedy or variety shows and other nickel and dime rewards.

Later on, I learned the truth about just how much the customer has to gamble in order to receive his / her first "free" buffet. It took $1,700 in circulated coin or cash to get that first free meal…I was shocked! Of course, the customer has no idea of the real cost since it's part of the game that Las Vegas offers up, but if you were to pay for the buffet yourself it would cost between $25 to $30 person. Talk about a rip off! Somehow though, the gambler feels they're getting something for nothing, which is the "perception of establishment benevolence" the casinos want to infuse into the mentalities of their patrons! Believe me…the only winners are the casinos, no matter what you hear as delusional whisperings, promising financial windfalls find their way into your ears!

I had no experience working (in the gaming or) casino industry having just moved to Las Vegas six months (earlier), but for some reason, I thought working on the famous Las Vegas Strip at one of the most elegant casinos in the world, would be a glamorous work environment. So, I eagerly sought work there first. Although I had applied at one of the premier establishments in town, I learned that soon there was going to be a brand-new upscale casino opening, so I applied there too, hoping to land a position there.

Truly, I was naïve…a wide-eyed innocent ready to give my all in this fantasy world of non-stop excitement. I had no idea what was in store for me…no predetermined expectations to go by, and that may be one of the reasons why I was hired so quickly. Casinos prefer "un-informed" female employees they can mold into becoming what they want over time. Needless to say, when I received the call from the guy who would be my direct supervisor, that I had been hired, I felt as though I had hit the jackpot!

I should've realized that it was a bad match for me since I didn't smoke, drink, or gamble…but I wanted a change. I was looking for a stable job with a good company with opportunities for advancement. Las Vegas was and is still a "right to work" state which means employees have virtually "no rights" unless they secure a job under the unions like Culinary or Teamsters, where you'll have protection or recourse if things go badly. Unfortunately, my job did not fall under a union…so I was on my own. My supervisor was quite happy to have a total "innocent" under his control!

A woman was assigned to act as my mentor. She was an energetic, middle-aged, casino hardened survivor of many years…soft on the outside, tough as nails on the inside. She was sweet to everyone…but could handle belligerent customers, as well as "back stabbing co-workers" with equal ease. She never lost her cool and could navigate the casino cesspools without offending anyone. She taught me the ropes and put me through the paces…explaining the basics but was careful about not sharing the whole truth with me!

She tried to protect me because she knew I was out of my element and basically clueless. Almost as soon as I started working there, my co-workers started hitting me up with (their) hard luck stories. They all needed various amounts of cash for food, clothes, their kids, sick parents and so on. They said they would pay me back out of their next paychecks. Being a trusting person, I was genuinely concerned for their well-being and helped them as best I could…until my mentor pulled me aside and told me to STOP IT…IMMEDIATELY!

This stunned me and I explained to her that it was my Christian duty to help others in need! She told me that many people who work in the casinos are "lying, degenerate gamblers, hooked on the rush of that potential win…the one that will make them instantly rich!" I never loaned those people money again…nor was I ever repaid a single penny by a single one of them…lesson well learned! About that time, I came to be informed (privately I might add) by my supervisor, "…that there were other ways to make a little more money if things got tight". Those ways involved providing him sexual favors! I told him "no thanks!"

I soon learned that casinos use many female employees as pawns, eventually making it a toxic and compromising environment for them. It's "a slow descent into Hell," as they groom you to become whatever they need or want in order to keep the "high rollers / whales" happy and content in their respective places of business! Nice looking female employees were pressured in various ways to comply, of course you have choices…but the consequences for *making the incorrect choice in their view, could be as bad as having your arms cut off…figuratively speaking of course!*

The atmosphere was indeed ruthless as fresh female recruits were used mercilessly to the casino's advantage. Exploitation is the norm. I believe I was hired specifically for my looks and their false belief that they could indoctrinate me with their agenda, and I would be compliant…they were wrong! Because I resisted their attempts on more than a couple of occasions (I was written up on the third offense) I was shipped off to the "Special Events Department" hoping that they could do something to "improve my poor attitude" (if you will).

One day, I was scheduled to work at a gift distribution event. It was for the VIPs…a few high rollers, politicians, and a few assorted celebrities. The gifts were very nice I thought…Waterford Crystal…front row seats to an Andrea Bocelli concert…vouchers for all expense paid trips and cruises…cars and so on. The people who even bothered coming to receive these gifts had an almost dismissive ambivalence about it. They had already lost so much money that these casino kickbacks were considered an insult by many of them!

Anyway…during my shift one particular gentleman came in to pick up his gift and returned five more times in the course of the evening just to chat and joke with me and my co-worker. He was pleasant with a quirky sense of humor. He was tall and nice looking…from the deep south, and said he owned a barge company on the Mississippi River…and…he was very wealthy!

During the course of our conversation, he asked me if I was working the high roller party scheduled for the next night. I told him that I was. "Great…I'll see you then!" he commented, and then he left us. After he left the room, my co-worker said to me, "…he likes you," which to me seemed ridiculous since I was a complete nobody. I didn't think much about it the rest of that evening.

The casinos monitor the high rollers / whales carefully and of course there are cameras everywhere. Everyone is under surveillance 24/7. The higher ups were watching and listening to our exchange(s) that night…unbeknownst to me! That next night, I showed up for the event wearing my uniform and was looking forward to working my first VIP party. Before I got into the ballroom, I was escorted to another room…there waiting for me was my supervisor, and another woman who was also a supervisor.

I thought I was in some kind of trouble but instead they were very welcoming and pleased to see me. They explained that the "southern gentleman" whom I had met the night before had enjoyed my conversation and wanted to "spend some time with me." They went on to explain that I would still get paid for a night's work at the party even though technically, I would not be there...plus...I'd get a nice bonus of $500...and (of course) I was free to accept any gifts or gratuities that the southern gentleman might offer me...of course I would! I couldn't believe what I was hearing. Then the woman supervisor handed me a low cut, sexy Black cocktail dress and high heels that the "gentleman" had purchased just hours prior...especially for me from one of their high-end fashion clothing stores!

"He'd like you to wear this she said gleefully waiting for me to take the items from her. I stood there like a deaf mute for what seemed like an hour before it sank into my head. I realized that in essence I was being "pimped out" to benefit the casino and one of their cash cows. My heart was racing and the pounding vein on the side of my head was about to explode when I told them "NO" ... and that they "...could all go to Hell!"

My supervisor told me that this was my last chance, or I'd be sent to the bowels of the casino as a "go-for" or something worse. I didn't care...I turned to leave and as I did so, the "southern gentleman" walked in! He had been listening all this time. I was mortified and everyone could see that I was visibly shaken. He was very apologetic and calm and asked me to sit down so he could explain. I did as he asked, and he said that he just wanted me to be his companion on his last night in Las Vegas.

He wanted to gamble and was hoping that I would bring him good luck by standing by his side and nothing more. Yeah...sure, I thought. He stated that his intent was no more than that, and that he hoped I would reconsider. He assured me that we would stay in the casino the entire time. Well...I couldn't afford to lose my job since I was relatively new and had no other prospects at that time, but I resented being set up and used like that. I decided to find a different job as soon as possible.

With that thought in mind, I reluctantly agreed to stay for three hours. He was a perfect gentleman, thankful to have my company...at first! He bet heavily at various tables and won for a while, then like most compulsive gamblers...he started losing. He became surly and verbally abusive as his losses increased. Before I left, he offered me $1,000 if I *would do some vile and abhorrent sex acts with him in his suite! BINGO…. I knew it! I declined his offer and left at 2AM, saying "goodnight and goodbye!"*

I never saw the "southern gentleman" again after that night, but when he returned to Mississippi, he let the "higher ups" know that he was "very displeased with me…and wanted me to be fired as soon as possible, or he'd go to a different casino to gamble!" That would be a competitor casino of course…

I was forced to leave soon after that, once again enabling the casino to continue to keep another whale in its greedy clutches. I can tell you first hand that I have never experienced such a dehumanizing, demoralizing work environment as I did working at that well known, highly respected Las Vegas casino on the Strip. As thrilled as I was to be hired at the beginning…I was even more thrilled to be leaving the godless, opportunistic padded sewer at the end!

If you were to ask me if things have improved for women working in the Vegas casinos now. Sadly, I would have to say…" nothing changes!"

7

SPECIAL FAVORS FOR THE MOB
TO CONDUCT FAMILY BUSINESS

When Caesars Palace opened on August 5, 1966, the weekend was for special guests only. It was not open to the public until Monday rolled around. Knowing several wise guys from the El Cortez who were now working the casino, I knew this weekend was going to be "Mob City," if you know what I mean. "Wise guys" (members of mafia crime families) were running Caesar's Palace, and this was a weekend of weekends. It was a first-class operation.

Did I ever hit the jackpot! I checked in a wise guy from one of the junkets who owned a parfum factory in Philly, PA. We had a great guy connection, and he took a special liking to me and this guy was a class act. Amongst his luggage was a very big box containing parfum, etc. Talk about the luck of the draw, not only did I get a hug tip, but he also gave me the box of parfum, and I became a big hit with not only my mother and sister, but the Goddesses as well; hey, you can't blame a guy.

Oh, yeah, my wise guy guest said he won $50,000 gambling on the flight over here. He said his luck was still going meeting me and wanted to make sure I would be the one to check him out when the junket was getting ready to leave, which I did. He preferred to call me "Cheech" (which is Frank in Sicilian) upon learning I was Sicilian which he was also. If I thought my first tip was big, I couldn't believe what he gave me for the second, as he won a ton of money saying I was his luck guy.

Little did I know at this time, that later he would be the main guy that started my stint as a specialist doing special favors for wise guys.

He did indicate that he planned on returning to Caesar's Palace when he had a chance so I told him when he decided to return, he could tell the front desk clerk that he wanted me to specifically to check him in. I told him I would be working the day shift from Tuesday through Saturday. I don't recall exactly how long it was when he returned to Caesars, but when he did, he asked the front desk clerk if I was working, and if so, he wanted only me to check him in. I was just coming back from a guest check-in when I saw my Philadelphia guy and went over to greet him. I also noticed he had two other guys standing next to him. After we all said hello, he told me he came here with two of his friends and asked if I could also check in these other guys. I said sure, not a problem. When a guest makes a special request for a certain bellman, the desk clerk always complies because it's allowed.

They were given suites next to each other (comp rooms), so it wasn't hard to get their luggage on a cart. On the way to the rooms, I found out these guys he knew were from different families, which did not surprise me. Las Vegas was becoming a boom town with mob guys already here and more coming in as well as law enforcement agencies, strike force, FBI, etc.

Based on how our conversations were going, I got the feeling they wanted to talk to me on a more personal basis. One of the guys asked me if I could come by after I got off work. I told him I wasn't allowed to do that due to hotel policy, but we could meet after my shift at the Tower of Pizza just up the street. The Tower of Pizza was owned by a loan shark, Jasper Speciale, who also worked at Caesars in the pit.

At the Tower of Pizza, we took a table away from other people. They first asked how long I have lived in Vegas and if I knew Vegas well. I said a few years and that Vegas was relatively small, but I felt it was going to grow big in time. I don't recall everything we talked about being this was 50 or more years ago, but I got the feeling this conversation was going to be very important based on their tone of voices and facial expressions. Being around wise guys since I was a kid, I sensed these guys intended to set up operations here with other families and were representatives of the big bosses from where they came.

My Philly guy and his two friends finally got around to ask me if I could do a "specific type of special favor" for them that dealt with their family business. When they mentioned "family business" I knew this could be dangerous for myself. Any time you are dealing with wise guys it can be very dangerous, but I was very confident I could do this without fear of making a mistake.

They asked me if I knew if there was any place in Vegas I knew of where a "private meeting" could be held away from prying eyes and ears. They didn't trust the hotel rooms that could be bugged or even rental cars. I told them "yeah, I knew a specific place where they could meet." I instantly knew what to do, and I said I could do it for them. When I told

48

them how I could do this they thought it was brilliant. To put them at ease, I said "no law enforcement agency will be able to crack my method of doing this for you guys because I'll never do it exactly the same way twice but you'll always be able to conduct your family business in privacy and you guys will always be safe and no names will ever be used by me so they could never ever be ratted out. I was speaking wise guy language when I said that and felt they knew they could trust me.

I had water skied just about every place on Lake Mead which had over 500 miles of shoreline with hundreds of coves and waterfalls to relax and see everything in front and back of you. I knew these places like the back of my hand and where you can find privacy and be relaxed.

At this time, I owned a 20-foot Chris Craft cabin cruiser that I used to use on recreational trips on Lake Mead and other spots on my days off. It definitely was a big hit with the ladies and a buddy, Benny Caldero, and I would enjoy nice little excursions to some rather "secluded private beaches" locations along the lake.

I later "up-scaled" my boat and got a 25- foot Chrysler Clipper. It had a larger passenger capacity and was definitely a step in the right direction as I provided this kind of service for quite a period of time. I never took them to the same location.

I was also aware not to give out my phone number in case their phone was wiretapped by law enforcement. This made it safe for me. I had a specific method I used when they intended to fly out here to contact and meet with me which I felt was foolproof. It was a safety deposit box where they could send a note of when they are coming in and where to meet them. I would destroy it after I read it. When I told them, they thought it was very smart to do it my way. I did not do this on a daily basis; only on a need to do. I always provided them with food and drinks and cigars if they wanted one. They would set a time for me to come back and get them as only I knew where they were.

Lake Mead was the safest place to take them to conduct their family business away from anyone, be it law enforcement or other wise guys. Now, in order to keep myself safe while at the same time to protect their identities I always referred to them as "Gentlemen or Hi Guys or Hey Guys." It provided us with a safety net, if, for any reason, a law enforcement official ever asked or questioned me if I knew or met this guy or that guy, my answer would be honest and true. "I have no clue who you are talking about, I have never heard of that name, and I would never answer another question by them. If they tried to play hardball with me, they would be talking to a wall.

I did not consider myself as having "worked with the Mob" or being a member of a family. My interactions with them were strictly to provide a specific, special type of service for them, nothing more. They never discussed their business in my presence, our talks were about life in general - sports, area growth, how big was the lake, and entertainers. When I came to pick them up, we stayed on the beach and they relaxed, barbequed, played volleyball and just had a good time. And I was well-compensated for my service.

Like I said before, I had been around wise guys since I was a kid. The experience I obtained being around them and working in their establishments was a great value to my growing up years. Simply put, they were businessmen highly skilled in their profession and they were to be respected when being around them or talking to them. They liked that especially when it came from a youngster which I was at that time. I gained an incredible amount of life knowledge from these guys, particularly from Babe.

By the way, I was still providing this service when I was arrested for the Krause murder.

8

PRELIMINARY HEARING
STATE OF NEVADA V. GERALD WEAKLAND

It's time I talked about some of the things that actually took place in my trials. Up to now, you've not been given any of the specific testimonies or information as to what took place in those courtrooms. We're going to delve into that right now, and I'm going to try to present these various testimonies in chronological order of the hearings or trial dates at which they were given, so that you may follow the story as it developed. I'll also be commenting here and there.

Gerald Weakland was arrested on March 13, 1974, for the Krause murder and robbery and there was no doubt that any testimony given by alleged victim Marvin Krause would be considered extremely impactful at Weakland's March 29, 1974 preliminary hearing. I believe you are going to find here some very interesting testimony given by Marvin Krause!

Inasmuch as he had been called previously as a witness by and on behalf of the State of Nevada and having been previously sworn in by the Clerk of the Court, Krause underwent "direct examination" by State Prosecutor, Robert Wolfe. I'm just going to hit what I think is relevant to Marvin's testimony regarding Hilda Krause.

Q.　*What is your address?*

A.　*2995 Pinehurst Drive.*

Q.　*Is that in Las Vegas, County of Clark, State of Nevada?*

A.　*Las Vegas, Nevada.*

Q.　*I would like to address your attention to January 14th, 1974, at approximately 5:30 a.m. Were you home at that time?*

A.　*Yes*

Q.　*Would you tell the Court what happened at that location on that date please?*

Q. *Did anything occur that would cause the intruders to separate you from your wife so that they would take her in the other bedroom?*

A. *No, nothing that I know of.*

Q. *Had the intruders begun to tie you up or Mrs. Krause prior to taking her in the other room?*

A. *I don't know. I know they had started tying me up. I am sorry. I know they had started tying me, but I don't know what they had done with her. I was lying face down.*

Q. *After Mrs. Krause had been taken into the other room, were you then struck by either of the people?*

A. *Yes*

If I remember correctly, Krause was then "cross examined" by Weakland's attorney, a guy named Howard Ecker. He questioned Krause about the head injury he sustained, and what he (Krause) did afterwards. That questioning went as follows:

Q. *Where were you struck?*

A. *On the back of the head.*

This is interesting…because when Metro Officer Robert Keiser drove up and saw Krause, he noticed blood running down the front right side of Marvin's face! If he was hit in the back of his head…why is there blood on the side of his face? Was it possibly his wife Hilda's blood who, according to the crime scene cops, stated their investigation revealed a violent struggle occurred in both bedrooms and Weakland testified she did not struggle with him? Somebody is lying here.

Q. *With what?*

A. *I can't tell you what.*

Q. *Was anything done with your overcoat at that time?*

A. *Yes. They threw it over the top of my head.*

Q. *Was this prior to or after you were struck?*

A. *Prior to, I believe.*

Q.   *Were you ever unconscious?*

A.   *Yes. It seemed to me that I was out for a while.*

Wait a minute…Officer Keiser's police report stated Krause said "he was conscious" during all this time…even though one of the suspects hit him in the back of his head with a blunt object!

Q.   *Now, did you have occasion to wake up after you were hit?*

A.   *Not until I…*

Q.   *When did you wake up*

A.   *I can't tell you the length of time I laid there.*

Q.   *But you did wake up? When you finally gained consciousness and you testified you were dazed, were you still tied, or did you free yourself?*

A.   *It seemed I freed myself somehow.*

Q.   *At that time did you know what you were tied with?*

A.   *No, I don't.*

Q.   *Then I believe you testified…what did you do after you freed yourself?*

A.   *I immediately went into the big room where my wife was laying…and I plugged in the phone, and I called the police.*

During that phone call, he made no mention of his wife lying two feet from him! Nor did he call for an ambulance.

Q.   *I believe from the small bedroom you proceeded into the master bedroom?*

A.   *Yes.*

Q.   *About how far is that?*

A.   *Oh, about six or seven feet. I don't know exactly it's not very far.*

Q.   *Did you call to your wife at any time?*

A.   *No. I didn't say anything. I just plugged in the phone.*

Q.   *Did you have occasion to see your wife after that?*

A. *That's where I saw my wife laying in the room there.*

Q. *From where you observed your wife, where were you standing?*

A. *Right in the bedroom, like two or three or four feet from her.*

Q. *From her toes?*

A. *Well, she was just lying there.*

Q. *How was she lying?*

A. *She was lying face down.*

Q. *Do you recall anything about her body (knife wound; bloody cords) as she was lying there, any other items?*

A. *No, I don't.*

What? When Officer Keiser went upstairs, he noticed a knife sticking out of Hilda Krause's back! When the second officer (Peter Dustin) arrived on the scene, Keiser ordered him to call Mercy Ambulance. Marvin claims he never saw the knife...or any other items (as he was asked by Wolfe), yet he says he was only 2, 3 or 4 feet from her? C'mon...really?

Q. *Did she move while you were there?*

A. *No, she did not.*

Q. *Did you touch her body?*

A. *No, sir, I did not.*

Q. *Did you bend over her?*

A. *No, I did not.*

Q. *Was she tied up at that time?*

A. *I couldn't tell you...I didn't take that close a look, that close of a look.*

Q. *About how long were you standing over Mrs. Krause before you went to make the phone call?*

A. *Not long, almost immediately I started.*

Q. *Where did you...what did you do after you stooped over her before you made the* *phone call?*

A. *I didn't stand over her sir. I immediately plugged in the phone and dialed the operator.*

Q. *This was the master bedroom in which your wife was?*

A. *Yes.*

Q. *And you dialed the operator?*

A. *Yes.*

Q. *What did you do after you called the police?*

A. *I went down stairs immediately and stood in front of the doorway or the garage and waited for the police.*

Q. *When you observed your wife lying on the floor in the bedroom, did you see any cord?*

A. *I didn't see anything around.*

So, now I ask you…having read Marvin Krause's answers cited above, if you were in a situation with your spouse lying on the floor two feet away from you, would you have called the Metro Dispatcher and specifically say, as Marvin Krause did, "I've been the victim of an armed robbery and assault with hands and fists."

Or…would you have called an ambulance, then the police, (again you're standing just two feet from your loved one) and attempted to aid him or her as best as you could? Marvin didn't even touch her! Ok, maybe he got his wish that he previously indicated to both Rosalie Maxwell and Geneva Blue that he wanted to get rid of his wife, and also hoped she broke her neck instead of her arm when she fell down the stairs, as I will provide you in more detail later. What an evil creep this guy must have been. Here we have these dirty cops and prosecutors calling Marvin Krause a "victim" who "didn't see anything" around: no cord, no blood splatter; wife 2 feet from him in a pool of blood and knife sticking out of her back; never mentions to the Metro dispatcher his wife has been murdered. Are you beginning to see the picture now of a police cover up?

I think too that you'd quite likely stay in the room (or at least in the house) ready to answer the door when the ambulance and / or the police arrived! C'mon, who's kidding who here? I'll grant you that this is speculation on my part, but I do know that Marvin Krause was a personal friend of then Sheriff Ralph Lamb, and several detectives with Metro. I can't help but believe that based on his "friendships" with many of the law enforcement personnel in Vegas, it didn't constitute "a strenuous leap of faith" for the testimony of Krause to be considered "gospel" by any of them who would listen.

Now do you believe an honest Non-Nevada prosecutor would have a good case against Marvin Krause had he been a "defendant" based upon his testimony cited above. And remember, Marvin Krause had been a suspect in a prior unrelated murder, and when a young prosecutor, Neil Galatz, went after Marvin Krause, the prosecutor was told to "back off." This was told to me by former Chief Justice E. M. Gunderson of the Nevada Supreme Court.

Okay, now, let's go over this "perjured" testimony once more by alleged "victim" Marvin Krause, and judge for yourself, if you could actually believe this testimony, then being questioned and prosecuted by an honest prosecutor without threats from Krause's mob ties, friendly sheriff and dirty cops.

So, here we go, upon releasing himself after being tied up he immediately went into the big bedroom where his wife was lying and plugged in the phone and immediately called the police and said "he" was the victim of assault with hands and fists; never mentions his wife was murdered with a knife sticking out of her back, as he's talking to the Metro Dispatcher; did not call an ambulance; that he was only a few feet away from his wife when he "observed" her body (which means he actually "saw" her body); didn't see anything around (no knife, bloody cords about her body as she was lying there; that he did not "touch" his wife or "look her over" or "aid" her or even "call out to her" and "couldn't tell" if his wife was "tied" up at that time (although he had observed her body). He didn't take that close of a look nor did he hang around long enough to "find out"; and he was "unconscious" during the time of this crime after being hit in the back of the head with a blunt instrument; after he called the police he immediately went down the stairs and stood in the doorway or the garage and waited for the police and when metro Officer Kaiser arrived, Marvin Krause told him "my wife is upstairs and knocked out" and was he never questioned by his cop friends why he lied to Officer Kaiser about this. Give me a break – this was a classic police coverup by the cops and prosecutors.

It's interesting to note that Marvin Krause was physically able to testify at Gerald

Weakland's preliminary hearing but not at my preliminary hearing. I believe Prosecutor Mel Harmon presented a doctor's note to the court that insured Krause didn't have to testify at my preliminary hearing as he was "allegedly" too sick. What a crock of shit that was. I believe Harmon knew Oscar Goodman would have made mincemeat out of Marvin Krause and turn the tables around in Rosalie's and my preliminary hearing. And that's the truth and the whole truth folks!

Okay, my turn to play the honest, fearless prosecutor. Here are the questions I would have asked him:

Q: *Mr. Krause, you testified you saw your wife lying face down, you observed her back, and you didn't see anything about, is that correct? No knife in her back, or next to her body or blood around her body, or scarf around her neck yet you were 2, 3, 4 feet from her? Didn't stand long over her body before you made a phone call. You did not touch her body or bend over her.*

Mr. Krause, showing you State exhibit 2.

Q: *Have you had a chance to look at this photo?*

Q: *To your knowledge, the person depicted in that photo, would that person be your wife, Hilda Krause?*

Q: *Your Honor, I would like to show the jury this photo before I ask Mr. Krause my next question.*

Q: *Now that you had a chance to review or see the photo of Hilda Krause, your wife, do you see the knife sticking out of her back? Yes or no Sir.*

Q: *Do you see two cords next to her body. Yes or no.*

Q: *Do you see any blood around her body? Yes or no.*

Q: *Does she appear to be dead? Yes or no Sir.*

Q: *Do you see the scarf around her neck? Yes or no Sir.*

Q: *And you further testified you were 2, 3, or 4 feet from her; is that correct Sir, when you saw your wife lying face down; is that correct, Sir, yes or no?*

Q: *Do you also see any blood next to your wife's body, as so depicted in State's photo, Exhibit 2; yes or no, Sir?*

Q: Mr. Krause, do you see the "SCARF" around your wife's neck, depicted in State's Exhibit 2? Yes or no.

Q: Bringing your attention to State's Exhibit 2. Do you see blood splattering around the bedroom, next to your wife's body, the bedroom walls and sheets on the bed? Yes or no, Sir?

Q: Mr. Krause, as you reviewed and looked at this photo, State's Exhibit 2, does your wife appear to you to be dead, with that knife sticking out of her back in plain sight? Yes or no, Sir?

Q: Yet is it not true, you told Metro Police Officer Robert Reiser, the first one to arrive at your residence and I quote, "my wife is upstairs and knocked out," which he wrote in his police report? Yes or no?

Q: Directing your attention once again Mr. Krause, at State's Exhibit 2, does your wife with a knife sticking in her back, appear to you to be "knocked out." Yes or no Sir?

Let me back up here a minute, assuming you are not a lawyer, particularly a criminal lawyer, do you know whether or not giving false information to a police officer may be a crime?

According to Officer Keiser's police report, when he went upstairs and found a female lying face down on the floor, with a knife in her back, he called the ambulance after checking to see if she and a pulse.

Now I ask you, were you ever questioned by uniform police officers or detectives why you "lied" to Metro Officer Robert Keiser, that your wife was upstairs and knocked out? She is lying face down and he testified he saw nothing.

Q: How can you observe a body and "not" see anything?

I'm sure you, as I, noticed all of Marvin Krause's contradictions and lies as he is testifying and this Prosecutor Wolf, let it ride. I rest my case.

9

THE WEAKLAND DEAL

Insert Cited below is the written deal struck between Gerald Weakland and the District Attorney's office on August 13, 1974. It was read to the jury by Mr. Howard Ecker.

Case Number 27870, in the Eight Judicial District Court of the State of Nevada, in and for the County of Clark. "The State of Nevada, plaintiff, versus Gerald Ronald Weakland, defendant.

Plea Agreement

Whereas Gerald Ronald Weakland is charged in Case Number 27870 with Count One murder and Count Two robbery.

And whereas Gerald Ronald Weakland has agreed to cooperate fully and has been cooperating fully with the District Attorney's office in regard to the prosecution of person charged with the killing and or robbery of one Hilda Krause, and on the condition that Weakland continue to cooperate fully and to testify at the trial of persons charged with the killing and or robbery of Hilda Krause.

And whereas Gerald Ronald Weakland has agreed to cooperate fully and has been cooperating fully with the Clark County District Attorney's office in regard to the cooperation of persons charged with the shooting and or kidnapping of one William Obernauer.

Now, therefore, it is agreed by and between the parties hereto that, one, Gerald Ronald Weakland shall be permitted to plead guilty of the charge of second degree murder in regard to the killing of Hilda Krause, and Gerald Ronald Weakland shall not be prosecuted for the robbery charge in Case Number 27870; two, Gerald Ronald Weakland shall be granted immunity from being prosecuted for the shooting and or kidnapping of William Obenauer; three, Gerald Ronald Weakland shall receive full credit for all the time he has served in the Clark County Jail since the date of his arrest on March, 13, 1974; four, the Clark County District Attorney's office makes no representations as to the possible sentence to be imposed on Gerald Ronald Weakland on the plea of guilty to the charge of second degree murder as the sentence to be imposed shall be decided solely by the judge who sentences Weakland on his plea to second degree murder.

Dated this 13th day of August 1974.

Signed, Gerald Ronald Weakland.

Signed, Roy R. Woofter, Clark County District Attorney.

Approved, Clark County Public Defender by Michael A. Cherry, Assistant, by Howard Ecker, Deputy

Looking at this plea agreement document one would believe, and it would appear to be professionally and ethically well-written, right?

Okay, so now that you have read this plea agreement which Weakland, the cops and prosecutors agreed to, it looks legit, doesn't it? Forgetaboutit!

Later on, you're going to find out the real truth behind this plea document and the "real" plea agreement they all agreed to. This plea agreement contains fraud, deceit, malice oppression under the law and corruption beyond what you can't imagine. I kid you not, in my opinion, based on what happened to me, I believe that the cops and Prosecutor Harmon were dirty and a disgrace to the badges they wore with dishonor.

WHY WAS WEAKLAND OUT TO GET ME?

By now, I'm sure you're asking yourself why Weakland would name me in the plot seemingly "out of the blue." I've had a lot of years to think about that, and I've developed plenty of different and yet possible theories. I'll run one of them by you now.

I learned that he had a grudge against me for a reason I never imagined. I mentioned earlier that at one time (1973) if I remember exactly, I was in partnership with Bill Underwood in a number of properties and a school of Martial arts. One day Underwood says to me "hey Frank, how would you like to obtain the pool concession at the new MGM being built? I know a way you can get it!" I told Bill, "I know nothing about pools and wouldn't know how to operate it… I'm satisfied being the Bell Captain at the Hacienda Hotel."

I also remembered that once when I was visiting with Underwood, I had a conversation with Weakland myself. At that time, Gerry was a pool boy who worked for Underwood, and in that conversation, I learned directly from him that he was trying to get the concession.

I figured, great, Gerry was the pool boy at Caesars and certainly would have more insight as to how to handle that kind of business. I told Bill I didn't want to undercut Gerry's chances to land that concession.

Underwood then goes on to tell me that Gerry was never going to get the concession because he once beat up the kid, I believe, of one of Caesar's Executives, and Underwood fired Weakland for that incident.

Subsequently, the casino/hotel/gaming network, being what it was at that time, there was little chance whatsoever of Weakland getting that spot, and apparently Underwood was giving me an early shot at going for it. That bit of information made me reconsider the opportunity and I then told Bill that I would take the "concession" only if you let Weakland know that I'm not stealing it from underneath him."

Obviously, Bill did not give that message to Weakland, as I think it's possible that

Weakland may have learned later that Underwood had talked to me about it and maybe he felt that I was the guy who slammed the door on his dream. That possibility was validated later on when I heard that Weakland had even told a couple of convict friends of his that he hated me because I tried to "steal the pool concession" from him, and that he wanted me killed! What?

I don't know...but it's at least one possible theory as to why Weakland had a "thing" about getting me into a situation which would ruin my life.

My "friend and business partner" Bill Underwood seemed to frequently have "suggestions" for me regarding opportunities I might want to explore. Get this...he came to me another time telling me that I should think about becoming a loan shark. Yeah... a loan shark for crying out loud! I couldn't for the life of me figure out why he would think that I would be interested in doing something like that. Everyone knew at that time that loan sharking was a business that one would not think about getting into without reservation, because that was the dome of Tony "The Ant" Spilotro.

In his book, Of Rats and Men, John L. Smith wrote, "Not long after Anthony Spilotro followed Frank Rosenthal to Las Vegas, a strange thing began happening to local gamblers, casino wise guys, illegal bookmakers and loan sharks...they began suffering violent deaths. The weapon used – a 22 high standard pistol with a silencer was wickedly consistent. Someone was sending a message that there was a new street boss in town, one who demanded not only respect but also tribute. Although no one ever seemed to see anything, the little guy was said to be responsible for the lengthy list of murders."

Well, this particular suggestion would've placed me on a rather distinguished list. Turns out that at one point in time during his tenure as the mob's "overseer of activities" happening in Vegas "Tony Spilotro had initiated a "campaign" to reduce the number of loan sharks in town. The manner in which this "campaign" was being carried out was not a pleasant one for anyone who had gained his attention, let's just say.

After I learned this, I began to wonder... could it possibly have been that if I had taken Bill up on his "suggestion," that I would have been a target for the "elimination" by one of Spilotro's "associates?" Scary thought for sure, but one that perhaps would not have been considered particularly absurd. Anyway, I came to view my "friendship" with Bill Underwood quite warily from that point.

MAXWELL, LAPENA, BOUTWELL
PRELIMINARY HEARING

The evening edition of the Las Vegas Review Journal newspaper dated Tuesday, January 15, 1974, featured a short article with a headline that read, "Contract kill ruled out in townhouse stabbing." The article stated, "…Officers said they had ruled out the possibility of a contract killing in the death of Hilda Krause, 64, who was beaten and stabbed to death about 5:30 a.m., Monday (January 14th) in a bedroom of her expensive townhouse at…. Her husband Marvin…was knocked unconscious in the apartment robbery…."

Keystone cop Homicide Detective Beecher Avants, a rogue cop, whom I will expose for you as you read on, made this ridiculous statement to the public when he adamantly stated that the mafia had no involvement whatsoever in the murder of Hilda Krause. Oh, really Beecher, how would you have personal knowledge of that? You just started your investigation into the Kruse murder and also stated any rumors Marvin Kruse may have been involved in the death of his wife was bull shit. He made these stupid statements without ever doing a full and complete investigation of the Krause homicide in the very beginning of the Krause case. Hmm, let's see. Maybe he watched too many TV detective shows where they catch the killers in one hour. No, that's not the answer.

First of all, Caesars Palace was controlled by the mob and every damn cop, including Avants and his boss, Sheriff Ralph Lamb, knew this. Avants' false statement to the public that Marvin Krause was not a suspect turned out to be a police coverup. Avants knew Marvin Krause was involved in his wife's murder and he covered it up as I will show this to the reader later on. So back to the Krause investigation. Based on a confidential informant's tip, the police's investigation led them to Caesars Palace employee Gerald Weakland whom they arrested on March 13, 1974, for the Hilda Krause murder/robbery.

On March 29, 1974, Weakland gave a statement, but not a true statement we were to learn later on, to the Clark County District Attorney which resulted in Rosalie Maxwell,

Thomas Boutwell, and myself being charged in the Krause crimes.

With Weakland's knowingly false statement as the foundation upon which the State proceeded to build its case against Rosalie Maxwell, Thomas Boutwell and myself, a preliminary hearing was convened on May 8, 1974, before the Honorable Magistrate, B. Mahlon Brown to determine if there was probable cause for Rosalie Maxwell, Thomas Boutwell and myself to stand trial for the Hilda Krause murder and robbery. The State was represented by Deputy District Attorney Melvyn Harmon and Charles Paine.

I'm just going to address some relevant and material questions and answers given to pathologist Dr. James Clark as to the cause of Hilda Krause's death and Weakland's answers as to how he claimed he murdered Hilda Krause and see if you notice or can figure out the clue or clues as to who really murdered Hilda Krause.

Dr. James Clarke was sworn in and Mr. Harmon began his questioning:

Q: *Is it Doctor James Clarke?*

A: *Yes, sir.*

Q: *Dr. Clarke, what is your profession?*

A: *I am a physician, specializing in pathology, and Chief Medical Examiner for Clark County*

Mr. Harmon: *Your Honor, for the purpose of this preliminary hearing, I wonder if the defense counsel will stipulate to Doctor Clarke's expertise in the field of pathology.*

Mr. Spizzirri: *I would be willing to stipulate on behalf of Mr. Boutwell.*

Mr. Crosby: *Solely for this preliminary hearing, on behalf of Mr. LaPena and Maxwell*

The Court: *So, stipulated*

Mr. Harmon: *Thank you*

Harmon then continued his questioning of the witness.

Q: *Doctor Clarke, were you so employed as Chief Medical Examiner for Clark County on or about January 15, 1974?*

A: Yes.

Q: Pursuant to your assignment as medical examiner for this county, do you perform autopsy examination?

A: Yes, sir.

Q: Did you perform an autopsy examination at Bunker Brothers Mortuary on January 15, 1974?

A: Yes, sir.

Q: Would you describe the subject upon whom this examination was performed?

A: The subject was an elderly woman, fairly slight build.

Q: I am showing you State's Proposed Exhibit 2. Can you identify that individual?

A: Yes, sir. That is a photograph of the body upon which I performed the autopsy.

Q: Was this autopsy performed January 15, 1974 at Bunker Brothers Mortuary?

A: Yes, sir.

Q: As part of your autopsy examination, did you perform an external examination of this female body?

A: Yes, sir.

Q: Would you describe that examination and your findings as a result of it?

A: The main findings of the external examination was a deep incised cutting and stabbing wound of the neck. This was much deeper on the right side of the neck and extended horizontally for about 13 centimeters, or about 5 inches. The wound was gapping, particularly on the right, and it measured up to 2 centimeters in width in this area on the right. In addition, above the stab wound was a deep ligature *groove almost completely encircling the neck, which showed a fabric pattern to it. This measured approximately 29 centimeters in length and extended horizontally from just below one ear to the opposite side of the neck, below the other ear. There was also...*

Mr. Crosby: *Your honor, is Doctor Clarke reading from something?*

The Court: *Are you reading from anything?*

The Witness: *No, sir. Maybe I should be. There was a deep depression with a fabric pattern on one side of the mouth involving the cheek that appeared to be a gag. The only other external finding was a superficial stab wound which was of minor importance.*

Q: *Did you perform an internal examination, Doctor Clarke?*

A: *Yes, sir.*

Q: *Would you describe that examination and your findings as a result of it?*

A: *With the exception of the neck, all the organs were in good condition, including the brain; including also the microscopic examination of these organs. The cutting and particularly the stab wound of the neck resulted in severance of the right external jugular vein as well as lacerations of the carotid artery. In addition, there was a complete severance of the vertebral artery in the deepest portion of the stab wound on the right. The cause of death was massive external hemorrhage from the severed arteries in the neck.*

Q: *Doctor Clarke, as a result of both your internal and external examinations, were you able to form an opinion by what instrumentality these injuries were inflicted.*

A: *As far as the fatal wounds were concerned, it was a sharp-edged, sharp-pointed instrument, presumably a knife.*

Q: *Did you find any evidence in your examination, both externally and internally of this female body, of death by natural causes?*

A:	No, sir. There are no other significant diseases that could have contributed to the death.
Q:	Did you form any opinion regarding whether these injuries were self-inflicted?
A:	In my opinion, they were not.
Q:	What is the basis of your opinion in that regard?
A:	The size and nature of the lacerations plus the presence of stab wounds in addition to the deep cutting wound in the neck.
Q:	Did the superficial stab wound in the back have any significance in that regard?
A:	Well, it would have significance in that it could hardly have been self-inflicted because of its location.
Q:	Were you able to form any opinion whether these injuries were accidentally occurred?
A:	In my opinion, they could not have been accidental.
Q:	Were you able to form any opinion regarding the time of death in regard to when the injuries were incurred?
A:	No, sir. The body had been refrigerated before the autopsy and I didn't attempt to estimate the time of death.
Q:	Can you estimate how long this person would have lived after these injuries were inflicted?
A:	I think the interval would have been very brief after the severance of the arteries. Probably not over a minute.
Mr. Harmon:	That concludes direct examination.
The Court:	Mr. Spizzirri?

Mr. Spizzirri then began his cross examination of the witness.

Mr. Spizzirri:	Doctor Clarke, what is the date of this post mortem examination?

A: *January 15.*

Q: *I show you what purports to be a copy of your report. Is that your report?*

A: *Yes, sir.*

Q: *Could you tell us if that date reflected in the first paragraph, is that a typographical error?*

A: *I assume it is. It says the 14th.*

Q: *Despite that fact that your report says the 14th, you are certain as you testify here today that it was the 15th?*

A: *Yes, sir.*

Q: *What time was this autopsy performed?*

A: *As I recall, it was the afternoon about two o'clock.*

Q: *Was that the first time you had seen the person upon which you performed your post mortem examination?*

A: *Yes, sir.*

Q: *Had you been to the alleged scene where the incident took place?*

A: *No, sir, I was not.*

Q: *Were you shown any photographs of the scene?*

A: *Not at the time of the autopsy, no sir.*

Q: *Were you provide with any information by any officers pertaining to the scene prior to performing your post mortem examination?*

A: *I think some general information, but nothing detailed.*

Q: *You didn't take this information into consideration when you formed your opinion as the cause of death?*

A: *No, sir, I didn't.*

Q: *You indicated the body had been frozen?*

A:	*Refrigerated. It wasn't frozen.*
Q:	*And that made it impossible for you to form an opinion as to when this person demised?*
A:	*Yes, sir. Any precise opinion would have been difficult to form.*
Q:	*Did you do any toxicology work on the person of this examination?*
A:	*I took some blood and urine samples which were submitted to the Chief Deputy Coroner, but at the time I completed my report, subsequently, I don't believe I had been informed of any positive findings.*
Q:	*You directed that these blood specimens be examined for the presence of any alcohol or narcotic substance?*
A:	*Yes, sir.*
Q:	*Could you determine from your examination the position that this person would have been in at the time she received these stabbing injuries?*
A:	*Well, only to the extent that the anterior surface of the body must have been exposed to sustain the neck wounds. I don't know what her subsequent position was before she died.*
Mr. Spizzirri:	*I have no further questions.*

Mr. Crosby then had his opportunity to cross examine Dr. Clarke.

Mr. Crosby:	*Did you refer to the stab wound in the back as superficial and of minor importance?*
A:	*Yes, sir.*
Q:	*Could you explain what you mean?*
A:	*It didn't penetrate. It barely penetrated the skin. It didn't penetrate any vital organs.*
Q:	*When you conducted your autopsy, was there any foreign article lodged in the body?*
A:	*No, sir, there wasn't.*

Q: How many stab wounds were there, in addition to the two wounds…in addition to the back wound and the 13-centimeter neck cut? How many additional stab wounds were there?

A: Well, I can only say there was evidence of more than one, from the appearance of the deeper portions of the right neck. It may have been three or as many as five or six, but I couldn't say with any certainty.

Q: Couldn't you see the wounds?

A: The external wound was one common wound and it was only the deeper portions that were separate cuttings of the neck muscles and arteries.

Q: Do you have any way of telling whether the neck or back wound was inflicted first?

A: No, sir.

Q: Would you explain what you mean by the ligature groove that you indicated was present?

A: It was an oval-shaped depression in the skin or groove that extended two-thirds of the way around the neck with the deepest portion in the front. It appeared to have been an attempt at strangulation by ligature with a cord or fabric applied to the neck.

Q: Is there any way to tell, Doctor Clarke, whether or not death could have been caused by strangulation prior to the stab wound?

A: Not with absolute certainty, except there was no evidence of trauma to the larynx or to the hyoid bone, indicating that pressure hadn't been great. So, in my opinion, she was not killed by strangulation.

Q: Your report reflects apparently there was an attempt at strangulation by ligature, presumably prior to the throat cutting. Upon what facts or observations do you base that presumption?

A: I think mainly on the extensive hemorrhage observed, because if she had been dead by strangulation when she received the wounds, she wouldn't have bled too extensively.

Q:	*Your reports indicate that attempt at strangulation was presumably prior to inflicting…prior to the throat cutting. Now, what would indicate that as opposed to the neck having been cut then the attempt at strangulation?*
A:	*Well, the bruising and discoloration associated with ligature and the presence of the small hemorrhages subcutaneously would prove that she was still alive in any event when strangulation was attempted.*
Mr. Crosby:	*No further questions.*
Mr. Harmon:	*No redirect.*
The Court:	*Thank you Doctor. Does that conclude your testimony for today?*
Mr. Harmon:	*In view of the motion, that will conclude our testimony for today, your Honor.*
The Court:	*Fine. We will continue at nine o'clock tomorrow morning.*

Little did I know at the preliminary hearing that pathologist Dr. James Clarke's medical findings on the actual cause of Hilda Krause's death consisted of two extremely favorable medical findings which exonerated both Rosalie Maxell and myself. One medical finding is detailed in "Quite a Harry Situation" and the other in "Federal Young Guns Uncover Type of Killer Who Killed Hilda Krause" and "Actual Innocence."

Okay, here are some clues of the real killer for you to figure out. I'm just going to do a synopsis of Weakland's 1974 preliminary hearing testimony under questioning by the prosecutor Mel Harmon on how Weakland claimed he murdered Hilda Krause. You will get a more detailed account of this testimony later on.

- Weakland testified that he tied up Hilda Krause with telephone cords and tape.

- Then he took her into the other bedroom and tied her hands to her feet.

- Then he went downstairs to the kitchen to get a knife and went back up the stairs into the bedroom where she was lying and hit her in the back of the head with his fists and knocked her out.

- Then he raised her head and cut her throat one time all the way across the neck without getting any blood on himself and then stuck the knife in her back with such great force that he broke the handle of the knife.

Now, I ask you, does that sound true to you as to how he claimed he killed her? Forgetaboutit, not even close to the truth as you will read on. Okay, on to testimony parts of Gerald Weakland, Robert (Bobby) Webb and Weakland's precious love for his wife, Gail Weakland.

Weakland was then cross-examined by Boutwell's counsel, Mr. Spizzari, who centered most of his questions to Boutwell's interactions with Weakland and Robert Webb, and what he did at the crime scene on January 14, 1974.

Finally, our attorneys, Douglas Crosby, an associate of Oscar Goodman and former prosecutor and public defender, and Oscar Goodman, were given the opportunity to cross-examine Gerald Weakland. And were they ever ready…Oscar Goodman informed the Court, "Your Honor, it's my understanding that Mr. Crosby is going to examine Mr. Weakland." So, Counsel Crosby went first and exposed the fact that Weakland was enjoying some sort of deal as a result of his testifying at this hearing.

Q: *Mr. Weakland, what are you getting in exchange for your testimony?*

A: *I'm to be charged with Second Degree Murder.*

Q: *Is that all?*

A: *I was given immunity on the Obernauer charge. They told me I'd be charged with Second Degree Murder; five to life with the possibility of parole in five years.*

Q: *They also agreed they wouldn't charge you with any robbery offenses including the Krause thing; is that true?*

A: *Second Degree Murder.*

Q: *Is that all?*

A: *That's all.*

. . . .

A: *The detectives have been approaching me for a long time for a deal.*

72

Weakland went on to testify about the numerous times Detectives Lee and Avants questioned him about both the Obernauer and Krause cases.

Q: *When was the next time you had any conversations with my law enforcement officials regarding the Krause case?*

A: *Just after the first of the month, because my wife and I are separated, and she was in the hospital.*

Q: *Excuse me, the first of what month?*

A: *March.*

Q: *Your wife was in the hospital?*

A: *Yes.*

A: *Her and I had a fight.*

Q: *She lost?*

Hmm. I wonder if she was the love of his life and his sparring partner? Weakland then went on to testify Detective Lee could get Caesars Palace to give Weakland $5,000.00 if he would say "anything" he told them.

Weakland further testified, "I didn't want their money but when I found out about the little girl, I told him if he made sure this little girl went back to his ex-wife, he would turn himself in and only him."

However, both Weakland and Prosecutor Harmon left out advising the Court and Counsel Crosby that Weakland in a violent fit of rage "hanged" the "little girl" with a belt and only a neighbor saved her life to which Weakland "was never charged" for attempted murder of his ex-wife Gail Weakland's daughter.

MY OH MY! Now that's what I call real injustice and it was how the "corrupt" State of Nevada practiced law. This little girl never got a chance to tell a jury how she almost lost her life from a crazy person who the State of Nevada was in bed with – Don't you think!!

Had Crosby and Oscar Goodman known about this horrific attempt by Weakland to kill an innocent child, as well as the Court being made aware of it, Weakland's credibility would have sunk to a new low. I have no doubt Prosecutor Harmon was relieved this evidence stayed silent at our hearing.

Further questions by Crosby were mainly a rehash of Harmon and Counsel Spizzari's questions, which were getting a little redundant. He concluded by stating, "Your Honor, at this time, I don't believe I have any further questions, subject to the right to call for the purpose of further cross-examination."

Mr. Goodman said, "I think the record should reflect as long as we're on the topic, there was destruction, which will be raised at the appropriate time, of a 'tape' which was referred to at yesterday's hearing." (Later on, in my story, I will address what I believe this tape that was destroyed really stated).

Now it was Oscar's turn to take a crack at Weakland and you will see for yourself that Oscar's aggressive questions caused Mel Harmon to panic regarding Weakland's credibility. Oscar went after Weakland as a possible serial killer and after Weakland's credibility. Oscar was relentless in his opening questions.

> Q: *Isn't it a fact, sir, you had a discussion with Mr. Webb concerning the killing of other people in the Clark County area?*
>
> A: *No.*
>
> Q: *Isn't it a fact you told Mr. Webb you killed this person as a result of getting paid money for killing this person?*
>
> A: *No.*
>
> Q: *Isn't it a fact you told Mr. Webb you could pinpoint the location where you buried the body of the person you killed in the desert?*
>
> A: *No.*
>
> Q: *You're saying you never had a conversation such as that with Mr. Webb?*
>
> A: *Right.*
>
> Q: *Are you telling me you didn't have repeated conversations to that effect, that you killed "other people with Mr. Webb?*
>
> A: *No.*
>
> Q: *So, if Mr. Webb says that, he's lying?*

A:	*He must be.*
Q:	*Did you tell Mr. Webb you killed this person by shooting him with a gun?*
A:	*No.*
Mr. Harmon:	*Your Honor, I'm going to object to any further questions along this line...I don't see the materiality of this.*
Mr. Goodman:	*We're going into the credibility as to statements of this witness.*
Court:	*How much further do you want to go? He's said no to all the questions?*
Mr. Goodman:	*He's also saying he didn't kill anybody else and didn't tell Mr. Webb that he killed anybody else other than Mrs. Krause and the Obernauer case. Mr. Webb, I'm sure is going to testify Mr. Weakland told him those things and I'm entitled to put that in the record and this Court is entitled to weigh his credibility.*
Court:	*I'd tend to agree.*

Let me tell you I truly believed Harmon was bent out of shape that Oscar Goodman would be able to establish and present evidence that the State's chief witness was actually "a serial killer" who had a lust for uncontrollable violence, was a psychopath and a pathological liar. Now, that's what I call an honest, good citizen who the State fell in love with.

Oscar, on his game, further asked Weakland if he had any other "secret" agreements with the State where he was given immunity not known by the defense regarding other crimes he may have been involved in such as other killings. Weakland said, "No."

I won't present all of it to you as it's too laborious to deal with, but trust me, I've not left out any pertinent information. I will say this, as Oscar Goodman attempted to expose Weakland's credibility, it certainly did have its effect on Judge Brown, and Mel Harmon began to feel that presenting Gerald Weakland as a credible witness was becoming a very difficult task, i.e., possible serial killer.

| The Court: | *This witness' credibility is minimal as it stands.* |
| Mr. Harmon: | *(sarcastically) That's your opinion.* |

The Court:	I'm the only one who can judge that.
Mr. Goodman:	He's the Court.
The Court:	I didn't say he has no credibility, I said very minimal.

Things were getting quite intense and at one point, Weakland himself was on edge and responded to Harmon's questions.

Q:	Isn't it true, Mr. Weakland that Thomas Boutwell was also present?
A:	When you started asking me questions...
Mr. Goodman:	Object, it's not responsive.
The Court:	No, it's not.
The Witness:	(Weakland) Hell, do you want to hear the truth or not? You're arguing.

By that remark by Weakland, voices heated and rose up as the defense and Harmon argued back and forth.

| The Court: | Yelling is not going to get any of us anywhere except to get me upset. |
| Mr. Goodman: | I've got nothing further. |

When Robert (Bobby) Webb was called to the stand, prosecutor Harmon made sure on direct examination he would never mention what Gerald Weakland told him about his propensity to murder other people.

I distinctly recall Doug Crosby whispering to Oscar that he wanted to go first and drill Bobby Webb about his plea agreement with the State because he had a gut feeling there was something, they weren't being told about Webb's true plea deal with the State...And was he ever right.

I'm just going to address a few questions and answers given to and answered by Bobby Webb as Doug Crosby began his cross-examination of Bobby Webb's immunity agreement with the State.

| Mr. Crosby: | Now prior to your testifying here today and prior to your giving statements to the Las Vegas Metropolitan Police Department on April 2, 1974, was there any promises made to you regarding |

immunity in this incident?

A: *Yes, there was.*

Q: *What was that promise, and by whom was it made?*

A: *I don't recall by whom it was made. It was made to my attorney that I couldn't be charged in this case.*

Q: *Isn't it true in the presence of the D.A. and Mr. Kauffman, you were promised that the only criminal action you'd have to be involved in regarding this matter would be a plea to a gross misdemeanor?*

A: *That is correct.*

Q: *And you wouldn't be charged with being an accessory or as an aider and abettor to the crime of murder.*

A: *That's correct.*

Well now, if Bobby Webb was PINNOCCHIO his nose would have stretched clear across the courtroom. Wait till you read later what he wasn't charged with and kept secret for 25 years by Webb and his nefarious partner, Mel Harmon, in what appears to be a conspiracy to frame me for a crime of murder.

Up next came Oscar Goodman and he wasted no time as he asked Bobby Webb about Weakland's propensity for killing and Harmon had a fit when Oscar asked Webb that question and immediately objected.

The Court: *What grounds? I'm going to allow it.*

Mr. Harmon: *I don't think the question is proper.*

Mr. Goodman: *I will try to rephrase it.*

The Court: *You understand Mr. Harmon, the leeway I'll allow.*

Mr. Goodman: *Did you ever have a discussion with Gerry Weakland concerning his propensity to kill?*

A: *His intention to kill?*

Q: *His propensity; his lust for killing.*

Mr. Harmon:	*I object to the characterization.*
The Court:	*To the use of the word, lust?*
Mr. Harmon:	*Yes.*

Heated arguments were at an all-time high between the defense and State prosecutors concerning Weakland's thrill to kill many people as Oscar continued to press Bobby Webb.

Q:	*You had a discussion with Mr. Weakland before he went out to commit the Krause murder in which he states he was, in fact, going to kill Mrs. Krause?*
A:	*Correct.*
Q:	*You had a discussion with Mr. Weakland concerning his killing of other persons, is that correct?*
A:	*He indicated at one time he'd kill someone else.*
Q:	*Just one time?*
A:	*That's all I can recall.*
Q:	*Not more than one occasion?*
A:	*No.*
Q:	*Do you recall when he said he killed someone else?*
A:	*No, I don't.*
Q:	*Do you recall giving a statement on a date "which is not even indicated on the statement to the District Attorney's office" concerning Mr. Weakland telling you he killed another human being?*
A:	*Yes.*

Okay, here is serial killer time as Oscar Goodman continued along this line and established Bobby Webb had heard from Weakland "three different times he'd killed people" and "had indicated that in his statement to the District Attorney's office."

As Oscar Goodman was questioning Bobby Webb regarding details of one of the killing incidents, Mel Harmon flew off the handle. Hey, am I seeing things – are these red horns starting to grow on his head as he angrily objected to Oscar's questions?

Q: Mr. Goodman: "Did he tell you in specific detail where he shot the person? Where he shot him and where he buried the body…?"

Mr. Harmon: That's a compound question.

The Court: Objection sustained.

Oscar really drilled Webb when he asked a number of questions about various specifics of killings Weakland spoke to Webb about. When asked whether he was certain of his facts and whether he just made things up, Webb testified he thinks he'd even taken a polygraph.

If you think Mel Harmon was upset before, he went completely bananas when Oscar asked Webb about another killing, Weakland spoke to him about. The victim was a "psychiatrist" and was supposed to have been murdered a year prior. I'll say this, Mel Harmon's face turned red with anger.

HOLD IT! Am I seeing things again? Did I just see red horns light up the courtroom at Oscar's question to Webb? Ask yourself, do you think the homicide cops Avants and Lee would like to investigate and solve another murder or murders by Weakland to put a feather in their caps. Remember they hailed themselves as the TOP COPS. Are you kidding me? They're at best incompetent, and at worst they're corrupt. It would have put an enormous task for the prosecutors to overcome to any jurors that their chief witness was actually a serial killer!

I thought maybe you would like to read a little more about Weakland's love for his ex-wife. I will make this short but relevant and material how much Weakland cherished his ex-wife, Gail Weakland.

Gail Weakland was on the stand. Oscar went into the situation where she had been hospitalized for a time. It was very intense questioning, showing Weakland's M.O. (modus operandi) to inflict brutal domestic violence in addition to have a propensity for killing as he (Oscar) had suggested during the Bobby Webb testimony.

Q: There came a time, did it not, when Mr. Weakland, beat you?

A: Several times.

Q: There was one time he beat you up to such a severe extent that you went *to the hospital.*

Weakland caused her liver damage and two weeks hospitalization. Still no criminal charges for the lovebird.

> *A:*   *Yes.*
>
> *Q:*   *When did that beating take place.*
>
> *A:*   *Which one?*
>
> *Q:*   *The one causing you to be hospitalized.*
>
> *A:*   *I've been hospitalized "three" times.*

Wow, I wonder if he sent her flowers?

> *Q:*   *Tell us about the various times you've been hospitalized as a result of Gerry's beating you?*
>
> *A:*   *One time he broke my nose very, very bad.*
>
> *Q:*   *Where was that?*
>
> *A:*   *That was a year ago, about September.*
>
> *Mr. Harmon:*   *You Honor, we move to strike that as immaterial.*
>
> *The Court:*   *Overruled.*
>
> *Q:*   *September 1973.*
>
> *A:*   *Yes, I think.*
>
> *Q:*   *When is the next time?*
>
> *A:*   *No, he had before that too.*
>
> *Q:*   *He put you in the hospital?*
>
> *A:*   *Yes, in about February of the same year.*
>
> *Q:*   *And the last time he put you in the hospital was when?*
>
> *A:*   *February.*
>
> *Q:*   *February 1974?*

A:	*Right.*
Q:	*Where did the beating take place?*
A:	*At our apartment.*
Q:	*What type of beating did he inflict upon you?*
A:	*I don't understand.*
Q:	*Did he hit you in the ribs? Stomach? Head?*
A:	*Stomach, the back, the head.*

Alright, I believe you get the picture now. So, let's see…we have testimonial evidence of Weakland as more than likely a serial killer; an ex-wife beaten to a pulp numerous times, attempted murder of a little toddler; top homicide cops who don't investigate criminal crimes of a serial killer because he is now a prosecution witness who beat up women and children and I believe possibly a mentally unbalanced prosecutor with red horns brightly shining and "no criminal charges" for their "Alter Boy" for these governmental agents with badges.

I ask you what do you think if you were caught up in a manufactured crime by a government of red devils?

I also think and believe "any woman or man" who reads this should be repulsed by the State of Nevada not charging Weakland for his numerous, horrible assaults on his ex-wife Gail Weakland. But then again remember how much Mel Harmon loves his "angel boy" Gerald Weakland.

It had been well over two months passed since the preliminary hearing ended on September 4, 1974. Both counsel Crosby and Oscar had filed numerous motions challenging the State's charges against Rosalie and me.

On that date, September 4, 1974, our focus (Rosalie and I) was on the final closing arguments that the State and our attorneys would be presenting to the Court. This being a death penalty case via execution in the gas chamber, we were definitely concerned what the Court's determination would be after listening to all the various testimonies; testimonies filled with false allegations, assumptions, hearsay and outright lies. The Court was to deal strictly with the facts as they related to Rosalie and me.

Doug Crosby represented both of us because Oscar Goodman was in Omaha,

Nebraska, working on a federal trial. The judge was okay with that…without belaboring you with the long arguments.

After final closing arguments the Court advised, "All right, thank you gentlemen, I'll inform you when I'm ready to make my ruling."

I believed Doug Crosby's representation for dismissal was excellent, but unfortunately under the law, probable cause only needed to be slight to be bound over for trial. It's really a tough battle to have a probable cause hearing to go in your favor. Very seldom are they granted, but Rosalie and I did not know that at that time.

On October 1, 1974, in a ten-page Court Order that was issued, both Rosalie and I faced the death penalty. Boutwell made a deal not to face the death penalty – so what else is new here?

Well, that was it, the decision was mind-boggling (execution via the gas chamber) later to be overwhelming proven as the biggest and most sensational mob murder coverup by the governmental State of Nevada in its entire history.

After Rosalie and I were bound over to face the capital charge of first-degree murder to the District Court, Oscar Goodman filed a brief challenging Nevada's Death Penalty Statute as unconstitutional at the time.

Unless you are one of us, who did not commit the crimes of a first-degree capital murder charge (and there are many), you cannot believe what it feels like to go into a courtroom, especially before a good old bias judged, and hear step-by-step how you can, and will be, executed in the gas chamber (if you lose).

It's been over 40 years now, but I can still feel the trauma and see it as if it was today. As I sat in that courtroom listening to the prosecutor (guess who) trying his best to "murder me," I cannot describe in words what I was truly feeling inside of me, the emotional and physical impact that plays into your mind and thoughts, as Oscar fought passionately and vigorously to save my life.

At no time did I show that bias Judge Carl Christensen any emotion that flowed through my mind and body, kept it to myself, as I listened as you are to be executed. What the cyanide pills (hydrogen cyanide gas) start to do when they suck out the very breath of your body, cutting off oxygen to the brain and heart, your body shutters, trembles, heaves while your organs start to shred, your skin turns purple and your eyes pop as you experience extreme anxiety and pain, then you lose consciousness and ultimately die as the power of the cyanide pills kill you.

I will always remember Oscar Goodman as the man (and friend) who literally saved my life. Oscar's argument before Clark County Judge Carl Christensen regarding the death penalty being cruel and unusual punishment, was absolutely brilliant, incredible and full of passion.

Unfortunately, as vigorous as his presentation was, after several hours of a heated battle with the prosecutor, Judge Christensen denied that motion.

But, let me say this to you, and I pray you will never have to go through this, as I did, due to a corrupt Nevada government, to this very day, I have never forgotten what I was put through by a corrupt State and its agents "who wanted to murder me."

Rosalie was not present during this death penalty hearing argument. I believe Oscar wanted to spare Rosalie what the horrors could possibly be for her to know the pain and suffering she would experience once strapped in the gas chamber chair if we lost at the trial.

12

WHAT WOULD OSCAR HAVE DONE
IF ONLY HE HAD KNOWN?

*"I don't know whether Frank LaPena had anything to do with Hilda Krause's murder,
but I do know something about defendants, and his actions have been those of a man who
was innocent! He passed up opportunities to get out of prison if only he would admit his
role in the murder . . . but he refused!" – Oscar Goodman*

Over the many years that I've known Oscar Goodman, I've come to regard him as one of my very best friends, and a man who loves the city of Las Vegas. Thousands of people know him as the now energetic, unendingly and unapologetically enthusiastic Las Vegas former Mayor of our fair city.

Still others know, as the result of him having been written about in a number of books that he had an illustrious career in the practice of law before entering the world of municipal politics. No doubt, many millions more remember him as he appeared as himself in the classic mob film "Casino."

As you know, Oscar represented me at my 1974 preliminary hearing involving the probable cause issue of the charge of first-degree murder. That charge carried a death penalty sentence, and Rosalie and I were definitely not thrilled about the prospect of having to face the ultimate penalty for a crime we did not commit.

Now, just in case many of you may be saying to yourselves, "Wait a minute, if the U.S. Supreme Court said the death penalty was unconstitutional, didn't that make it unlawful for any state to incorporate it: Aren't there now states that still carry out capital punishment?"

Yes, there are, and here's a very brief explanation as to how that's so. Capital punishment had been carried out by a majority of states and the federal government for various crimes, especially murder and rape, from the creation of the United States up to the beginning of the 1960s. Until then, ". . . save for a few mavericks, no one gave any credence to the possibility of ending the death penalty by judicial interpretation of constitutional law," according to abolitionist Hugo Bedau.

There were no executions in the United States between 1967 and 1977. In 1972, the U.S. Supreme Court struck down capital punishment statutes in *Furman v. Georgia,* reducing all death sentences pending at the time to life imprisonment. Subsequently, a majority of states passed new death penalty statutes, and the court affirmed the legality of capital punishment in the 1976 case of *Gregg v. Georgia.*

The situation of *Furman v. Georgia* was unique in that the U.S. Supreme Court considered a group of consolidated cases. The lead case involved an individual convicted under Georgia's death penalty statute, which featured a unitary trial procedure in which the jury was asked to return a verdict of guilt or innocence and, simultaneously, determine whether the defendant would be punished by death or life imprisonment.

The last pre-*Furman* execution was that of Luis Monge on June 2, 1967. In a 5-4 decision, the Supreme Court struck down the impositions of the death penalty in each of the consolidated cases as unconstitutional in violation of the Eighth and Fourteenth Amendments of the United States Constitution.

In stark contrast to what many believe, the Supreme Court has never ruled the death penalty to be *per se* unconstitutional. The five justices in the majority did not produce a common opinion or rationale for their decision, however, and agreed only on a short statement announcing the result. The narrowest opinions, those of Byron White and Potter Stewart, expressed generalized concerns about the inconsistent application of the death penalty across a variety of cases, but did not exclude the possibility of a constitutional death penalty law.

Stewart and William O. Douglas worried explicitly about racial discrimination in enforcement of the death penalty. Thurgood Marshall and William J. Brennan, Jr., expressed the opinion that the death penalty was proscribed absolutely by the Eight Amendment as cruel and unusual punishment.

The *Furman* decision caused all death sentences pending at the time to be reduced to life imprisonment and was described by scholars as a "legal bombshell." The next day, columnist Barry Schweid wrote that it was "unlikely" that the death penalty could exist anymore in the United States. Schweid was premature in that declaration. Capital Punishment is a legal penalty in the United States, currently used by 31 states, the federal government, and the military.

Back to my friend Oscar Goodman. I discovered that we had something in common when I learned that he actually first came to Vegas the same year that I did-1964. He was admitted to the Nevada State Bar in 1965 and had served as a Clark County Deputy District Attorney in 1966 and 1967. Having become later a senior partner in the law firm of Goodman, Chesnoff & Keach, he put aside his duties at the firm during the years he had served as mayor.

It certainly was fortunate for me that by the time I became one of his clients, Oscar had established himself as one of the top attorneys in the country having been once "named one of the 15 best trial lawyers in America" by the National Law Journal.

His considerable knowledge of the letter of the law versus the spirit of the law when combined with a fiery intensity he often exhibited as he went about the task(s) of defending his clients, earned him an impressive reputation as the attorney you'd want to have on your side at any and all times.

In his book, *Of Rats and Men*, author, John L. Smith, said of Oscar, "Investigations by law enforcement agencies had an effect on Goodman with what he saw as lawlessness on the part of the government." Never one known to be reluctant to provide his point of view, Oscar Goodman has been quoted as saying, for example, "Someone has to be willing to speak out against government excess." "It's a shame what's happening in this country. The government's aggressiveness exceeds the bounds of fair play."

During the course of the years that he was practicing, Oscar faced off against some of the toughest prosecutors the State of Nevada had to offer. One of the most noted of these was Mel Harmon. Harmon handled some 300 felony cases. Over 130 or so were murder trials. I guess you'd have to say that in his own way, he was every bit as formidable as adversary as any defense attorney could ever have to encounter.

However, tales of Harmon's prosecutorial practices have been the stuff of myth and legend. On a number of his cases, he routinely denied the defense information that would be beneficial to them in the presentation of their arguments. This certainly was evident during the handling of my case.

I wasn't the only defendant to have been the recipient of Harmon's unique style of prosecution. The Nevada Supreme Court finally had been made aware of enough of the stories, and declared that on more than a few cases, the State of Nevada prosecutors in Clark County, and Mel Harmon in particular, had routinely failed to comply with constitutionally mandated discovery obligations by withholding materials exculpatory and impeachment evidence from accused criminal defendants.

Mel Harmon had openly disparaged the disclosure requirement imposed by the U.S. Supreme Court's landmark decision in *Kyles v. Whitley*, 514 U.S. 419 (1995), as "very fine for judges to write about . . . a legal fiction."

They went on to find that Harmon refused to turn over exculpatory and/or impeachment evidence in the case of *Jimenez v. State*, 112 Nev. 610, 918 P.2d 687 (1996). In *Jimenez*, the Court noted that Harmon himself had stated that, "even if he had the information, he would not have felt a duty to disclose it to the defense." *Jimenez* at 690.

I can assure you that if Oscar had only known of the tons of information that Harmon hid from him during those hearings, he would have blown his stack, and proceeded to rip Harmon a new one via proper, yet spirited expressions of displeasure. I'm sure all within the parameters of judicial decorum.

The list of exculpatory information was considerable and included such things as:

- When prosecutor Mel Harmon and D.A. Roy Woofter concealed from Oscar, Rosalie and I that a different prosecutor had been originally assigned this case and refused prosecution, which you will learn later "why."

- That D.A. Woofer then assigned Mel Harmon, the worst nefarious prosecutor in Nevada history, to take over the prosecution of Rosalie and I, and as such, the presumption of innocence just didn't exist at that point, as you will learn later.

- That Mel Harmon allowed and intentionally knew Gerald Weakland was committing perjury that Rosalie and I hired Weakland to murder Hilda Krause, and the State's theory of the crime never existed, which will be explained in more detail later.

- Harmon hid from Oscar that prior to the 1974 preliminary hearing, Weakland named two other individuals, not Rosalie or I, as having hired him to murder Hilda Krause, that will be explained to you later on.

- That both Mel Harmon and homicide detectives refused Weakland a plea bargain deal for naming the other two individuals as having hired Weakland to murder Hilda Krause. Why? You will learn later.

- Mel Harmon concealed from Oscar that Marvin Krause *personally* knew Weakland's accomplice, Robert (Bobby) Webb, who helped Weakland plan the murder of Hilda Krause.

- That Harmon concealed from Oscar, that he (Harmon) was in possession of a video-taped statement linking Marvin Krause hiring Bobby Webb to commit a violent crime of robbery with use of a deadly weapon upon a person who Marvin Krause didn't like. You will learn more about this later on.

- That Harmon concealed from Oscar, that he (Harmon) was in possession of a video-taped statement, where Marvin Krause personally solicited three cocktail waitresses from Caesars Palace to help him (Marvin) find someone to plan a "fake" burglary at his residence to steal his wife Hilda Krause's jewelry and furs so he could collect insurance money.

- That Harmon concealed from Oscar that "Harmon knew the real identity of the third person at the crime scene who actually murdered Hilda Krause." and it wasn't Weakland which 22 years later Harmon admitted to this unforgiving fact.

I could go on with this sickening laundry list of pieces of information that Oscar was not given the opportunity to address on my behalf, but I am feeling pretty confident now that you've got the picture. I'll stop here about these omissions that prosecutor Mel Harmon committed while attempting to derail Oscar's ability to defend Rosalie and I.

There is absolutely no doubt in my mind that had Oscar only known the facts that have been described here, the results of the preliminary hearing would have been significantly different. Harmon's ends justify the means style of prosecution was despicable and gave so much credence to Oscar's statement that, "Such actions are reflections of a Gestapo mentality, and are becoming a matter of course in Las Vegas."

Let me tell you this, when a prosecutor or cop does not disclose material evidence favorable to a defendant showing someone else committed a crime, they both become a disgrace to the truth-seeking function of the Court, and they insult the integrity of the judicial system. That is precisely what they did to me.

To this very day, I have maintained only the highest regard for Oscar, and he and I still occasionally see each other. It happens now more often than not at the National Museum of Organized Crime and Law Enforcement-more casually known as the Mob Museum.

I'd never be presumptuous enough to ever claim to possess the legal acumen that Oscar has. I will say that whatever legal knowledge I was able to acquire while I was incarcerated, I do try to apply with the same zeal in the quest for justice that I observed Oscar demonstrate on many occasions.

13

A GODDESS GOES TO TRIAL

On July 20, 1976, after having spent just over two years in the Clark County jail awaiting her day in Court, Case 29339, the State of Nevada v. Rosalie Maxwell got under way. I was in the new city Jail at this time during her trial, working as a trustee.

Before Rosalie's 1976 trial began, Oscar Goodman was judicially removed as my counsel, due to an alleged conflict of interest. Leonard Gang and Donald Wood were court-appointed for Rosalie. Talk about the luck of the draw. Rosalie struck gold when Gang and Wood became her attorneys. Leonard Gang was a former District Court Judge and Wood was a former prosecutor from Nebraska who later moved to Las Vegas, Nevada. Me, I ended up with two losers: Randy Mainer and Bill Skupa, who never once visited me when I had the death penalty hanging over my head. I was, as a result of their negligence, forced to file my first ever motion before the Court to remove these two attorneys which was granted.

Getting back to Rosalie: There were approximately 27 witnesses called during her trial; many who'd been called as witnesses in our preliminary hearing a couple of years earlier.

Judge James Brennan performed the roll call of the jurors and the alternates, and they were sworn in by the clerk. The clerk then read the formal charges against Rosalie that had been lodged by District Attorney, Roy A. Woofter, and of course, Melvyn T. Harmon, Deputy District Attorney. The reading concluded with "…to the charges just read the defendant has entered a plea of not guilty."

Judge Brennan instructed the jurors that they would be allowed to take notes during the trial; the jurors were given pads and pencils.

In a criminal jury trial, the prosecution always goes first. I'm going to make this short and sweet and I feel it may pique your interest as we move along here. Here is the prosecutor Larry Leavitt's Opening Statement:

I would like to advise you at this time that what I am doing now is making an opening statement, and as the Court has told you, my comments and the comments of any of the attorneys in this case are not evidence. The only evidence that you will hear and see will be in the form of testimony from the witness stand and physical items that are introduced into evidence during the course of this trial; . . . .

The defendant in this case, Rosalie Maxwell, at the time of this occurrence was a cocktail waitress at Caesars Palace Hotel. She was married to an individual named Don Maxwell, but she had been separated from Don Maxwell for some period of time.

. . . For approximately three years preceding this incident, Rosalie Maxwell had been carrying on an affair with Marvin Krause, both of them having worked at Caesars Palace

. . . Rosalie would meet with Marvin when Hilda Krause was in town approximately twice a week at the Sands Hotel and other places in exchange for this Marvin bestowed upon the defendant gifts of jewelry and money.

. . . Rosalie Maxwell, the defendant, and Frank LaPena were aware of the great wealth possessed by Mrs. Krause and they decided that they were going to acquire some of that wealth and the way to do that was to eliminate Hilda Krause so that Rosalie would be free to become much closer to Marvin Krause, perhaps even marry him.

. . . In order to accomplish this end, . . . a meeting was held between Rosalie Maxwell, Frank LaPena and Jerry Weakland. At that meeting, a plan was developed whereby Hilda Krause would be murdered.

. . . The terms of that deal were that Jerry Weakland was to receive one thousand dollars down, with ten thousand dollars to come sometime later, perhaps within the year after, according to Rosalie Maxwell, she was able to acquire some of the money that would be left to Marvin Krause.

. . . The defendant and Frank LaPena advised Jerry Weakland to make this look like a robbery, and the defendant removed one thousand dollars in cash. . . from her dresser in her bedroom where that meeting took place. . . . On Monday, January 14, 1974, Jerry Weakland carried out his end of the bargain.

. . . I would ask you on behalf of the State of Nevada to listen to all of the evidence objectively and open-mindedly and give us your complete and undivided attention, and I am sure that at the close of all of the evidence in this case, you will find that this defendant is guilty as charged.

Please keep in mind I will prove to you that the prosecutor Larry Leavitt was deliberately lying to the jury that Rosalie Maxell and I advised Gerald Weakland "to make this look like a robbery." This was a monumental lie right from the start of the 1974 preliminary hearing that would have resulted in our charges dismissed by Judge Mahlon Brown had Oscar known about this lie.

I would also like you to pay attention to what this corrupt prosecutor inferred to the jury that Rosalie Maxwell wanted Hilda Krause out of the way so she could marry Marvin Krause, knowing this was also untrue; but like I say, you be the judge as I put this all together for you.

Now here is part of defense attorney, Leonard Gang's opening statement:

Ladies and Gentlemen, it's unusual for the defense to make an opening statement right after the State makes its opening statement. Usually, you reserve it until your opportunity to present your part of the case. However, I think in this case it's a rather unusual case. It's going to be a very lengthy case and because of the nature of the evidence and the testimony that you're going to hear, I'm going to make a statement now. I will be very brief.

The State has told you and you have been advised that this trial may take two to three weeks, that there is going to be some 30 or 31 witnesses. Yesterday we marked and identified some 60 photographs. These will be a tremendous volume of evidence and number of witnesses. They are going to present a quantity of evidence but not quality.

I want you ladies and gentlemen to keep in mind throughout this case what does the evidence have to do with Rosalie Maxwell? The State will present a witness by the name of Gerald Weakland who is the confess murderer in this case. His testimony will indicate that an alleged meeting occurred between Gerald Weakland, Frank LaPena and Rosalie Maxwell. We dispute that. It is our position that that meeting never occurred and that Rosalie was not present at that meeting.

This is a real-life story. It's a sad story but it's real life and you are participants in it. This story is well put together by the police, 'although great police work did not solve this crime as you've been informed.' There was an informer who gave the police some kind of a tip which led to Gerry Weakland. We don't know the name of the informer. That's not been presented to us, although it was requested, and we don't have an opportunity to examine the informer in open Court.

I'm sure Harmon or Leavitt will do a good job in putting forth the evidence and they are experienced prosecutors. The judge will keep order in the Court, will instruct you on the law to be applied to the evidence.

I sincerely hope that the case will be well tried by the defense, when it's over, I'm convinced that not only will you fail to be convinced of my client's guilt, beyond a reasonable doubt, but that you will be convinced that she is innocent.

Now, I ask you to keep in mind, as you read Leonard Gang's statement, did his reference to Mel Harmon and Larry Leavitt bring in mind anything like MARC ANTONY'S speech before the citizens of Rome? Let me say this, I thought how subliminally brilliant it was to imply surely Harmon and Leavitt were "honorable men" (yeah right), who based on their experience would present their case very well…the fact law enforcement and the State may "not" have been totally forthcoming to the defense, regarding their knowledge of the confidential informant notwithstanding. I wondered if a juror or two might've thought the same thing.

But there was one thing I didn't have to wonder about: Yes, great police work did not solve this crime, as Leonard Gang argued, "Great Police Work Covered It Up." This I will prove to you during the conclusion of this book.

I'm not going to bore you with a lot of questions and answers from a six-week trial. What you are about to read is the heart of the defense's attack against the State's charges upon Rosalie Maxell, starting with Gerald Weakland's 1976 trial testimony.

Gerald Weakland, having been first duly sworn to tell the truth, the whole truth and nothing but the truth testified under direct examination by prosecutor Mel Harmon who immediately attempted to try and establish the date, time and place where this alleged murder for hire contract was established; a very critical and material part of both Rosalie's defense as well as mine, that no murder contract ever existed.

Q: *by Mr. Harmon:*

As a result of your telephone conversation with Frank LaPena on Friday, January 4, 1974, did you have occasion to go to the Greenbriar Townhouse area?

| A: | Yes, I did. |

...

A:	Yes, that's the Townhouse where I went to meet Frank LaPena.
Q:	Do you recall what time of the day or night it was?
A:	Between 7:00 and 10:00.
Q:	Is that A.M. or P.M.?
A:	P.M.
Q:	by Mr. Harmon:
	Your Honor may the record show the witness has identified Rosalie Maxwell.

Then Weakland, out of the blue, shocks the entire courtroom ignoring Harmon's question and said under oath: "This lady had nothing to do with this crime, any statements I made against her I lied about; and I did it on my own to protect my family."

WOW! What the hell just happened? Without a doubt the morning's proceeding were thrown in a tail spin as Weakland caught everybody off guard with his testimony about Rosalie. After this bombshell exploded in the courtroom a recess was called for everyone to get their heads straight back on.

Harmon continued:

| Q: | Mr. Weakland my last question this morning was" What did Rosalie Maxwell do? You responded: "This lady had nothing to do with this crime." Were you saying she did nothing after she came to the door on January 4, 1974? |
| A: | I'm saying this lady had no involvement with this crime. |

BY THE WITNESS:

Your Honor, I made a statement this morning that this lady had nothing to do with it. I have been harassed from these people from jump street on this.

BY THE COURT:

Wait a second, for the record harassed from the people from what?

BY THE WITNESS:

> *I'm talking about homicide detectives on this case about these people,*
> *this lady, I told the Court this morning I made a false statement against*
> *her. I've been drilled by this gentleman here. I've had to go along with*
> *this thing so I could get in here and try to clear up this thing. ECF*
> *VOL. 7*

Like Leonard Gang stated in his Opening Statement, we are going to dispute that any meeting between Weakland, Rosalie Maxwell and myself ever occurred. The prosecution subpoenaed Ms. Jean Crow, Personnel Clerk at Caesars Palace whose testimony backfired against the State's theory of the case and the charges against Rosalie and myself. I'm going to make this short and sweet.

By Mr. Leavitt:

Q: *Would you state your full name, please?*

A: *Jean Crow.*

Q: *Mrs. Crow, what is your occupation?*

A: *I'm a Personnel Clerk at Caesars Palace.*

By Mr. Gang; Cross-Examination:

Q: *Can you tell us from looking at those sheets what period of time—*
        what shift Mrs. Maxwell worked?

A: *6:00 in the evening until 2:00 a.m. in the morning. ECF Vol. 10*

REDIRECT EXAMINATION:

Q: *Mrs. Crow, are you able to determine from the record that you brought*
        with you to court today what Mrs. Maxwell's ordinary days off were
        during the year of 1974 specifically in the month of January?

A: *Well, the latest card I have here in here shows her days off as*
        Wednesday and Thursday. ECF Vol 10

There can be no question that the State's case against Rosalie was very weak and I believe the jurors noticed that also. When Jean Crow was the custodian of Records at Caesars Palace testified that Rosalie Maxwell was in fact at work at 6:00 p.m. on the night of January 4th and worked until 2:00 a.m. on the morning of January 5, 1974, the jurors had to believe the State failed to prove beyond a reasonable doubt Maxwell was not guilty of the state's charges against her when the documentary evidence showed she had not been at her townhouse in attendance at the alleged meeting as Gerald Weakland testified.

I believe this powerful exculpatory and material evidence coming from Mrs. Jean Crow had to weigh heavily on the jurors' mind because Gerald Weakland's testimony Rosalie "had nothing to do with this crime, any statements I made against her I lied about", was corroborated by Mrs. Jean Crow's testimony on January 4, 1974, she was a work on a Friday night between the hours of 6 p.m. to 2: a.m. Bingo! No Murder for Hire Contract Ever Existed just as Leonard Gang argued.

Not only was this a devasting blow to the prosecutor's case, the fact that the State's theory of murder, Rosalie wanted Hilda Krause out of the way so she could marry Marvin Krause and get all of Hilda's wealth and then murder Marvin Krause within the year, also did not exist and here is why:

You recall prosecutor Larry Leavitt in his Opening Statement said about Rosalie Maxwell: "She was married to an individual names Donald Maxwell." What they didn't tell the jurors was Rosalie Maxwell neither prior to nor after the murder of Hilda Krause sought to divorce her husband, Donald Maxwell. Well, hello, and good ridden to the State's theory of the case, refuting Weakland's testimony Rosalie wanted to marry Marvin Krause after the demise of his wife Hilda Krause.

Just to make matters worse for the State was the testimony of State witness Lt. Hanlon you may find very interesting. Here is Lt Hanlon's testimony on direct examination by prosecutor Mel Harmon. You will get the point of what this testimony revealed as to whether Gerald Weakland was a LIAR.

By Mel Harmon

Q: *Lt. Hanlon, directing your attention to July 19th and 20th of 1976, were you present in my office when Gerald Weakland was interviewed?*

A: *Yes.*

Q: In your presence was a description given by Weakland as to how Hilda
            Krause was killed?

A: It was.

Q: What did he say?

A: Mr. Weakland described that he walked over and stood over and
            loosened the bounds of Hilda Krause where he personally tied her
            hands. He leaned over and 'strangled her' he thought to death. He
            did strangle her. Momentarily thereafter, he was somewhat in doubt,
            and went to the kitchen and obtained a large knife, came back upstairs
            where she was, once again went over to her, picked up her head by the
            hair, pushed a knife through once and dug it back through her throat.
            He backed up a step or two and drove the knife as hard as he could in
            her back.

Mr. Harmon: That's all we have, your Honor.

The Court: Do you have any cross?

Mr. Gang: With the Court's indulgence for just a moment.

The Court: Surely.

Mr. Gang:

Q: Mr. Hanlon let me ask you one question. You're not familiar with
            the statements Mr. Weakland said prior to January 19th and 20th,
            1976, are you?

A: Not fully, sir, no.

Q: And you are not familiar with his testimony in the preliminary hearing
            transcript?

A: not too close, no sir.

Mr. Gang: All right, I have no further questions, Your Honor.

...

Did you catch it? Did you catch this inconsistent piece of information? If you did, you might wonder if the jury caught it also. According to Lt. Hanlon's testimony, Weakland told Harmon he "strangled" Hilda Krause, yet when Detective Chuck Lee testified earlier, and was questioned by the defense, he (Lee) said Weakland never told him he strangled Hilda Krause. So, which was it? Did Weakland lie to the police, or did he lie to the D.A.? My contention is he lied to both! And I hope you agree with me. You will learn and read later how this played on the prosecutor's quest to hold Weakland as a credible witness who doesn't lie for the State.

Based upon what the jury heard during Weakland's 1974 preliminary hearing testimony, I don't believe the jurors bought Lt. Hanlon's testimony as truthful.

Oh, yes, before I forget, even Mel Harmon went so far as to admit before the jurors, their theory of the case wasn't right regarding Detective Whitney's police report of the informant when Mel Harmon said: "Arguably, there are things in them apparently given by the informant, which are inconsistent with the state's 'theory of the case,' meaning the informant completely impeaches everything Weakland said about the Krause murder, and that's the real reason they tried every which way to prevent us from obtaining (Joseph Costanza) as a very strong witness against Weakland and the State's charges against Rosalie and me.

Ok, it's now crunch time for closing arguments by the State and the Defense. I'm mainly going to address the Defense's closing arguments because I feel they were great. Like I said before Leonard Gang and Donald Wood were brilliant. Here is Donald Wood's closing as he places a chart on an easel for the jury to see. The chart was a calendar showing the witnesses who testified, and the order in which they appeared indicating he'd be referring to the calendar during this representation. I shall cut to the short and just get to the meat of his presentation before the jurors.

Donald Wood:

> I want you to know right now, Rosalie Maxwell is not guilty of these crimes. A little over a month ago, capital punishment under the statute pertaining to her was declared unconstitutional so for about twenty-six months she was confined with the understanding that if convicted she'd be put to death, and you were advised at the outset, this is not a capital case.
>
> The State's theory is Rosalie Maxwell and Frank LaPena hired

Gerry Weakland to rob Marvin Krause and murder Hilda Krause, probably the most attractive theory about the case is the State's theory is not supported by the evidence.

The State's theory came to light as a result of two crimes; the Krause case and a crime which proceeded it, the Obenauer crime: The two perpetrators, Weakland and Webb having been involved in that incident.

They faced charges for attempted murder, kidnapping and robbery... then the Krause incident, Weakland faced murder, robbery and deadly weapon and he made a deal. Weakland makes his deal and brings in Rosalie Maxwell. 'She hired me to do it.'

Bobby Webb plotted the Krause murder. He was in on it. He said he sent one of his friends and he got a gross misdemeanor and then part of that deal, the D.A. is going to appeal to get him placed on probation. Alright, I call our attention to the fact, Weakland is the principal accuser against Rosalie Maxwell.

'This lady had nothing to do with this crime... I'm saying this lady had no involvement with this crime... Your Honor, I made a statement this morning this lady had nothing to do with it. I've been harassed from these people from jump street on this. I made a false statement against her...if you want to send this lady to prison, you're going to have to find someone else beside me to do it... I've already stated this lady had nothing to do with this crime. I will answer no further questions.'

The defense had come here prepared to take on this one witness. He was really the principle accused, there are no other accusers of any significance. This is the man who comes in here and takes the oath like everybody else and he recants. He left his tracks with inconsistent statements. Rosalie had to be here for some reason in the first place. Obviously, somebody accused her or made a statement implicating her, and it was Weakland, and he walks in here and says 'she had nothing to do with it.'

Okay, well, as I say, it reversed the course of the lawsuit, we are no longer defending her against Weakland. Once Weakland does what he does, what's there to defend against but prior inconsistent statements over which we've no control. How do we defend against a prior statement? That's history, that's history.

I suppose when one's charged with contract murder the first question is 'well, when does he say the contract was made?' Weakland said, 'I imagine it was 2 or 3 weeks before it happened the exact date, I'm not sure approximately eighteen to twenty days.'

Now, the preliminary hearing for the first time, Weakland is cross-examined. Somebody else is after him to pin it down.

Q: *When was the first time you became aware of this contact?*

His answer: I imagine it was eight-ten days before maybe it was the last of December. I believe it was a Friday night between eight and nine in the evening.

The last Friday was December 28th and you know Rosalie worked those hours on that date. That's in evidence.

He comes in here on July 21st, took an oath, and it was a great temptation to say, he told you this woman had nothing to do with this, therefore believe him. We're not going to tell you he was an honest man July 21st; we're telling you he was a liar on March 29th, April 1st and May 9th, 1974… Mr. Harmon suggested we have to be in the position of saying he was truthful to you in the trial, he was truthful two years ago.

Our position is he is not worthy of belief. The truth is not in him and if you believe that, if you believe he's not worthy of belief, then you should acquit Rosalie Maxwell. It's just that simple. If you believe him when he testified in this trial that she had nothing to do with it that's fine, that ends it. She's not guilty. But if you find and if you believe he's unworthy of belief, then that ends it too, and she should be acquitted. So, we don't have to vouch for his credibility.

The State wants you to believe a fairytale. She's going to marry Krause, but she's married.

Marvin had another adult female companion, didn't he? Oh, you, they saw somebody else coming in. I submit to you her contacts with Avants, and Lee are more consistent with innocence than that of guilt. Remember, Chuck Lee said she was cooperative.

The Court: *Thank you Mr. Wood. Any further answering argument?*

Mr. Gang: *Very, very brief, Your Honor. After six weeks of trail, Mr. Harmon and I have finally agreed upon something. I agree Gerald Weakland is a liar no question about it, he's a liar.*

Mr. Harmon say the question is "When is he lying?" That's not the question at all. The question is: When did you say to yourselves, I believe Gerry Weakland lies, statements or some of them beyond reasonable doubt.

I want to tell you one other thing and I'm finished.

You should not convict on the testimony of murderers, thieves, robbers, prostitutes, dope addicts, felons and liars.

And the police who failed to fully search for the truth. Their investigation stepped up when Gerald Weakland said what they wanted to hear.

I guarantee you if you spend two more years in the Clark County Jail and you never opened your mouth, and you never said one word to anyone, there'll be someone who, for the right deal, will be willing to say and will be willing to testify under oath you confessed to them. Thank you very much.

The Court: *Ladies and Gentlemen of the jury, the case is submitted to you for deliberation and decision. If you would go with the officers in charge of you and select a foreman, deliberate and reach a verdict.*

And so, it ended. The day had been quite long. It was 7:45 p.m. and Rosalie Maxwells fate was now in the hands of the jurors.

At 6:36 p.m., August 20, 1976, Rosalie Maxwell, after being found not guilty, was free to begin to piece her life back together and attempt to put the ordeal of the past 2 years behind her. I watched on the TV screen where the news media made a huge story of her acquittal and I had good reason to feel optimistic that a jury would do the same for me.

14

QUITE A HARRY SITUATION

On Perhaps titling this chapter as I have lets you know right away the point of view I have regarding Harry Reid. I imagine that his name is familiar to many of you, as he has certainly gained notoriety as one of our country's notable political figures in recent history. The now retired former Majority leader of the U.S. Senate (from 2007 to 2015) enjoyed a 30-year career, serving as one of the "voices of the people" of the State of Nevada.

He began his rise to that "lofty position of responsibility" entering politics in 1968, when he (then the city attorney in Henderson, NV) won election to the Nevada Assembly. In 1970, he was selected to become running mate to his former boxing coach Mike O'Callaghan and winning the election, served as Nevada's Lt. Governor from 1971 to 1974. After serving in that office, he launched two unsuccessful campaigns… trying to become a U.S. Senator and later Mayor of Las Vegas.

It was during his "disappearance from the public arena" that our paths crossed landing him in the position of being my court appointed defense lawyer at my 1977 Nevada trial.

Recalling my first attorney-client meeting with Harry Reid at the City Jail, I believe was in late 1976, and it was not one in which I would consider him to be, in my gut feeling, a person who possessed a force of nature/power. He spoke too softly for me, no strength in his voice. He started off by telling me "The State wants you real bad," words to that affect. Not, how we are going to go "after" the State due to the false charges against me. I didn't know anything about the guy.

His comment made me feel like I was the most evil person on the planet, which immediately triggered my distrust in him. Boy was I ever to learn my gut feeling was right. Harry Reid and his co-counsel Bruce Alverson, unbeknownst to me at this time were civil attorneys not criminal attorneys with Alverson "never" doing a murder case before and going up against the so-called best prosecutor in Nevada. What really pissed me off was Reid "lied" to me that he had done about 100 jury trials, leaving out they were probably civil cases.

Neither Harry Reid nor Bruce Alverson had any right to accept my case, neither one was qualified to take on a case of this magnitude. In my opinion, I was later to learn through my own ability to do criminal law, Reid and his co-counsel didn't know their ass from a hole in the ground about criminal law. With the criminal law experience that I have today, I would have had my case dismissed at the early stages of my March 1977 trial or acquitted before the jury; something Reid and Alverson should have done had they known what they were doing.

Yep, like Oscar Goodman put in his book (Being Oscar), "when I took the bar, the judge who supervised the group had nice things to say about me. It was said 'Harry Reid was the best young CIVIL LAWYER and Oscar Goodman was the best young criminal lawyer among the batch admitted during those years'".

In their so-called preparation for my trial, I don't recall Bruce Alverson coming to see me to let me know how they were progressing in their investigation. Reid sent an investigator to see me and to waste my time. The witness list I provided him to combat the State's charges against me, "went nowhere" as I found out later.

Years later, I couldn't believe the News Media described Reid as a "tough" guy who boxed with Governor O'Callahan as his trainer. Reid is lucky he never stepped into the boxing ring with me when I was fighting, I would have hit him so hard, I would have knocked his ass into the next century. My trainer was Tippy Larkin. a.k.a. Antonio Pilliteri, World Light Welterweight Boxing Champion from Garfield, N.J. No one ever lasted one round with me. I was also trained in Martial Arts by Ken Hanselman, youngest J.D.I. in Marine Corps history at 17 years old. What I saw and learned from my own experience with Reid, he was no tough, guy; he was a wimp and a weakling. Mel Harmon ran over Reid and Alverson like a locomotive train.

Okay, now that I got that off my chest, Let's get back to my case and their representation to throw me under the bus.

Like I stated in "A Goddess Goes to Trial" the State's case against Rosalie Maxwell was very weak and mine was no different had I gone to trial with real criminal defense attorneys who studied the trial transcripts of Rosalie's 1976 jury trial. At Rosalie's 1976 trial, Leonard Gang and Don Wood presented evidence before the jurors that Rosalie was still married to Don Maxwell before and after the Hilda Krause murder. This evidence tore apart the State's theory of the case and Weakland's March 29, 1974 murder confession and preliminary hearing testimony that Rosalie and I hired him to kill Hilda Krause so she could marry Marvin Krause within the year; then "kill Marvin Krause" within the year to inherit the Krause fortune. This evidence played big with her jury that acquitted her later.

A critical part of my defense was to also prove no murder for hire contract ever existed between Weakland, Rosalie and myself. This was actually a simple, but powerful defense for Reid and Alverson to present on my behalf, just like Gang and Wood did for Rosalie when they destroyed the State's theory of the case, proving Weakland lied that Rosalie wanted to marry Marvin Krause after Hilda Krause was murdered.

Big question: why didn't Reid or Alverson produce evidence at my trial that Rosalie, neither prior to nor after Hilda Krause was murdered sought to divorce her husband, Donald Maxwell. These two incompetent attorneys never bothered to send their lame duck investigator over to the County Records to show Rosalie never initiated any divorce proceedings against her husband. Were these two bought off or just plain dumb. So, what have we here? "The State's Theory of Homicide and the Defense's Failure to Defend Against It."

Let's go to another "State's Theory of Homicide and Defense's Failure to Defend Against It." As you may recall in Rosalie's jury trial how Gang and Wood, in their excellent presentation proved before Rosalie's jurors no murder for hire contract ever existed on the date, time and place Weakland testified he met Rosalie and I at her townhouse on January 4, 1974, between 7 and 10 p.m. and entered into a contract to murder Hilda Krause when Mrs. Jean Crow, who was the Custodian of Records at Caesars Palace testified Rosalie was at work at 6:00 p.m. on the night of January 4th and worked until 2:00 a.m. on the morning of January 5, 1974.

At my March 1977 trial, Mrs. Jean Crow, was called by the State, like at Rosalie's trial. She testified she was the personnel clerk at Caesars Palace for 5 years; she brought certain records with her from Caesars Palace as the Custodian of Records. She brought with her the personnel files of Marvin Krause showing he was first employed as a box-man and at the time of his termination he was the Manager of the Slot Department.

BY MR. HARMON

> *Mrs. Crow, I'm directing your attention to two documents which make up the personnel file on Rosalie Maxwell...*

Q: *What basically is this document?*

A: *It's just a shift schedule change. She works 6 hours on those days: Monday, Friday, Saturday and Sunday and on the swing shift.*

Q: *Does this document show what hours Rosalie Maxwell was working during December 1973 and January 1974?*

A: *Let's see, I can't read the date on here; looks like February 1973 she was working 6 p.m. to 2 a.m.*

VOIR DIRE EXAMINATION

Q: *Do you have any records any place that would indicate that Rosalie Maxwell worked any other hours from the date of February 1973 up to the time she left?*

A: *I don't have them in my file, we could probably get them. It would be on microfilm.*

Q: *Would it be proper to assume that unless there is some shift change in your file, that these would be the hours that she was working?*

A: *Uh-huh.*

MR. REID: *Nothing further your honor, we would agree with the introduction.*

WHAT? Where is your head going Harry??

As you may recall, Mel Harmon took an ass whipping from Gang and Wood. The alleged murder contract took place on January 4, 1974, at Maxwell's townhouse.

Harmon stated:

Q: *As a result of your telephone conversation with Frank LaPena on Friday, January 4, 1974, did you have occasion to go to the Greenbriar Townhouse area?*

A: *Yes, I did.*

By Mr. Harmon:

            Were you saying she did nothing after she came to the door on January 4, 1974?

106

Mel Harmon realized he made a serious mistake at Rosalie's trial, adjusted his argument of an alleged contract murder meeting of January 4, 1974, without any objection by Harry Reid for altering the facts in evidence, when the State takes a position, they are stuck with it. Why didn't Reid produce the exact same testimonial evidence that Gang and Wood did at Rosalie's trial to prove no murder for hire contract ever existed on January 4, 1974?

Now, Alverson starts to recross Jean Crow and asks a dumb question:

Q: *Just briefly, your Honor, is there an indication whether or not Rosalie Maxwell's "marital status" changed from 1966 until the date of her termination?*

A: *We are not usually notified unless they fill out a new W-2 or something.*

Hey, Alverson: like I said before, all you had to do was to use your investigator for that question and you would have found out Rosalie "never ever" sought a divorce from her husband; how simple was that for you to do? Did he do this on purpose or was it his inexperience as a criminal defense attorney?

A little while back I decided to do a little research on Harry Reid's legal career. It was quite interesting to say the least. What I found was a person glorifying himself as an attorney who took on impossible cases to trial amongst other things.

Are you ready for this one: CONTACT HARRY REID 1-866-716-7343

"Every American is entitled to equal justice, no matter their rank in society, equal justice by not equally unfair Justice. Reid is an intensely faithful Mormon but holds his bible close to his vest. Back in the Vegas of the sixties and seventies, Reid was a 'hot shot lawyer' known for being the lawyer of last resort. He would take the cases no one else would take, either because they 'were impossible to win' or paid no money or both. He would defend people down on their luck, 'OR HE FELT WERE WRONGLY ACCUSED.' He took more than a hundred cases to trial, a number almost unheard of today."

Really? Are you serious? Is this a joke? Reid a hot shot attorney who took more than a hundred cases to trial. I wonder being a hot shot attorney, did Reid ever win one, such as a murder case getting an acquittal. I don't think so. In my personal opinion, Reid couldn't cross-examine a grape. I don't recall him arguing criminal case law like Harmon would do and Oscar Goodman during my 1977 murder trial. During my 1977 trial, I don't recall Reid arguing criminal case law like Harmon and Oscar Goodman did during my 1974 Preliminary Hearing.

There's been a sort of "urban legend theory" that Reid's return to political prominence/ascension came as a result of his handling my case. The Hilda Krause Murder was considered the most sensational murder case in Nevada at the time and Reid was certainly getting a lot of exposure as the lead defense attorney in the case.

Now, I will say this, Reid, at one point, attempted to prove that Marvin Krause may have been the one who had his wife murdered and Harry was going down the right road, but Harry made a left turn instead of a right one. I will explain.

On January 27, 1977, prior to my March trial, a "discovery hearing" was conducted as I and my attorneys tried to learn the identity of the Confidential Informant (later identified as Joey Costanza) who had provided information to the State that later determined to be very favorable to me. Geneva "Genie" Blue was questioned by Harry Reid at that hearing. Her testimony would promote a strong consideration of the theory that Marvin Kruse was possibly the person that had his wife murdered. The exchange between Genie Blue and Reid went as follows:

BY MR. REID:

Q: *Did you know a man by the name of Marvin Krause?*

A: *Yes.*

Q: *When did you first know Mr. Krause?*

A: *July, around July of 1966.*

Q: *How did you get to know him in July of 66?*

A: *I worked at Caesars Palace at the time; he was slot manager at the time.*

Q: *Did you know him from 1966 up through and including January of 1974?*

A: *Yes sir. (AA Vol. 1p 11, ll. 20-29)*

Q: *You had conversations with Mr. Krause about his wife, Hilda or conversations that took place?*

A: *There were conversations that took place.*

Q: *Who was present when these conversations took place?*

A: *Rosalie and myself.*

Q: *And Mr. Krause?*

A: *Marvin Krause (AA Vol. 1, p. 13, ll. 25-31)*

Q: *What was said and by whom about Mrs. Krause?*

A: *It was said by Marvin Krause. Mrs. Krause had fallen down the stairs and she had either fractured or dislocated her hip and was immobile and it was something to the effect of "why couldn't it have been her neck" (AA Vol 1, p 21, ll. 5-9)*

About six months later, after Marvin Krause commented about his wife not breaking her neck or her hip, etc., in the presence of Geneva Blue, Marvin Krause made the following remarks on how he wished he could figure out how to get rid of his wife, Hilda Krause. Geneva Blue responded to Harry Reid's questions as follows:

A: *And so, Marvin made a statement to the effect, he said, well, he said, 'They say good things come in three'. He said, 'For me, bad things would be good things in three,' or something to that effect. He said, 'Maybe next time I'll be rid of her…'*

Q: *Now, were there other times during this period from 1970 through Christmas of '73 that he said derogatory things about Hilda Krause?*

A: *Yes, quite often when he was drinking.*

Q: *What was the type of language he would use?*

A: *Not the language I would use.*

Q: *In referring to his wife?*

A: *Yes.*

Q: *Explain to the court what you mean?*

A: *Very foul, really foul language, street language. (AA Vol 1, PP 21, ll. 23-32. P 22, 1-7)*

Q:	Is there anything significant about approximately Christmas time of 1973, the last time that you were present with Mr. Krause socially?
A:	Yes, that would have been when he gave Rosalie her gold piece for Christmas, and he gave it to her early before Christmas.
Q:	Did he refer to his wife at that occasion?
A:	That there would be a better present coming later. (AA Vol 1, P. 23, ll. 8-18)

Unfortunately for me, the trial judge, who also never sat on a murder case, denied Reid's discovery motion and the testimony of Geneva Blue that her testimony was hearsay, so the jurors would not be able to judge for themselves all this evidence Reid tried to bring forth to the jury.

All Reid had to do was file an "Interlocutory Appeal" (A Writ of Mandamus) to the Nevada Supreme Court that would have led my case to be dismissed or be acquitted. Reid should have also done the same in order to get the Nevada Supreme Court to overrule the Judge on Geneva Blue's testimony. However, Reid is not a real criminal defense lawyer who knows how to cite case law off the top of his head; same for Alverson.

How do I know this: I personally won this issue in the Nevada Supreme Court years later when I researched the law. The Court, in their August 31, 1983, granted me a Writ of Mandate in Case No. 14640; where they factually determined and found:

- The transcripts of the September 29, 1982, grand jury contained statements by Weakland manifesting confusion as to the parties involved in the murder.

- The informant has advised police of statements which are inconsistent with Weakland's testimony before the grand jury and Weakland's testimony in the prior proceedings.

- The significance of the informer's testimony is manifest for petitioner to be able to cross-examine Weakland based upon the factors cited above.

- The value and importance of the potential testimony of the informant was necessary for a fair determination of the issue of guilt or innocence.

- The defendant had a right to inform the jury of those facts from which they could determine the informer's credibility.

I believe you can see for yourself, I had very strong issues that the jury was entitled to hear at my 1977 trial, and I don't believe I need to say any more about Reid and Alverson on these issues.

Here is a couple more things I want you to know about Reid and Alverson's representations on how they threw me under the bus, then I'll get down to the nitty gritty you should find very, very interesting.

During my 1974, preliminary hearing, the corrupt cops and prosecutor Harmon, placed a sleaze bag lying murderer on my tier who made up a false story that I had confessed to him that I had hired Gerald Weakland to murder Hilda Krause. Oscar Goodman tore this guy, Bill Fish, to pieces where magistrate Mahlon Brown made a factual finding determination and threw out all of Fish's testimony as underserving of belief.

Based upon criminal law, Fish's testimony was precluded from being heard by the jurors, since it was found to be underserving of belief. Due to Reid's incompetent knowledge of criminal law, Reid, instead of preventing this, allowed it to be heard by the jurors which prejudiced me before the jurors despite my testimony that I never said that to Fish. I wonder how you would feel if something like this happened to. This is the case that piece of shit Reid did not research and preclude at my 1977 trial. *State v. Havas*, 91 Nev. 611, 540 P.2d 1060 (1975), the Nevada Supreme Court held, "that both the District Court and this Court are bound by a magistrate's factual determination."

How do I know about this law years later doing my criminal law research, "I found this law." Yeah! A hot shot criminal lawyer, who doesn't know how to research, cite or argue criminal law.

Also, Reid and I got into a big, heated argument over Reid's having me wear "jail clothes" during my trail before the jurors. Can you believe what this dumb ass had me do? This made me look guilty in front of the jurors' eyes. It took all my restraint not to knock Reid out with one punch. I did realize that I had done that I would have been in a world of more trouble.

Let's go to another issue concerning Reid's representation of me. As you may recall earlier, I presented evidence by Oscar Goodman going after Gerald Weakland's lust for inflicting brutal violence upon his ex-wife Gail Weakland. However, at my 1977 murder trial, Reid only asked a couple of questions to Gail Weakland about his violence against her nor did he aggressively go after Gerald Weakland about his propensity to inflict severe brutal violence upon Gail Weakland and her young daughter, "whom Weakland tried to murder," like Oscar Goodman did at my 1974 preliminary hearing. Gail Weakland's testimony went as follows:

A: *One I was afraid to tell because I knew I didn't think they would pick up Gerry ever, and if he thought I talked 'he got his hands on me, he would have killed me'.*

Well, I hope you agree with me, Reid had a golden opportunity to show the jurors Weakland was a serious possible serial killer as Gail Weakland seriously believed Weakland would have not only murdered her but her child as well when Gail Weakland stated Weakland "hung her daughter by the neck with a belt" and would have murdered the child if a neighbor hadn't stopped him."

What the hell were you thinking Harry for not going after this evidence, like a hot shot criminal defense attorney would have done to show the jury, Weakland would even murder "a child" for no real reason other than his own personal lust to kill anyone, as well as framing a person for a crime that person did not do.

Did you do this on purpose Harry or were you just plain incompetent as an alleged criminal defense attorney. I find it very difficult to believe in my opinion you were that stupid having all that alleged trial experience. My thoughts are you did this on purpose to help the State convict me.

Hey, Harry, why didn't you argue strongly to the jury, "WHY" wasn't Gerald Weakland, 'charged with attempted murder' on Gail Weakland's daughter and, go after the dirty cops and prosecutor. The jury certainly would have been interested why Weakland was left off the hook regarding the child. And why didn't you find out the neighbor's name to subpoena him as a defense witness and present him as a hero for saving the child's life. Neither you nor Alverson can give me one damn excuse for not presenting this evidence before the jurors.

The jurors should have been given the opportunity to know and evaluate what was this young child feeling when she was being hung by the neck by Weakland. Was she petrified she was going to die and what did she do to have that low life Weakland try to kill her? This child had to be scared to death, what mental, emotional scars then and over the years did she experience? She should have been subpoenaed by Reid, so the jury would have first-hand knowledge what the child suffered at the hands of Weakland and evaluate what a monster Weakland really was.

Yeah, hot shot criminal attorney. In my opinion, you're a joke to call yourself a criminal defense attorney. I believe a 10-year-old kid could outlawyer you. As you read this, do you yourself believe Reid should have subpoenaed Gail Weakland's daughter and the guy who saved her life. You be the judge…

What you are about to read next you may understand the frustration what these two attorneys put me through. I will put this in order for you step-by-step and hopefully you will come to the same conclusion I did, but, at a later date, as I shall explain. As I do this I shall be arguing before the Court and jurors, what Alverson and Reid did not. Now, please understand, and put yourself in that courtroom, when you are sitting next to your attorneys, the trauma of facing a life sentence for a crime you did not commit is quite unnerving and your concentration can easily be impaired as your life is at stake, and certain testimony and evidence, etc., can easily pass you by. It did for me, my mind and concentration were not clear during the early stages of my case as the State was falsely trying to execute me via the gas chamber.

On March 29, 1974, Gerald Weakland gave a (false) statement and confessed to murdering Hilda Krause on January 14, 1974, and under questioning by Charles (Chuck) Lee stated the following:

Q: *You said you went down to the kitchen and got a knife. Would you describe the knife?*

A: *Yes. It was approximately 10" long with a brown wooden handle, a bread knife with 'weavered edges' for cutting bread.*

During my 1974 preliminary hearing, I had no legal training or school on legal matters. I would not know until many years later that the Pathologist/Coroner, Doctor James Clark's autopsy, medical findings and determination as well as his expert testimony regarding the murder of victim Hilda Krause would become and had always been, the very best defense witness for my innocence. Also, how Hilda Krause was really murdered and the real type of person it was WHO murdered Hilda Krause, which I will disclose later.

A lot of what you are about to read was presented at my 1974 preliminary hearing, however, Dr. Clarke was far more specific and detailed at my 1977 trial on the cause of death of Hilda Krause. Your attention is directed to his "CERTIFICATE OF DEATH" where he medically determined at #(c) cause of death was from homicidal traumatic "incised cutting and stab wound, neck."

Now, I will remind you, prior to Weakland's March 29, 1974 confession, Lead Detectives Avants and Lee had reviewed Dr. Clarke's Autopsy Report on Hilda Krause's cause of death.

In addition, both Reid and Alverson should have thoroughly reviewed and evaluated the 1974 testimony by Dr. Clarke at the preliminary hearing and the autopsy report before Dr. Clarke testified at my 1977 trial. That information could have blown Weakland out of the courtroom, despite Weakland saying at my 1977 trial, that I had nothing to do with the Hilda Krause murder by going after Weakland '74 preliminary testimony and March 29, 1974, confession.

Alright, you and I are going to get right to the meat of the testimony of Dr. Clarke and then you can see for yourself how corrupt the State and its witnesses are, except Dr. James Clarke, who told the truth. Pay close attention to what Dr. Clarke is actually and specifically testifying to, as to his 1977 testimony as follows:

BY MR. HARMON:

Q: *What is the nature of your duties as a medical examiner for this*
             county?

A: *The duties consist mainly of performing autopsies in the case of*
             *sudden death or homicidal deaths 'to determine the **exact cause** of*
             death.'

MR. ALVERSON:

             Your Honor, we would stipulate as to the doctor's expertise in
             medical and related fields.

MR. HARMON:

Does this include his 'specialty' as a pathologist?

MR. ALVERSON:

Yes Counsel.

MR. HARMON:

Thank You Counsel, 'we accept' the stipulation

THE COURT: *Thank you gentlemen, the Court will accept the doctor as an expert in the field of pathology*

…

A: *…In the neck there was an incised cutting wound extending completely across the neck from left to right.*

Q: *Dr. Clarke, in layman's terms what do you mean when you refer to an incised cutting wound?*

A: *That means it 'cuts, through the skin like a surgical incision.'*

Wow! An incised cutting wound that cuts through the skin like a surgical incision. Many years later, I became curious as to the definition of the medical word "incised." Here is what I found in the medical dictionary of definition of, "incised wound"

Incised – Adjective

3. Medicine/Medical. Made or cut cleanly as if surgically; not ragged; an incised wound

Incised – Adjective

3. (of a wound) cleanly cut, as with a "surgical knife"

Medical Dictionary – Incised definition of a cut or wound: made with or as if with a sharp knife "or scalpel"

When the State accepted Dr. James Clarke's specialty as to the exact cause of death of Hilda Krause, the State accepted the pathologist's medical fact that Hilda Krause was murdered by a "killer" who used a surgical/type of knife blade that cut through her skin like a 'surgical incision," that cut cleanly; **like a scalpel,** clean and well-defined, leaving a **straight edge pattern line** and **not a jagged or serrated edge knife with "weavered" edges that would leave an uneven pattern incised wound.** You be the judge, and hope you agree with me.

Anyone with an ounce of a common sense, (like a defense attorney) and especially a homicide detective would know a serrated bread knife with "weavered" edges would not leave an incised wound on a victim, it would leave a ragged or jagged cutting wound. Hilda Krause was murdered by no other weapon except a surgical type of knife blade that cut through her skin like a scalpel.

That being said, knowing Hilda Krause was murdered by someone who used a surgical type of blade knife that cut through her skin causing an incised wound, and not by a serrated bread knife with weavered edges, homicide detectives, Beecher Avants, Chuck Lee and Ray Lyons, based on their long training and experience knew or had to have known that Weakland was lying during his March 29, 1974, statement/confession, video confession and subsequent testimony, about the specific type of weapon/knife that was truly used to kill Hilda Krause and all three homicide detectives made a decision "not" to follow up on any leads or clues or evidence either physical or oral that would have led them to **WHO** the person was, or could have been, that used the surgical scalpel type of blade knife to kill Hilda Krause.

This is one of those rare cases where the conduct of the police measured against the factors set forth above deprived me of my life, liberty and pursuit of happiness and due process of law. There can be no dispute that led Homicide Detective Beecher Avants, who oversaw all police procedures and investigations, including the autopsy findings by Dr. Clarke as to the specific type of incised cutting and stab wounds, showed that Hilda Krause was not murdered by a serrated type of bread knife with weavered edges. Nonetheless, I believe they manufactured this crime against me.

Furthermore, the surgical scalpel knife blade used to kill Hilda Krause, "MYSTERIOUSLY DISAPPEARED" from the crime scene, someone got rid of it. What does this mean, the real killer has yet to be brought to justice and is still at large, but we are going to look at some viable theories of who it may possibly be, so you are going to be a part of this mystery. Now, if you think I'm going to get the proper justice as you read the amazing evidence I uncovered, "Forgetaboutit."

We are now going to review more of Dr. Clarke's Autopsy findings of his 1974 preliminary hearing testimony to pinpoint what he testified to which both Reid and Alverson should have been able to notice and argue to the jury that contained two (2) exoneration issues (the knife and who didn't do it).

Q: As part of your examination, did you perform an external examination of this female body?

A: Yes Sir.

Q: Would you describe that examination and your findings as a result of it.

A: The main findings of the external examination was a deep incised cutting and stabbing would of the neck. This was 'much deeper' on the 'right side' of the neck and extended horizontally for about 13 centimeters, or about five inches. The wound 'was gapping' particularly on the 'right' and it measured up to two centimeters in width' in this area on the right.'

Q: Did you perform an internal examination Doctor Clarke?

A: Yes Sir.

Q: Would you describe that examination and your findings as a result of it?

A: With the exception of the neck, all the organs were in good condition including the brain; including also the microscopic examination of these organs the cutting and particularly the stab wound resulted in severance of the 'right' external jugular vein as well as lacerations of the carotid artery. In addition, there was a complete severance of the vertebral artery in the 'deepest portion of the stab wound on the right'. There was also a fracture of the traverse process of the cervical vertebrae close to this 'severed artery'. The cause of death was massive external hemorrhage of the severed arteries in the neck.

CROSS EXAMINATION

BY MR. CROSBY:

Q: How many stab wounds were there in addition to the two wounds—

in addition to the back wound and the 13 centimeters neck cut?
How many additional stab wounds were there?

A: *Well, I can only say there was evidence of more than one, from the appearance of the 'deeper portions of the right neck.' It may have been three or as many as five or six, but I couldn't say with any certainty.*

When reading the 1974 and 1977 trial transcripts, I was picking up on this. Without realizing it, Pathologist, Dr. James Clarke is exonerating me and neither Reid or Alverson is picking up on the fact that the Autopsy Report and Dr. Clarke's testimony is providing overwhelming evidence of innocence on my behalf in my case.

Now I had a reason for using bold lettering and underlines. They are clues for you to figure out and solve for yourself.

Doctor Clarke's Autopsy Examination findings and trial testimony delivers a grand slam home run that exonerates me. My hot shot attorney and inexperienced co-counsel had no idea how to use this powerful, material exculpatory medical evidence on my behalf. Come on Harry! How the hell did you not see this. This Autopsy Report and testimony on the actual cause of Hilda Krause's death how she was actually murdered and by WHO, is staring you both in your face and you blew it… Were you guys so inept or did you do it on purpose. There is nowhere on the face of this planet, I believe, you did not see what was in front of you.

I ask you how simple can this be for a criminal defense attorney to argue exonerating facts supported in the record. Can you figure out **what's missing**? If not, you will know later on as I did. But, still, I say Reid nonetheless is a lawyer who should have figured it out because he had it in his possession. Now, when I came upon this evidence years later, I immediately knew the answer how the State started to frame me and the type of person who dunnit and who didn't do it. Okay, here is a specific clue to **"what's missing."** You have read Dr. Clarke's Autopsy Report/testimony. Now, here is the big clue. Weakland is, was, a professional boxer. See if you can put two and two together and figure out what kind of person this was who actually murdered Hilda Krause.

I later came to know one specific thing about the significance of this. There is no question in my mind that Mel Harmon knew and was hoping Reid and Alverson would not figure it out. They didn't – or did they? You will be the judge, since this evidence was in the court of record, and ask yourself could you have figured it out, had you seen, read and evaluated this medical evidence?

Just a few more things before I sign off on Reid and Alverson. As I said before, Reid's private investigator was useless. Here is a list of witnesses I gave the investigator, never used by Reid or Alverson at my trial, to discredit the State's witnesses, that I testified to years later:

- Melinda Swerigan to testify that on the day Weakland alleged he had come to the Hacienda Hotel to get a payoff from me for the Krause crime, Weakland was actually applying for a job.

- Otis McClindon and Tillis Banks, who testified at my 1974 preliminary hearing to testify that certain monies paid by me to Weakland's wife was a $50 loan and not a payoff for Mrs. Krause's murder.

- Camille Dixon, Brian Clayton, Richard Grisham, and other neighbors to testify that I did not have a meeting with Webb on November 28, 1973.

- Nurse Haley to testify as to jewelry that Krause was wearing when he was brought to emergency on the day of the murder/robbery,

Wait till you read the next one. A police report generated by Detectives Beecher Avants, Chuck Lee and O.R. Lyons, dated March 13, 1974, indicated that the detectives had interviewed Gerald Weakland's family a week earlier on March 6, 1974, and the detectives were made aware that Weakland did not murder Hilda Krause. The report said that Lois Weakland (aka Sam), the wife of Leo Weakland, overheard Jerry and Leo talking in their kitchen. In that conversation, Lois heard Jerry say to Leo, "**she was alive when I left.**" (APPENDIX 1).

So, in essence, Lois told cops that her brother-in-law, Gerry Weakland, was involved in the Hilda Krause murder...**but did not murder her**. That's right... I was stunned and immediately became pissed off to the truth. Since I was able to discover this March 13, 1974 report, then I thought that there was no way in hell that Reid and Alverson had missed it. This March 13, 1974 police report corroborated Dr. Clarke's autopsy Report/Testimony, physical evidence at the crime scene and DNA which you will learn later. Weakland did not murder Hilda Krause and the damn cops and prosecutors always knew this. Therefore, the jurors in my 1977 murder trial never heard that "**Weakland in his own words" denied that he murdered Hilda Krause.**

I will say this Harmon did not conceal this police report from the defense. It was Reid's responsibility to discover this March 13, 1974 police report that was in the "police files" as the lead attorney. I ask myself and you, the reader, WHY didn't they use that investigative police report that was not hidden, and, in the discovery police files, on my behalf against the State's charges against me? You be the judge.

That info in the hands of any real defense attorney would have made mincemeat of Weakland and his testimonies, and/or claim regarding my involvement in this horrific crime.

- A.G.A. Exh. "N-2" at P. 648, ll. 15-20

- Appellant's Supplemental Opening Brief pages 6-8; pages 9-15

Now, here comes another biggie for you to evaluate that Reid didn't, but why?

During our 1974, preliminary hearing, Mel Harmon was questioning Lt. Beecher Avants about his February 5, 1974 interview with Rosalie Maxwell, about a **mafia hit** man, Charles White, a.k.a. Charlie **"the knife"** that went as follow:

BY THE WITNESS:

> I asked her if she knew a man names Charles White, also known as Charlie the Knife. She said she did…not that she had but three months prior to the murder that Marvin Krause had been in the coffee shop at Caesar's Palace and this man apparently was sitting with Mr. Krause. After this man left, he (Marvin Krause) was questioned by the police as to why he was sitting with this individual, and Marvin was quite upset because of this.

Mind you, this 1974 transcript is supposed to be read and evaluated by Reid before my 1977 trial. So, let's see some of the questions I put together that Reid did not.

Hey, Harry, why didn't you question Avants about his knowledge of Marvin Krause socializing with a mob hit man named Charlie the Knife?

Was tough guy Harry Reid afraid of the Mob? Only he would know the answer to that question.

Was Marvin Krause connected to the Mob? You bet your ass he was and big time. And there was no excuse for Harry Reid not to find out Marvin Krause was connected to Mob Boss Santo Trafficante Jr. and that he obtained some ownership in the Hotel and Casino de Capri in Havana, Cuba which opened in 1957.

Marvin Krause was also connected to the Mob Enforcer, Tony Spilotro, which I obtained evidence Spilotro was close to Marvin Krause and you already read about Charlie the Knife. You will read more about Charlie the Knife near the conclusion of my story.

So maybe Reid may have been afraid to go down this road, I don't know, but it's a passing thought. Always the strong possibility it was a mob hit that Reid wanted to stay away from or maybe he was told by someone it would be in his best interest to forgetaboutit! And remember Hilda was murdered by a knife. Let me tell you, it was well known during this time period the Mob owned cops, prosecutors and judges, witnesses, etc. They were businessmen but also violent killers who had the power to control the city. It was scary in many ways.

As I previously stated, Harry was on the right track in naming Marvin Krause as the possible suspect who wanted to see her dead and prosecutor Harmon in fact, concealed that issue from Reid. I will say this Reid's argument was good, I won't take that away from him. This was a major exculpatory issue, but I don't believe Reid would have run with it. Nor was he smart enough to do so in order to get me acquitted, since he didn't with the other meritorious issues of showing innocence.

This was Harry Reid's argument before the Court:

MR. REID: *Your Honor, I will attempt to show through Geneva Blue that Marvin Krause is probably the person that had his wife killed or certainly an inference can be made from these proceedings.*

Trial Transcript 2569. ll. 20-23

MR HARMON:

      It certainly is. He represented before that this witness was going to establish an inference that 'Marvin Krause had his wife killed' T.T.F. p. 257

Let me say this that low life piece of shit, **knew** Reid was on the right track, and **concealed what Weakland really said in the beginning of his confession to get a plea**

bargain. I will reveal and disclose it later.

> MR REID: *Okay your Honor, we have a right in a proceeding before this court in an attempt to show why it's important that we be able to interrogate an informant who, in our opinion would lead us back not to LaPena or Maxwell but to Marvin Krause. As an offer of proof, the testimony from this woman would be that on many occasions she was out socially with Marvin Krause, he made all kinds of remarks how he wished the bag of bones would blow away referring to his wife. How he wished how he could figure out some way 'to get rid of her…' It's my contention that the perpetrator in crime is Marvin Krause*

T.T.F. 2571-2572

As I stated above, the Judge heard Blue's testimony, but denied before a jury to hear and evaluate it. Had Reid known criminal law, he could have appealed the two denials to the Nevada Supreme Court by filing an Interlocutory Appeal. With the Justices on the Court at that time, there is no doubt in my mind that we would have prevailed.

No question in my mind, Harry the Horse cost me to lose 9 years out of my life throwing me under the bus. Mister Hot Shot Lawyer, how did "YOU NOT" know?

SENATOR HARRY REID'S RISE TO POWER

(A PASSING THOUGHT)

Was it his representation of me, in what was called during the Mob days the most sensational homicide in Nevada history that got Reid's pollical career stated over again? You Be the Judge.

Was it at the expense of me, who was actually innocent and framed by law enforcement officials that Reid saw to it that I would be found guilty? You Be the Judge.

Did Harry Reid get his political career started again by possibly allowing the State to convict me, and was later rewarded with a very powerful political appointed position as the Chairman of the Nevada Gaming Commission? You be the Judge.

Serrated bread knife with wavered edges "not" real murder weapon, that mysteriously disappears at the crime scene. How did "hot shot" defense attorney, miss this where years later I did not when I reviewed coroner's death certificate of the actual cause of Hilda Krause's death? You be the Judge.

Rosalie Maxwell was acquitted on August 20, 1976. Her attorney Leonard Gang, tells Reid, "follow what we did at Rosalie's trial and Frank should be acquitted." Reid didn't. You be the Judge.

Leonard Gang and Don Wood, destroy Detectives Beecher Avants and Chuck Lee's credibility at Maxwell's trial, however, Reid let the detectives commit perjury and damage my credibility... You be the Judge.

Leonard Gang told me years later, that Reid helped the State find me guilty when he put me on the witness stand and "**never asked me if I hired Weakland to commit this crime.**" The news media hammered me on this issue and the jury agrees that I never denied that I committed the said crime while on the witness stand. You be the Judge.

Reid never investigates to let jurors know that the victim's husband, Marvin Krause, was heavily connected to Crime Boss Santo Trafficante Jr; Chicago Enforcer, Tony Spilotro and mob hit man, Charlie the Knife, and also a close personal friend of the Clark County Sheriff and Detective Beecher Avants and that Marvin Krause was once accused or under investigation of a murder. You be the Judge.

I got into a heated argument with Reid because he had me wear "Jail Clothes" during the trial before the jurors. No doubt, in my mind, I believe he did this to help the State find me guilty. You be the Judge.

Reid does not file an Interlocutory Appeal before Nevada Supreme Court Regarding Informant Issue that would have possibly led my case to be dismissed that traverses Weakland, Thomas Boutwell and Robert Webb's testimony nor, files a Motion to Dismiss criminal charges on my case based on real weapon mysteriously disappears at crime scene. I believe Reid allowed the State to continue to "frame" me. You be the Judge.

POLITICAL CAREER

1964 to 1966   Became City Attorney for Henderson, Nevada

1970 to 1974   Became youngest Lt. Governor in Nevada History at age 30

POLITICAL CAREER IN DOWNHILL SPIRAL

| 1974 | Lost to Paul Laxalt for U.S. Senate Seat |
| 1975 | Lost to Bill Briare for Mayor of Las Vegas, Nevada |

I'm of the opinion that these discrepancies in Reid's handling of my defense played a major role in my being convicted on April 10, 1977, of First-Degree Murder and Robbery with Use of a Deadly Weapon. When the jury came back, I noticed a couple of women were sobbing. I knew my life was over. Never before in my life had I experienced this kind of emotional pressure waiting to hear the jury verdict, "Guilty." No! This can't be happening to me, this is a bad dream, but reality took over.

During my sentencing hearing I received, "life without parole, plus an additional 40 years." I can't really tell you what was racing through my mind at that time as there are no words that can describe it because I was far too numb. My thought process knowing I was going to die in prison for crimes I never committed is beyond anything you can possibly imagine.

There's a theory that's been going around for years that Reid's appointment to be Chairman of the Nevada Gaming Commission shortly after that trial was a "reward for meritorious service," if you get my drift.

My Next Destination: "WELCOME TO HELL." THANKS HARRY!!

15

BELIEVE ME, YOU CAN'T REALLY KNOW

There are a lot of perceptions and images that form in our minds when we watch TV and movies or read stories in books and newspapers and so on. Some of you have perhaps even had opportunities to talk to friends, associates or (God forbid) relatives or loved ones who've been through some pretty tough life experiences that others have had the good fortune to have avoided in their own lives.

I can (almost) guarantee you…there are some things that unless you've personally experienced them, you simply cannot really know! Oh sure, you may feel at different times, either sympathy for, or empathy with others, but there's a tendency to incorrectly use those words to describe one's feelings. In general, 'sympathy' is when you share the feelings of another; 'empathy' is when you understand the feelings of another but do not necessarily share them.

I think you may find this next exercise uniquely challenging. I'm going to tell you a number of things that I experienced over the past 40 plus years. As you read the following, I want you to begin every sentence with the words, "You can't really know…" and reflect on whether or not you find yourself feeling sympathy, realizing that after some internal reflection(s), you share my sentiments, particularly if you have had similar experience.

Or… (and this might be interesting and quite personally revealing), whether or not you find yourself empathizing with my statements, fully understanding it, but not particularly sharing (or agreeing with) my feeling(s), because you've never been in a situation like that!

I'm now going to take you down memory lane with me, and believe me, you would never want to experience what I tell you:

- "You can't really know… the emotional, demeaning, embarrassing and shocking impact of being charged with a death penalty crime you did not commit.

- The humiliation of being arrested, taken to jail, fingerprinted, mug shots, stripped down, thrown into a cold cell, charged with a capital crime.

- The overwhelming charging document, "it's you against the whole state of Nevada."

- Waiting for your first attorney visit, who will explain what the State is going to attempt to argue against you.

- Clueless as to what your attorney is preparing to defend you and argue against the State witnesses and legal arguments arising during your Court proceedings.

- Chained like an animal to and from the courtrooms; humiliation and degradation when people look at you in the courtroom as being on display for the State's entertainment.

- Listening to State witnesses committing perjury, powerful lies, and you can't say anything or expose your anger or disbelief. And all the State has to show is probable cause, which is slight, to have you bound over for trial which is easy when they have coached their lying witnesses on what to say to get you bound over and conceal evidence that refuted the charges, they made against you.

- Purposely placed by the detectives and prosecutor, while in the County Jail known as the "ten-man tank" where the criminally insane are or were housed; Freddy Puser, who thought he was Elvis Presley, talked to his imaginary bird over his shoulder and insisted you pet him while out on the tier; Cuban who actually ate his shit or threw it against the walls; the Wolfman who howled – yeah, that's where the prosecutors and detectives had me housed; behind the scenes scumbags. My mail was read, and my phone calls were recorded. Jail trustee, Joe Recendez told me this information.

- Preparing for a death penalty hearing.

- Listening to what procedures are implemented when you are going to be executed and what the gas chamber pellets will do to you once released.

- The actual preparation by correctional supervisors, wardens, etc., just before they take you into the gas chamber and when they actually strap you in. Step by step, what the gas chamber is like when the pellets fall down near your legs/ankles and how long it might take before you succumb to the deadly gas fumes, tearing your insides apart.

- Looking at the four walls in a cell trying to keep your sanity to not get claustrophobic, being fed like an animal through the bars during lockdown or walking the chow hall and you have 15 minutes from the time you sit down to finish your food. Wearing jail/prison clothes as I did that mark you as a criminal, despite no evidence in my case to support it.

- The stench and smell.

- How many crazy things run through our mind as you waste away in both the County and City Jails? I spent four (4) agonizing years that can't be put into words, waiting…waiting…waiting day after day as my lost years went by waiting for my trial to start.

- What kind of judge are you going to get? Good, bad, fair. I got a dummy who never presided in a murder case before, plus a defense attorney likewise. WOW! How lucky can a guy get?

- Boy, did I ever learn the hard way. There is no such a thing as a fair trial. It's a fallacy on the Constitution and a defendant. Prosecutors who hid evidence of innocence which was done in my case. Prosecutors conceal exculpatory and material evidence; cops lie, state witnesses lie; cops putting words in your mouth to the jurors and judges, "that you didn't say to them."

- What a farce, "Innocent until proven guilty." I's really the other way around, "Guilty till proven innocent; an extremely difficult uphill battle to achieve." Why? Because most jurors will side with the cops and have already made up their minds after the lying prosecutor reads off the charges the defendant is facing in his/her opening statement.

- Let me tell you this and I kid you not, waiting for the jury verdict, is mind boggling, stress beyond words.

- You wonder what really goes on in the minds of a juror as you are trying to read them. Their "eyes" and facial expressions gives them away. If they smile, you are good; if they have tears in their eyes, you are sunk. Is their decision based on hatred, scorn, getting even to the accused? I don't really know; I am not a mind reader.

- Then the judge during your sentencing who sided with the prosecutors 99% of the time, gleefully tells you how much he is going to punish you while the prosecutor smirks to himself with his deranged psycho mentality and evilness only he and the devil can share with each other.

127

- Uninformed citizens do not realize there is nothing more frightening by what the government and police who possess such power can do to innocent people and a judge who can make rulings against you that can actually commit you, like my 1977 trial judge, who later quit the bench, and you guessed it, he became a prosecutor.

- I will say this, most but _not_ all district court and appellate justices only look at what the state alleges and focus their attention on the state's argument. Yes, we still have good judges and cops who are honest; not corrupted by the legal system and they tangle with the bad ones.

- Fighting with your attorney, whom you do not trust as I did with Harry Reid.

- Let's talk about fighting. One thing for sure when you enter Hell, a world beyond your imagination, you are going to be physically tested whether it is the County/City Jail or Prison. Your survival depends on your "heart." You fight, win or lose, you gain respect among the gladiators. Don't fight back, show weakness and you are in serious trouble. They will turn you into a "punk" (sexual attacks); make your family or love one put money on their books, bring in drugs. Your only chance for survival to keep physically safe is to P.C. up (go into Protective Custody). You will be locked in your cell 23 of 24 hours with one hour for exercise in a secured area. It's hard time, but it keeps you alive.

- I'll just say I never P.C'd Up.

- Granted, on April 10, 1977, I was not sentenced to the "death penalty." What I got was worse. A life sentence without parole can be viewed as somewhat of a "slow death" which is exactly what I received.

- Nevertheless, through unadulterated strength of mind, perseverance, and an undying faith in the legal system to see justice served, I fought to restore what I had maintained was "mine alone," my innocence.

These are just a few of the types of thoughts that came into my mind in the beginning of my ordeal. I'll tell you right away my feeling(s) regarding point number one. When I was charged with Hilda Krause's murder, I couldn't believe this was really happening to me. First, (of course) because I didn't do it, nor had I anything to do with it. Second, because it was absolutely ludicrous for anyone to think that I would do such a thing to any woman! Of course, the arresting officers didn't know me from Adam, but hell… anyone else who really knew me would know how insane this premise was and here's why:

My mother was the foundational rock upon which I built my whole life! She was a beautiful, gentle, caring, loving soul, who also happened to be a fabulous cook! She was kind and funny… and an angel of the Lord. As I said earlier in this tale, (certainly prior to Nino introducing me to his friend Laurie) I learned so much from mom about how to simply be a good person in this world.

I lost my mother due to heart failure on January 25, 1970, and my whole world crumbled before me. My sister Candi was a stronger person then I was regarding the loss. I had never known pain and heartbreak such as that before. I blamed myself for not being more attentive to her health needs and it crushed me. I begged God for forgiveness for not being a better son. Despite taking her to a heart doctor for surgery and seeing to it that she took her medications on a regular basis, I felt that there could've been something more that I should've done to save her.

I loved my mom more that words can say…she is never out of my mind! It was she who instilled in me a tremendous faith in the Lord, taught me to demonstrate true strength of character, and most importantly the "real deal" regarding how to treat and be respectful of the women I would encounter in life. As a result, I have always cherished and treasure the relationships I have established with the women in my life!

Arresting me, charging me with planning to kill a woman that I didn't even know, was the wrong thing to do, I can assure you. I was determined that I would vigorously fight those who I discovered to be behind this "insidious" attack on my status as a law-abiding citizen. Over the next 40 years, I learned of the existence (in Nevada's legal system) of dirty, corrupt cops and prosecutors. I learned that there were witnesses who had provided information that would've helped my defense. I also learned of evidence that was never allowed to be mentioned to the jury (in my trial by the way) for reason I could not fathom.

How many of you would not want to receive vindication against wrongdoings inflicted on you for 25 plus years of your life? I decided that I was going to fight the low life, evil devils in the justice system with every fiber of my being! I really want them to regret accusing me of participation in one of the most heinous crimes the State of Nevada has ever seen. This was a crime that I would never and could never commit!

These thoughts, "You can't really know…" only covered the thoughts I had while in jail awaiting my first trial. So now, unbelievable to me, after Rosalie Maxwell was acquitted of all charges in her trial, I go through my trial and I'm convicted of murder and sentenced to life! What… I'm going to prison?

I pray that none of you ever have to experience what you just read nor what you are going to read next as you reflect these thoughts of going to the "Big House:"

- "You can't really know…" what it is like to meet the warden for the first time realizing that this person will be the person who decides what you do, day in and day out for the rest of your life.

- What it feels like to be in quarantine for a month before you're assigned a bed and the unit that will be your new home for probably the rest of your life.

- What will it be like where you take your first walk on the yard not knowing what to expect and what awaits you?

- How you'll deal with your emotions, your mental state of mind, your nightmares, keeping your eyes open and being well aware of your surroundings, never allowing yourself to be trapped in a corner.

- What it's like to hear the sound of the steel doors trapping you in a tiny cell. "NO ESCAPE", can't get out, you are physically trapped in a tiny room and the walls coming down on you.

- What it is like to have cellmates who smoke, or are dirty, smelly, drug users, "head cases," different personalities clashing with each other, fights, arguments and some getting murdered via shanks, strangulation, etc. Yeah, and I celled for a time with a serial killer, Pat McKenna, considered one of the deadliest killers in Nevada history.

- What your nerves go through for the anticipated wait for the cell door to open so you can walk out the door. What the unbearable noise in a rotunda when the guards start yelling or threatening you or shooting near you in your direction. The shots sound like and explosion especially in a rotunda building where I was housed for a time.

- How to survive during race riots, killings, stabbings, beatings, watching your back, your sides and what and who was in front of you; rapes, guys screaming who are weak.

- Told when to wake up, what to wear, what to eat, food poisoning, the "mystery meat" that eventually kills you, fed in a cell during lockdowns, rooms trashed during cell searches while you are ordered to strip down during searches and to spread your cheeks and cough; mouth also inspected for contraband; it's pure humiliation.

- What it's like transferring from one prison to another chained up like an animal, belly chains, ankle chains, long hours on the bus. Goon squad guards screaming at you to either get on or off the bus. I was transported 24 times from one facility to another.

- Knowing about the drugs everywhere, guys overdosing or being stabbed over drugs or beaten or murdered sometimes over non-payments or homosexuality.

- How to survive amongst the Gangs, White Supremist/Aryan Warriors, Brotherhoods, Mexican and Cuban, Columbian Mafias, Bloods, Crips, Garson Parks, Muslims, Australians, South Africans, Italians, Sicilians, Native Americans; all kinds of nationalities – you name it, they were there.

- What it's like to sleep on bunks made out of steel, dirty mattresses, spiders, scorpions roaming the cells, snakes on the tiers, mice and rats, pigeons and millions of roaches.

- What it's like to survive a prison riot, with a swat team firing bullets into the building where you are celled.

- The devastating loss of your family, freedom and animals who were part of your everyday life as you realize just how disconnected you are from the outside world.

- The despair of sickness and aging in prison, what it does to you emotionally and physically as it creeps upon you each and every year as you age.

- Doing my own legal work fighting for my life, if I don't win, I die in prison.

- What it was like wanting to die so it would end praying to God to rescue me from this Hell or bring me home to a better place.

•   No, you don't really know what I went through, only I do, and other innocents like me.

Don't laugh… when I said that I get asked, "how did you do it," these are the kinds of things that people are referring to! Making it through these kinds of experiences really tests a person's ability to handle stress levels that are very foreign to most people who have no clue as to what it is to be caught up navigating through your justice system. Some indeed sympathize… others recognize that they are more empathetic, but it doesn't matter which of those one discovers about themselves…no one can accurately anticipate what these thoughts and living conditions will have on them until they experience them firsthand!

We are not done yet. There will be a number of other thoughts that I'll be challenging you to reflect on. They'll be found later in my story! Now it's time once again for you to take another journey with me to the land beyond time.

16

THERE'S NO PLACE LIKE PRISON!
FROM "PORTER" TO "LAW CLERK"
TO "SENIOR LAW CLERK"

If the title of this part makes you think of the chant that Dorothy said in the classic 1939 movie, "The Wizard of Oz," then I've evoked the image or thought exactly as I hoped you'd identify it! Throughout this part, as I tell you about my experiences in the "hell holes" that are home to some of the worst members of humanity you could ever imagine, you won't be at all surprised discovering yourself chanting this title as you read!

In 1977…the day finally came when I was told to, "roll it up… you're traveling!" You are taken to a holding tank where you're to wait for the prison guards to come and get you with their chains. They arrive, and they chain your belly and your ankles. You're put on a bus with plastic seats and given a bologna sandwich. Yeah, a good hearty meal of nourishment with nothing to drink. After everybody is loaded up, the bus in slow motion begins to travel and not fast.

This was one hell of a long ride from the Clark County Jail to the Northern Nevada Correctional Center in Carson City. I believe after the one pit stop that you're given to relieve yourself; it took well over 10 hours to arrive at our destination. Either 10 days or two weeks later after I went to "classification" to find out where they were going to send me, I was told I was to be shipped to "MAX" at the Nevada State Prison. Upon classification again at "MAX," I was placed on the fourth floor of the main housing unit.

Wow…what a beautiful cell! Steel bed with chains (suspending it from the ceiling) to hold it up, a mattress only an inch thick, wood splintered toilet, dirty walls and floor, and…my famous broken window where all my new furry and/or multi-legged friends could crawl through day or night! Spiders, scorpions, mice and rats, snakes, pigeons, and of course…millions of cockroaches. Due to a lawsuit for using DDT to spray the cells, they were not sprayed for 5 years.

The main concerns for the guys on the 4th floor was the rattlesnakes slithering down the corridor and guys yelling for the guards to kill them. We also had bull snakes sneaking in from my broken windows in front of my cell. Lucky me, I was placed in the most dangerous cell on the 4th floor tier. To be honest, these snakes made my hair stand up, as well as the scorpions and spiders. Night time was the worst and I slept very little, as I felt I needed to be alert. Learning to play the games, it cost me a few bucks that I had on my prison account, I was later able to get some candles which I kept lit at the bottom of the door cell to help keep out the critters. Anyway, when the Warden decided to open the yard again, in my mind and thoughts I knew there was going to be a huge adjustment for me to be meeting some of the most criminally violent guys who some did not give a thought of killing someone over stupid shit. If you show weakness, you are in serious trouble. I never showed weakness; they noticed that; they never bothered me.

Getting back to when I arrived at "MAX," the place was still on "lockdown" due to two murders on the yard. I believe about 6 weeks later we were lifted off lockdown. My first time on the yard, I noticed the Law Library was just ahead. I spoke to the officer in charge and asked if there were any job openings available. He told me there were, but I first must request that the classification committee give permission for me to work there.

I did and was assigned as a Law Library "Porter" for a whopping $5.00 a month salary. No problem... I just wanted to read and study the law books and did I ever study! Somehow through the grace of God, I took to the study of law like a duck to water. I realized that I was able to understand just what the justices were actually saying when they either overturned a conviction or affirmed one. I was able to use both types of decisions to my advantage. A huge opportunity availed itself when the prison opened a paralegal course for inmates. I jumped at it!

I took the course called "Criminal Law, General Use", and on August 25, 1978, I graduated with a Grade of A+. I was then allowed to work as a "Law Clerk" and my salary doubled to $10.00 a month! I spent a lot of time with the "old timers" who were not allowed to work in the Law Library. It's a bit of a misnomer to say they were not "allowed." It would be more accurate to say that they were not given access to the Library (by the Warden and the guards) because of their considerable legal acumen gained as the result of having been incarcerated there for many years! It was really a shame too...these guys were true "jailhouse legal eagles," and I would consult with them often because of their vast knowledge so I could better help the guys.

It became so gratifying when I found myself assisting in the overturning of murder cases and getting reduction in sentences for some of the guys. Curley Robbins was the first murder conviction I helped get overturned on a jury instruction, and to both of our surprise Curley was not re-prosecuted. Several months after his release, I was told to go to the Property Room as a package was sent to me.

Well, I'll be damned. Curley bought me a 12-inch color TV. A note had come with it: "Have a great day brother, can't thank you enough for saving my life. God Bess You!" Now that touched my heart. He didn't need to do that, but he did! Curley never went back to prison again, at least not in Nevada. I believe he went back East… I have no idea what happened to him after that.

I prepared a number of documents and achieved a bit of success in getting a lot of positive results on my own behalf. Apparently, work of my abilities got around, and I guess you would say that I was certainly considered a "jailhouse lawyer" among many of the guys with a paralegal degree.

My mentor while I was in Nevada State Prison was an attorney, Tom Perkins. I never forgot what he said to me. "It's not about innocence or guilt. It's about who is best prepared when they walk into the courtroom. That's the one who walks out a winner!" Was he ever right!

Throughout my years in the Nevada State Prison, I never presented my client's cases until I was fully prepared to help them in the court system. I thank God for giving me this gift in winning a plethora of cases for them.

As a Senior Law Clerk, I assisted clients that included the Italian Gorillas, Italian, Sicilian, Mexican, Cuban and Columbian Mafias, The Hell's Angel, the Aryan Warriors, the Aryan Circle, the Bloods and the Crips, Garson Parks, and Native Americans… as well as non-gang affiliated inmates and convicts.

My intense approach to learning the law and apparently my success at applying it on behalf of others, resulted in eventually my being brought to the Warden's office. I had no idea exactly what I was being "summoned" for and what a surprise that turned out to be. Unknown to me, it seems that all of the gangs and their shot callers had engaged in a meeting with the

Warden. At that meeting, they "expressed" to him their "wish" to have me named the "Senior Law Clerk," because they found in me someone who really fought for them. They went on to say to him that the "tendencies to resort to violence" had subsided in many of them as they recognized that they were having a chance to get out of prison.

Now…this "wish" as I referred to it did take on a more "strident meaning" when it was also made quite alarmingly clear to Warden Gary True, that if he determined that he was not going to promote me to "Senior Law Clerk," they were going to kill Paul…the current holder of that position…mission accomplished! They obviously got their point across, and the Warden ordered me to his office.

I was told that I was going to be named to that position. I told the Warden I was not qualified to take that position as it carried a heavy load. I could see the frustration on his face as I kept refusing to take that position. Then… and only then, he said the magic words to me: "Frank, I will give you anything you want within reason. Please take the position."

Whoa…did I really hear what I think I just heard? Did I really hear the Warden "literally plead with me" to take the new title? Wait…is that now the "Hallelujah Chorus" from Handel's "Messiah" ringing in my ears?

Why yes…I think it just might be! I thought to myself, this is too good to be true, but I'm going to go for the gold. I said, "Okay, Warden, I would like to be housed in the dorm, where I could have freedom to walk, and I want you to let me choose my own Law Clerks!" Well…that did it.

Gotta throw this observation in at this point because I learned that selecting competent, "Law Clerks" was going to be more of a challenge that I first imagined. The dangers of handling convict cases could be a pressure cooker with the lives of inmates at stake on occasion! That was the point I was originally trying to make when I told the Warden I believed I was not qualified to be named "Senior Law Clerk." It carried a lot of pressure not to make stupid mistakes. However, I believed God gave me this gift to achieve much success in assisting these guys adequately as well as in my own cases.

The specific incident that I'll tell you about now didn't result in a loss of life…but it shouldn't have led to one of my Clerk's having an "unfortunate accident" shall we say. I happened to place on my Law Clerk staff, a very cocky, jive talking inmate. He talked about how great he was, and I'm telling' you…to hear him tell it, he was a reincarnation of Spencer

Tracy as Henry Drummond from the classic, "Inherit the Wind!" What this guy "inherited" was an extremely exaggerated ability for self-assessment.

Anyway…I basically just ignored a number of his dumb comments and gave him a chance to "live up to his own hype!" What a disaster…I learned he was truly dumb in ways of the law, and just talked a lot of shit. One day in a very excited voice, he told me he'd just won a major move on behalf of his client, a gang banger who was a member of the Bloods. When he told me what he'd done, I immediately knew he was in danger.

He filed a motion on the guy's criminal post-conviction case, are you ready for this, "To deny discovery in his case pending a hearing." Holy shit, you're supposed to file a motion "for discovery of evidence and know what discovery you are seeking!" Needless to say, he got "stuck/shanked" (stabbed by an inmate…most likely the guy he screwed up on) for his effort.

I immediately filed a motion on the Blood's case for reconsideration to strike his prior motion, and to accept his present motion for discovery. The district judge was gracious and granted my said motion. This incident definitely made me much more wary regarding the qualifications of guys who wanted to become Law Clerks. Back to the story…

So, Warden True agreed to my terms and Bernie Ybarra and I received a big room to live in. That is where I met my little furry friend to be, "Mickey Mouse" and…get this…I was now making a whopping $40.00 a month salary. Believe me, I didn't simply take this newly acquired responsibility for granted. I set about earning every cent of my significantly improved salary.

One of my big victories for the guys on the yard was when I challenged the Director of Prison, Wolff, in a civil rights law suit called, Mickel v. Wolff. The case involved a prison built "Sweat Lodge" supposedly for the Native Americans in the facility, but they would not allow them to use it. I sued the Director, Chaplain Fry and the Warden. It was nothing personal with me, just business for the Native Americans. I eventually won a 15-page decision before federal judge Edward Reed, granting Native Americans access to the "Sweat Lodges" to purify themselves according to their religion.

They made a "7-tiered choker" for me that goes around your neck. Each tier indicated the level or "ranking" of your status as a Chief. Think of it as being a 1-star to 4-star General. I was made a "Chief and Holy Man with the wrist bands of the four winds." That I must say was quite an honor that I have always cherished.

I would have to say that my biggest "win" ever resulted in getting an inmate who was nicknamed "Bam Bam" an acquittal of over a hundred felony charges. I don't remember his real name…everybody simply knew him as the character from the Flintstones! Anyway, "Bam Bam" was in the Medical Infirmary to undergo some type of surgery. At this moment, I do not recall whether it was for a major or a minor surgery. When he woke up, he was in severe pain and asked for pain medication. The doctor refused him, and the guard told him to shut up!

Now, back then, the guard was carrying his weapon. "Bam Bam" begged the doctor for pain medication and was again refused. "Bam Bam" then jumped the guard, took his weapon away, and threatened the doctor for pain medication. He also took the jail house keys and while still holding the doctor and the guard hostage, he called out to one of the gang members to unlock the whole prison!

That was the start of a prison riot…and it was a huge one. The child molesters' cell doors were opened, and the guys tortured them so bad that they all ended up in a hospital. S.W.A.T. came in and there was a gun battle with bullets flying all over the tiers. There were smoke bombs and gas bombs being used, and the place had indeed turned into a war zone. I hit the floor and put a wet towel over my head and didn't move one inch.

When it was all over, "Bam Bam" was charged with over a hundred felony counts. To the Court's surprise, "Bam Bam" said he would represent himself when his public defender tried to plead him out. Well…here we go, Bernie Ybarra and me. We prepared all of "Bam Bam's" legal work for him, from his opening statement to his closing statement to the jury. We centered our argument on the premise that none of this would have happened in the first place if only the doctor had given "Bam Bam" pain medication. Well, to both the prosecutor and court's absolute shock "Bam Bam" was acquitted of all charges. He was later shipped off to Walla Walla Prison in Seattle, Washington.

Oh yes, I almost forgot, I was always ready to provide legal assistance on behalf of any inmate, but I had a standard rule that I'd given to myself. I would not do legal work for a low life sexual predator! My two exceptions in all my years were based upon my belief (after doing research and investigations) that the two guys who had been charged with that were in fact innocent, but I was able to prove that these two could not have physically done the crimes.

Medical physicians provided me with their expert opinions that these two guys who were accused of sexually assaulting children could not have committed their said crimes based upon the fact they both possessed "enormous organs." Such organs would have ripped open the child's insides, and each child's insides were intact.

Each doctor said It was "medically impossible" for the guys to have done such an act. Their previous attorneys never produced such expert testimony on their behalf at their trials. Each one was granted an evidentiary hearing on the merits of what I wrote for them. I do not recall what the outcome or the hearing was since I was still at "MAX," but I did not see these guys anymore.

It was never lost on me that being the "Senior Law Clerk" required me to be very diligent, efficient, and professional, and the pressure to "not make stupid mistakes" was enormous! However, I believed God gave me this gift to achieve much success in assisting these guys adequately as well as in my own cases.

Now that I mentioned what my biggest win was, I will tell you what was the most rewarding and enlightening piece of litigation that I ever did, which is still close to my heart today and will be forever. This litigation even surpassed the work I did one on my own behalf as it resulted in the saving of the life of a convict's little girl. The work I did was documented by Pat Harbour, at the time a school teacher and notary public at Nevada State Prison.

How this came about almost or possibly could have resulted in my Law Library runner Johnstone getting violently killed.

I recall going to work in the Law Library one morning and there was a note on my desk. It was from Marty Everson and a nasty note accusing me of being a heartless p**k and not coming to see him in solitary confinement (the hole). In the prison system, if someone has a beef with you, you better confront them to find out why and I did.

When I asked Marty why the nasty note, he told me he told my runner Johnstone to let me know that his daughter needed lifesaving surgery, but his wife's religion would not allow the doctor/surgeon to touch her daughter; however, the doctor told Marty's father if one parent gave him permission, he could perform the surgery.

Marty told Johnstone he needed me to help him do legal work in order to get his daughter operated on. I told Marty that Johnstone never told me this. Well, let me say, the emotions at this time were flying. Tough guy Marty started to break down and I could feel his pain and anxiety, and did I ever feel the pressure to help him ASAP.

"Alright, Marty, I'll be back; just give me a little time to see how I can help you and your daughter." Man, my mind was racing a mile a minute as I was stressed on how I was going to figure this out. I went back to my office, sat down, took a long deep breath, let it out, closed my eyes, prayed and asked God to help me save this child and he did. Boom! All of a sudden, I knew exactly what to do, but never did before. God had given me the wisdom on how to prepare "a limited Power of Attorney" allowing Marty's father to act in his stead.

After I finished the document wherein Marty gave his father the right to act on his behalf, getting the child the surgery and medical help, she would need after the surgery, I immediately told Pat Harbour I needed his help as a Notary Public to legalize the document. Pat went with me to see Marty and witness Marty's signature. As soon as this was done, Pat left the prison and went to Marty's father and both left to go to the doctor and the precious little girl was saved by the surgeon "who had blessed hands." Pat Harbour was a "hero" in my mind with his quick actions. I merely did what I was trained to do with God's guiding hand.

Prior to my waiting to hear any news if the child was ok, my nerves were on edge and more so when one of the officers came to my room and told me Warden True wanted to see me. When I arrived at the Warden's Office, Pat Harbour was also present. When I saw the warm expression on the Warden's face and Pat's smile, I knew that the little girl was out of trouble. Warden True came up to me and shook my hand and complimented me when he said," Frank... many of the officers here, including myself, believe that you didn't commit the crimes you are in here for. Your recent actions in saving that child's life convinces me of that even more now. Killers don't go around saving lives, Frank. They have no conscious ... but you do.

Wow! I can't really tell you what the impact of Warden True's words meant to me. Later, when I went back to my dorm room, sat down with my thoughts and felt I knew for the first time in my life what a surgeon doctor must feel like when they save the life of a human being. There are no words.

Okay, the child was on her way to recovery. Time for me to deal with Johnstone. During our conversation, I asked him why he hadn't made me aware earlier that Marty's daughter was in danger of losing her life. Johnstone, a former biker, looks at me and says, "Fuck Marty and his little girl!" When that asshole gave me that callous answer, I slowly got up from my desk, walked over to him and grabbed him by his hair; then slammed his face onto the desk! I picked up a mop handle and hit him in his back and legs and knees.

I also picked up the mop bucket and smashed it over his head saying to him, "you fucking punk! You nearly got that child killed". I continued telling him, "You'd better P.C. up (protective custody) you low life piece of shit because if the guys find out what you did, especially if they learn it from Marty, they'll kill you!"

One of the correctional guards seeing what was happening and knowing the reason it had occurred, called out to administration. "We have a man down. Appears he slipped on some water and banged his head pretty hard!" If it can be considered something to his (lousy) credit, when the investigators tried to find out how Johnstone sustained his injuries, he didn't "rat me out."

I have to admit that was one of the very few times I ever lost control of my temper! It completely infuriated me thinking about what might've happened to Marty's little girl, and Johnstone's comment made be lose it. Last, but not least, Marty was so grateful for my help and his expressions of gratitude for my efforts was an incredible reward enough for me. Let me just say this, when you save a life, you never, ever forget it.

Wait till you read about the next one. Bet you wouldn't figure this one out from everything you have already read in my story/book. As strange as it may seem to you, nonetheless, it's true; I actually saved the life of Gerald Weakland. Yeah! Incredible as it may seem, the guy who tried to put me in the gas chamber.

Despite Weakland doing muscle work and bringing in drugs for the Aryan Warriors, many of them hated Weakland. And there came a time, when 15 Aryan Warriors decided they were going to kill him, where they had him cornered, for testifying against me, but couldn't without first getting my permission. Charlie Cooper, 3rd in command of the Aryan Warriors came to the Law Library, told me what they wanted to do, but out of respect came to me first. I left the Law Library, went to where Weakland was cornered and was scared begging for his life telling the guys he said at my 1977 trial that he told the jury that he lied that I hired him to kill Hilda Krause. During this time, I was known as the "shot caller," being I did all the legal work for everyone in the Joint. They respected me. I stood in front of all of them and I told them, "You're not going to kill him, he did say at my trial that I did not hire him to kill that woman. I'm dealing with him through the court system." I also knew if they had killed Weakland, I would get all the heat and if just one of them got weak and said I ordered Weakland's death, I would again have to fight for my life. Wait till you read what the l low-life psycho did to me later. Yeah, folks, it's one for the books. Many years later, the court system became aware of it played up by the media.

There were times when in order to try to create (or engage in) "lighter moments" in what was certainly on a daily basis not the most pleasant place to be (it's not supposed to be, I get that!), I find myself doing some pretty unusual things. I have to admit that some of those things were on the high end of some fun. I specifically recall that one of those was kind of hilarious.

Ok, time to have a little fun at Devils Island. You see, we had many jack rabbits running around the prison yards, and this one particular time I decided to take it upon myself to see if I could catch a jack rabbit running on the yard. Okay, so imagine the picture of me trying to run fast enough to catch a jack rabbit.

Not only am I making a fool of myself, but I was entertaining the tower guards who were laughing their heads off! The jack rabbit was zigzagging around the yard running from a dummy (me) with quite ease. Needless to say, my meager effort to capture "that rascally wabbit" was quite comical. I was not even getting close to that fast-moving cottontail, when one of the guards got on his horn laughing as he said, "Nice try LaPena!"

When you're doing time for no crime, you begin to make adjustment in your daily life to try to make things perhaps a little beneficial to yourself in whatever small way possible. I got to test out my culinary skills (such as they were), when another inmate (Clarence Morgan) and I, volunteered to work in the kitchen one day a week. This turned out to be quite beneficial to us, while at the same time providing us with a little bit of fun. Let me explain.

One of the tasks we were assigned was to make was ice cream on the weekend for the guys. Clarence and I decided to be a little bit "creative." Okay I admit it was downright, "sneaky" as we played around with the ingredients required to make the ice cream. You see, the "Head Chef" in charge of everything in the kitchen was a real "juicer" and we don't mean he was a fan of fruit. Nope, not at all. His "juice of preference" always possessed a more "alcoholic ancestry!"

The guy had numerous bottles of whiskey hidden in the kitchen's back room, where the ice machine was. Being "good Samaritans," Clarence and I poured some of the alcohol into the ice cream machine, then served said, "tangy delicious 40 proof dessert" in cups, to the delight of the convicts!

Not to be forgotten (of course) were the tower guards and Cell Sergeant in the main building. I saw to it that each of them received a full carton of our "booze infused ice cream." It's called playing the game and here's how it works. The guards have to pay for their meals. So, in the kitchen I made several big cheeseburgers for each tower guard and presented it to them along with their carton of ice cream. Now inasmuch as I've said that an exercise such as this would definitely have to be found to be beneficial to me, I would also take the liberty of preparing a bit of a "care package" for myself. I would wrap in foil apples, oranges, tomatoes and a few other snackable tidbits, and picture this…I'd walk out of the kitchen and onto the yard, my jacket over my arms, with the food in both sleeves! I'd stop at Post One, and the guy there would say to me, "Are you clean, Frank?" "Yes sir! Oh, I have a carton of milk for you send down the pail." The pail was lowered, and I would put in it his sandwich and carton of "Milk." Then I go to Post Two and do the same thing.

After taking care of those two, I'd go to the Cell Sergeant and making sure no one could see us, I'd give him his sandwich and carton of ice cream. The Sergeant then checks me out for contraband, never touching my clothes and says, "You're clean!" Okay, then I'm off to my cell where I had a styrofoam ice chest and I'd place in it all the food I "borrowed" from the kitchen.

Not a bad haul for the week, if I do say so myself. I always remembered the one very important "rule of the game," and that was to never piss these guys off, and they will not bother you. It's part of your learning to survive within the system. I learned it, used it and survived it!

You may just be wondering how I cooked some of my food I borrowed from the kitchen. I obtained a metal coat hanger and extra toilet paper, which I would roll up in a ball with a hole in the middle. I would put the meat in the corner of the clothes hanger, light my toilet paper and cook my meat. Like I referred before, when you play the system, or better, know how to, you learn many different ways to survive.

17

MY ANIMALS...MY PETS...MY FRIENDS

B.J. was a rescue in California. I went there to see a friend of mine. Upon leaving and driving back to Las Vegas, I saw an animal shelter and decided to stop and look around. I wasn't looking for a pet at this time nor had I previously thought about getting one while in California, but as I look upon it today, it was God directing me to stop and get one of his angels. Just one look at the little stinker and I was done for. That beautiful little face just stole my heart and I rescued her. She was just a baby. I believe just eight weeks old. I asked the owner/employee what type of dog she was. He said she was part Corgi. I asked what kind of food I should feed her. There was a pet store next to the shelter and after obtaining what I needed, I called my new friend and angel, Baby Jane (B.J.).

When I arrived back at my house, my mom, Katherine, sister, Camille, and nephew, Scott, all went bananas over B.J. She stole everyone's heart. Years later, after mom passed, my sister, nephew, niece and her military husband, left my residence to go to a military base. I came to find out that my precious little B.J. died when a supposed friend looked after her while I was incarcerated in the Clark County jail. It tore my heart out. The pain was excruciating. An asshole by the name of Kasalyn made a snide remark about the loss of my baby. I hit that big jerk so hard in one punch that I knocked him out cold. When he awoke and I was sitting on his chest, I made him apologize or I was going to break every bone in his body for insulting my dog.

When I was in prison, I had an unusual assortment of pets that shared my living space, shall we say. There was a bird, a mouse, and believe it or not, a Black Widow Spider! We had a mutually beneficial relationship. I fed them, cared for them, provided them with shelter and warmth. They enabled me to maintain my sanity! Each of them came into my life in different ways.

What would you say if I told you that many people don't know that Mickey Mouse spent time in prison? You'd think, "C'mon Frank, where'd you get that from?" I'd tell you again, "No, seriously…Mickey Mouse spent time in prison!? Then I'd look at you and smile and tell you, "Okay…so it wasn't "the" Mickey Mouse, but rather one of my little furry friends who came to mean so much to me! Here's how that all came to be.

In the last chapter, I told you that as one of the conditions of me taking the Senior Law Clerk position, I wanted to have my own dorm. Warden True agreed. So, to the dorm I went, with Bernie Ybarra who would be my roommate. We had a big room with lots of space. While Bernie and I are settling in, we hear the tiny patter of feet in the room, and we notice that we have a tiny field mouse that's taken up residency with us! We decided to see if we could catch him. That stinker was really fast on his feet and kept eluding us.

So, we got a big box that we were going to put him in once we caught him. Oh yeah, it took hours of frustration to catch that tiny baby because he was so elusive. Finally, we caught the cutie pie. He desperately tried to climb out of the big box to no avail. The next day, I had one of my clients make a big house for my new fury friend.

I got some cheese and crackers for him. My client made a great plastic mouse house with green grass and two water sites. One to drink from and one to bathe in. Once he became aware that he was not going to be hurt, he calmed down and didn't try to run away. I was fascinated by how clean he was. He would use his tiny paws, put them in the water and clean his face and body. I couldn't believe my eyes.

As time went on, he became my little buddy. He would run up my arms and sit on my shoulder when I was typing up writs, motions, doing research, etc. At times he liked the warmth of my hands and would sit in them and fall asleep. I named him Mickey…of course. I had him for a little over four years as I was waiting for the Nevada Supreme Court's decision on my homicide case and hopefully getting ready to go back to the Clark County Jail.

Bernie said if I got a favorable ruling by the high court, he would take good care of Mickey as Bernie also like the little stinker. I believe that Mickey lived two more years when Bernie later told me that our little angel friend passed on. Mickey had a good, safe life, and I thanked God for bringing him into mine!

Mickey was not my sole companion. I also had "Tweety" bird. One day as I was playing basketball with convict John Layton, this baby bird flew right into my hand and stayed there. What a surprise and a spiritual one I believe. At first, I didn't know what to do, but it did not fly away. So, here I go again with having another angel on my hands. I attempted to place him on my shoulders and he, to my surprise, complied and stayed there!

Now I eventually had two "kids" to take care of. I'll finish that story later, and I imagine that you're not going to let me get away with not telling you about the Black Widow Spider…right? I found her going up the wall in my cell, and I wasn't going to kill her. I had a real large glass jar, so I put the jar against the wall as she was climbing so she fell into the jar. I made enough holes in the lid so she could breathe. I took two metal sticks so she could move around, and I fed her (you guessed it) cockroaches. I studied her and her movements. Her webs were fascinating as she made them. I will leave out some of the details of her eating habits, so you won't feel squeamish. I used a glove and long tweezers to remove her food. She too lived a good long life away from predators.

One of the things that breaks my heart when I watch TV, is to see the commercials for entities such as the ASPA and the Humane Society. I, like so many of you, look at the faces of the "angels with fur" that God put on this planet being caged inhumanely, terrified and depressed.

Shelters are incredibly lonely places for dogs although safer in shelters then being chained to a house or wandering the streets. But unfortunately, there is no doubt, I believe, that listlessness is all but inevitable for a dog in a shelter. They sleep on cold kennel floors, are overlooked time and time again by prospective adopters and have limited social action. They need a fluffy bed and toys to play with for stimulation or time to cuddle. These little acts can completely transform a dog's spirit.

To me animal cruelty is unforgiveable. I see fear and sorrow in their eyes. I see their bodies, sometimes racked with bruises, and suffering from malnourishment…trembling, shuddering as they perhaps ponder their current environment. I wonder if they're capable of thinking what their life expectancy is…then I say to myself, Of course they are."

Why wouldn't they be able to understand, contemplate their situation in life? If we've been given the capacity to reason by our creator, isn't it possible that perhaps to a lesser extent our animal friends have been given the ability to conceptualize beyond the natural law of "survival of the fittest?"

It's in part "déjà vu" to me because I can personally relate to the horrors they've experienced. More than anything, I truly pray to God that one day I might establish an animal sanctuary. I feel that it's now the thing that has given purposed to my life at this point. I would love to be able to give these angels love, safety, friendship and freedom from cages. They would have the ability to roam, run, and play...never again to be locked up and left alone to wonder what's happening to them!

Yes...that's my prayer to God. I know what they go through and suffer the fear in their precious eyes and trembling bodies. On April 15, 2015, my wife and I found and rescued "Samson" from death row. A "bait dog" racked with bruises and scars we couldn't touch his body, malnourished skin and bone, cartilage torn in his left ear, trembling, petrified, sensed his life was about to end...Forgetaboutit! He's safe, runs freely, plays with lots of toys and tug of war with me, has three doggy beds, spoiled to the core and is a very, very protective Rhodesian Ridgeback and Boxer mix.

Yeah, without a doubt I identify with these furry angels quite strongly...so much so that if I were President of the United States, I would issue an Executive Order that would make it unlawful in every single shelter and animal rescue foundation, to put an animal down except for reasons involving terminal illness with no chance of survival.

The commission of such an act would constitute a federal crime, punishable with mandatory prison time...no probation and no parole! That sentence would be served in a maximum-security prison with the perpetrators placed with the hard cases.

Now, if I were a judge presiding over an animal cruelty case, and there was overwhelming evidence against the defendant, I would not allow the DA or a slick attorney to plea bargain in my court. There would be no allowing a scumbag to slink away with only a slap on the wrist. Nope, that would never happen in my court.

I'd probably get some nickname like Judge "Maximum Frank" LaPena and anyone found guilty of cruelty to an animal would find themselves in dire straits! Okay...so maybe that's a pretty significant indication of how I might not be exactly unbiased in my point of view. I'll live with it!

I hope and pray someday that I will attain my goal of setting up the animal sanctuary, shelter, rescue. Those who are animal lovers and are as serious about animals as I am, will understand my enthusiastic stance regarding those who do them harm.

Many of you probably think that I'm seeking some kind of monetary compensation from the State for all they illegally put me through. Damn right I am, and I deserve it. Let's face it that would be a really great result from all the horrors that I have suffered and my precious animals.

However, believe it or not, I'm telling my story more to expose the corruption I found in the legal system and to inform the masses of what could possibly (heaven forbid) happen to them if they become the target of injustice perpetrated by the State.

Yes! I truly believe God has a plan for me to receive compensation and establish an animal sanctuary for my furry angels. Hmmm! "Spats Animal Haven," feel safe, secure and happy. "Adopt or get wacked" and "Don't forgetaboutit!" You can take that to the bank.

In closing, I would like to relate to you as you read my story and those of you that are also animal lovers. You know there are not any words that can describe the hurt and pain we all suffer in losing our precious angels, and yes, in my own words, they are God's gifted angels he allows us to care for his kids until he determines that they are to come home to him and await our arrival to once again be with them. And this includes all those angels who didn't have a home. We are blessed.

| | | | |

Dear Frank,

We truly cannot thank you enough for linking arms with us and saving lives this past year!

Even through the health and financial difficulties our community continued to face through 2021, your compassion and generosity never failed. You helped us save 15,759 animals last year and to find forever homes for Bowser, Megan, Jasper, and Finn (pictured above from left to right) as well as thousands of other shelter pets like them.

If you have any questions about this letter, your donations, or how your support is impacting and saving lives, please let us know at (702) 955-5972.

With sincere gratitude,

Daryl Sprague

Chief Marketing and Development Officer

The Animal Foundation is a Nevada 501(c)3 nonprofit organization - Federal Tax ID# 88-0144253. No goods or services were received in consideration of this gift, unless otherwise noted.

18

<u>2 YEARS WAITING FOR TRIAL DECISION</u>
<u>SIX YEARS WAITING FOR APPEAL</u>
<u>HERE WE GO AGAIN</u>

If I don't believe you can ever imagine what it was like as I was sitting in my Taj Mahal cell when I heard in a loud voice by one of the guys, "Frank the Nevada Supreme Court overturned your conviction." At first, I wasn't sure if I had heard right. One of the guys was listening to the radio. I yelled out, "Are you sure?" "Yeah, Frank, it's all over the news." On April 13, 1982, the Nevada Supreme Court reversed my contract for hire murder conviction. Wow! Nine (9) years of intense fighting with the State had finally come to a halt or so I thought at that time. As I sat on my bunk, tears started to flow from my eyes, a stress that you cannot begin to imagine was lifted off my shoulders. As I tried to gather up my thoughts, my fighting spirit ran right through my body. This time I was well-trained in criminal law and intended to kick some ass since I didn't know on what issues the State Supreme Court reversed my conviction.

Approximately two days later I was told to "Roll-Up" you're traveling. Sgt. Mills, who always treated me decently, came to my cell and asked me if he could have "Tweety-Bird". Mills absolutely loved Tweety-Bird. He was the one who bought bird seed for him. Mills had a big office and now and then I would take Tweety over to the Sgt's office and Tweety liked him and would fly on his shoulders. So, I knew Tweety would have good life with Sgt. Mills.

Honest to God, as happy I became with my reversal, it was emotionally hard for me to leave my "kids" I was attached to and loved, but life must go on.

Well, the ride back to Clark County Jail was far different then the ride I took to prison. This time I was transported by a van with soft cushion seats and the ride was much faster.

The Nevada Supreme Court reversed my contract murder conviction and remanded my case for a new trial on the grounds that admission of Weakland's statements incriminating me constituted reversible error. The Appellate Court concluded that the State had improperly withheld the "benefits of a plea bargain or promise of leniency until after a purported accomplice (i.e., Weakland) had testified in a particular manner". *LaPena v.* State, 643 P.2d at 244-45.

I was sent back first to have a Preliminary Hearing due to the Appellate Court's language and I appeared before Magistrate Joseph Bonaventure (a good judge) in my opinion, a straight shooter. This time, I had to act on my own case because one of my appellate attorneys, Richard Wright, had withdrawn from representing me due to a mysterious occurrence. His law partner, a former U.S. Attorney, suffered an "untimely accidental fall off of a mountain" …yeah, that's true.

For the next couple of months, while Bonaventure tried to get an attorney to represent me, I continued to represent myself, and, I will say this, I managed to hold my own, citing case law time and time again against the State's superstar, "cheater" prosecutor Harmon. Judge Bonaventure was so impressed with my knowledge of criminal law he even asked me if I wanted to continue to represent myself.

Knowing criminal law as I did at this time, I said, "No, your Honor, as you know, under Gideon v. Wainright, 372 U.S. 335, the Supreme Court ruled that States are required under the Sixth Amendment to the U.S. Constitution to provide me with an attorney in my criminal case, since I was unable to afford one."

Well, as expected, prosecutor Harmon objected for some dumb reason and I countered him by telling the Court "Your Honor, Mr. Harmon has no standing under the law to object whether I should be court appointed by counsel since I am indigent." Judge Bonaventure told Harmon his objection was overruled.

I kid you not, every day his courtroom was packed with attorneys refusing to represent me mostly telling the Court my case was so long they would be in financial trouble because it would take an enormous amount of time to read and research my case to prepare for a new trial. In the meantime, Harmon was going nuts because he couldn't argue against what the attorneys used for excuses not to represent me.

I will refer to Bonaventure as Judge Joe. Alright, I'll get to the point of all this and clarify my arguments and law supporting my issues. Judge Joe, in a frustrating attempt to get me counsel wanted to appoint the Public Defenders' Office to represent me. Harmon, hearing that started to sing "Happy Days are Here again," but I shut that down really quick. This turned into a long day of arguing the facts and criminal law. I told Judge Joe, "Your Honor, that would be a conflict of interest because that office represented Gerald Weakland during his preliminary hearing, his March 29, 1974 confession statement and during Weakland's plea agreement with the State, legally as I know the law, they cannot represent me." I also recall saying something to the effect, "Your Honor, if Mr. Miller from that office is court appointed to represent me, I would demand my Public Defender to disclose to me everything Weakland told them; and if they didn't disclose that information to me, I would sue them for 'attorney malpractice'". But I knew under the law they couldn't violate their attorney privilege regarding Weakland… Hahahaaaa – was I having fun sending Prosecutor Harmon up the wall. Not one time before Judge Joe, did Harmon outlawyer me. I was kicking his ass and his red-faced expressions were showing it.

Anyway, being street wise, I had a gut feeling Judge Joe was going to give me a lot of leeway so, I decided to give him due respect, take his frustration off his shoulders, and, I said something to this affect, "Okay Your Honor, temporarily I'll go with the Public Defender's Office." Judge Joe, to my surprise then basically said, "Frank, I'm going to allow you to be co-counsel in your case and issue an Order to the Clark County Jail Commander that you are allowed every day access to the Law Library to allow you to do your legal work, and if anyone denies you let me know. ok"; "Yes, Your Honor, I very much appreciate that." As soon as I was allowed into the law library, I immediately researched informant law and found a great one which dealt smack on point with the facts in my case trying to get the identity of a confidential informant (C.I.). Jones v. Jago, 575 F.2d 1164 (1978) (Sixth Circuit Court of Appeals)

In Jones v. Jago, that informant, like mine, was in a position to have knowledge concerning the involvement or 'non-involvement of the real parties' involved in a murder. The Jones Court concluded the non-disclosure of the informant's statement was a violation of Jones's right to due process as described in Brady v. Maryland. In Jones, as in my case, the State knew about an informant who "possessed personal knowledge" of the parties involved in a murder where it makes no reference to the defendant, (exactly like informant Joseph Costanza told Metro Detectives Weakland never mentioned either Rosalie Maxwell or being involved in the crime Weakland asked Costanza to take part. When questioned by cops Avants and Lee, Costanza said, "He did not know me' never talked to me' Did not know what I looked like; If he ever saw me on the street, he would not recognize who I am".

So, when I finished my Motion for the Identity of the "Very Reliable Informant" I submitted it before Judge Joe. In addition, I filed several more motions. If I recall I believe during one of my oral arguments before Judge Joe, he made reference that he might let Weakland's prior statements and testimony be stricken from the record as underserving of belief. Harmon blew his top and decided to try and take my case out of Judge Joe's Courtroom by way of a Grand Jury Indictment that could pass Justice Court and go directly to District Court. I believe when Judge Joe read my Informant Motion he was going to rule in my favor and throw my case out. Here's why!

In Joseph Costanza's initial statements to the police, he identified two individuals with Weakland when Weakland met Costanza "six weeks before the murder" of Hilda Krause on January 14, 1974. Costanza's description of the two individuals were remarkably similar to the actual physical characteristics of Thomas Boutwell and Robert Webb. Now, I ask you, the reader, how did Costanza in his statement know that the first name of one of the individuals was "TOM" and that this "Tom" was a football player? And, again, I ask you, how did Costanza also know the other person was a football player? Both Boutwell and Webb testified in judicial proceedings they were football players. Meaning they both committed perjury that Weakland told them about the crime plan just before January 14, 1974. Costanza would have impeached their testimony.

Boutwell committed perjury when he testified that he never knew the name or the location of the Krause residence until the 13th of January 1974, and further perjured himself that was the date he met with Weakland for the first time at Webb's residence. Costanza would have impeached Boutwell's testimony.

Robert Webb also committed perjury when he testified, he never knew the names of Marvin or Hilda Krause or the location of the Krause residence until January 12, 1974. Costanza would have impeached Webb's testimony, as according to his statements to the police. (ROA, pp. 446-449)

The statements of Costanza also revealed Boutwell and Webb were the same two individuals he recognized at the Rib Cage Restaurant with Weakland after the Krause murder as being the same two people he met six weeks prior to the Krause murder. As a matter of fact, Boutwell, Webb and Weakland admitted Costanza was at the Rib Cage Restaurant talking to Weakland on that occasion. The police themselves had characterized Costanza as a "very reliable" informant. Therefore, if Costanza was telling the truth, the prosecution's house of cards case would have been shattered by his testimony.

At no time prior to my 1974 preliminary hearing, neither Oscar Goodman nor Douglas Crosby was provided with the police report concerning the informant Costanza or the "oral" statement Costanza gave to top cop Beecher that were in the possession of the District Attorney's Office. In the oral statement Costanza stated:

"I had no knowledge of Frank LaPena being involved with Gerald Weakland in the Krause murder and he had no further information to provide the police as he stated, 'I've told Mike Whitney everything.'"

Weakland also stated and testified he gave Krause the "watch" to his "Honor Brother", Joseph Costanza, to which Costanza told the police that was a "lie" and Weakland testified he gave me Krause's "ring", another "lie." Webb testified he got rid of this evidence by throwing the watch and ring into a garbage can.

I hope you can understand just how important informant Costanza's testimony would have been favorable and material for me at my 1977 murder trial. You be the judge of that, and I hope none of you who read my life story, will ever be subjected to what you are about to further read, notwithstanding what I have already revealed to you earlier. The path of corruption continues as follows:

Harmon, knowing Judge Joe was providing me with a fair preliminary hearing, then elected to dismiss the murder and robbery charges and seek an indictment against me before a Grand Jury. Boy OH Boy, here we go again!

When Weakland testified at both Rosalie Maxwell's 1976 trial and my March 1977 trial, Weakland, under oath, said all his statements and prior testimony against us was a lie and was pressured by Metro Detectives to testify against us. Let me tell you, Harmon and his corrupt cops were livid when Weakland said we had nothing to do with the murder of Hilda Krause, so they charged Weakland with two counts of perjury for his testimony at our trials.

The jury convicted Weakland, but the Nevada Supreme Court reversed his conviction. In doing so, it held that there was "No Overwhelming" evidence that Weakland committed perjury. Basically, meaning at Weakland's perjury retrial he stood a good chance of being acquitted. *Weakland v. State*, 615 P.2d 252-254 (1980) So, behind closed doors Mel Harmon and Metro Detective Beecher Avants decided to give Weakland two sweetheart deals with the cooperation of Judge Paul Goodman. Wait to you read this!

First, Weakland was allowed to plead to two counts of perjury by way of an "Alford Plea" in March 1981 and would receive a sentence of probation pursuant to the terms of this agreement. However, after "five" useless hearings, the plea agreement was actually consummated and, (are you ready for this?) during each of those hearings, the conversation always revolved around the status of my Krause appeal. (ROA p.2369-70)

Can you believe this; Harmon and his criminal Detectives made a plea deal with Weakland to testify against me in later 1981, over a year even before my Krause conviction was reversed on April 1, 1982". No, question I believe Harmon knew my Krause conviction would be reversed due to his unethical tactics in my case, so they charged Weakland with 2 counts of perjury for his testimony at our trials. They also decided in their retaliation for his recantation at Rosalie's 1976 trial to punish Weakland by placing him in more restrictive security level. Weakland testified so at my March 1977 trial. EOR 3587-4983.

Beecher Avants was furious at Weakland for disclosing to both our jurors that Avants (Homicide Detectives) pressured him to testify against Rosalie and me. Avants wanted revenge and sent a blistering letter against Weakland to the Nevada Parole Board. It was a beauty, I'll say that knowing Gerald Weakland to be an extremely uncontrollable person during his fits of rage, the State kept a watchful eye on Weakland's prison activities. Here is what the Devil Lucifer said about Saint Weakland.

On December 14, 1978, Avants sent a poison pen letter to the Nevada Parole Board, where he makes reference to (1) their police files which contain other incidents relating to Weakland's brutality; (2) Weakland beat numerous prisoners; (3) Has been an agitator in prison; (4) was involved in an escape plan in which there was a plan to use deadly weapons; (5) Weakland pistol whipped Marvin Krause; (6) He kidnapped, robbed and shot Willis Obenauer and left him to die (7) he beat his own wife, Gail Hodges, (Weakland) causing liver damage and two weeks hospitalization; (8) He admitted to Webb burying a man in the Sunrise area and beat prisoners in the jail and prison and, of course let's not forget; (9) Saint Weakland, hung his step-child by the neck with the belt. Wow! Based on that, do you, the reader, think, on his own, Weakland+ without help would have won his freedom with the Nevada Parole Board? I don't think so, do you?

Aww! Wait till you read this. Avants wasn't through with his vented revenge against Weakland, so he sent another love letter on behalf of his prize pupil Weakland to the Parole Board. Wait till you read this – Avants described Hilda Krause's murder and Weakland's violent and depraved nature in detail. Here is what this two-faced hypocrite cop wrote:

"A person of this background should not be considered for parole… there is no room in society for this kind of behavior that this man exhibits. We feel strongly and we urge the Parole Board to deny Gerald Weakland's application for parole" EOR 528

Avants sent a similar letter later. He argued that:

"Weakland does not deserve any leniency whatsoever, I hope and pray that Weakland will be denied parole at this hearing." EOR 5227

Mel Harmon (aka Crime Boss Mel) weighed in too. He called Weakland:

"Really the lowest kind of human being and among the most dangerous type of person **who** can be at large in a community or a state." Harmon explained that the District Attorney's Office, "opposes (Weakland's) Parole at any time in the foreseeable future. I strongly recommend Weakland be made to serve a substantial period in prison before he is seriously considered for parole release." EOR 5222

My! Oh My! Oh My! What beautiful letters law enforcement officials wrote on behalf of Weakland to the Parole Board. What you are about to further read to may disgust you by what Harmon and his "Halo" Boys wrote to the Parole Board regarding Saint Weakland, but first let me say this.

Listen, within the legal Judicial System, it's not uncommon for lawyers, i.e., defense attorneys, prosecutors, judges to socialize with each other. I know this personally, as years later, I worked for a criminal defense attorney as a paralegal. They would come over to Carmine Colucci's office, share stories and drink a lot of booze. As I previously inferred, I believe Harmon knew through the grapevine that Nevada Supreme Court was going to overturn my murder conviction.

All that being said, after my Krause conviction was overturned on April 13, 1982, that sneaky little P…K and his Outlaw gang of crime busters, gave Alter Boy Weakland a second plea deal and let me tell you, as I believe you will agree, it was a dandy, to get Weakland's cooperation again. In Weakland's new plea deal, the State and Beecher Avants would stop

155

writing 'negative letters to the State Parole Board objecting to his parole. Are you ready for this? In return they would also write "favorable" letters on behalf of Weakland to the Parole Board, however. They held back the "favorable" letters "until Weakland testified." On September 28th, Weakland signed his second plea deal with the State.

On September 29, 1982, I was indicted again for the Krause murder on the testimony of Gerald Weakland and Irwin Fish, a convicted nefarious murderer, whom Justice of the Peace Mahlon Brown had previously found Fish's testimony to be so unreasonable he threw out all of Fish's testimony as underserving of belief. Yep, that's the truth folks, that low life, pathological psycho liar, Weakland, whose life I actually saved in prison, when the Aryan Warriors had Weakland cornered and ready to shank him to death, lied once again that I hired him to kill Hilda Krause. How was I able to save his life? I was the "Shot-Caller: at that time doing the majority of all the convicts' cases. Ironically, they nicknamed me "Big Frank", not because of my size; they respected my toughness and intellect and most importantly they trusted me, and I fought like hell for them to get them justice and never failed them.

Counsel Mills questioned Jerry Blackman as follows:

Q: Do you know the defendant Frank LaPena?

A: Yes, I do.

Q: And do you have knowledge as to his proclamation towards violence?

A: Yes, I do.

Q: Was there an incident or several incidents which occurred in the Nevada State Prison while you were an inmate there which gave you an opportunity to observe Mr. LaPena in regard to that propensity for violence?

A: Yes, there were several occasions when other inmates who knew Gerald Weakland. They talked to Frank about virtually killing Weakland and Frank would not allow that to happen.

Q: Did you know that of your own knowledge he did not allow that to happen?

A: Yes.

Mr. Mills: I have no further questions.

Without a doubt, it was easy to see why Weakland made that second deal, the poison pen letters were devastating AGAINST Weakland, and he came to realize he was more than unlikely to ever see the light of day if the State kept sending them. Well, what would you expect from an evil lowlife, woman, child beater, serial killer, who absolutely had "no conscience", is insane, pure evil, uncontrollable, violent beyond words and totally crazy, a psychopath?

That second deal also included the Chairman of Nevada's Parole Commission, Bryan Armstrong publicly stating, "it would be favorable (to Weakland) if he came back and testified against me." Listen and read this horse shit:

After Weakland struck his second deal and testified on September 29, 1982, before the Grand Jury against me, the District Attorney's Office and Metro Homicide Detective told the Parole Board that Weakland was "fully cooperative" and "testifying truthfully" and they asked the board to "consider Mr. Weakland's cooperation in its subsequent proceedings." EOR 5253

According to the Grand Jury Transcript the State had agreed if Weakland testified against LaPena, "...the homicide and D.A.'s Office won't write any more letters to the Parole Board" (ROA pp. 2120-2121) Weakland testified that (1) He lied at both of Rosalie and my trials when he testified neither of us had anything to do with the Krause Murder (Note: remember what I just wrote – ROA p.2154) and (2) He had plead guilty to second degree murder and sentenced to a term of five years to life; ROA pp. 2155, 3085.

Alright, I'm indicted on Weakland's testimony I hired him to kill Hilda Krause. "This is another clue." When Weakland testified at my 1977 Krause trial, homicide detectives "pressured him" to testify against me, Weakland was telling the truth, as well as all his statements and testimony against me was false. What, you just read of Weakland's September 29, 1982, Grand Jury testimony was known perjured testimony by Weakland. As I said before, the corruption continues.

You will be going with me down a path of additional corruption of the likes you can't even begin to imagine as you read one... Let's get back to the Parole Board Farce and analyze this together and let's see what we come up with as suddenly, according to Harmon and Metro Detectives, Weakland is no longer a threat to society. "He's a good guy" our new Choirboy.

Oh Yeah!

Although I was not present at Weakland's parole board hearing I'm going to use my own interpretation of how I believe what Mel and his three lumps of shit said to the Parole Board in Weakland's favor, either by letter or in person. Don't laugh, it may be true.

Oh please, pretty pretty please, roses are red, violets are blue, we love Weakland as much as you do too, Mr. Chairman and members of the Parole Board. Please give this sweet, innocent looking, law-abiding menace to society serial killer a break and release him upon society, and don't be concerned if this insane monster (we now adore) commits any further crimes of brutal, savage violence. We will see to it he won't be prosecuted by **us** because we need our Choirboy Weakland's testimony against Frank LaPena, the one we framed. (Was Harmon on his knees when he asked the Parole Board for this)

If anyone was a menace to society, law-abiding citizens can thank Mel Harmon and his gang of corrupt cops. Weakland, true to his behavior being among the most dangerous persons who can be at large in a community or state, once paroled before my 1989 May trial, went on a cover-up crime spree physically terrorizing decent citizens, where he beat some of them senseless, wrote bad checks, beat up a war veteran in a wheelchair; beat the living shit of his then wife Doreen Weakland, caught with a shot-gun that carries a federal life sentence, violated the conditions of his parole numerous time and parole officers were told "not" to violate him. I attained all this evidence at a later date and his crimes were so many I'm only going to put the Exhibits here as proof of what he did such as: Exhibits B – B-1, B-2; C-1, C-2, C-3, C-4, C-5. C-6; E; F-1 and F-2. (Nevada Revised Statutes) Weakland murdered inmate Lloyd Paulette on January 25, 1977, never prosecuted NRS 200.030; Weakland attempted murder on Ronald Dean Smith on May 17, 1980, found guilty at disciplinary hearing, never prosecuted, NRS 200.010; NRS 205.130 (e) (Fraud) 1990, never prosecuted; NRS 205.090 (Forgery) 1990, never prosecuted and NRS 200.471, 200.481 (2) (Assault and Battery) never prosecuted. The Grand Jury was never made aware of Weakland's horrendous crimes when he gave testimony before them. So, there you have most of it. One thing is for damn sure, prior to my 1989 Krause trial, Harmon and Avants, did everything within their power to make Weakland appear before the jurors "Trouble Free." You be the judge of that.

After I was indicted, Gary Gowen, Esq., was court appointed to represent me. All of the motions I had filed before Judge Joe, once indicted, were transferred to a District Court Judge. I finally ended up with a good, fair Judge, Thomas O'Donnell. I had been in the old county jail for about a year when I was granted bail before Judge O'Donnell. At that time, I was placed in 3G, third floor of the County jail and eventually waiting to be released on Bond, which Rosalie had put her house up as collateral for me. If my memory is correct, my bail in 1974, was set at One Million dollars by Magistrate Legates. After my Krause case was overturned, I believe it was set at One Hundred Thousand dollars, but I got it reduced to Fifty Thousand.

SPECIAL FAVORS FOR MOB ENFORCER TONY SPILOTRO

During this time, I learned that among my well-known fellow "residents" was Tony Spilotro. In January 1983, Anthony "Tough Tony" Spilotro was indicted for the May 15, 1962 killings of mobsters Billy McCarthy and Jimmy Miraglia in Chicago. This case became known as the "M & M Murders," McCarthy's scrotum was ice-picked, and his head was placed in a vice where it was squeezed until one of his eyes popped out! I'm sure that Miraglia's demise was equally unpleasant.

One day I hear some cop calling out my name. As I go to the cell bars, I see several cops out there and one of them says to me, "Frank, come out here", as he opens the cell door. "What for?" I ask. "Everything is okay, Frank, just come with us, alright?" Now from the tone of his voice, I did not detect any danger, so out I go walking down the 3rd floor corridor.

As we turn to the left, there is a holding tanks and I recognize Tony Spilotro in the tank. Spilotro calls me over and the cops placed themselves on each end of the corridor to seal it off if anyone comes down the hallway! Tony asked me if I knew what his circumstance was, and I said yes.

He goes on to say, "I'm concerned that someone might want to make a name for themselves by testifying in court that while in the County Jail, I admitted to them that I killed the two guys in Chicago." He then asks me if I knew a way that "could be prevented". I told him, "Yes, I know a way you can protect yourself from that. I can prepare affidavits which you will need to make everybody sign that you came in contact with".

"That affidavit will state that you have never talked to them about your homicide case, and that they do not know anything about your case in Chicago. Then, if for any reason they

159

will appear to testify against you they will be committing known perjury as a result of either favors or threats from the prosecutors and said affidavits will be sworn to under lawful oath!".

A big smile came onto his face as he was pleased to hear my suggested answer to his question. He shook my hand and thanked me for my help. "However..." I then added. "At this time, Tony, I have no access to go to the law library to make up the affidavits." Right there, Tony calls one of the officers over and asks him if I could use the law library to do some work for him.

Well, the cops and I went to the law library and they told everybody to clear out! I typed out the affidavits and made hundreds of copies. Then I returned to Tony with them. As I gave the copies to him, he said thanks, then surprised me, "Do you want me to take care of Weakland for you? I said, "no I'll deal with him myself." "Now...even the cops here in this jail must sign the affidavits." He said nothing to me, just nodded.

So, my job, or favor as I looked at it, was to see that nobody appeared at his trial to testify against him that he admitted to them he committed the M and M Murders. Nobody from the Las Vegas County Jail did. You will read more about what appears to be Tony Spilotro's "personal" involvement in my Krause case.

The day I made bail and walked down the stairs of the County Jail; attorney John Momot was waiting for me. He handed me an envelope that contained some money from Tony Spilotro. Later on, one of Spilotro's associates asked me if I knew how to obtain the identity of police informants. I said, "Yes, I personally set new law in the State of Nevada on that specific issue" and I provided them with a copy of my legal work as such.

In 1983, upon my release, after meeting with John Momot, Esq., Gary Gowen was waiting for me and drove me to Rosalie's house, where I stayed for a while, trying to find a job. It was tough, really tough. Metro detectives did everything they could to deny me a Sheriff's Card to prevent me from working in a hotel-casino. I eventually obtained my Sheriff's Card, but Metro wasn't done with me. Ali Damaventi and John Cody, Bell Captain Supervisors hired me at the Hilton to work the valet parking. I never finished my shift as they were told to fire me stating a metro detective called executive Davis and told him, "you have a killer working at your establishment." Happened again at the Sahara and Bally's Hotel and Casino. They were doing their best to prevent me to make a living.

Rosalie, Lynn Brady, and I decided to go to the local 631 Teamsters Union and enroll in the union. We were sent out to the Las Vegas Convention Center during a CES Electronic Convention. I was assigned to Supervisor Tommy Thomson who would later become my best friend ever. When Tommy read my name on the work sheet, he said, "I've read a lot about you in the papers and TV, and you got a raw deal in my book." Tommy made me feel at ease and said, "come on I'll show you where we are going to build this exhibit." "Have you ever done this type of work before?" "No". "Okay, did you bring any tools with you?" "No." "Do you know how to read a blueprint?" "No". "Did you bring any lunch with you?" Tommy laughed and said, "Alright, Frank, here's a screwdriver, just walk around and pretend you know what you are doing, I've got your back". Tommy, by the way, bought me lunch.

That folks, was the beginning of the best friendship in my life. I never in my life met a more kind, generous person than Tommy. I'm talking about he was that way with everyone he came in contact with. Tommy was the most loved person I ever met. Tommy used his "juice" from the Union Hall to get me work at the convention center with him. However, I needed more work time and since I was good at criminal law, I went to work for a criminal attorney, Carmine Colucci, as a Paralegal. Carmine was great to me as well as his top Legal Assistant Zoe. Zoe helped me in so many ways around computers and around the office. She was awesome.

Just for the heck of it, I did an interview for a job that was open for a Limo driver. To my surprise, I was hired at the Little White Chapel and my pay level rose quite higher than working in the law office.

In the meantime, attorney Gary Gowen and I were pounding the State for more info concerning informant Joseph Costanza and Harmon and Metro were adamantly opposing it. Unfortunately, for me, my District Court Judge Tom O'Connell passed away from a massive heart attack. Another Judge was supposed to be picked randomly; that's a joke, folks, because the D.A.'s Office controlled that with their power. But one other Judge made a comment if my case was assigned to his court, he was going to toss my murder charges out the window. There was a specific reason this Judge wanted my case, and Harmon did everything he could to prevent that, and the D.A. Office got the Judge they wanted who denied my third motion to get Costanza. Gary Gown and I appealed the denial via a Writ of Mandate to the Nevada Supreme Court.

What you are about to read amounts to the worse case in Nevada history. What oppression under the law means pertaining to the most corrupt prosecutor Mel Harmon and his nefarious gang of metro cops. It took me "eleven years" after I was first arrested to find this out based on Harmon's concealment tactics. This may startle you, it sure did me, as I was present when Gary Gowen was orally arguing my case on the District Court's denial of Costanza when Chief Justice E.M. Gunderson stopped Gary Gowen who truly believed there were police reports and prosecutor reports that appeared to be missing from the time Weakland was "first" arrested to the present time. You are not going to believe how Chief Justice Gunderson totally shocked everyone in the appellate courtroom when on April 11, 1985, Gunderson said something to the affect, "Counsel you are getting into an area that has troubled me for a number of years," that Weakland had made **three statements** as to who hired him to murder Hilda Krause, **"the first one that incriminate 'Marvin Krause' as the individual who hired Weakland to kill his wife"**, as follows:

> *A number of years ago a person who was on the District Attorney's staff at the time was talking to me in Carson City about this matter. He is now a District Judge. So, I say that he was up there, for some purpose I forget what, but we were talking about this case and he indicated to me that Mr. LaPena was not the first individual that Weakland incriminated. That, in fact, as I recall the story, Mr. Weakland was first inducted in the course of the investigation to incriminate Mr. Kraus and claims that, you know, was trying to bargain for his freedom by incriminating Mr. Kraus, and evidently that was discussed as a possibility to purchase Mr. Weakland's testimony in exchange, you know, by agreeing to give him a lesser sentence in exchange for testimony against Mr. Kraus and ultimately that was decided against following conversations between the District Attorney's Office and the police department then Mr. Weakland was induced to say or offered to say that another individual, not Mr. LaPena, had engaged him to kill Mrs. Kraus. And again, this was discussed and finally decided that they wouldn't bargain for Mr. Weakland's testimony on that basis… in any case, Mr. LaPena was the third person that Weakland was willing to incriminate under entirely different stories in exchange for favorable treatment. (AA Vol.3, pp.77-78).*

Are you as concerned, as I am "WHY" were the other two suspects **"NOT"** charged for the Hilda Krause murder/robbery?

Let's talk about the first suspect Marvin Krause and here's the big question. How would the prosecutor and his Metro detective Avants know Marvin Krause "did not hire

162

Weakland" to kill Hilda Krause since that case was in its early investigative stages? I have no doubt in my mind Marvin Krause "hated" me so much he used every bit of his "juice" in law enforcement to set up and help frame me. This town was loaded with dirty cops and the good cops suffered from it. I obtained proof Marvin Krause socialized with then Sheriff Ralph Lamb who I believe protected Marvin Krause and I later learned Krause was protected by Mob Enforcer Tony Spilotro.

Yep, Marvin Krause kills two birds with one stone; gets rid of his wife and me at the same time. Something for you to think about, Okay! Don't forget Marvin Krause was a suspect in an unrelated murder, and a young prosecutor, Neil Galatz, who wanted to go after Krause "was told to 'Back off'." That's a hell of a lot of power no matter how you look at it. Would you agree?

Time to look at the second suspect Weakland names as the person who hired him to kill Hilda Krause. I always wondered WHO was the second person Weakland names to hire him to murder Hilda Krause. That person's name has never surfaced, WHY? Was this person so powerful or dangerous, cops, prosecutor or maybe a judge was scared to name him. Interesting, isn't that? And again, how would Harmon and Detective Avants know that this second person did not hire Weakland to murder Hilda Krause when Weakland confessed it was the second person who hired him to kill Hilda Krause?

Did Napoleon Bonafarte and his partner Lucifer ever question this second suspect that Weakland names? You can bet your ass they didn't. I was their "fall guy" and they pressured Weakland to make sure I would be.

District Court Judge Addeliar Guy's statement to Chief Justice Gunderson regarding Weakland's three statements clearly and overwhelmingly showed beyond a reasonable doubt I had nothing to do with the Hilda Krause murder and robbery and was 'actually innocent'.

What kind of justice is there when the State knows you are actually innocent of a crime, yet use perjured testimony to arrest, prosecute, convict and send a person to prison for the rest of their lives, or in my case to successfully seek the death penalty? It's truly sad, the State would stoop so low in corruption. When a prosecutor does not disclose material evidence favorable to a defendant showing innocence, the prosecutor becomes a disgrace to the truth-seeking function of the court and insults the integrity of the judicial system and that is precisely what they did to me. You be the judge. I lost my life, my dignity, you do not really know what I endured. My nightmares are indescribable, so please understand my aggressive writing. These bastards also caused the **deaths of my animals**, which emotionally tore me apart; Yes! I'm going to tell it like it is. We have lots more to read and if you think I will get any justice from this, guess what!! Forgetaboutit!!

Gary Gowen, Esq., was considered by the local judicial system here in Las Vegas, NV, as an "Outsider." Gary worked mostly in the Reno, NV area, if my memory is correct. I liked Gary; he was aggressive and smart and being an outsider, he did not let anybody push him around; no fear of cops, prosecutors or judges. He wasn't a good ol' boy. But Gary was a kind of a strange duck. He did unusual things about his representation of me. For instance, after several years together preparing for my second Krause case, he suddenly disappeared without telling anybody neither me or the trial judge or the State. Guess where Gary went? Sailing around the ocean in his 50 plus foot boat. Gary had been appointed to my case on November 2, 1982 and continued as my sole counsel until January 29, 1986. Gary later turned up in Court and didn't understand why he had been relieved from my case. I didn't like losing Gary who had more than five (5) years invested in investigating my case. Gary told my new counsel LaMond Miller he would gladly help in any way he could since he had abundant knowledge of evidence obtained in my case.

I will say this Gary had a big pair of Gulunies. On December 8, 1983, Gary went after Avants, Chuck Lee, prosecutors Harmon and Schwartz and Weakland in a hearing before Judge Thomas O'Donnell regarding undisclosed police and prosecution reports concerning Informant Costanza and statements made by Weakland before law enforcement officials. Gary just knew they were hiding something, and he intended to get to the bottom of it. It would later be evident it was about Weakland's **three statements:**

BY MR. GOWEN:

Q: *You have made several statements to the police with regard to your involvement in the murder of Hilda Krause?*

A: *Yes. (ROA P., ll. 10-12; AA Vol. 3, P. 124-125)*

When, on April 11, 1985, Chief Justice Gunderson informed Gowen that Weakland made three statements as to who hired him to murder Hilda Krause, naming me as the third one, Gary was beside himself. The State engaged in selective prosecution by only accepting Weakland's third statement that it was me. Mel Harmon and Avants, I believe, made sure

Weakland's three statements would never be listed as a part of the Krause investigation record. "And, it wasn't, according to Justice Robert Rose on December 12, 2003." I wish Harmon was a cockroach, I would have fed him to my Black Widow Spider pet, then again, I wouldn't want to poison my Black Widow Spider.

Remember what I said above about the Krause case being in its early investigative stages and law enforcement did now know when Weakland confessed who Weakland was going to say hired him to kill Hilda Krause. You are going to read what the prosecutor "admitted to" in his Opening Statement before the jurors on May 9, 1989:

So, although Jerry Weakland was arrested, the police 'did not know who else was involved in the crime. They did not know the motive for the killing and the robbery. The police and the District Attorney's Office then 'reached an agreement' with Weakland. Gerald Weakland was allowed to plead guilty to second degree murder if he 'told all' he knew about the killing and if he agreed to testify in court."

Yep, they "reached an agreement alright" but only after they pressured Weakland to go back to the drawing board and name me. I hope you agree with me, this was a classic case where the State engaged in selective prosecution by only accepting Weakland's 'third' statement: it was me.

Even more interesting is how the State knows Marvin Krause was not involved in his wife's murder since the State has always argued Weakland's statement and testimony are true and believable. That being the case, **why wasn't Weakland's FIRST statement then believable that Marvin Krause hired him to murder his wife?** What evidence did the State know about to refuse Weakland naming Marvin Krause as the culprit who hired him to murder his wife? I'll tell you what **"NONE."** That also goes for the second statement it was someone else other than me who hired Weakland to do this crime **"NONE"**

Whey they break the law they become criminals and as an organization of people they become a criminal activity, a governmental gang who break the law. Yes, they are gangsters who wear a badge in dishonor. Like Oscar Goodman would say, "I'll take the black hats over the white hats any day", "I'm with you Oscar".

Let me just go back a bit to say something that has irked me for a very long time among other things. After Rosalie and I were arrested, our homes were searched for the Krause "watch and ring" by Metro Detectives (Avants and Lee). No watch or ring of any fruits of the crime were found (ff 360-3601) Weakland stated he gave the Krause "ring" to me and Krause "watch" to Joseph Costanza, who told Avants that Weakland "lied", and he gave the Krause "watch" to him. Weakland's accomplice Webb testified he threw the "watch and ring" in the garbage can. Gail Weakland said she saw Weakland hide the watch. Nurse Haley, who wanted to testify, said: Marvin Krause gave her the "watch and ring" to hold for him when he was admitted at Sunrise Hospital on January 14, 1974. My Oh My! This is a story in itself, would you agree?

Anyway, what got me hot under the collar, besides all those liars, after searching my house, Avants and Lee later came back to my house, broke into it, and were caught red handed by my next-door neighbor, Brain Clayton. He asked what they were doing in my house? They told him they were looking for evidence of a crime. I later learned from Geneva Blue two very special jewelry gifts that Frank Sinatra and Liberace gave me "disappeared" from my jewelry box. I have no proof they stole them, but my gut feelings told me otherwise.

1989 SECOND TRAIL GETS UNDERWAY-CONVICTED AGAIN

Prior to my 1989, second trial, the State offered me a plea deal for time served. I believe almost anyone would've taken that deal in a heartbeat. I turned it down without a second thought and it cost me many more years in prison. No way on earth was I going to plead guilty to a crime I did not commit, especially one involving a woman. I believe during my second trial they were nervous Justice Gunderson and Judge Guy would have shocked the jurors about the three statements Weakland confessed to leading to my acquittal for being innocent in the Krause case.

Justice Gunderson's statement to Justice Rose regarding Weakland's three statements on December 12, 2003, at Pardon's Board Hearing:

Justice Rose: *What was the reaction of the D.A. if they were there at that hearing?*

Justice Gunderson: *I don't recall that there was any reaction by the D.A.'s office. But you know it has always been my belief that one of the reasons that the D.A.'s Office wanted to get Mr. LaPena to plead guilty and were willing to let him off as I believe with time served, was because they didn't want the possibility that those facts would emerge in a very uncomfortable way for them."*

Justice Rose: *What I was wondering if this could have been a Brady violation, which is the Withholding of evidence by a prosecuting agency.*

Justice Gunderson: *Yes, and I agree with that, and I've always felt that, and I can understand why they wanted to put the case to rest and were willing to make a deal that would   bury the issue."*

Justice Rose: *Thank you.*

On October 26, 1988, LaMond Mills and George Carter were appointed to represent me in the Krause case. The following occurred at the hearing:

THE COURT: *This is Case NO: C59791 will you make your appearances for the record.*

Mr. Harmon: *Your Honor, Mel Harmon on behalf of the State.*

Mr. Carter: *George Carter for the defendant.*

Mr. Mills: *LaMond Mills for the defendant.*

Gary Gowen: *Gary Gowen for the defendant. (Out of nowhere Gary just decided to shop up in Court after abandoning me and decided he wanted to go sailing.*

Mr. Mills: *He is going to be acting as a witness. He is not functioning as an attorney in this matter, Your Honor.*

Prior to my 1989 trial, I had several meetings with both counselors along with my private investigator, Michael Wysocki (Former Metro Detective). Wysocki had interjected his knowledge of witnesses and records that were necessary to obtain in order that relevant and material evidence that would be presented on my behalf during my trial proceedings.

During these meetings, Wysocki stated that counsel interviewed and issued subpoenas of defense witnesses, Rosalie Maxwell; Gary Gowen, Esq.; Melinda Sweeigen; Judge Addelair D. Guy; Former Justice, E.M. Gunderson; Anthony Bruno; Otis McClendon; Tillman Banks; former Metro Lt. Hal Miller; Camille Dixon; Brian Clayton; inmate Nathan Kimmel and Freddy Walker; Nurse Haley; Judith Hill, Esq.; Frederick Pinkerton, Esq; and that Michael Wysocki's testimony was crucial since he possessed a great deal of knowledgeable facts which would have refuted the testimony of State witnesses, Gerald Weakland, Thomas Boutwell,

Robert Webb, Beecher Avants, Charles Lee and most import, "The State's Theory Of The Case." I had requested counsel to have investigator Wysocki check the records at the County Clerk's Office for the years 1973 and 1974, to provide evidence that Rosalie Maxwell 'never' initiated any divorce proceedings against her estranged husband, Donald Maxwell, prior to or shortly after, the homicide of Hilda Krause. These important crucial defense witnesses were **not** called on my behalf by Mills or Carter. **Here I go again more attorney fights**.

Mills' failed to call Rosalie Maxwell who was my most critical witness to support my theory of defense, that 'no murder contract ever existed.'

On May 2, 1989, prior to my second trial, in my presence and investigator Michael Wysocki, Counsel Mills interviewed Rosalie Maxwell for approximately two (2) hours extracting vital information from Maxwell which went to the very heart of the charges against me. Rosalie Maxwell was the one person, other than myself, who possessed personal knowledge that I never met or knew where Marvin Krause lived or that he was married.

Rosalie Maxwell informed Counsel Mills that during the time of her relationship with me, she informed me that despite her separation from her husband, "SHE WOULD NOT DIVORCE HIM." She also told Counsel Mills if he would check the county records, he would find that "she did not initiate or attempt to initiate any divorce proceedings against her estranged husband, Donald Maxwell, prior to or shortly after the January 14, 1974 homicide.

More importantly, Maxwell advised Counsel Mills that detectives Beecher Avants and Charles Lee "interviewed Donald Maxwell" and were told by him that Rosalie Maxwell had not initiated any legal divorce proceedings against him in 1973 or 1974.

Rosalie also informed Counsel Mills with evidence tending to show both Gerald and Gail Weakland Hodges for seeking revenge against me and Rosalie by informing Mills she was personally present when Bill Underwood pleaded with me to accept the pool concession at the MGM Grand Hotel since Bill was unable to get Weakland that position because Paul Ross, the hotel manager would not place Weakland in that position due to Ross's knowledge that Weakland previously beat up a pool boy resulting in the boy's family initiating a law suit against Caesars Palace. This meeting occurred at the Sun Deck Restaurant out by Caesars pool in late 1973, where all three parties were having lunch together. Rosalie told Mills this time she was willing to testify on my behalf.

Prior to my 1989 trial, I questioned Counsel George Carter if he had read my 1974 preliminary hearing transcripts, 1977 trial transcripts and investigative police reports and State witness statements. I wanted Counsel Carter to be adequately and properly prepared for the presentation of both State and Defense witnesses. Counsel Carter told me he had not nor intended to be since he felt he wasn't being financially compensated enough by the low allowance Courts give attorney on court-appointments.

He also said his agreements with other Counsel LaMond Mills was that he was to do all the legal writing and **"NOT"** the examination of witnesses.

However, to my surprise, Counsel Mills allowed Carter to present arguments, examine witnesses and because of Carter's lack of preparation and due diligence he was making serious mistakes on facts and examination of witnesses and when I tried to correct him on facts, he rejected my assistance. I then told him, "When the court states its' time for a break, I'm going to break your jaw." Unfortunately. the jury saw me lose my temper and this was not a good thing for me. After a lengthy talk all parties agreed it would be in the best interest for me that Counsel Carter remove himself from my case. Upon Carter filing the said Motion, the Judge denied it. I was now stuck with this lame duck and it showed during the rest of my trial.

My former Counsel Gary E. Gowen's testimony was extremely crucial to my defense as he possess personal knowledge from his telephone talk with Informant Joseph Costanza with linked Gerald Weakland and Marvin Krause together in December 1973, planning of a subsequent fake robbery which resulted in the death of Hilda Krause.

On April 16, 1989, trial counsel Mills spoke by telephone to former Counsel Gary Gowen for a half hour, and on April 17, 1989 spoke to Gowen for a half hour, yet, unbeknownst to me. Counsel Mills never revealed to Gary Gowan what date my trial was to commence.

Trial Counsel Mills was well informed Gary Gowen possessed a vast knowledge of facts in his nearly six years of investigating my case and was more than willing to testify for me.

Gowen's testimony would have corroborated Investigator Michael Wysocki's investigation that the "two items of property Marvin Krause claimed to have been stolen from him were actually turned over to him by the admitting nurse," Nurse Haley. Her testimony was critical since it impeached both Marvin Krause's statement and Weakland's testimony of the "Watch and Ring." Both Wysocki and I informed Counsel Mills that Nurse Haley was willing and able to testify and shed light on the truth of this matter. She was not called to testify on my behalf by Mills.

Investigator Wysocki possessed valuable knowledge of a personal nature, as well as Counsel Gary Gowen of my character in addition to vast knowledge of facts refuting the State's theory of the case and Weakland, Boutwell, Webb, Avants, and Lee's police reports and testimony. Investigator Wysocki informed both Counsel Mills and Carter yet was not called by them on my behalf.

I will give credit where credit is due. On May 9, 1989, Mills did a very terrific job of cross-examination of Weakland's credibility and caught Weakland in a monstrous admission that no contract murder ever existed that should have resulted in an acquittal by the jury or moving the (biased) trial judge to move Harmon to dismiss all charges against me. Yeah! Right and the cow can jump over the moon. Anyway, George Carter finally did some good cross-examination, but the rest of it, forgetaboutit! Ditto for Mills also. No Justice Gunderson, Judge Guy, Gary Gowen, Rosalie, Wysocki, but in the '77 trial, Weakland had testified several times concerning what different dates he "allegedly" went over to Rosalie Maxwell's house, and entered into an "alleged" contract (to commit) murder between Maxwell and myself. Prior statements and testimony showed that the trial revealed that Weakland said under oath, this "alleged" contract murder meeting occurred on January 2nd, a Wednesday night…on January 4th, a Friday night… and around the first week in January 1974, which he stated also happened on a Friday night!

At no time during the three different dates Weakland "allegedly" went over to Maxwell's residence and entered into an "alleged" contract murder; nor did he ever depart from his testimony that this "alleged" meeting took place other than on a Friday night between the hours of 8:00 p.m. and 10:00 p.m.

Counsel Mills pressed Weakland for a "final" determination as to what precise date of the three dates he previously testified to, was the alleged date. The case record herein clearly and conclusively established that Weakland stated January 4th, a Friday night was the date, when he testified under direct examination by Mills!

Q: *State your name sir*

A: *Gerald Weakland*

Q: *And you're the same Gerald Weakland who testified earlier in these proceedings?*

A: *Yes. I was originally contact by Frank La Pena back in December. I imagine it was the first week of December 1973. I believe I testified when this originally first started was in December, that…you know Frank and I first had contact about this case, and he kept in contact with me constantly.*

Mr. Mills: *I am going to now use this transcript for the purpose of impeachment, rather than recollection. Sir, do you recall testifying in the preliminary hearing?*

A: *Yes.*

Q: *Do you remember giving the answer approximately three weeks before the 14th of January, just 'after' Christmas? Do you remember that answer?*

A: *Yes.*

Q: *Do you remember being asked the question, now did you become aware of it, and do you remember giving the answer, I was contacted by Frank LaPena and then you went on to point out Mr. LaPena in the courtroom? Sir, isn't it true that at that time, in 1974, you testified that you first became aware of this when you were contacted by Mr. LaPena after Christmas, approximately three weeks prior to January 14, 1974?*

A: *Yes.*

Q: *A short time after you testified that you had a meeting with Rosalie Maxwell in her townhouse. Do you recall that testimony?*

A: *With Rosalie and Frank, yes.*

Q: *And do you recall approximately what time of day that meeting took place?*

A: *I believe it was 8:00 and 9:00 that evening. It was a Friday evening.*

Q: It was a Friday evening. And do you recall approximately how many days that that was before January 14, 1974?

A: I believe it was right after the first of the year.

Q: Mr. Weakland, drawing your attention again to the preliminary hearing held in 1974, I draw your attention to page 52 of that preliminary hearing and ask you to read lines 27 through 30 to yourself, sir.

A: With Rosalie and Frank; yes.

Q: And do you recall approximately what time of day that meeting took place?

A: I believe it was 8:00 and 9:00 that evening. It was a Friday evening.

Q: It was a Friday evening. And do you recall approximately how many days that that was before January 14, 1974?

A: I believe it was right after the first of the year.

Q: Mr. Weakland, drawing your attention again to the preliminary hearing held in 1974, I draw your attention to page 53 of that preliminary hearing and ask you to read lines 27 through 30 to yourself, sir. I am showing you additionally…additionally a transcript from your "entry of plea" dated February 4, 1975 and draw your attention to Lines 15 through 17. Have you had an opportunity to read lines 27 through 30 of the preliminary hearing transcript?

A: Yes.

Q: And lines 15 through 18, of the plea down, dated February 4, 1975?

A: Yes.

Q: Do these refresh your recollection as to how long before January 14, 1974, you allegedly met with Rosalie Maxwell and Frank LaPena at her townhouse?

A: Yes.

Q:	*And how long was it?*
A:	*Ten days.*
Q:	*And that ten days was a Friday...was it not?*
A:	*I believe it was. Yes, it was, sir.*
Q:	*So, it's your testimony that ten days prior to January 1974, on a Friday and I believe the Court has taken judicial notice that would be January 4, 1974.*
THE COURT:	*That I have no dispute on Mr. Mills.*
Q:	*The one ten days before would be a Friday, January 4, 1974, and that's your best recollection at the time that you made these statements when you met with Rosalie Maxwell?*
A:	*And Frank LaPena, yes.*
Q:	*Thank you. I believe that it was at that time, at that meeting on January 4, 1974, approximately 8:00 p.m. is when you received the details, allegedly were given a map and received the details who the victim was going to be, that he worked the early hours that it should be done on a Monday or Friday, isn't that true sir?*
A:	*Yes.*
Q:	*And prior to that time, you had not received that information... prior to January 4, 1974. (sic) the specific information and the map?*
A:	*I didn't get the map until that time, no sir.*
Q	*But isn't it true you also were first told about the detail or work schedule of Mr. Krause on that...at that time as well?*
A:	*Yes.*

Now, I have to admit that Mills did a very good cross-examination of Weakland concerning the date, time and place that the "alleged" murder contract meeting occurred!

Then my other Counsel, George Carter tore into Weakland's lies concerning the "alleged" meeting, when he presented Ms. Jean Crow, the Personnel Director of Caesars

Palace Hotel and Casino, who testified that the timecard records of Rosalie Maxwell, conclusively showed she signed in to work at 6:00 p.m. on January 4, 1974, a Friday night and signed out of work at 2:00 a.m. January 5, 1974.

When Ms. Cross testified on the 18th of May, she was given direct examination by Mr. Carter. That exchange went as follows…

Q: State your name for the record.

A: Jean Crow.

Q: You are the same Jean Crow here a few days ago and testified?

A: That's correct.

Q: You are the Custodian of Records at Caesars Palace?

A: Right.

Q: Pursuant to request by myself, have you had occasion to search the records of Caesars Palace relating to one Rosalie Maxwell?

A: Yes.

Q: Did your research those records specifically with an eye toward whether Miss Maxwell worked on January 4th, a Friday, 1974?

A: Yes, I did.

Q: Did you find the records necessary to make that determination?

A: I did.

Q: What did the records reflects as to whether Rosalie Maxwell worked on that particular day?

A: They show she worked from 6:00 to 2:00 a.m. that day.

Q: Are those records kept in the ordinary course of business?

A: Yes, they are.

Q: Did they appear to have been tampered with since the time they were made?

A: No.

Q: *Is there any reason, at this time, for you to believe these records are not accurate?*

A: *None.*

THE COURT: *And I am to understand that what you have testified to here is January 4, 1974, that from 6:00 p.m. there was a sign in and at 2:00 a.m. a sign out?*

THE WITNESS: *Correct.*

No question Mills scored a major hit against the State when he made Weakland "admit" according to Rosalie's documentary work schedule by Mrs. Jean Crow, Rosalie was at work from 6:00 p.m. to 2:00 a.m. during the date, time, and place Weakland testified a murder for hire contract was entered into between the three of us.

What you're going to read next is going to show you what this piece of shit, old prick said as he went ballistic on both of my attorneys for scoring a huge point against the State and a fit of anger for a judge trampled all over my rights to a fair trial as he did everything, he could help Harmon convict me such as:

THE COURT: *(to Deputy District Attorney Harmon) I need some opposition to these motions then. There is nothing here in the **file to indicate you care.** (ff,2262)*

THE COURT: *Mr. Harmon, I am denying any attempt by them to mess with Mr. Costanza. (ff. 2463)*

THE COURT: *No such thing has been deemed hostile. The other thing you have now hanged the testimony you elicited from him (Weakland) when you cross-examined him regarding the date when he went to see Rosalie Maxwell. (ff.4012)*

THE COURT: *I have a letter addressed to Judge Wendell, a copy went to the District Attorney's office, 'Attention to Mr. Harmon'. The date is February 7, 1987. It was received in Department 9 on February 7, 1987 and forward to my office. In regard to Mr. Frank LaPena…I do not know the man, never met him, and if I passed him on the street, I would not know him. Regarding Mr. Jerry Weakland, **I have no***

175

knowledge of his connection with Mr. LaPena." (ff. 4311-
4313) (Emphasis added)

He also became incensed when we asked for a jury instruction regarding the clearly false testimony of Weakland stating he told Costanza of my involvement in the hired murder and more incensed when we asked for a jury instruction that the State failed to prove any murder for hire contract ever existed.

How about a little humor folks, O'Boy, O'Boy talk about injustice as it relates to a fair trial. Hmm, let's see here, O'Yeah! I went to trial with **five (5) prosecutors** against me in my case: The Judge, Mel Harmon, David Schwartz, LaMond Mills and George Carter. I stood no chance of winning; but I hoped the jurors paid attention to Mrs. Jean Crow's testimony. They didn't. Well, I do have to admit something at one point during my trial, I wished if the Judge had been a football, I would have kicked his ass over the Goal Post for 15 points and a bottle of rum.

I believe if the jury had heard what the testimony of Chief Justice Gunderson and District Court Judge Guy would have testified to regarding Weakland's three statements it would have turned the tide of evidence in my favor to a possible acquittal, and I also believe that the Judge would have backed off a bit with this tyrant attitude.

I'm going to go back a little to LaMond Mills cross-examination of Weakland strictly on point to what you're going to read as to how Weakland claimed he killed Hilda Krause. This might throw you off some, but then again you may figure it out from my previous clues, who the type of person it was who really murdered Hilda Krause.

On May 9, 1989, Weakland was cross-examined pertaining to the specific, precise, detailed and described physical attack and injuries he claimed he inflicted on Hilda Krause, and the events on how he allegedly murdered Mrs. Krause. Keep a keen mind as you read this, ok:

Q: *And you tied up Mrs. Krause?*

A: *Yes.*

Q: *And how did you tie her up, Mr. Weakland?*

A:	I tied her with her hands behind her back. (ROA P. 3078)
Q:	Did you simply cut her throat? Did you stab her or cut her?
A:	I cut her.
Q:	Did you take one cut?
A:	Yes (ROA P. 3082)
Q:	Did you get any blood on yourself, Mr. Weakland?
A:	No, not that I recall. (ROA P. 3083)
Q:	Had you gagged her?
A:	I believe I did, yes.
Q:	Then what did you do, Mr. Weakland?
A:	I left.
Q:	Did you go back and check Mr. Krause?
A:	No, I didn't I wanted to get out of there (ROA P. 3084)

On May 18, 1989, Gerald Weakland was recalled as a witness by my Counsel LaMond Mills and testified as follows:

Q:	Did you tie up both the hands and feet of Mrs. Krause?
A:	According to what the transcript says, yes. (ROA P.4008)
Q:	And what did you use to tie up Mrs. Krause's hands and feet, sir? (ROA P. 4009)
A:	A cord.
Q:	Did you stab her in the throat? (AOA P. 4011)
Mr. Schwartz:	Your Honor, I am going to object. (ROA P. 4011)
The Court:	Objection overruled.

Mills continues with his questioning:

| Q: | Did you do anything else to Hilda besides strike her in the back of the neck and cutting her throat? |

A:	*As I was leaving, I believe I stuck the knife in her back.*
Q:	*Did you do anything else to her?*
A:	*No.*
Q:	*Did you ever try to strangle her?*
A:	*I don't believe so. (ROA P. 4012)*

Counsel Mills did not go any further on this. Didn't put his testimony on a blackboard before a jury and use Dr. Clarke's testimony before the jury. He didn't compare them against one another to show the jury that Weakland was lying about how he claimed he murdered Hilda Krause!

Q:	*Your testimony is you took **one** cut and cut her from **left to, right?** (Emphasis added)*
A:	*Yes.*
Q:	*That was sufficient?*
A:	*Yes.*

Alright folks, you have finally come to the last clue. LaMond Mills just nailed it right on the head. Come on LaMond, you're a highly experienced former prosecutor with the U.S. Attorney's Office and criminal defense attorney. Think: Weakland just handed it to you, you got it, you are dead right on target. Weakland just testified under oath that he told you and the jurors **he did not murder Hilda Krause**. Pay attention to what he just testified. Don't play dumb.

Prosecutor Harmon is praying you won't figure out what Weakland just said, because if you do, you will blow Harmon right out of his shorts. No question in my mind Harmon knows what it is because that piece of evidence is in Harmon's possession.

Time for you to win the most sensational murder case in Nevada history, LaMond. Don't blow it LaMond, damn it, he did, or did he on purpose? Had you only looked closely at what Dr. James Clarke's Autopsy Examination and Report that was in your possession as a police report and actually compared it to what Weakland just "admitted" you would have finished the State's star witness' credibility permanently and I would have been exonerated, despite that clown Judge.

I will tell you later when I accidently came upon this incredible evidence it only took me a New York Minute to figure out who this type of person was that murdered Hilda Krause, and it wasn't Weakland. And I will tell you later my theory of why I believe Weakland confessed to a murder he didn't commit.

As for Lamond Mills, the lead attorney, he should have discovered it before my 1989 trial, used it as an Opening Statement and closing statement, put this testimony on a blackboard before the jury and use Dr. Clarke's testimony and Autopsy Examination Report to show that Weakland was lying about how he claimed he murdered Hilda Krause.

I'm going to play "Lawyer" right now for what I believe Mills should have argued before the jurors based upon what you previously read. Ok? Mills Opening Statement should have been very short yet powerful and right to the point. All LaMond Mills had to say was:

> Ladies and gentlemen of the jury, as I stand here before you the evidence in this case, which I'm going to present to you, will prove, and I believe shock you into possible disbelief, confessed killer Gerald Weakland did not murder Hilda Krause. The evidence I intend to submit will prove beyond a shadow of a doubt this did not happen, despite Weakland's proposed testimony before you and what the State just told you that Weakland murdered Hilda Krause. The evidence in this case will also provide two highly respected defense witnesses who will testify. The State pressured Weakland to incriminate Frank La Pena in order to get his plea agreement sealed. Ladies and Gentlemen the evidence in this case will prove beyond a reasonable doubt that Mr. LaPena had absolutely nothing to do with the Hilda Krause murder and robbery and has been unjustly crucified by the State's beyond what you can't imagine since the inception of this case and I ask you bring back a verdict of not guilty.

Here is what Mills said in part; couldn't believe it!

> There was a tragic murder that simply not denied. Gerald Weakland appears to have been the person who brutally murdered for hire.

You dummy whose side are you on? Didn't you look at and evaluate any research of

Dr. Clarke's Autopsy Report and testimony? The real issue is who stood to gain from that murder - who really caused that murder to take place." You stupid idiot, you had the answer to that question through Justice Gunderson and Judge Guy on the record, where the hell did you study law, in kindergarten?

Upon the conclusion of my 1989 trial, as I was waiting for the jury to come back into the courtroom with their verdict was pure torture as I can best describe it. My stress level was skyrocketed and heart pounding. I strained my eyes looking at the jury to see if they were smiling or serious or wouldn't look at me. Once I saw their faces, I knew I was a dead man once again.

So, when, on May 20, 1989, when I heard their verdict of guilty on all counts there went my second trial of…untold truth in the land of…no justice… I can't even begin to tell you the mental torture I was about to begin all over again knowing the horrors I was to relive once more. There is no way to explain this to you.

I couldn't believe it, here I was six years of freedom gone and back to hell once again. For six years while out on bail I fought the State of Nevada with every fiber of my body and soul, not knowing during this time, just how far the State went into concealing material exculpatory evidence of innocence from me prior to my 1989 trial.

On June 27, 1989, I was sentenced to life without the possibility of parole, to die in prison. It's a long, agonizing, slow death you have no idea exists within the walls of hell. Justice was not only blind, but apparently unable to conclude that witnesses the caliber of Weakland, were untrustworthy after listening to countless discrepancies to his testimonies!

Was I angry? You bet your ass I was, and I targeted the trial judge who did everything he could to help the State convict me. On sentencing, I adamantly pronounced I was innocent of these crimes. My voice was so loud it was bouncing off the courtroom walls, and the judge moved backward in his chair, possibly thinking I was going to go after him, despite me being in chains! The bailiff, who incidentally wasn't a fan of this tyrant judge, told me later that I scared the shit out of him (the judge) with that outburst. I responded by saying that he deserved it for running a kangaroo court on me.

My thought process however was one day I would like to piss on his grave, but that's another story. Well, here I go again back to the Big House and Super Max living amongst snakes, scorpions, spiders, pigeons, cockroaches and finding "new pets" and freezing my ass off.

The long ride to Super Max chained like an animal was torturous in itself. The site is surrounded by mountains and lies in a valley and the weather is absolutely freezing during wintertime 20 to 30 below zero. When I arrived, I was met by the "Goon Squad… the baddest of the bad" among the correctional guards.

They took pleasure in screaming at us as we got off the bus. You're immediately threatened to obey every command they give you. In the reception building you're told to "put your nose and toes to the wall", and don't move an inch until called by the counselors and warden. Move and you get the end of their night stick.

Without a doubt based upon my legendary courtroom battles and mind fights while locked up like a caged animal, I have undergone various forms of torture doled out by various entities in the State of Nevada and its prison system from April of 1974 to the present time. Federal law defines torture as "the intentional infliction of severe physical or mental pain or suffering". Dr. Vincent Lacopino, an adviser to the non-profit Physicians for Human Rights said that "Torture leaves long term psychological scars, humiliation and isolation leave their mark. The brain clearly can become conditioned by extreme fear and stress and be damaged psychologically for a very long time".

"The brain is never the same as it was before", said neurologist Bruce McEwen, of the Rockefeller University. Stress and trauma can damage memory systems… psychological torture undermines the very ability to think, and it doesn't leave any marks.

On June 27, 1991, while incarcerated at the Ely State Maximum Prison I suffered a severe mental breakdown. This was triggered by my having my trial appeal denied by the Nevada Supreme Court…and learning of the passing of my dog Solomon all in the same week. These two losses were mind boggling, and I went down for the first time in my life.

The correctional guards who watched me and knew my character noticed that something was wrong with me. I became non-responsive in conversation and had a faraway look. It was they who suggested that I needed help and told Dr. Kay Knight (the prime psychologist) "Frank is not the same person anymore, he needs help."

Dr. Knight started to treat me and prescribed Prozac for me and expressed her opinion regarding the severe depression, loss of family, my freedom and animals that I was suffering from and how it affected me. I felt hopeless, unloved, lost and out of control of my situation.

The Prozac did me a lot of good as I noticed that not only did my depression start to diminish, but I became much more, "mentally sharp." This manifested itself by enhancing my ability to perform legal research and do my writings just as proficiently as I had previously been able to do during my stay at Nevada State Maximum Prison in Carson City. I asked Dr. Knight if the Prozac was responsible for my so called "brain enhancement." She said, "Yes…something about the neurons in your brain become more active."

The Prozac had my brain in high gear…but it also altered my personality believe it or not. Among the side effects I was experiencing, was that my language in interactions with other people became aggressive. I was told that I should get off the medication as it definitely was making me act differently than many of the guys had been used to. I told Dr. Knight that I didn't want to take the medication any longer, as I felt it had done its job. I was no longer depressed, and my fight spirit had returned.

Now, during this time frame, one of my appellate attorneys Gary Gowen wrote me a letter expressing his dismay with the Nevada Supreme Court's ruling and said he would like to come to Ely and visit. I wrote him back and asked him if he would bring all the legal files relating to my case. To my surprise, he not only brought me my files, but an electric typewriter as he had received permission from Warden Wolff to do so.

Well, let me tell you, I thoroughly went through these legal files and I couldn't believe my eyes when I saw and read the specific police report. To my amazement, I found the following document that would have had a bombshell effect on my case against the State.

As I previously told you, a police report generated by Detectives O.R. Lyons, Charles "Chuck Lee and Beecher Avants, dated March 13, 1974, indicated that the detectives had interviewed Weakland's family a week earlier on March 6, and they (the detectives) were made aware that Weakland did not murder Hilda Krause! The report said that Lois Weakland (aka Sam), the wife of Lee Weakland (Gerald's brother) overheard Gerry and Lee talking in the kitchen. In that conversation, Lois heard Gerry say to Lee, "she was alive when I left!"

So, in essence, Lois told the cops that her brother-in-law was involved in the Hilda Krause murder…but did not murder her. That's right…I was stunned and immediately became pissed off with all my 1977 and 1989, trial attorneys, wo didn't use this police report on my behalf against the State.

It doesn't take a genius to figure out, when the said detectives who were present when Weakland made his murder confession/statement on March 29, 1974, he knew Weakland was lying about killing Hilda Krause, according to the Detective March 13, 1974, police report.

With this March 13, 1974, police report, my trial attorneys, Harry Reid, Bruce Alverson, LaMond Mills and George Carter, should have blown Weakland and the State right out of the Courtroom. If I was able to easily discover this March 13, report there is no way in hell that all my trial attorneys had missed it.

Despite this powerful evidence of ineffective counsel, would it be enough to get me a new trial, knowing I was subjected to die in prison. I prayed to my Savior Jesus for his help and assistance. And he listened when the right hand of God was dispatched to me. He directed me to uncover a substantial amount of evidence concealed by the State at my 1989 trial.

This evidence came to me that I will now disclose, by inmate Samuel Song, whom I had previously known at the Southern Desert Correctional Center in Indian Springs, Nevada, which later proved to be very reliable that:

- Prior to my 1989 trial, he knew Weakland committed numerous felony crimes at Bally Grand Hotel and Casino in Reno, Nevada, where Weakland maintained a $300.00 casino credit line.

- He was associated with other ex-convicts both prior to and after my May 1989, trial, a parole violation and "known" by Weakland's parole officer.

- Prior to my 1989 trial, Weakland in a fit of rage, brutally assaulted his wife, Doreen Weakland, whose parole officer knew of this felonious assault and was requested "not" to initiate charges against Weakland by law enforcement officials who possessed knowledge of this assault.

- Weakland committed other felony crimes (Forgery) when he took his wife, Doreen Weakland's credit cards and forged their name in order to obtain money to pay for his gambling debts and habits

Okay, so how was I going to prove these allegations Sam Song gave me since I would need an investigator to substantiate this information? Well, let me say, I believe Jesus was not through guiding me in this new-found evidence.

To my utter delight and surprise, I received a letter from one of my best friends and former business partner in California. Wow, what a blessing, Danny LaMere, said he been trying for years to locate me and wanted to know if there was anything, he could do for me.

I wrote Danny, told him of my new founded evidence but needed money to hire an investigator; said I knew one in Las Vegas, named Anthony Pitaro... I can't tell you the feeling that went through my body and mind when Danny wrote me back and told me he hired Anthony Pitaro to investigate my case.

Anthony Pitaro forwarded a letter to me that he had been retained by Danny LaMere to investigate my case and requested all information I had to begin his investigation.

On October 22, 1991, I was informed by correctional officer, Harold Neveau, to call private investigator, Anthony Pitaro who confirmed the following:

- Weakland's credit line at Bally's Grand Hotel in Reno, Nevada, was "suspended" in June 1989, for issuing bad checks with insufficient funds while gambling heavily at the said Hotel.

- Weakland issued five (5) additional bad checks totaling Four Thousand One Hundred and Seventy Dollars (4,170) at Bally's Grand Hotel in Reno, Nevada in 1990.

- Doreen Weakland had her credit cards confiscated by the bank, where her credit had been established, due to her husband's compulsive gambling habits and that Doreen Weakland (in the presence of Sam Song's wife) on several occasions had to borrow money from the ex-convict, Jesse Dearman's wife in order to pay her living expenses.

- Weakland's boss on two or more occasions paid off the bad checks Weakland wrote at Bally's Grand Hotel.

- Weakland wrote numerous bad checks in Lake Tahoe, Nevada, at the Stateline Hotel and Casino, formerly the Sierra Hotel and Casino and four (4) or five (5) bad checks at the Western Village Hotel and Casino, 815 Nichols Blvd., in Sparks, Nevada and Western Village filed a criminal complaint against Gerald Weakland in Justice Court, Sparks, Nevada and investigator Pitaro believed Bally's Grand Hotel had also filed a criminal complaint against Gerald Weakland.

- Weakland had also wrote bad checks prior to my 1989, trial at the Bonanza Hotel and Casino in Reno, Nevada.

- Doreen Weakland's son who eventually ended up in prison at S.D.C.C. in Indian Springs, Nevada, may have been provided with special treatment by law enforcement agencies in return for Doreen Weakland's "silence" in "not" revealing or filing criminal charges on Gerald Weakland for physically and feloniously assaulting her "prior" to my 1989 trial.

- Doreen Weakland waited until after my 1989 trial before she separated from Gerald Weakland.

From the evidence investigator Anthony Pitaro was able to obtain and provide me contained in his sworn affidavit as well as Sam Song's sworn affidavit he provided me, I believed I had a meritorious issue of deliberate and willful suppression of relevant, material and exculpatory evidence concealed from me by the State of Nevada and its agencies at my 1989 trial. In addition to that there was no doubt in my legal experience my trial and appellate attorneys denied me reasonable, effective assistance of counsel, prior to, during trial and on my appeal which I will later explain.

The following is the moral transformation testimony by Gerald Weakland during my 1989 trial:

BY MR. SCHARTZ:

Q: *Now, you testified earlier, Mr. Weakland, that you had been in prison for how many years?*

A: *About 14 years, 10 months, 14, 18 months, something like that.*

Q: *And presently are you married?*

A: *Yes, I am.*

Q: *And do you have any children presently?*

A: *I had four children from my first marriage. The lady I am married to has two children.*

Q: *Are you currently employed?*

A: *Yes, I am.*

Q: *Why are you testifying today?*

A: *You know, I lost my values in life there a few years back. My family*
                       stuck through with me through this whole thing, my children and
                       everything. They have had to contend with the news and school and
                       everybody, every time it comes up. And they have constantly stuck with
                       me. And I owe that to them, and I want to do what's right.

This testimony was untrue. It was false and perjured.

Despite gaining a plethora of material exculpatory evidence concealed from me by the State of Nevada and its agencies, I still needed the mind set I once had to put it all together in order to get the Courts to agree with me.

One day, I was sitting in my single cell, trying to figure out how to initiate my Petition activity. I suddenly felt at peace, no stress, no worries, and I swear on my mother's grave, a cloud came down over my cell, a divine intervention, and I was told how to start my Habeas Petition. I just started typing on my typewriter and I didn't stop…didn't go to chow…just ate what I had from my commissary. I was on a new roll…I had regained my purpose…my new mission had begun.

On March 27, 1992, I filed a proper person Petition for Writ of Habeas Corpus for Post-Conviction Relief in State Court before Judge Thomas Foley, my 1989 trial judge, which to my dismay, I knew would be an exercise in futility due to his extreme bias in my case. Nevertheless, I was going to give him and the State a ton of material exculpatory evidence to their disliking.

On June 3, 1992, I filed a Memorandum of Points and Authorities in support of my Habeas Petition for Post-Conviction and Evidentiary Hearing. I argued inter alia in part: "The State's actions in concealing for 18 years the true nexus of Gerald Weakland and alleged victim Marvin Krause's relationship and secret agreements with both Gerald Weakland and Joseph Costanza, the State would assist them in an past, present or future crimes they committed that amounted to an outrageous, grossly shocking conduct as to violate any sense of justice and must be malum in se or amount to engineering and direction of 'criminal enterprise' from start to finish which had prejudiced me for 18 years.

These arguments were submitted by me in my said Habeas Petition. I argued Investigator Anthony Pitaro's Affidavit, corroborated Attorney Gary Gowen's Affidavit that Gerald Weakland had a secret agreement with State law enforcement officials they would assist him in any future crimes he committed.

The prosecutor (Schwartz) by leading Weakland in regard to his now good character/values not only introduced erroneous testimony but succeeded in preventing the truth from being introduced before me, the trial court and jury.

Weakland was permitted to create for himself a respectable alibi false background paying himself off as a good citizen doing the right thing for society as well as for his family and his own person, where in truth and fact, Weakland's testimony concerning his good character was false, especially since Weakland's crimes for writing bad checks without sufficient funds, assault for beating his wife unmercifully, ex-felon in possession of a firearm, attempt murder on inmate Ron Dean Smith, made Weakland a prime candidate for another life sentence as a habitual criminal if he refused to cooperate and testify against me at my 1989 trial. The State knew Weakland's testimony was false and allowed it to go uncorrected.

The excerpts from my 1989 trial transcripts shows how the State was vouching for Weakland's credibility on false grounds:

MR. SCHWARTZ:

> Clearly, Gerald Weakland's believability is crucial. He is the case. He is the case. He is the State's main witness. He has testified. They have had an opportunity to cross-examine him, call him back today and cross-examine him again if you will. They have had ample opportunity to attack Gerald Weakland's credibility and this jury has witnessed that.

What a lie, what an incredible lie by prosecutor Schwartz before the jury. Weakland's believability was indeed crucial, but I was not provided with a fair opportunity to attack Weakland's credibility nor the trier of fact to evaluate the real credibility of Gerald Weakland, a psychopath who wears the mask of a normal man but possesses the skills of a highly cunning killer and con artist with dynamic personalities who can easily fool his victims and a jury with superficial charm.

The existence of possible criminal charges and parole revocation proceedings was a huge factor for Weakland to testify in a manner that the State wanted and moreover demanded, if Weakland wanted to continue his present life as a free person. Thus, I was denied the opportunity to present vital impeachment evidence which could seriously have affected the jury's assessment of Weakland's credibility.

Without a doubt, Weakland since 1974, had a secret agreement with State law enforcement officials and subsequently Robert Manley of the Nevada Attorney General's Office that as long as Weakland agreed to testify against me in any present or future proceedings Weakland need not worry about murder charges being lodged against him. Since there is no statute of limitations on a murder charge and convictions that have occurred, even without a body, Weakland was subject to and a prime candidate for prosecution on the 1972-1973 murder he had made many admissions to regarding the individual he bragged about burying behind his brother Gordon Weakland's, house in addition to the 1977 murder of Lloyd Paulette, which former Deputy Attorney General, Robert Manly knew Weakland committed.

Robert Manley knew Weakland murdered inmate Lloyd Paulette on January 25, 1977, but refused to prosecute Weakland, even though he had evidence to do so, for the said murder. Attorney Frederick C. Pinkerton, of Reno, Nevada, who represented inmate, James Russo in a criminal case that Weakland was supposed to be a witness in, also possessed information conducted by his investigator, Gary Smith, of Weakland's murdered inmate, Lloyd Paulette on January 25, 1977, prior to my first trial that started on March 1977.

Talk about what a corrupt legal system the State of Nevada is. I had obtained Gerald Weakland's prison movement sheet which revealed it had been "altered" to show Weakland was not housed in Administrative Segregation on January 25, 1977, at the Nevada State Prison in Carson City, Nevada on the day he murdered inmate Lloyd Paulette. However, I successfully obtained an affidavit of an inmate who verified Weakland was called in the said Unit and witnessed Weakland murdering Lloyd Paulette.

Well, here is another one for you to read about. Robert Manley, prison investigative correctional officers and high-ranking prison executives, knew Gerald Weakland was guilty of the attempted murder of inmate, Ronald Dean Smith, that occurred on May 17, 1980, at the said prison. "Weakland was actually found guilty during his disciplinary hearing by Warden Gary True and prison counselors, to which I had obtained a copy of the said hearing. However, the despicable, unlawful and unconscionable actions of these crime fighting law enforcement agencies, especially Robert Manley, falsely and knowingly prosecuted inmate, John Layton #11108 for this heinous crime knowing full well Weakland committed. This special disciplinary committee possessed strong evidence that Weakland was guilty of the brutal attack and use of a deadly weapon (garrote) upon inmate, Ronald Dean Smith, and willfully suppressed their knowledge of this crime in order to get Weakland to testify against me at my September 29, 1982, grand jury hearing, which occurred prior to my indictment.

QUESTIONS

Did Gerald Weakland murder Lloyd Paulette? Indeed, he did. Was a garrote used by Weakland to murder Lloyd Paulette? Yes it was. Did Weakland assault and attempt to murder Ronald Dean Smith with a deadly weapon? Indeed, he did. Was a garrote used by Weakland in his attempt to murder Ronald Dean Smith? Indeed, it was. Did Attorney General Manley and prison executives know Gerald Weakland attempted to murder Ronald Dean Smith? Indeed, they did, they found him GUILTY of such at his special disciplinary hearing.

These so called "White Hats" of justice created a sham, farce and mockery of justice upon the trier of fact and myself, where Weakland knowingly lied. The only agreement they had was to stop writing derogatory letters against him before the Nevada Parole Board.

Turing to another issue I wrote and argued in my June 3, 1992, memorandum of Points and Authorities in my Habeas Petition. On July 23rd, 1991, in a telephone conversation with Counsel, Gary Gowen, I learned he possessed knowledge given to him by informant Joseph Costanza during a telephone conversation which linked Weakland and Marvin Krause together in the January 14, 1974, fake robbery and murder of Hilda Krause.

Counsel Gowen specifically informed me that Costanza said to him: Weakland told me that the person he was going to rob 'is the same person who told Weakland where the person he was going to rob lived; what time he left for work, what days of the week it was appropriate to rob him. That this guy who provided Weakland with this information was an official at Caesar's Palace and "they" had planned this together long before December 1973.'

The impact of this information absolutely stunned and shocked me that for approximately eight (8) years Counsel Gowen never revealed this vital and very critical information to me. Talk about ineffective assistance of counsel. Wow, why did he do this to me?

This also takes us to the real issue, did Costanza, like Weakland, possess a secret agreement with the State and other law enforcement agencies they would assist him in past,

189

present or future crimes he committed, as long as he agreed to keep his bargain in keeping 'silent' about his true knowledge of the real parties involved in the Krause incident? Yes, he did. This type of action is known amongst law enforcement agencies throughout the country as the "Blue Wall Code" i.e., special favors and undisclosed secrets within the circles of law enforcement, you scratch my back and I'll scratch yours.

On March 31, 1991, during my ORAL arguments before the Nevada Supreme Court, Justice Steffen questioned prosecutor Schwartz:

Q: *What was the motivation of Costanza with the police? Just to somehow ingratiate himself in a general way or was he in, do you know of any specific bargain for assistance he got? Obviously, he is on the other side of law enforcement most of the time.*

SCHWARTZ

A: *I don't know of anything he received for cooperating. But I do know he had a checkered record down there. He had been arrested several times for loan sharking and some other crimes, that I'm sure Michele Whitney is the officer he confided in to you help me and I'll help you in the future and if I get into a jam Michele Whitney will remember I helped, he'll help me. When we piece it back together, we were talking about the Krause residence.*

I further wrote in my habeas petition that I was denied reasonable, effective assistance of Counsel prior to, during my trial and oral arguments in violation of my sixth and fourteenth amendments to the United States and Nevada constitutions.

In order to state a claim of ineffective assistance of counsel sufficient to invalidate a judgment of conviction, I had to demonstrate trial counsel's performance fell below an objective standard of reasonableness that counsel's deficiencies were so severe they rendered the jury's verdict unreliable.

I also had to prove prejudice and show there was a reasonable probability, but for Counsel's mistakes the result of the proceedings would have been different and further identify the acts and omissions of counsel's unreasonable performance.

I've handled big major criminal cases when I worked as a Senior Law Clerk at both the Nevada State Prison, Indian Springs, and High Desert and Maximum State Prison Ely State Prison. Besides my own story, I have sad stories, enlightening, intense and very funny and extremely dangerous stories.

THE NINJA WARRIOR AND ME

After I filed my March 27, 1992 Habeas Petition, a new twist in my life was about to occur between a California inmate and myself.

I had no idea that I had become a known entity outside the state! On May 7, 1992, I was appointed by Central District of California Magistrate, Volney V. Brown Jr., to the case of *Interstate Compact Inmate, James Allen Hydrick v. James Gomez, Director, et al*, Case No. CV-92-314-WMB (APPENDIX 2). This one is definitely for the books. Wow! I'm not aware of any federal case where a judge or magistrate appointed a convict to represent a defendant in another state instead of a Federal Public Defender or private attorney.

I was tasked with filing a "Traverse to Respondents Return to Petition for Writ of Habeas Corpus: pursuant to 28 U.S.C. Sec. 2254 by a person in State custody on behalf of Mr. Hydrick. Okay…so that's a lot of legalese…let me break it down. A "traverse" is a common law term and is "a denial by a defendant of a plaintiff's assertions or claims." The system of common-law pleading has been replaced throughout the United States by Code Pleading, and by rules patterned on the system of pleading in Federal Civil Procedure, but lawyers still use the word *traverse* for denial.

A "Writ of Habeas Corpus" is "an order issued by the court of law to a prison warden or law enforcement agency holding and individual in custody, to deliver that prisoner to the court so a judge can decide whether or not that prisoner had been lawfully imprisoned and, if not, whether he or she should be released from custody."

I was told that Hydrick had been transferred to Ely State Prison, Nevada from California because (believe it or not) all the convicts wanted to test him and kill him, to achieve status for themselves! Hydrick claimed to be a "Ninja Warrior" from the "Shadows of Iga Society" in Japan. His martial arts expertise and skills had been featured on the T.V. Show "That's Incredible" hosted by Kathy Lee Crosby and John Davidson back in the '80s.

Encountering this guy for the first time was an experience to say the least! He was considered so highly dangerous that he was actually "sealed" into his cell… that's right…"

sealed." He was literally chained and welded into his cell. I counseled him to write a letter to the warden indicating that such a setting represents a violation of his 8th amendment right against cruel and unusual punishment. If there was ever a fire, he could be burned alive in his cell.

I'll never forget...I was called into the Warden's Office (Warden Wolff) and he was smiling when he told me to sit down. As I do so, he handed me a document stating that I had been court appointed to represent a California inmate transferred here to Ely. This guy could actually levitate off the ground...he did it for me! Holy crap, it was cool. I tried it and fell to the ground in a split second.

Wolff arranges for me to have a conference room to meet with and talk to Mr. Hydrick. So here he comes...handcuffed and belly-chained to the max, with members of the "Goon Squad" escorting him with fear in their eyes! WHAT? That's right...this guy had a presence that exuded danger and power within him. I stand up when he comes into the room. He looks dead into my eyes and says, "Are you Mr. LaPena?" I said, "Yes, I am."

He then says, "Gentlemen, I want to confer with my attorney...in private...under the attorney client privilege! I'm not going to cause any problems here gentlemen!" Then...holy shit... in a split second he had the chains off and he sat down! The "Goon Squad" guys were so startled they absolutely froze. Now mind you, the guards never removed the cuffs and chains. I immediately said, "He just wants his hands free, so he can write things down for me."

Having somewhat eased the tension of the moment, I started to confer with my client about his case. BUT...before we started, he asked me, "How would you like me to address you?" I said to him, "Just Frank will do." He went on to say, "Your reputation for doing legal work is well known in California!" Needless to say, I was both surprised and at the same time quite pleased to hear that sort of commentary.

If memory serves me correctly, he had been accused of sexually assaulting or abusing two of the kids who had attended his school of martial arts. He swore he never touched those kids but nevertheless was convicted. Afterwards, things took a very interesting turn as the prosecutor on that case who had positioned himself as working to "help the kids," was later accused by them of the very same offenses!

Due to my being transported back and forth several times from Ely to the Clark

County Jail and courtrooms, I fell out of touch with Mr. Hydrick. One of the times I that I was transported by bus to Ely State Prison, he was no longer there. I later learned the Federal Magistrate ruled in his favor. Long story short I eventually won his case.

On August 31, 1992, without appointing counsel or conducting an evidentiary hearing, Judge Foley denied my Habeas Petition for Post-Conviction relief. I then appealed his denial to the Nevada Supreme Court. Oh yes! I almost forgot Judge Foley's "brother" was informant Costanza's attorney. You get my drift now about his kangaroo court. These "two brothers" made sure I would never be able to get Costanza as my defense witness. What do you think? Do you agree?

On November 1993, the Nevada Supreme Court, in a unanimous decision, issued an Order of Remand reversing Judge Foley's denial of my Petition for Post-Conviction (APPENDIX 3). I'll skip to the chase and get right to the merits of their Order:

> *When a petition for post-conviction relief raises claims supported by specific factual allegations which, if true, would entitle the petitioner to relief, the petitioner is entitled to an evidentiary hearing unless those claimed are repelled by the record. Hargrove v. State, 100 Nev. 498, 686 P.2d 222 (1984). Having reviewed the record on appeal, we conclude that appellant's petition for post-conviction relief raised claims supported by specific factual allegations which, if true, would entitle appellant to relief. Accordingly, we vacate the order of the district court denying appellant's petition for post-conviction relief, and we remand this matter to the district court with instructions that the district court conduct an evidentiary hearing.*

It is so ORDERED.

Never one to sit back and let the trial court rule on what issues I raised in my Habeas Petition in an evidentiary hearing setting I attacked the State again and raised a huge red flag that caught them off guard, and it was a beauty as I think you will agree as you read this. You already read Weakland's 1989, May 9th and May 19th, trial testimony. On November 29, 1993, while I was still representing myself, I filed a MOTION TO DISMISS my 1982, grand jury indictment, inter alia, on the grounds I was factually innocent for allegedly hiring Gerald Weakland to commit a murder that Gerald Weakland, "did not commit."

The Central Question in the La Pena case is, "**WHO** attempted to and in fact, used a scarf to gag Hilda Krause with? **WHO strangled** Hilda Krause **'before'** Weakland allegedly cut her throat **one** time only? **WHO** used a cord or rope to **strangle** Hilda Krause causing her to suffer a ligature groove mark around **her neck? WHO, reinserted that knife again into the same wound Weakland claimed he originally** caused her; **WHO stabbed** Hilda Krause **'twice'** in the back portion of her neck? **WHO** caused that **violent struggle** to occur in the bedroom where her body was found? **WHO** caused all that blood splattering to occur, and, **WHO** untied the cord from her hands and feet? The major central question her is, **WHO** did **all** those criminal acts upon Hilda Krause? If Weakland didn't as he claims he did not, **WHO DID?** And whoever did, then that person is **the real killer** of Hilda Krause. I have always maintained this was a who dunnit murder case. What do you think? You be the judge.

ON NOVEMBER 24, 1993 THE NEVADA SUPREME GRANTS ME A NEW EVIDENTIARY HEARING

When the Nevada Supreme Court on November 24, 1993, issued its Order or Remand in my favor, I later learned Judge Foley had passed away and a new Judge, The Honorable Gene Porter was assigned my case.

David Schieck was court appointed to represent me. On September 10, 1994, Schieck had the Court transport me back to the Clark County Jail so we could introduce ourselves and start preparing for the Court hearing. At this time Dave asked me if I would give him "one year" to prepare for the evidentiary hearing. He said it would take him that long to read all the transcripts and investigate my case thoroughly.

This was very hard for me to do. I would have to literally give up a whole year of my life so he could properly prepare to represent me. I said "ok", but I felt every second of it. I had researched David Schieck's legal history and was pleased to find out he had been very successful in overturning convicted criminal cases. He had a successful history before the Nevada Supreme Court. It appeared to me I finally had an outstanding criminal defense attorney.

Now, I also had a long history of being able to let the Court allow me to be co-counsel in my case. That allowed me to file petitions and motions via my appointed counsel granting me permission. I knew my case better than the new attorneys did. Every time I did that it drove Harmon nuts because defense attorney was cautious about attacking Harmon about his unethical tactics, except Oscar Goodman, Gary Gowen, and me. I pulled no punches going after that unethical p***k. I believe I was the first one to call Harmon a liar to my face which I did before Judge Porter.

Like Oscar Goodman, I was relentless, never quitting, and unafraid in attacking the State of Nevada, and, like a warrior soldier, I attacked, and attacked and kept on attacking the corrupt enemy the State, and on July 26, 1995, I filed before Judge Gene Porter, a Motion For Specific Discovery of Brady Materials Not Previously Disclosed By The State, i.e., the identity of the 2nd assailant at the January 14, 1974, Krause crime who physically strangled, stabbed, used a scarf and cord that caused the victim to suffer a ligature groove mark completely around her neck and who engaged in a violent struggle with the victim, none of which Weakland claimed he committed on Hilda Krause. A.G.A. Exh. "N-1", pgs. 194-278.

On August 8, 1995, the Honorable Gene Porter granted my Motion for Specific Discovery of Brady materials Not Previously Disclosed, and, thus, the Court made a "factual determination" that a second assailant existed in the murder of Hilda Krause. A.G.A. Exh. "P" pages 2-3-4. When I found out Judge Porter granted my specific motion, "I thought this was the beginning of the end" for the false charges against me. Yeah! Right! Forgetaboutit! (see Criminal Court Minutes, APPENDIX 4).

I MAKE HARMON ADMIT BY HIS OWN WORDS THAT
HE KNOWLINGLY FRAMED ME

I believe the normal court time to conduct an evidentiary hearing is anywhere from a few hours to a whole day. Mine lasted for five days: October 16th through October 20, 1995. This time both Rosalie ad I testified, and Judge Porter concluded that my testimony was "credible." Dave Schieck, I believe, started with my 1989 trial attorneys and did a very good job proving they were ineffective during my 1989 jury trial, but let's get to the main issue of Weakland's 1989, trial testimony and October 17, 1995, evidentiary hearing testimony, where Schieck goes a little deeper into Weakland's claim on how he claimed he murdered Hilda Krause much better than Lamond Mills did. Pay close attention because I'm going to stop at one point and let you solve this homicide coverup by Harmon. Caren Benjamin did a newspaper article on me entitled, 'MURDER WAS THE CASE." (APPENDIX 5). I'm going to just submit a small piece of it for you to get the gist of what I've been writing in my book.

LaPena's case was handed to defense attorney David Schieck who, despite having represented a number of Nevada's more notorious murderers, found the file a little daunting. "It's like representing a piece of legal history," he said, "The further I got into the case, the more I realized that it's even more than that. Frank's case is really part of the history of Las Vegas."

I was in high school in 1974. When I look back at the names and people involved on both sides of the case, I was in awe for a period of time." As Schieck read through testimony and documents, awe transformed into something closer to disgust. He believes police and prosecutors were at best not telling his client's former attorneys all they knew about the case and at worst hiding evidence. He also found new witnesses who claim they have knowledge that could have acquitted LaPena years ago. In the evidentiary hearing…Schieck presented one of them.

The man, Teodoro Martinez, worked as a busboy in the late 1960's at the El Cortez, where Weakland was a waiter. Martinez testified that the Krauses had been regular customers of the once posh gourmet room and had asked for Weakland, their favorite, by name. Martinez's story, Schieck maintains, creates a crucial link between the Krauses and Weakland, who swore he never talked to Marvin Krause until the day of the murder.

I'm only going to submit Gerald Weakland's 1995, testimony as it strictly related on how he claimed he murdered Hilda Krause. On October 17, 1995, Gerald Weakland took the stand and testified under direct questioning by Counsel David Schieck as follows:

GERALD WEAKLAND

Having been called as a witness by the Defendant, being first duly sworn, testified as follows:

DIRECT EXAMINATION

By Mr. Schieck:

Q: Could you please state your name and spell your last name for the record?

A: Gerald Weakland W-e-a-k-l-a-n-d

Q: And Mr. Weakland, you currently reside in the Reno area?

A: Yes, I do.

Q: And what's your current custody status?

A: I'm on parole.

Q: And how long have you been on parole?

A: Since 1988.

Q: Do you recall what month in 1988?

A: August.

...

Q: Now, again I'm going to ask you some questions concerning January 1974, and what occurred and what your testimony was concerning that, okay. And I'm not—if you need refer to your testimony let me know and we'll show it to you.

A: Okay.

Q: Now, we've already established that you have your statement on March 9, 1974, during your preliminary hearing, you gave a statement at that time.

A: Okay.

Q: Do you recall during that statement admitting that you had sliced the throat of Hilda Krause once?

A: Yes.

Q: Okay. And, again, when you testified in 1979, excuse me 1989 at Mr. LaPena's trial, you indicated that you had only sliced her throat once, is that correct?

A: I believe, yes.

Q: Is there any reason that you need to change that recollection and that testimony?

A: **No.**

Q: Okay, so, your testimony is clear in your mind, as the events are, that

197

you only sliced her throat once?

A: *Yes.*

Q: *Okay. And you did not stab her into the throat or neck area, is that correct?*

A: *No.*

Q: *No, it's not correct or no, you didn't.*

A: *I mean, no, it's correct. I slit the lady's throat. I did not stab her in the throat. No.*

Q: *Now, when you went over to the Krause residence you took a satchel that contained various items, is that true?*

A: *Yes.*

Q: *Okay. Including stocking masks and gloves and things of that nature?*

A: *Yes.*

Q: *Okay. Did you take a scarf?*

A: *No.*

Q: *At any point did you gag Hilda Krause with a scarf?*

A: *Gauze, I think but not—no.*

Q: *Gauze but not a scarf?*

A: *I think, yes, but no, scarf, no.*

Q: *And just so we're clear what are you talking about when you say gauze?*

A: *I may have had some gauze. In fact, I don't even remember to tell you the truth.*

Q: *If I were to tell you that your statement in 1974 said you had gauze, would you have any reason to contest that that was true?*

A: *No. I'd have to see it. But I think I had some gauze with me, I'm not sure.*

Q: Just so I'm clear when you say gauze you mean like cotton gauze.

A: Yes.

Q: Okay. Clearly not a ladies' scarf?

A: No.

Q: Okay. Did you at any point put a ladies' scarf around Hilda Krause's mouth?

A: No.

Q: Now, there were a number of law enforcement individuals present when you gave your statement including Chuck Lee and Beecher Avants, is that true?

A: Yes.

Q: Along with Mel Harmon, your attorneys—

A: Right.

Q: At any point did anyone advise you that Hilda Krause, was found with this scarf around her neck?

A: Not that I recall, no.

Q: But you recall that it wasn't you that placed the scarf around her neck?

A: No.

Q: And Tommy Boutwell was with you?

A: Yes.

Q: To your knowledge, did he?

A: No.

Q: Do you have any explanation as to how a scarf got around her neck?

A: I never knew of a scarf, so I don't know anything about it.

Q: In connection with either preparation for your preliminary hearing or for any of the statements or testimony you've given have you ever seen *the autopsy report prepared by Dr. Clarke?*

A: *No. I have never.*

Q: *Has anyone involved with this case, and again I'm talking about the same people that we've established, has anyone ever discussed that autopsy report with you?*

A: *No.*

Q: *Okay. Now, that autopsy report which we've admitted into evidence here indicates—let me go back. Included in what you took in the satchel was some cord, is that correct?*

A: *Yes.*

Q: *Okay. Electrical type cord?*

A: *Yes. I believe it was telephone wire cord if I'm not mistaken.*

Q: *And you've testified and gave a statement indicating that you used that cord to tie up Hilda Krause?*

A: *Yes, I believe we did.*

Q: *Tie her hands and her feet?*

A: *Yes.*

Q: *At any point did you use that cord to strangle Hilda Krause?*

A: *I may have I don't recall.*

Q: *And if I were to represent to you that in previous testimony you indicated that you had not.*

A: *I don't—like I say, I think I hit Miss Krause behind the head. I don't you know, I don't think I used it, no.*

Q: *If I were to indicate to you that the autopsy report that's admitted into evidence that there was a ligature mark, around her neck above where she had been – her throat had been-cut, did anyone **ask** you about that when you gave your statement?*

A: No. They didn't.

Q: Did anyone ask you if you had strangled Hilda Krause?

A: I don't believe so. I, you know, I tied her hands and feed, I'm not sure
        if I tied it around her neck or whatever. I don't remember.

Q: But you remember the "scarf"?

A: I don't remember the scarf. I've—did not have the scarf.

Q: Is this the first time anyone has asked you questions concerning whether
        or not you'd attempted to strangle Hilda Krause?

A: I don't recall any questions concerning whether I tried to strangle her.
        I may have. Some may have asked me before, but I don't remember
        it.

Q: Do you recall testifying in May of 1989 when asked the question: Did
        you ever try to strangle her? Your answer was: I don't believe so.

A: That's what I'd say to you now, I honestly don't believe I did.

Q: And, again, no one involved in this case asked you to explain the
        ligature markings around her neck when you gave your statement?

A: No.

Q: Now, your statement and your testimony indicate that you slit her
        throat once and then stabbed her in the back; is that correct?

A: Yes.

…

Q: Now, if I were to tell you that the autopsy report of Dr. Clarke that's
        been admitted into evidence indicates that at least one and perhaps more
        deep stab wounds were inflicted into the right side of the neck of Hilda
        Krause with a great deal of force would that surprise you?

MR. HARMON: Through the original cutting wound?

MR. SCHICK: Yes. Through the original cutting wound.

THE WITNESS: *I believe I shoved the knife this way (indicating)and then pulled it back. I—you know, as far as I believe it was one cut.*

Q: *Just one cut across the neck?*

A: *Right.*

Q: *After you made that slice did you reinsert the knife again?*

A: *No.*

Q: *When you gave your statement…March 1974, did anyone ask you, involved in this case, concerning the fact that there was a deep stab wound to the right side of the neck that went through the wound, the cutting wound?*

A: *No.*

Q: *No one told you that the statement that you were giving was inconsistent with Dr. Clarke's report?*

A: *No. They did not.*

Q: *And up until today has anyone asked you that question?*

A: *I don't believe I ever ben asked, no.*

Q: *Up until I just asked you these questions had anyone told you that information?*

A: *No.*

Q: *And again, Dr. Clarke's autopsy report describes the stabbing wound that I've talked to you about. There were one or more stab wounds extending very deeply into the neck. These stab wounds extend down to the lateral processes of the cervical vertebrae with a fracture of one of the lateral processes. There is a compete severance of the vertebral artery on the right. No one ever ask you about that wound that was inflicted on Hilda Krause?*

A: *No. I just told them how I did it and that was it.*

What is your opinion as you just read Weakland's October 17, 1995 testimony?

202

Alright, let's rehash Gerald Weakland's October 17, 1995 testimony before the Honorable Gene Porter.

On October 17, 1995, during Weakland's last given testimony, before the Honorable Gene Porter, Weakland testified: 1) That he sliced Hilda Krause's throat one time only and did not need to change that recollection and testimony given by him in 1989, at my trial; 2) That he did **not stab** her in the throat or neck area, E.H.T. at P.245; and 3) Again testified he did not stab her in the throat, E.H.T. at P. 247.

Weakland further testified: 4) He did not take a **scarf** with him nor did he gag Mrs. Krause with a scarf, E.H.T. at P 247; 5) That he did not put a ladies scarf around Hilda Krause's mouth, E.H.T. at p. 248; 6) That no one ever advised him that Hilda Krause was **found** with this scarf around her neck, and, that it wasn't him that placed the scarf around her neck, E.H.T. at P. 248; 7) That he never knew of a scarf and didn't know anything about it, E.H.T. at P. 249; 8) That he doesn't remember the scarf and did not have the scarf, E..T. at P. 251.

Weakland also testified: 9) He tied up Hilda Krause's hands and feet with a cord and said, **"No"** when asked by Counsel Schieck if he used that cord to **strangle** Hilda Krause, E.H.T. at P. 250; and, 10) That he had not been asked by anyone if he had strangled Hilda Krause, E.H.T. at P. 251; 11) In his statement and testimony that he slit her throat once and then stabbed her in the back and that was the extent of the cutting that he did with the knife and, demonstrated how he cut her throat with the knife from **"left to right,"** E.H.T., P. 251 and 252; 12) That after he sliced her throat **"He did not reinsert the knife again,"** E.H.T.at P. 253; 13) That he didn't scatter any blood and detectives at no time talked to him about blood they found splattered about the bedroom E.H.T. AT p. 257; 14) That she was **still** tied up when he left the knife in her back and didn't check to see if she was still alive, E.H.T. at P. 258.

Okay, now that you have formed your own opinion of what you just read, the next thing I want you to review with me and I hope you picked up on it; is the way Weakland used certain words when he responded to Counsel David Schieck's questions when Weakland said, "I just told them I did it and that was it." What was your take to these certain words Weakland used, like: "I believe"; "I don't recall"; "I don't remember"; "I don't think"; "I don't believe so"; "I'm not sure"?

My spin on his testimony and use of certain words indicated Weakland was just making it up as he went along regarding how he killed Hilda Krause. Nothing Weakland said, as you just read, was backed up by the physical evidence. There is only one rational way to explain his testimony and confession to the police and prosecutors: "Weakland did not possess first hand guilty knowledge of how Hilda Krause died" WHY? Because he did not kill her; someone else did. Without a doubt, the State's charges against me were false, fabricated and manufactured. That's the truth, the whole truth and nothing but the truth.

You recall what I said before to pay attention so you can solve this homicide cover-up by Harmon to its conclusion. Unfortunately, Counsel Schieck, did not pick-up what Weakland just showed when he demonstrated how he claimed he sliced Hilda Krause's throat from "left to right." Had Schieck noticed what I noticed when I read the Autopsy Examination Report years later, I believe Schieck would have moved the Judge Porter, to pressure Harmon to dismiss all charges against me.

I could not believe what happened later, after my 1995 evidentiary hearing concluded, we were all ordered to file briefs challenging each other as to the merits of the evidence produced at my hearing…Talk about a shocker. It was the devil himself Mel Harmon in one of his responding briefs who admitted to the fact, a Second Assailant Existed, was present and participated physically in murdering Hilda Krause.

STATE ADMITS TO A DIFFERENT KILLER KEPT SILENT BY MEL HARMON FOR 22 YEARS

In their own words, The State of Nevada admitted to the fact, "a second assailant" actually existed and participated in the murder of Hilda Krause, when prosecutor Mel Harmon himself wrote in his Opposition to Petition for Post-Conviction Relief, at p. 18 dated July 24, 1996 (APPENDIX 6). Mel Harmon admitted the State had possession of information regarding the existence of a Second Assailant, meaning the State knew the "identity" of a "different killer" who murdered Hilda Krause and has kept that person's identity "secret' for, at the time, "22 years" and present time "over 40 years" and never charged him for the Hilda Krause murder. Adding injury to insult and lying, the State said, "All information in possession of the State regarding this 'second assailant' was disclosed." I don't know who's a bigger liar – Harmon or Weakland.

- So, who hired the Second Assailant to murder or possibly assist Weakland in the murder of Hilda Krause?

- What motive, reason or purpose would this person have to "gain by killing Hilda Krause?

- How could Gerald Weakland have not known Hilda Krause was "strangled" before he allegedly cut her throat or not see the perpetrator (Second Assailant) not strangle her?

- Why didn't experienced homicide detective Avants and Lee after reviewing the autopsy report, Weakland's March 29, 1974, murder confession, initiate a police report/notes?

- There was a Second Assailant at the crime scene. Were they a part of a conspiracy to cover up the tracks of the real killer of Hilda Krause? What do you think?

- How did the Second Assailant escape from the crime scene?

- How did Mel Harmon come into possession of information to acknowledge the existence and viability of the Second Assailant?

- Why did Mel Harmon, who knew the identity of the Second Assailant, fail to have Avants or Lee arrest and charge the Second Assailant for the murder of Hilda Krause?

- Was this Second Assailant so dangerous that Harmon was afraid of him that he may have threatened Harmon's family?

On August 16, 1996, in a Minute Order, Judge Porter found that I received ineffective assistance of counsel at my 1989 trial and granted my Petition for Post-Conviction Relief and my conviction and sentence were vacated (APPENDIX 7). On October 10, 1996, Judge Porter entered his Findings of Fact, Conclusions of Law and Order granting me a new trial.

At this time, I would like to go back a little bit right now and talk some more about Rosalie, as it personally affected me a great deal. The last time I saw Rosalie alive was on October 20, 1995, when she testified at my evidentiary hearing when Judge Porter requested her presence in the courtroom to give testimony. But first I would like to say this.

On February 25, 1997, while housed at Indian Springs prison, I just felt that morning that I needed to talk to her and couldn't get this feeling out of my mind and I knew I had to get to her. Rosalie, at this time, had been placed in a hospice facility and, about two weeks prior to this day, we had talked on the phone. It had sent chills through my body when she told me she had about two more weeks before she would pass. She said, "Please don't worry yourself sick, stay strong, and I will be alright." I can't tell you what went through my emotional state of mind when she told me that.

I had been trying to get enough money and collateral put together to make a hundred-thousand-dollar bail and was feeling a lot of pressure that I may not be able to before she died. I wanted to say goodbye to her in person. Nurse Ruth was Rosalie's hospice nurse and when I would call, Ruth would pick up the phone and hand the phone over to her. On February 25, 1997, when I called Rosalie, Nurse Ruth answered and I asked her, "Is Rosalie awake?" Ruth, in a soft voice said, "I'm sorry, Rosalie just passed away." I only remember at that moment that I slowly hung up the phone and went some place to be alone. From that point on, I very seldom held a conversation with anyone. I don't know but once in a while I kind of thought about that morning as I was having this strong feeling that I must talk to her. Rosalie was somehow at that time sending me a message of good-bye. On June 6, 1997, I made bail.

Back to Rosalie's testimony, one more thing before I forget. When Rosalie decided she did not want to do any more chemo treatments she began to get worse and wanted to do something for me. She wanted to leave her house and care for me and put it in my name, but when she did her last chemo, her alleged girlfriend, Linda, took Rosalie to a shyster lawyer named Bucky, who I know, and Linda got Rosalie to sign over all of her property to Linda. Rosalie, according to Lynn Brady, was so out of it she did not know what she had done. Anyway, Linda dies shortly after Rosalie from a heart attack. However, when Rosalie found out that Judge Porter ruled in my favor, she was thrilled for me.

One week after I made bail, I went to work for Attorney Carmine Colucci again and was happy to see Zoe who ran the law office. Free once more with a good job and being with special friends in my life. Trying to adjust to a new world and life all over was not easy. I had lost so many years; I could never get back and the free world was kind of scary not knowing what the free world was like anymore. I was fortunate to have friends and family help me to put my life back together. In prison, you live in the dark ages and life passes you by. I called it "The Walking Dead." You have no real life any longer. Getting back to Zoe. God bless her. She had met and married a great guy named Bart. Like before, Zoe helped me around the law office, and like me, Zoe was an animal lover. Bless her heart.

I was anxious to see my special friend Freddy Leipsizer who had put up $4,000.00 cash along with a family member who put up the rest of the money to get me out. I pretty much stayed home most of the time after work. Tommy was always inviting me over for dinner and could he ever cook. There was Annie, Tommy's boss, their son, Stephen and mom Flo. What a great family. Tommy would drive me around if I needed to go somewhere. While I was out, Tommy told me Lynn Brady was elated that I was free and anxious to see me. Lynn Brady, like Rosalie, was a cocktail waitress at Caesars Palace and had a striking resemblance to actress Janet Leigh.

It was big hugs and smiles and relaxation. During our conversation, Lynn told me something she believed I didn't know about my case and it was a blockbuster.

I knew Lynn had been subpoenaed by the State at my 1974 Preliminary Hearing, but I did not know why. Harmon told Magistrate Brown the real reason he decided he was not going to use her as a witness. Lynn told me when she was sitting down in the hallway, she recognized a man who had attacked her in November 1973, put a gun to her head, tied her up and threatened her life and robbed her. This low-life criminal was none other folks then Robert (Bobby) Webb, Weakland's accomplice in the Hilda Krause murder. And she screamed when she saw Webb. Harmon was immediately in a panic and told Lynn to calm down. He had Detective Ray Lyons interview her and have her make a taped statement. She also had a great deal of information that she personally knew that Marvin Krause had hired Webb to commit the crime against her and it was Marvin Krause who actually hired Weakland to do a "fake" robbery at his residence to steal his wife's jewelry and furs.

Can you, my reader, just imagine what Oscar Goodman would have done to Webb and Mel Harmon with evidence that Marvin Krause hired Bobby Webb to commit a robbery with the use of a deadly weapon on Lynn Brady and that Marvin Krause tried to get Lynn Brady to find someone he could hire to do a "fake" robbery as his residence to steal his wife's furs and jewelry. Oscar would have torn them apart. I don't believe our preliminary hearing would have reached its conclusion like it did.

At this time, I had no reason to use it unless the Nevada Supreme Court upheld Judge Porter's favorable ruling for me. Appeal briefs had been filed and I was awaiting the Appellate Court's decision.

Although things were going okay for me, I was still missing something. I needed comfort and companionship to keep me grounded and stop my loneliness – a forever pet. Problem was I didn't want to go through losing a best friend anyone. It's too heartbreaking if you know what I mean. Despite my feeling confident that I would prevail at the Nevada Supreme Court level on my request for a new trial, I didn't want to chance going through that all over again for both the animal and me. I made a hard decision to wait and if all goes well, I was going to rescue a furry angel to be my companion. Without a doubt, they are the perfect companion during the good and bad times.

I worked for Carmine Colucci for about a year then decided I wanted to do something else. A friend of mine, Jim, was a manager at a night club and asked me if I would like to work at his club. I said sure and he hired me as a bouncer. Jim felt with my life experiences that I had the ability to calm down the possibility of any physical confrontations. Jim also had other bouncers working there who appeared intimidating but lacked my everyday experience dealing with people. I neither tried nor did date any of the women there. But I did flirt with them in a friendly way. Can you blame a guy? I'm not sure how long I was at that club, when a guest and I had started talking about gold. He asked me if I would be interested in learning "aqua mineralogy." It's abstracting gold from water. A special type of water machine had the ability to suck up the ground dirt with a water hose and send it through the machine. The gold would attach itself to the metal plates and when the water came out the other end, it was purified.

I was only there about two weeks when I got a call from Sandy Shaw. She asked me, "Are you sitting down or standing up?" "Why," I asked. She told me that the Nevada Supreme Court had just ruled against me. My issues were solid backed by supporting evidence. I was in Arizona at the time at the facility to learn the aqua mineralogy. I called David Schieck and told him where I was. I believe that he said that prosecutor Schwartz wanted to issue an all points directive to "catch me"-piece of shit lying prosecutor. I told David that I would turn myself in the next day as soon as I get back to Vegas. I was an hour away from Mexico and could have easily entered the Mexican border and disappeared. But I didn't. The next day I turned myself in at the Clark County Detention Center, told the officer I was Frank LaPena turning myself in. Are you ready for this? The Metro officer said, "We don't have any record of you, no warrants, nothing to hold you in here, come back tomorrow, maybe your name will be placed in our file." So, I left and went over to a friend's place to sleep there and the next day went back to the jail. Well, I didn't really sleep, my stress level skyrocketed. Still, I couldn't believe it. Back to the Big House to die another day. My third trip back to prison and third death sentence of a Walking Dead Man. Yep, December 7, 1998, my Pearl Harbor day.

My head was still spinning when I was sent to Indian Springs Correctional Center. I felt like I had lived in a time-warp zone, one moment in a city surrounded by people, the next moment in prison going back and forth. This can't be real, but it was. There are no words contained in the dictionary that can define what it mentally feels like to be free, then imprisoned, free, then imprisoned, then free then imprisoned. What I experienced was pure mental torture.

Once I cleared my head and slowly read the Nevada Supreme Court's 1989, split decision reinstating my conviction and sentence, I was furious. I couldn't believe my eyes reading the ridiculous language the Court used to deny me a new trial.

In the meantime, David Schieck filed a Petition for Rehearing before the Nevada Supreme Court that they misapprehended and disregarded numerous facts upon which District Court Judge Gene Porter based his decision when he ordered a new trial and found that my 1989 trial attorneys were ineffective and that I had demonstrated at the evidentiary hearing that I was actually and factually innocent of the crimes for which I was convicted. From the language they used to deny me a new trial, I just knew they would deny my Petition for Rehearing. And they did. On October 8, 1999, the Nevada Supreme Court issued an Order Denying Rehearing.

In the real world, a Judge or Appellate Court can use any type of language they want in their rulings. They can overturn your conviction or deny it, they have that power over your life.

The legal system portrays an image of fairness, that it can do no wrong. That is the biggest farce upon the American people as a whole. Cops can frame anyone they choose. Cops plant evidence, fabricate evidence, commit perjury under oath. Some prosecutors withhold, conceal and suppress evidence that puts their cases in reasonable doubt and use perjured testimony or any means whatsoever to convict a person and some judges and justices demonstrate a depraved indifference to human life by ignoring evidence of innocence.

Don't get me wrong on how I feel about cops. We have great cops who hold their badges in honor. I have many family members who are heroes as well as friends. I just hate the bad ones who slipped through the cracks during their training and afterwards. I even risked my own life to save a metro officer.

Getting back to Keystone Cop, Beecher Avants, who testified that I admitted to his lying buddy Chuck Lee that I was pimping about 25 or more girls at the Hacienda and then 10 or more which I ran as steady girls and that I smoked marijuana incessantly. Remember going back to my childhood in New Jersey, I never forgot what wise guy Babe drilled into me about, "Never tell anyone what you have done or intended to do, if you keep your mouth shut, no one will ever know you existed, and never let anyone know what you are thinking." Both Avants and Lee were liars as I never said anything to them about pimping girls at the Hacienda, or about smoking marijuana period. These two lying pieces of shit were professional liars inflaming the jury against me. They were putting words in my mouth that I was also nervous at the times during their interrogation of me, which never happened. Then that cockroach Harmon would put my credibility against Avants and Lee before the jurors knowing the jury would believe the police officers over my testimony. It's a trick that I later learned that a prosecutor uses at trial proceedings if the defendant takes the stand. By the way folks, when Detective Chuck Lee retired, he bought Sherri's Ranch Brothel in Pahrump, Nevada. Lee and his partners poured millions into modernizing the Bordello industry and became a "legalized pimp"; bought 300 acres of land in Nye County and co-founded Courtesy Automotive dealership. Wonder where an honest cop gets millions of dollars? Hmm! I wonder. I wonder if Avants and his cockroach were his best customers with discounts?

It was so difficult for me to believe I was back in prison. The loss of my freedom and reincarceration had taken its toll on me causing me emotional stress, extreme anxiety, shock and trauma returning back to hell. I started to suffer severe headaches, nose bleeds, high blood pressure and severe depression, but the power that God instilled in me would not let me give up.

Listen, you can knock me down, and think you won… forgetaboutit! I will bounce right back up and continue to fight, never quit, never surrender. I will fight till the end. And boy! You have no idea how many times I was knocked down by the State and got right back up to fight another day. Like my mom told the doctor when she said, "your son will never walk again." "You don't know my son, he will walk again, he's a fighter, never quits, never gives up."

When you're dancing with the devils unfortunately you are in the hot seat. You will see for yourself when you read the opinion written by Justice Bob Rose in State v. LaPena, 114 Neev.1159, 968 P.2d 750 (1998) where Rose and the majority in a split-decision, wrote around my specific detailed facts showing innocence and acted as a "13th juror" in denying me a new trial. His written opinion, His written denial is "Reprehensible", "Appalling", "Disgraceful", "Deplorable", and, also, "Judicial Criminal".

Justice Rose and his majority actually invented testimony that did not exist in the record in their 1998 opinion. It's fraught with misleading statements, testimony and facts. They set aside their law as they wish and rule over and around my meritorious facts that were specifically detailed and presented to them by me and David Schieck.

The Nevada Supreme Court's decision in State v. LaPena, supra, (1998) is one of the worst, if not the worst and corrupt judicial decisions ever made by the majority as that Court actually turned a blind eye by overlooking and misapplying unrefuted factual evidence clearly supported in the record showing actual innocence. You will see for yourselves that decision written by Justice Rose is a sham. State v. LaPena, supra, is a political, corrupt, inept, incompetent and cowardly decision. I don't know that real reason he wrote such a ludicrous decision, but it was rumored Rose was possibility facing criminal charge with the Clark County District Attorney's Office, who prosecuted me. Was he pressured by the D.A. Office, not to rule in my favor? I don't know, dirty politics maybe, but what I do know, his ruling against me was preposterous.

Now, you have along with me, Weakland's testimony enough times for you to form your own opinion and what your opinion is as to Justice Rose's ruling. At times, I will write this like I'm speaking to Justice Rose and the majority who sided with him.

This is part of the Nevada Supreme Court's written opinion by Justice Rose in State v. LaPena, supra:

> *An autopsy revealed that Mrs. Krause had been strangled with a rope or cord "prior" to having her throat slit, Id. At 751.*
>
> *That she had sustained several stab wounds to her neck, 'after' her throat had been slit, Id. At 751.*
>
> *Weakland maintained he 'had not' strangled or stabbed her in the neck, Id. At 759.*
>
> *(Although) the autopsy showed multiple stab wounds in Mrs. Krause's neck and strangulation as the cause of death, Id. At 759.*
>
> *Weakland maintains that he never stabbed or strangled her, Id. At 759.*

On December 3, 1993, LaPena filed a motion to dismiss the indictment based upon an alleged lack of evidence and a 'colorable claim of factual innocence'. LaPena's Motion to Dismiss was subsequently consolidated with the PCR Petition, 'and LaPena presented evidence in support of dismissal at the evidentiary hearing', Id at 754

From the language of Justice Rose's written decision, would you the reader, agree that Justice Rose and his majority "acknowledged Weakland did not either strangle or stab Hilda Krause in her neck area as being "true"? The record cited above is crystal clear the Nevada Supreme Court "made no adverse finding" regarding Weakland's testimony he never strangled nor stabbed Hilda Krause in her neck. Id. 750, at 752-759.

What I'm mainly going to do right now is for your benefit to review different areas of arguments and evidence I submitted in many issues before the Court and how easily Justice Rose disregarded my evidence and wrote around it, to what I believe he and his majority wanted to A their buddies in the District Attorney's Office to deny me justice… Aww! Come on Rose, you can't really be that stupid to not see overwhelming evidence of innocence I provided your Court. Ok, now I'm going to expose you to my readers as my evidence I presented to you couldn't be any clearer that justice was not properly served as Weakland's testimony on how he claimed he murdered Hilda Krause is a crock of shit. **It didn't happen, and you know damn well it didn't.** Here we go:

LaPena continues to assert his factual innocence and sets forth the following reasons why the testimony of convicted murderer and perjurer Weakland should not have been believed and why the indictment should have been dismissed.

*It is LaPena's assertion that Dr. Clarke trial testimony corroborates LaPena's theory of defense that Weakland did not kill Hilda Krause due to the complete differences between Weakland's account of **how** the homicide occurred and what Dr. Clarke's autopsy showed. If Dr. Clarke is to be believed, then Weakland is not the murderer and LaPena 'cannot' be convicted as a co-conspirator and accomplice.*

This Court's own recitation of specific historical facts as to the actual cause of Hilda Krause's death and Weakland's denial of that cause is indisputable and compelling evidence that the State failed to prove beyond a reasonable doubt every element of the crimes with which LaPena was charged in a violation of his Fifth and Fourteenth Amendment rights guaranteed to him by the United States Constitution.

By the facts stated by Weakland in his own testimony, he could not be the actual killer of Hilda   Krause and LaPena is therefore innocent of this crime and wrongfully and unjustly convicted. The evidence is clear that Hilda Krause was actually murdered by someone other than Weakland and also means these two specific indisputable facts exonerates LaPena as the alleged contract killer

Dr. Clarke's findings and conclusion that Mrs. Krause was strangled with a rope or cord prior to her throat being cut 'has been recognized and accepted' as 'true' by both the State and this Court in its written opinion in State v. LaPena, *968 P.2d 750 (1989).*

Thus, the State cannot impeach Dr. Clarke's credible testimony (Harmon stipulated to his expertise) without calling Weakland's lies believable. Dr. Clarke's medial findings presented by Mel Hamon to prove that Hilda Krause was strangled before her throat was cut prove that Weakland's third confession implicating LaPena was not worthy of belief.

Furthermore, this Court's recitation of facts in terms of LaPena's Motion to Dismiss that and LaPena presented evidence in support of dismissal at the evidentiary hearing again shows this Court 'should not have reinstated his conviction and sentence, where they actually determined LaPena presented evidence that warranted dismissal at his evidentiary hearing. State v. LaPena (1998) at 1165.

Do you agree the State itself is telling the Nevada Supreme Court that they acknowledged and accepted themselves, what I just cited herein? In plain language the State framed me, and Rose's Court helped them also.

Here is what Justice Rose said to all that I argued above:

LaPena theorizes that Mr. Krause killed Hilda Krause after Weakland left the Krause residence on the morning of January 14, 1974. LaPena relies on the fact that Weakland has consistently stated he killed Mrs. Krause by slitting her throat, 'although the autopsy report showed multiple stab wounds in Mrs. Krause neck and strangulation as the cause of death. "Weakland maintains that he never stabbed her or strangled her. Weakland did not check to see if Mrs. Krause was alive when he left. LaPena asserts that all of this exculpatory information (No it was facts Rose) combined with Martinez's testimony at the evidentiary hearing demonstrates his factual innocence and his trial counsel's failure to

213

properly investigate the case. We disagree.

Disagree to what? Have you lost your senses; this evidence speaks for itself. You yourself acknowledged and accepted Weakland's testimony to be true that he didn't strangle Hilda Krause nor stab her in her neck area. Since Weakland didn't do that, common sense will tell you someone else did. Were you reading my appellate briefs with your eyes closed or were you deaf during our oral arguments before you or were you experiencing memory problems?

I don't understand you; at times you have given me justice and then turned it around like your prior rulings never existed. Are you nuts or an idiot with a brain? You are supposed to be an intelligent man with common sense and not a judge beyond to just have a pulse.

By oh Boy! Wait till you read how Rose and his majority ended this innocent issue and how I'm going to ream him for doing so:

> *Mills testified that efforts were made to uncover a connection between Weakland and Mr. Krause, even if counsel had created a stronger connection between Weakland and Mr. Krause 'there was overwhelming evidence that LaPena hired Weakland to commit the murder'.*

You Stunod, are you getting senile? You admitted in your written decision that Weakland did not cause the death of Hilda Krause. Where the hell did you ever learn to write law - in reform school? Overwhelming evidence that I hired Weakland to murder Hilda Krause? Are you kidding me? You've got it backwards Rose. The factual evidence is overwhelming. I did not hire Weakland to murder Hilda Krause. Did you forget Chief Justice Gunderson and Judge Adelair Guy who was present when he was assigned as the first prosecutor in my case Weakland told Guy "Marvin Krause hired him to murder his wife Hilda Krause". Did you also forget sleazebag prosecutor Mel Harmon concealed for 22 years that he personally knew the identity of a second assailant at the crime scene who attacked and murdered Hilda Krause. And, you are doing what the State has always done in this case, avoiding the truth. You, Mr. Justice Robert Rose are a disgrace to the American System of Jurisprudence. You have tarnished the robe you wear. Hey! Rose, this isn't your first rodeo, your historical facts precisely state: "The actual cause of Hilda Krause's death was due to her being strangled and stabbed in the neck area multiple times, and that Weakland maintained he never strangled Hilda Krause with a scarf or rope or cord nor did he **ever** stab her in the neck

214

area. State v. LaPena 750, at 751-752 & 759." Now, do you and your majority remember what you wrote as I even cited it for you?

Okay, let's address another stupid ruling made:

Counsel extensively cross-examined Weakland on inconsistencies between Weakland's testimony as to what he did to Mrs. Krause and the findings of the coroner. 114 Nev Ad. Op. 124 at Page 11

having concluded that LaPena was properly convicted at this 1989 trial we affirm the district court's denial of LaPena's motion to dismiss the charges against him. 11 Nev A. Op 124, at P.22"

Properly convicted? I was properly framed for a crime you know damn well I didn't do. You coward. What is it you don't see that anyone with an ounce off common sense can see? This was conclusive compelling exonerating evidence I provided you and your majority. Tell me and my readers that you're a pea brain idiot! How can I be charged with the murder since Weakland did not kill Hilda Krause?

You have a big ego Rose, so let's do this, how about putting your big ego up against little O' me! How about you and I debate my case together on National TV, i.e., Fox News, CNN, Anderson Cooper, 2020. I'll crush you like a grape, I know the real facts of my case inside and out, as I can hold my own against you any day in the week, and when I get through exposing you on National TV, your legacy as a Justice will be forever tarnished. I will expose you before millions of viewers for your corrupt ruling. Another thing, I never had a prosecutor outlawyer me one on one, including Napoleon Bonafart, the one who moonlights as a Wolf and Howls at the cars on the freeway.

When the reader reads what you also did to me in your deplorable opinion, I believe they will hold you in disrepute. I have read thousands of Appellate Opinions but never have I ever seen an Appellate Court in its opinion cross the line like you did in State v. LaPena supra. In one of my briefs filed with the court, I stated that the majority of justices invented testimony that did not exist in the record, that ultimately denied me my freedom.

APPELLATE PERJURY

What you are going to read now, I call it "Appellate Perjury", where Rose and his majority "Lied" about the evidence they ruled upon. Do you think I'm going to receive justice from this different Nevada Supreme Court where I'm accusing some of their Brethren Justices for falsifying evidence in their ruling against me? Forgetaboutit.

This is my own writing contained in my March 26, 1999, Habeas Petition:

> LaPena also submits the majority of the 1998 Court engaged in more than obvious impermissible inherently incorrect and extremely objectively unreasonable determination of facts, not supported in the record, in light of the evidence presented by LaPena in the State court proceedings to the point that Court ruled in their opinion on "*facts that did not exist in the record*" to deny LaPena his P.C.R. Petition as follows:

THE COURT:

> Mr. Krause reported that after the assailants left his home, he untied himself and went upstairs in an attempt to aid Mrs. Krause," State v. LaPena, (1998) 750, at 751-752.

These fact findings by the Court are totally incorrect and objectively unreasonable, as he "never" went upstairs to **aid** his wife," and testified in March 1974, he **never "aided or touched"** his wife at Weakland's preliminary hearing as follow:

BY MR. ECKER:

Q: Then I believe you testified…what did you do after you freed yourself?

A: I immediately went into the big room where my wife was laying, and I plugged in the   phone and I called the police. A.G.A. Exh. A-7, at P.65, ll. 9-13.

…

Q: Did you call out to your wife at any time?

A: No. I didn't say anything. I just plugged in the phone. A.G.A. Exh. A-7. At P.65. ll. 20-22.

Q: Did you touch her body?

A: No, I did not.

Q: Did you bend over her?

A: No, I did not." A.G.A. Exh. A-7, at P. 66, ll. 9-12.

THE COURT:

Weakland maintained that LaPena, an acquaintance to whom he owed money had approached him at the end of December 1973 and asked him to kill Mrs. Krause. State v. LaPena, (1998) 750, at 752.

These fact findings by the Court were both totally incorrect and extremely objectively unreasonable and belied by the record in light of the evidence presented at the 1995 evidentiary hearing, by Detective Beecher Avants, that "Weakland was **always bumming money from Joey Costanza, a known shylock, and, that Weakland owed money to Costanza.** A, G, A, Exh. "N-1", at P. 311, ll. 5-6; & P. 316, ll. 3-5. Also, the Parole Progress Report, 1982, Agenda, Exhibit G, admitted at the evidentiary hearing showed Weakland stated:

> *...he became deeply indebted to loan sharks through his heavy drinking and gambling, he owed, 'thousands of dollars' he could not pay. Through the use of coercion and threats against his estranged wife and children, he felt at the time, he had no choice but to perform the contract murder.*
> **(Emphasis added)**

The State never proved LaPena was a shylock, or used coercion or threats against Weakland's family, or that **Weakland owed gambling debts to LaPena**, and LaPena at his October 20, 1995, evidentiary hearing testified the only time he gave Weakland money was for a $50.00 loan as a favor to Bill Underwood who shorted Weakland in his payroll. A.G.A. Exh. "N-2" at P. 604, Lns.17-23.

THE COURT:

> *Weakland never names anyone else other than LaPena as the person who hired him to kill Mrs. Krause." State v. LaPena, (1998) 750, at 760.*

These facts cited by the Appellate Court are not supported in the records and, are inherently incorrect and extremely objectively unreasonable in light of the evidence presented by LaPena in the State court proceedings, that "Weakland first **named Marvin Krause as the person who hired him to murder his wife,"** See A.G.A. Exh. K, A.R.B., AT P. 23-24, and LaPena, at his October 20, 1995, (evidentiary hearing) testified:

BY MR. SCHIECK:

Q: Mr. LaPena, did you hire Jerry Weakland to do anything to either of the Krauses?

A: *No, I did not.*

Q: *Did you have any involvement in the death of Hilda Krause?*

A: *Absolutely none whatsoever, A.G.A. Exh. "N-2" at 648, ll. 15-20*

On July 23rd, 1991, C.I. Costanza in a phone conversation, told LaPena's counsel:

GARY GOWEN: "Weakland told me that the person he was going to rob is the person 'who' told Weakland where he lived; what time he left for work; what days of the week it was appropriate to rob him; that this guy who provided Weakland with this information 'was an official' at Caesars Palace and 'they' had planned this together 'long before' December 1973. A.G.A. Exh. "M", at P. 39, Ins. 21-28.

THE COURT:

Also, Webb testified at the 1989 trial that Weakland had told him that LaPena and Maxwell 'had hired him to kill Mrs. Krause. State v. LaPena, (1998) 750 at 760

This factfinding by the Court is completely incorrect and egregiously and extremely objectively unreasonable as no such testimony exists in the record, in light of the evidence presented in the state court proceedings as Webb testified: "the second night he told me the plan between a man and his girlfriend". A.G.A. Exh. A-6, at P. 76, ll. 5-7.

THE COURT:

Weakland's accomplice Boutwell, also testified that LaPena had orchestrated the plan to kill Mrs. Krause. State v. LaPena, supra, 750, at 760.

These 1998 fact findings by the Court are **so outrageously incorrect** and extremely objectively unreasonable, in light of the evidence presented in the state court proceedings, **as no such testimony exists in the record**, as Boutwell testified he never met LaPena, as follows:

BY MR. HARMON:

Q: *State your name please?*

A: *Thomas Boutwell.*

...

Q: *On January 14, 1974, did you know Frank LaPena?*

A: *No. A.G.A. Exh. A-5, at P. 198, ll. 9-13.*

Q: *Did you know Rosalie Maxwell.*

A: *No. A.G.A. Exh. A-5, at P. 198, ll. 9-13.*

BY MR. CARTER:

Q: *Had you ever seen LaPena before?*

A: *No.*

Q: *Had you ever heard Mr. LaPena's name mentioned before?*

A: *No." A.G.A. Exh. A-6, at P. 33, Ln. 25; P. 34, ll. 4-14*

LaPena urges This Honorable Court should find and conclude the 1998, Nevada Supreme Court opinions of specific historical facts identified above was not fairly supported by the record and was outrageously incorrect and extremely objectively unreasonable. Yep, a classic case of APPELLATE COURT PERJURY!

Well, I don't think anything else needs to be said about what you just read. I'm not trying to influence you here; you judge for yourself what you think. I hope you understand as I'm writing this life story of mine, I'm reliving nightmares once more that I tried to block out of my head. So, if I kind of sound-off with some anger here and there, please know it is very difficult for me not to.

On March 26, 1999, I launched a new war against the State and some justices and filed another Habeas Petition on the ground of Newly Discovered Evidence covered up by Napoleon Bonafart and his nefarious criminal gang who hid evidence that connected Marvin Krause and Weakland accomplice Robert Webb in committing criminal acts together. I also filed a Motion to Dismiss my Indictment on February 8, 2000 on the grounds that the State's own evidence, showing that another person, not Weakland, had committed the actual murder of Hilda Krause, establishes conclusively the State did not prove all the elements of the crimes charged in the indictment against me. The most essential element of the crimes charged is missing, namely, who, if anyone, was hired to do it. I intended to shove this argument right down their throats again.

Now on to the newly discovered evidence. At the September 20, 1999 evidentiary hearing, Lynn Brady, testified that in 1973, 2 months before the Robbery/Murder, the victim's husband, Marvin Krause, asked her and two other people to help him pull a fake robbery of his residence to steal his wife's jewelry and furs so he could collect the insurance money. When the three people refused, he asked them if they knew someone who would do it or if they could put him in touch with someone that would do this for him. Again, the three refused. Lynn Brady told the prosecution about this in 1974 and provided a taped statement. The prosecution kept the oral and taped statement information quiet for 25 years and always argued before the jurors and judges that it was LaPena who masterminded the fake robbery of the Krause residence knowing all along that it was Marvin Krause who was the real mastermind behind the fake robbery, not LaPena. See testimony of Lynn Brady as contained in Appellant's Amended Opening Brief filed June 27, 2002 (APPENDIX 8).

19

WHAT THE MAY 22, 2003, NEVADA SUPREME COURT AGREED WITH ME BUT DID NOT RULE IN MY FAVOR IN THEIR ORDER OF AFFIRMANCE

The Nevada Supreme Court entered its Order of Affirmance on May 22, 2003 (APPENDIX 9). You have already read some of what the December 7, 1989, court ruled. Do you think I am going to finally receive justice from the Nevada Supreme Court in 2003 after I harshly accused some of their "Brethren Justices" of falsifying evidence in their ruling against me? Hahaha, I think you know the answer to that one.

I will cite to the record and then make some comments to their ruling. You will see they start out like they are going to give me some Justice, then watch as they take it away as follows:

> LaPena claims that the State violated Brady in failing to disclose the tape-recorded statement of Lynn Brady, a friend of LaPena. LaPena claims that Brady's statement was favorable to the defense because it supports LaPena's theory at trial that the murder victim's husband, not LaPena, was "the mastermind" behind the crime. The statement also connects Mr. Krause and a State witness, Bobby Webb, to a prior criminal scheme where Mr. Krause hired Webb to commit crime against Lynn Brady at her place of employment. LaPena claims that this part of the statement could have been used as impeachment material," at P. 3.

> Cause can be shown by proving that the State withheld the evidence. Prejudice can be shown by proving that the withheld evidence was material", at P. 4.

> The Court first determined Lynn Brady's statement (leaving out what she testified to) would have been favorable to the defense at P. 4

> The part of the statement regarding Mr. Krause's plan to have himself robbed and his wife murdered would have been corroborated by the defense theory that **'LaPena did not**

plan the crimes' at P. 4 (Emphasis added)

The alleged robbery by Webb at the instigation of Mr. Krause may have been used as impeachment material. Thus, these parts of Brady's statements were favorable to the defense. at P. 4

The State asserts...it was not required to disclose Brady's statement because the defense could have discovered it with due diligence. We disagree, at P. 5

Because the State failed to disclose favorable evidence to LaPena we must determine if this...evidence is material. We conclude that it was not..., at P. 5

Webb's alleged robbery of Brady was not material because whether or not he would have been charged with a crime was too speculative. at P. 6

We conclude that LaPena failed to demonstrate prejudice to overcome the procedural defaults with respect to this Brady claim.

LaPena also attempts to overcome the procedural defaults by making a claim of factual innocence. He claims that because Weakland's testimony regarding how Weakland killed Mrs. Krause does not coincide with the physical evidence contained in the autopsy report (they leave out Dr. Clarke's testimony on how she was killed), Weakland could not have been the person who killed Mrs. Krause and therefore LaPena is innocent. We conclude that LaPena has failed to make a credible claim of factual innocence. (They conveniently left out the State via Mel Harmon actually admitted a Second Assailant existed and participated in the murder of Hilda Krause and Harmon knew the identity of this Krause killer)

What do you mean an "alleged robbery?" This was not an "alleged robbery," it was an actual robbery by Bobby Webb. Who do you think you are kidding? This court has purposely ignored Lynn Brady as an actual robbery victim, and she made out a police report to Detective O.R. Lyons plus a taped statement identifying Webb as the robber and attacker at Dr. Zack's office.

Webb's robbery of Lynn Brady was not material because whether or not he would have been charged with a crime was too speculative? Get outta here! You should have been thinking the opposite. This was a classic case of a coverup by Napoleon Bonaparte. Did this court forget Harmon told Lynn Brady that Webb was a strong witness against me and not to mention that at that particular time, the Court should have used plain common sense, the State wasn't going to charge Webb with those crimes, nor Marvin Krause, they needed Webb's testimony and put a hammer over his head that he better testify against me or he would be going to prison for a long time. At the trail level it was up to the jury, not this Appellate Court, to decide if Webb should have been charged with Lynn Brady crimes, as well as Marvin Krause who hired him to do so.

Lynn Brady possessed personal knowledge that in late 1973, just two months before the robbery/murder of Hilda Krause, Marvin Krause personally asked Lynn Brady and two other people to "help him" pull a "fake" robbery at his residence to steal his wife's jewelry and furs so he could collect insurance money. All 24 jurors have always been led to believe, and they did, by the State and Weakland, it was me who was the mastermind who had planned the proposed fake robbery, and the jurors used the testimony against me in their decision to convict me.

When the State used this false evidence and perjured testimony to convict me and the jury bought this false evidence and perjury to convict me, how would the Nevada Supreme Court in its 2003, Order of Affirmance rule it wasn't material where, the State determined 'it was material' enough of them to argue before all 24 jurors it was me as the mastermind behind this 'fake' burglary/robbery". A.G.A. Exh. "A-9

Listen to the rest of this nonsense: "Because LaPena's petition is untimely and successive, he must also demonstrate good cause and prejudice for failing to raise this claim earlier. We conclude that LaPena can demonstrate cause for failing to raise this claim earlier because the existence of Lynn Brady's tape-recorded statement was not disclosed (via Mel Harmon) until 1998, when she was contacted by LaPena, however (here we go again) we conclude that LaPena cannot demonstrate prejudice."

Can you believe this. They agree the State of Nevada withheld this evidence. I prove cause and prejudice on my claim, therefore, they withheld evidence "is material." They also agree the withheld evidence of Mr. Krause's plan to have himself robbed and his wife murdered would have corroborated my defense theory that I did not plan the crimes and may have been used as impeachment material and was favorable to my defense.

Are you reading what I believe I'm reading here? In trying to read into this it sounds to me like the Appellate Court is saying I produced evidence I did not plan these crimes. What do you think? Their reasons for denying my appeal made no sense.

Well, folks, you judge for yourself if this evidence was material for me to have it brought before a jury. If you were a juror would you have wanted this evidence submitted before you to decide if it was material enough for me to get a new trial on newly discovered evidence? Anyway, Carmine Colucci filed a Motion to Allow Oral Argument Before En Banc Court (APPENDIX 10) (response) to the Court's May 22, 2003, Order of Affirmance. I liked it; hope you do too.

During this time period as Carmine Colucci and I were waiting for the Appellate Court's decision on my March 26, 1999, Habeas Petition, I became ill and was placed in the medical section of the infirmary. I believe it was just after September 11, 2003, that I was transferred to Northern Nevada Correctional Center Medical Hospital in Carson City, Nevada for prostate surgery. In the meantime, the Nevada Supreme Court denied the Motion to Allow Oral Argument Before En Banc Court. I then filed a Federal Habeas Petition and received two Federal Court "convict haters". Twice they denied me justice and twice I appealed them to the 9th Circuit Court of Appeals who overturned their bias rulings.

Anyway, after my surgery while housed at the medical hospital, one of the counselors visited me and asked me a very surprising question. "Mr. LaPena, do you want to stay here or go back to High Desert Prison 'Pending your Pardon's Board Hearing"? "Huh", I couldn't believe what I had just heard. Are you ready for this? Chief Justice Deborah Agosti, who wrote the May 22, 2003 Affirmance Opinion against me, "sponsored" me to be placed on the Pardon's Board for clemency. Not, only her, but the Director of Prisons, Jackie Crawford, also sponsored me to appear before the Pardon's Board. I asked the counselor for permission to use her office phone to call attorney Carmine Colucci. He was elated when I told him the news and immediately said he would represent me before the Pardons Board. Carmine and Zoe then put together a packet of letters from people asking the Pardons Board to grant me clemency. Carmine and Zoe worked hard and had a lot of people writing favorable letters on my behalf. Carmine contacted former Chief Justice Gunderson and asked if he would testify on my behalf at the Pardons Board. Well, did he ever. I truly believe retired Chief Justice E.M. Gunderson came forward at my December 12, 2003, Pardons Board hearing and presented overwhelming testimonial evidence that I was "actually innocent" of the most sensational publicized contract murder, where the State concealed and covered up that Weakland first named Marvin Krause, as the person who hired him to murder his wife and not me. I believe this was the first time in both Nevada history and maybe the country, where a Chief Justice of the State's Highest Court ever testified for a prisoner. Remember it was Justice Gunderson who dissented in his 1976 Opinion that there was no probable cause to arrest both Rosalie and I for the Hilda Krause robbery/murder. I want you to know in writing this book about my life I am in my own way honoring Justice Gunderson for everything he said about this travesty of justice because his words were never truer. I wish he were alive today as to this final clue I shall give to you. I believe Gunderson would have a great smile on his face and say" "I told you so."

At that Pardons Board hearing, both Justice Rose and Agosti gave me a "Yes" vote for clemency along with the other Nevada Supreme Court Justices. How do you figure that, after both wrote opinions denying my Habeas Petitions? Guilty conscience maybe? I don't know.

On that day, the Pardons Board commuted my sentence from life without the possibility of parole to life with the possibility of parole. Unfortunately, even after that, twice the Parole Board denied me parole and was heavily scolded for doing so. Carmine Colucci later told me that Governor Kenny Guinn and Chief Justice Deb Agosti wanted me paroled ASAP. Life can be really screwy at times, don't you think?

I was finally granted parole on February 8, 2005, I was released from High Desert State Prison. But it was the day before, February 7th, Correctional Officers told me to start rolling up all my property and needed me to sign some paperwork. I had 22 boxes of legal work put onto a cart.

Let me tell you, it was a long day and night, and my anxiety level was sky-high. This was going to be the FINAL FRONTIER for me being freed for the third and final time. At 4:00 a.m. I was told to start getting ready for transport.

After eight more years living in hell, I was for the last time, shackled in chains and placed in a van and transported to the headquarters of the Parole and Probation facility. When I arrived and the chains were unlocked and removed, I began my "Freedom Walk". I just started walking nowhere in particular, just looking at buildings, stores, streets, sidewalks, smelling free air. All of a sudden, a car pulls up next to me and guess what, I will never forget it was Zoe who came to pick me up. Holy cow! What a surprise. Carmine already knew before I did, what date that I was to be released. But what happened next just stunned me.

When Zoe had pulled up, she started talking to this gadget. "Carmine, I found Frank; he was walking down the street."

Are my eyes deceiving me? "What! What is that in your hand that you are talking to Zoe?" "It's a cell phone Frank." I couldn't believe my eyes this tiny thing in Zoe's hand was a "telephone." Wow! Just then it flashed through my head how much of this world has passed me by. Big smiles, lots of hugs at Carmine's law office, but I couldn't get over the cell phone image and what it did. So, Carmine told me they were going to give me a cell phone the next day. Carine and Zoe were absolutely God Sent to me with all the help they were giving me. Carmine already had an apartment for me with get this "free rent" from one of his clients, a class guy, named Robert Lawson, who owned the apartment building.

Okay now for my next surprise. Zoe later said, "Come on Frank we need to go grocery shopping to get you settled into your new place." At the grocery store Zoe asked me what I would like to get. I said grapes, oranges, apples, bananas, juice drinks were all I wanted. Now, get this, we get to the cashier and I go into my pocket to pay for my groceries and Zoe stops me, takes out a card, places it in a machine, I looked stunned. "What are you doing Zoe?" "It's a debit card to pay for the groceries and the money is extracted from my bank account." Huh! "They can't do that Zoe, that's illegal." "No, Frank it's how we pay for things we want." I'm speechless. The reality of this new world I came into struck me like lightning. I was totally bewildered. I knew then I would need a lot of help adjusting to today's society.

The next day, February 9th, I walked to Carmine's office and they had a cell phone for me. Zoe took her time showing me how the cell phone worked. Getting to the part where I was to speak into the phone as a voice mail which kind of made me feel foolish talking to a phone, Zoe suggested I leave a message like "Sorry I missed your call, will call you back'. However, I decided to say something different so when someone called me, and I missed the call I said: "What in the hell are they going to think of next".

I waited about a week or two I believe, then went back to work for Carmine. Coming out of the dark ages to the present time in 2005, was unnerving. I was lost in this world of computer, electrical gadgets, cars, etc., etc. I was now beginning to start my life all over again.

And, I was blessed to have friends, especially Tommy Thomson who couldn't do enough for me. It was approximately one month after I had been out, Tommy called me wanting to know if I needed to go shopping. I said yes. It was early March 2005; Tommy comes over to my place and has a female with him. Very striking, elegant, classy looking and beautiful. He saw me staring at her and Tommy said, "this is my sister Betty." Your sister? I've known you for over 20 years Tommy, you never mentioned to me you had a sister. "I have three (3) more Frank and they are all married." Well, I'll be darn, what a nice surprise. I wanted to buy a watch, so Tommy took us to Target. Betty helped me pick out a watch. There was no question in my mind Betty was once a beauty queen, and, of course, I later learned she had been one. Betty was just visiting Tommy and their family as she was living in Texas. I did notice that Betty started to visit Las Vegas more than usual as Tommy always called me when she was in town. I did attend Betty's 60th birthday in Las Vegas. I didn't stay long because I felt uncomfortable with crowds. What was funny, Betty was trying to fix me up with some of her girlfriends I wasn't interested in any of them. None compared to Betty.

Okay, I'm getting a little ahead of myself, so let's go back to Carmine's law firm. After I had been working for Carmine for about a month and a half, he asked if I wanted to take a walk with him. We ended up a Bob's Bail Bonds. The owner, a client of Carmine's was Robert Murry. Bob was a former detective with Metro's Intelligent Unit, knew all about me and surprised me when he said, "I personally know you had nothing to do with the Krause murder." I asked him what he knows that I don't know. He responded he still had a family to think about, so he couldn't tell me. I'm thinking what in the hell can scare a detective. None of it made any sense to me. So, I dropped it. But what really caught me off guard was he offered me a job as a Bail Bondsman. Are you ready for this- $600 a week? That was enormous money to me. I then went to work for Bob. Carmine was happy I got the job. Now I'm making good money, so I got a larger apartment with a garage and a nice car. What's next on my agenda, you guessed it, no secret here, a furry angel to rescue.

My search however took me a little longer as I was dead set on rescuing another Sheltie, like Solomon. I couldn't get it out of my head that I let Solomon down by refusing to accept a guilty plea deal where he would have lived out his life with me. You see, Solomon was really special. He was amongst a group of abused dogs that Rosalie told me about. Rosalie had talked to this lady who rescued abused animals. Rosalie was partial to Shelties and this lady told Rosalie she had a Sheltie, so Rosalie and I went to look him over. When I saw Solomon and he saw me, he came to me when I called out to his name immediately. The lady was very surprised and happy as to how Solomon reacted to me. She told Rosalie and myself that in the eight months he was under her care he would not go to anyone who was interested in adopting him. I assured her he will always be safe, and I would give him a loving home. God, he was absolutely beautiful, and we became best buddies for life. To this day I carry a heavy heart missing him, but I know I will see him again as well as all my furry angels I lost. I enclosed his picture in this book for you to see.

My search for another Sheltie like Solomon did not work out too well. I should have known better you can't really replace them as they all have different personalities. It was Saturday and I went to PetSmart where they were showing Doggie Adoption Day. Again, I didn't see what I was looking for so for whatever reason I went into the PetSmart store and found myself walking past the Cat adoption cages. I wasn't looking for a cat, but I saw this incredible little long-haired black and white cat, with very piercing green eyes. Wow! I had to admit this was a beautiful looking angel. She was looking dead straight at me. I decided to take a closer look and the attendant noticed both of us and said something like, "She's got her eye on you, she likes you." She is really pretty, but my mind was set on a dog. Ok! I started walking elsewhere but I kept getting drawn to look at her again. So, I sneak my head around the corner, so she can't see me. That little stinker is looking right at me. I couldn't fool her. That's enough, time to go, what the hell am I thinking. Sunday rolls around and all of a sudden, it's on my mind that someone might adopt that pretty little cat. I need to find out. I went back to PetSmart. I snuck around the corner like I did before so as not to be seen. Well, I'll be a USC Trojan, she caught me looking at her. Okay, I'm done for, she wins. Went to one of the workers at the store, said I want this little cutie pie cat, named Sheba…never had one before but I'm committed to take care of her for life. I buy all the essentials to owning and taking care of a cat. Off we go to my two-story apartment. No sooner do I open her cage door she bolts up the stairs like a rocket. In the meantime, I'm trying to figure out where to place her food bowl, sand box, water bowl. All done, now time for us to get to know each other. One big problem. I can't find her, looking everywhere, no sign of Sheba. Where in the dickens can she be? I can't believe I can't find her. I know she is in the house, but where? Every day I check to see her food is gone, sandbox needs cleaning, water bowl is down, where the hell is she? Ok! It's my 3rd night and I'm in bed watching TV. All of a sudden, I feel first, then see, this little gorgeous animal had jumped on the bed, walked up to me and laid her head between my chest and arm. I 've had her for 15 years now. Am I blessed or what!

Now more about Nurse Betty. This was Tommy's nickname for his sister Betty. She did Home Health Care for an agency in Texas. Betty is well educated obtaining her Master's

Degree in counseling and other degrees. I had a different name for her later on. Like I said Nurse Betty started coming out to Vegas more than usual but for a good reason; we started dating and kept it from her family. After I proposed to this beautiful woman, we were married on January 25, 2007. I chose the 25th of January because that was the date my mother went to heaven. I wanted it to be a day to celebrate joy, not sadness. Now, Betty was aware of my time in prison, and she took time to learn what the corrupt State did to me and how I suffered from it. I was on lifetime parole and each month I was required to report to my parole officer at their headquarters. Betty has a great sense of humor. She now called herself, "Warden Betty," when she liked to boss me around. She is an animal lover and had an incredible, beautiful female Akita-German Shepard named Hope and we later added Star, a gorgeous black lab. Two dogs and a cat, both Hope and Star loved Sheba and vice versa. She slept between Hope and Star. These two beautiful angels have now passed, and we now have Samson, Rhodesian Ridgeback Boxer mix and Sheba.

Back to Court. Having finished all of my State issues and proceedings, I was in federal court arguing the merits of my issues presented to them. As I said before, I had two haters, who had no business being federal judges. When I made parole and was released from custody, I was required to notify in writing the Federal Court Judge I had moved and provide the court with a filed stamped copy of my new address. I have always been very self-conscious in following Court rules and procedures. Six days after I was released from prison, on February 8, 2005, I filed a Notice of Change of Address by personally going down to the Federal Court Building and filing it. On February 14, 2006, a year goes by and I don't understand why I haven't heard anything from the Federal Judge. On April 5, 2006, Judge Pro entered an Order and Judgment dismissing my Federal Habeas Petition. I didn't know this, until out of curiosity, I went to the Federal Clerks Office to check on my case and was informed by the clerk my case had been dismissed for failing to inform the Judge my change of address. The clerk states there is no record of me filing such a notice.

More than a year later, I filed a Motion to reopen the matter stating, "Due to my very serious inadvertent failure/mistake to provide the court with my change of address, I sent a change of address to the Court of Appeals (9th Circuit) on February 14, 2005 and believed I had sent the Judge a filed stamped Notice of Change of Address. This POS denied it on August 3, 2007.

Seven years later, just before June 1, 2012, while going through some of my legal work that was left, after throwing away more than 20 boxes of legal work because I was no longer fight my case in Federal Court, I came upon my file stamped Change of Address date February 14, 2005. Talk about being hot under the collar with the stupid federal Judge Pro. Well, I insulted Judge Pro for his egregious negligence for allowing this to happen. Pro knew he had no choice but to reinstate my Federal Habeas Petition or the 9th Circuit Court of Appeals would have reversed him. I knew this bias POS would deny my Petition which he did. And, again the 9th Circuit granted me a Certificate of Appealability on actual innocence as one of my issues (APPENDIX 11).

20

DNA PROVES LAPENA INNOCENT

Prior to finding my February 2005 change of address in 2012, I decided to test my legal brain on DNA. I got the idea from Franny Forsman who was the Director of the Federal Public Defenders Office. Franny told me there was no time bar against a defendant who wanted to have DNA testing to prove their innocence. Franny is in a class all by herself. She is absolutely brilliant and more important a genuine good person.

On June 10, 2011, I filed a Post-Conviction Petition Requesting a Genetic Marker Analysis of Evidence Within the Possession or Custody of the State of Nevada (APPENDIX 12). You will now know how DNA Petitions first get started. My case was assigned to the Honorable District Court Judge Abbi Silver. I thus began a new era on DNA litigation. In doing so, I knew I better study up on this subject. I read articles on Alec Jeffreys from the U.K. who invented "Touch" DNA that resulted in thousands of cases providing great results.

On October 25, 2011, the Honorable Abbi Silver **granted** my DNA Petition and ordered that the hairs impounded in my case from the victim Hilda Krause would be subjected to genetic Marker analysis.

On November 3, 2011, I'm still representing myself and holding my own against prosecutor, Marc Schifalacqua before Judge Silver. It was a status check on the DNA testing where the D.A.'s office contacted Metro Homicide who was going to assign a particular detective to either get the evidence (hairs from victim Hilda Krause's hands) or retrieve the evidence somehow for testing or getting out. Hairs were found in both of Hilda Krause's hands. If DNA reveal those hairs belonged to Marvin Krause "I win." Remember, Marvin Krause had testified he never touched his wife while she was lying two feet from him.

On April 17, 2012, I'm still going strong litigating my DNA case by myself and filed a Motion for specific DNA blood testing as you can see by the caption, but I would like to direct you to p. 5 Lns.6 thru 9, PKG#6, and you will see later where I go with it (APPENDIX 13).

Surprise! Surprise! Surprise! Wait to you read this. Prior to my Supplemental Motion being filed, that you just read, the Nevada Legislature enacted a new Nevada Law, an Intermediate Court called a Court of Appeals. It helped ease the heavy load of cases before the Nevada Supreme Court. A defendant or civil litigant could appeal from a District Court decision to the Court of Appeals instead of directly to the Nevada Supreme Court.

During my DNA court proceedings before Judge Abbi Silver, she was court appointed by the Governor to sit on this new three judge panel. Oh boy, it looks like I'm going to lose my judge and start all over with a new judge.

Her appointment to the Court of Appeals required her to distribute all her present and pending cases to other District Court Judges (Administrative Order of Assignment APPENDIX 14). But guess what? Having presided over my DNA case for several years, she wanted to finish it to the end, so she requested permission from the Nevada Supreme Court to allow her to keep my case to its conclusion.

I filed a Supplemental Motion on May 5, 2015 (APPENDIX 15). What do you think as you read this? I feel very strongly I obtained exactly what the Court said I needed to solve regarding an Unknown male whose DNA was all over the cord that was used to strangle Hilda Krause. I previously argued in my DNA Motion that District Court Judges have granted many defendants DNA Petitions and Motions for a new trial based on "**Unknown Male Perpetrators**" and supported that argument with case files. The State responded to my supplemental motion and I personally did the reply to the state's response. Enjoy your new knowledge of DNA law.

During another hearing court proceeding before the Honorable Abbi Silver, on September 15, 2015, she stated the following:

> THE COURT: *So, the Court believes that the issue is: 'do these DNA results from last January that we just received, January 15, do they effectively impeach Weakland's testimony on how the murder happened? Because if he's lying about how the murder happened, then he could be lying about who put him up to killing Hilda Krause. Pgs. 8 & 9.*

> THE COURT: *Now, these are things that the Court thought of, but that's a full impeachment. pg. 15*

> THE COURT: *And if at the E.H. you bring in witnesses that can explain this and*

232

say, 'looking scientifically, and then perhaps asked, 'Look at Weakland's testimony', no struggle. A quick slit, right. That's what he testified to Is that enough?''; P. 16 (LaPena Note: one slit did not cause her death, Multiple stab wounds to carotid and vertebral arteries did)

THE COURT: "Somebody's got to look at what's happened here and see whether or not it fits with what Weakland says because the only evidence in this case is Weakland testimony; P. 17

THE COURT: "And, again, like a coroner, a Jordan, A green, somebody that the State perhaps has used, somebody, a consultant to go after those issues that the Court has brought up 'along with putting it against Weakland's testimony from the 1989 trial.' P. 20

When you have read specifically what Judge Silver was getting at, she then did an amazing thing for me, the last part of what you just read. Judge Silver Court appointed an exceptional crime scene analyst for me. On that she had used in the past when she was a prosecutor. She made a strong suggestion to one of my attorneys that Joseph Matvay would be a good choice for us to use so my attorney said that would be fine and she assigned Matvay to my case. I believe Judge Silver wanted to really find out what happened at the Krause crime scene on January 14, 1974, and Matvay had the experience and ability to do just that. Matvay was an expert capable of performing a crime scene reconstruction or sequencing as to what occurred at the crime scene. I was really excited to find out for myself. Matvay had served 35 years with the Las Vegas Metropolitan police Department and the last 20 years with Metro as a CSI Supervisor. Appointed as my defense witness, he was now considered an enemy of the State. What he didn't expect is that he ran into a roadblock by the State in attempting to obtain evidence so he could reconstruct the crime scene.

Did the State suppress the evidence that crime scene analyst Matvay needed to reconstruct the crime scene? Top Cop Beecher Avants parading himself off as a great homicide investigator and his top sidekick Chuck Lee's investigation at the crime scene was a farce, a complete incompetent investigation or it was done on purpose as a coverup. I believe it was done on purpose so no physical evidence could tie Marvin Krause as being a possible part of his wife's murder.

Matvay was not able to reconstruct the crime scene or do any sequencing due to a lack of documentation as Top Cop Avants' investigation was lacking in many respects. Avants was solely responsible for Metro to conduct a proper investigation. Mr. Top Cop conducted a "bad investigation" at the crime scene and afterwards.

My evidentiary hearing on January 30, 2017 turned out to be a disaster for me as my two alleged criminal attorneys threw me under the bus, especially the idiot I had talked about before whose name I refused to divulge. I couldn't stomach this POS attorney. Laziest and worst attorney I had in over twenty years. Totally useless. Prior to my evidentiary hearing, I had prepared the perfect questions to go after Criminalist Craig King. One of my questions was extremely important to ask Criminalist Craig King because of the two electrical cords found by CSI Jerry Keller, one cord was on the right side of Hilda's body and the other cord was "around her neck." I had no doubt that whoever strangled Hilda with the cord around her neck his DNA would be more than present for Craig King to get a full DNA Profile through CODIS. I also knew through my research on DNA that a "TINY" DNA Profile can be copied many times and create a sufficiently large pool of DNA for analysis.

Prior to this hearing, I had a personal talk with Guyman, told him I couldn't stand this other attorney, didn't want him on my case any longer as he's worthless. Guyman said he could do this all by himself. Later all three of us had a meeting. I told the worthless attorney he will not question Craig King. We argued this back and forth then the POS said he would use my questions. The P…K was lying to me.

Man, did they pull one over me at the January 30, 2017 hearing. They both lied to me at the table when they said Judge Silver did not want to hear about Lab Item 1.1, 1.2, and 1.3. Then the POS tells me he is not going to use my questions. I came right out of my seat and they tried to quiet me down.

So, what does prosecutor Marc DiGiacomo do? Right out of the gate he starts questioning Criminalist Craig King about Lab Items 1.1, 1.2, and 1.3 and no objection from attorneys. At that moment I felt like I was going down the tubes. And I sure did. That's bad enough I thought. Then Guyman never asked Matvay about the video I gave him that contained 164 pictures of the crime scene. Matvay said I believe he was provided with less than 70. Right then and there I should have stood up and objected to the representation of both attorneys. My mistake for not doing that.

What broke the camel's back came when prosecutor DiGiacomo argued the poor handling of the cords contaminated the cords to the extent that the unknown DNA could have been left by any number of prosecutors, court personnel or jurors over the course of 43 years. No objection by either of my attorneys that DiGiacomo's argument is pure speculation and conjecture.

Not one single piece of evidence was submitted by DiGiacomo that any prosecutor, court personnel, juror, defense attorneys or Judge since 1974 to 1995 ever handled the cords.

My attorneys should have argued to the Court to ask DiGiacomo if he personally interviewed all my defense attorneys, prosecutors on my case, court personnel, jurors, judges who sat on my case since 1974, 1977, 1989 and 1995 to obtain this whether or not the personally touched the cords by their hands. That was the perfect question to ask the Court to challenge his wild exaggeration of the alleged cord handling. As for me I should have stood up and objected because I was only one in Judge Silver's courtroom who had personal knowledge about the cord handling and told her not one time did my defense attorney, prosecutor, juror, judge or court personnel ever touch the cords with their hands; that the cords always remained in a sealed bag. What I should have done was ask the Court to dismiss my attorneys who I believe threw me under the bus. I became really upset with myself for not doing that. I believe I could have won my DNA Petition by myself.

Actually, I can't fault Judge Silver for buying into DiGiacomo's argument as it was my attorney's fault for not challenging it and it was a very big issue used against me. Had this issue been challenged properly I believe Judge Silver would have ruled my way.

Anyway, on August 3, 2017, The Court denied my DNA Petition on DNA evidence. So, as you can understand, my DNA Petition was to get enough DNA evidence in my favor to get myself a new trial and once obtaining that DNA evidence at a trial level to get an acquittal. The Court was not addressing an actual innocence claim. I will say this no judge ever worked harder on my case than Justice Abbi Silver. Wish I had Abbi Silver as my defense attorney, no doubt in my mind that I would have been acquitted, because she has a brilliant legal mind and is as tough as nails!

However, when Justice Silver made her ruling, "While the DNA results are favorable to Mr. LaPena to the extent, they further impeach Weakland's depiction on how he murdered Hilda Krause, they do not contradict evidence presented at trial, nor impeach Mr. Weakland on the natural point of employing Mr. Weakland's service or whether another person committed or assisted with the murder." I believe Justice Silver inadvertently forgot I had in fact submitted evidence of the last part of her ruling to obtain a new trial.

Weakland first admitted to prosecutor Addelair Guy that Marvin Krause **employed his services** to kill Hilda Krause. On July 26, 1996, prosecutor Mel Harmon admitted into the record "**another person had committed and assisted**" in the Krause murder whose **identity** was known by the State when they stated, admitted and acknowledged they were in possession of information regarding a Second Assailant at the Krause crime scene and the DNA showed an "Unknown Male" strangled Hilda Krause with the electrical cord that was found by CSI Metro Officer Jerry Keller around Hilda Krause's neck. None of this cited above was cumulative as they, the 1989 trail jurors, were never presented with this evidence to evaluate for a not guilty verdict.

There was no question in my mind that Craig King was going to see to it that I did not have a full male profile of the Unknown Male Strangler. Didn't trust him as far as Chuck Norris could throw him, nor the D.A.'s office who had members that were famous for covering up evidence, along with their Metro Cops. Avants-Lee should have been arrested for the way these two Keystone Cops messed up the crime scene. Top Cop Best Investigator – they couldn't investigate a peanut butter sandwich properly. Go on the internet and look up McKenzie v. Lamb, 738 F.2d 1005 (9th Cir. 1984) where Metro's good old boys tried to frame two innocent guys. "We do things the way we please out here" (including covering up crime scene, arrest innocent persons). Lowlife scum with a badge.

I prepared this motion due to my distrust of the LVMPD, DA's office, and criminalist Craig King. Judge for yourself if you think I was justified in filing this motion. I prepared and gave this motion to that piece of shit attorney. The p…k didn't file it and when I found out, I jumped all over him, but I also had to be careful of myself since I was still on Parole. You take what I wrote here and put 2 and 2 together why this nefarious law enforcement officials did or didn't do.

21

MOB ENFORCER TONY SPILOTRO THREATENS CONFESSED KILLER, GERALD WEAKLAND "YOU WILL BE DEALT WITH IF YOU SAY ANYTHING ELSE ABOUT MARVIN KRAUSE OR ROSALIE"

Why do suspects or persons of interest confess to crimes they did not commit? Well, the truth of the matter is that lots of people confess to murder they did not actually commit. Here are some circumstances why some do. For example, bad cops aggressively drilling an accused with no defense attorney present or some with low IQs, some retarded that could go on for very long periods of interrogation. Using the bad cop first, then the phony good cop second who cleverly put thoughts into their minds until the person begins to believe they did the crime and the dirty cops giving the slow thinking or exhausted person clues from the crime scene to get a confession and arrest and a conviction of which they will testify later against the person. There are a plethora of cases like that. Other confessions have been from being physically beaten up by the cops who will lie about it. Then you also have defense attorneys, either lazy or very incompetent who conduct no investigation on your behalf and then scare the suspect or defendant into taking a plea bargain for a lesser sentence if facing the death penalty or life without sentence.

The question as to WHY would Weakland confess to a murder he did not commit came up several times during my court proceedings by both the State and my attorneys. Viable answer – Mob Enforcer Tough Tony Spilotro. I believe Spilotro made Gerald Weakland an offer he could not refuse. Either confess to the charge of the Hilda Krause murder and get the heat of Marvin Krause or he and his family dies. I will explain in more detail as you read on.

Spilotro came here to Las Vegas around d 1971. By 1974, at the time of the Hilda Krause murder, one could easily conclude the only loan shark (alive) making big money in Las Vegas was Tony Spilotro and his Hole in the Wall Gang.

Without a doubt, Tony Spilotro, "the Enforcer" called the shots in Las Vegas during his reign from 1971 to 1986. It was noted that Chicago Godfather, Tony Accordo, sent Spilotro to Las Vegas to oversee the Outfits Casino business holdings. I was to later find out Tony Spilotro on a personal basis knew both Gerald Weakland and Marvin Krause. In my opinion, especially MOB "enforcers," love big money, and enormous power. Killers whose savior is Satan.

All locals in town during the 1970's knew that Las Vegas was run by the Mob. It doesn't take a genius to figure out that Marvin Krause, who was heavily connected to and controlled by the Mob, was doing the slot machine skim for the Mob of which Tony Spilotro, the Enforcer, was the overseer of the Chicago Outfit of their take at Caesars Palace. Marvin Krause knew that if he wanted all to be well in his own little world, Tony Spilotro would have to be happy at all times.

You recall that I previously told you that I did some legal work for Spilotro. He thanked me and to my surprise, he said, "Do you want me to take care of Weakland for you?" I said, "No, I will deal with him myself." Wow! Twice I had Weakland's life in my hands and all I had to say was one word "YES" and Weakland's dead. But I'm more into saving a life, not taking one.

It should have dawned on me right then and there that Spilotro and Weakland actually knew each other but I had other things on my mind at that time.

I had received a couple of letters from Greg McWilliams who knew Weakland both in and out of prison, and what Weakland was really like on the streets with gang bangers. A real nefarious human who loved to inflict brutal physical pain on people. I'm sure you recall other acts that Weakland's brutality that I have written about in this book.

Wholly crap! I don't know if any Hollywood writer could make up a factual or fairytale story as crazy as mine which has so many twists and turns. It's like a puzzle that couldn't be put together. So, let me tell you what was in Greg's letter dated March 20, 2001, which really caught me by surprise as I shall relate to you (APPENDIX 16). And use your own interpretation as to what this letter may mean to you okay? I have my own possible theory which I will point out to you.

In that letter, among the things that McWilliams wrote were the following:

Hey Frank . . . in late '74 or '75, I met G.W. (Gerry Weakland) in the old Clark County jail . . .he told me that the Krause incident was an inside move put together by Marvin Krause and that you had nothing to do with it and would be acquitted and compensated for your inconvenience.

McWilliams went on to write:

. . .it was all a strategically arranged situation with you all going through the motions to derail any chances of the State making a case against M.K. (Marvin Krause). G.W. found out that I was arranging my bail through Dale Phiefer (Burton's Bail Bonds) and he (Weakland) stated he knew Dale. When I got out, I mentioned this to Dale.

I was told in no uncertain terms that if G.W. said anything else about M.K. or Rosalie, he would be dealt with, and if I ever saw G.W. again I was to relay that to him. Supposedly, Spilotro, Fat Herbie Blitzstein, and the "Hole in the Wall" mob was backing M.K.

I pointed out some of the things I know about your case to Oscar G. (Goodman) who as you know represented Rosalie at one point, and who I hired . . . in 1989. Oscar expressed to me that he was well aware of how royally you had got screwed around, and claimed that one of his regrets was that he hadn't stayed on that case and crushed Mel Harmon and G.W.

Greg further went on to state in his letter:

I don't know if you are aware of it or not but G.W. tried his hand at hustling as a pimp prior to the Krause incident. A very heavy-handed operator he turned out to be a gorilla pimp. He clashed with some of this Carson & Compton mob over a couple of hookers who G.W. was putting pressure on. This situation escalated and at least one of the women got seriously hurt – real sadistic brutal stuff.

Well, I 'll be a California Condor! How about that! Weakland being a brutal, heavy-handed gorilla type of street pimp prior to the Krause murder. Here's a factual street check. Street pimps make a ton of money trafficking women, especially the violent, brutal ones. Even more interesting is that Gerald Weakland testified how broke he always was before the Krause murder and that I had given him a lot of money prior to Hilda Krause's murder. That lying piece of shit had more money from pimping and trafficking then I ever had.

Now I want you to join with me and check this out and see if you agree with me ok? Greg's letter inter alia brought into question an interesting theory that I will explain to you as you read on regarding Weakland's street crimes and loan shark debts to the Mob. It could be that Weakland didn't give Mob Enforcer Tony Spilotro his "street tax" that Spilotro mandated from street criminals which Weakland was. Just maybe Weakland was a vicious street thug that thought his physical boxing skills and violent actions could stop a bullet from a Mob hit man and his crew. You be the judge as you read on.

Rosalie Maxwell and Mob Enforcer Tony Spilotro. Really? Seriously? When I read the part of Greg's letter about Spilotro warning Gerald Weakland that he better not say anything else about Rosalie Maxwell being involved in the Krause murder or he would be dealt with by Spilotro that was a shocker to me. Well, what do ya know, Rosalie was being protected by Mob Enforcer Tony Spilotro. WOW! Well, I reckon I heard it all now.

Questions about Rosalie Maxwell. Did she personally know Tony Spilotro? Did Marvin Krause introduce Rosalie to Spilotro? When and where? Did Marvin Krause ask Spilotro to look after Rosalie since Marvin was in love with her and on several occasions asked her to marry him? Would that be the reason that Spilotro threatened Weakland if he ever said anything again about Rosalie being involved in the Krause murder, he would be dealt with by Spilotro and his Hole in the Wall Gang? By the time I found out about this from Greg in 2001, there as an apparent connection between Spilotro and Rosalie. Rosalie had passed on in 1997. Wonder why she never told me? Just curious and I should be don't you think? No doubt our conversation would have been interesting.

As for Marvin Krause, it seems that Spilotro had the responsibility to assure Marvin Krause that he would not become a suspect or charged in any way for his wife's murder. Needless to say, if Marvin Krause found himself embroiled in a murder investigation, it would put a significant crimp in Krause's ability to perform his tasks for the Chicago Outfit.

When Weakland first named Marvin Krause as the person who hired him to murder his wife, Hilda, Spilotro (who had some members of law enforcement in his pocket), got word of it. Yeah! Based upon Weakland's personality, it would appear that Weakland was pushing his luck with Spilotro in more ways than one by naming both Marvin Krause and Rosalie in the involvement of the murder of Hilda Krause. It caught the ire of Spilotro. One thing for sure, it wasn't healthy to be on the wrong side of Mob Enforcer Tough Tony Spilotro and his Hole in the Wall Gang.

Spilotro had to make sure Weakland would learn that if he were to mention both Marvin Krause and Rosalie Maxwell's names again, that certain "associates" of his (Spilotro's) would pay Weakland a visit and it wouldn't be simply to ask him, "How ya doin?"

Spilotro's main man was a guy named Frank Cullotta. Cullotta was the leader of the Hole in the Wall Gang who were a bunch of guys who had been responsible for a number of burglaries, murders and other kinds of criminal mayhem in Las Vegas. But I'm not sure if Cullotta was in Las Vegas in 1974-1975 though it probably did not matter because Spilotro's numerous associates reached as far as other states other than Nevada.

Getting back to Dale Phiefer (Burton's Bail Bonds). Dale was a known big-time bondsman. I have no doubt that Dale knew Tony Spilotro and members of the Hole in the Wall Gang. I met Dale many years later and he was a very pleasant person. Small world, isn't it? Anyway, I have no knowledge if Greg relayed Spilotro's threat to Weakland later on or if Dale did since Weakland and Dale knew each other, and Dale did have the ability and authority to visit Weakland in the county jail, but somebody relayed that information.

It didn't matter if Weakland was in the county jail or prison. If Spilotro wanted and ordered Weakland and his family dead, you could take that to the bank that it would happen. Remember, to insult of defy Tony Spilotro was a sure death wish not only for Weakland but his family as well. Judge for yourself as you read Gerald Weakland's testimony recantation at Rosalie's trial in 1976, and what I learned later from Weakland's granddaughter. I believe had Spilotro dispensed "associate" Crazy Larry Neuman to take care of Weakland and his family, they would have ALL been whacked if Neuman caught up with them. It was said, Neuman loved to kill people for the thrill of it. He didn't need a real reason to do that.

Alright, you have read enough in my book, although there is more to know Weakland did not murder Hilda Krause, and the big question is, WHY did Weakland admit to a murder he obviously did not commit? I hope you agree with me that Weakland most likely had a greater fear (Spilotro) than the criminal justice system to protect himself and his family.

You recall I previously argued: Weakland's own admission was that he owed thousands of dollars to loan sharks in 1974, or earlier, would certainly indicate Weakland owed Spilotro and Costanza money. But Weakland was not fearful of Joey Costanza (his Honor Brother as Weakland called him). I believe Weakland could not pay even the "vig" (interest) back in 1974 and he knew Spilotro was a vicious debt collector.

What can be confusing to me and possibly you is that Weakland made a ton of money as a street pimp and trafficker just before the Hilda Krause murder. It's hard to imagine a guy like Weakland made tons of money and gambled it away so fast he needed loan shark money to keep continuing his gambling habits. Okay, let's try and work on this puzzle together and see what we can come up with.

You recall, I earlier stated that during Rosalie Maxwell's trial in 1976, Weakland adhered to being in fear for his family's life. He testified as follows:

> By Mr. Harmon: May the record show that the witness has identified the defendant, Rosalie Maxwell . . .

> A: This lady had nothing to do with this crime, any statements I made against her I lied about, and I did it on my own to protect my family.

I'm not exactly sure what date it was, but I believe it was 1989, when housed at Indian Springs correctional facility, I met Ernie Davino, a member of the Hole in the Wall Gang. Ernie and I lived on the same tier and we spoke several times. Ernie told me in no explicit terms when he finished his State sentence, he had to do another sentence in federal court of a crime he confessed to "that belonged to Tony Spilotro." Simply told to take the rap or die.

Weakland made his point well taken when he testified at Rosalie's trial that he lied about Rosalie's involvement in the Krause murder to protect his family. However, I do not believe anyone (except Spilotro) that knew what Weakland's thought process was or truly meant by that testimony, i.e., you take the rap for the Krause killing or your family dies, and I'll excuse the thousands of dollars you owe me, and better not say any more about Rosalie being involved with the murder of Hilda Krause or I'll deal with you in my own way. Capisce?

Another incident that I will point out is that in January 2019, Weakland's granddaughter visited me at my residence to let me know she loved her grandfather, Gerald Weakland, who was kind and protective to her. Shannon was very nice, and we had a pleasant conversation. While talking Shannon Mateo relayed to me, I believe, her father, Weakland's son, remembered many times that Weakland told his family words to this effect: "We have to move right now, no time to waste." This occurred even in the middle of the night. Why move instantly now? Simple! The Mob was looking for him and Weakland knew or sensed they were on his tail. When you owe money to the Mob and fail to pay, you and your family are in great danger. As Weakland stated in his 1982 Parole Progress Report you read earlier. This isn't a brain twister. The coercion and threats to Weakland and his family came from an obvious deadly loan shark who gave Weakland no choice to either murder Hila Krause or confess to it according to Weakland although Weakland's murder confession and testimony was beyond belief.

It makes sense, take the rap for the murder to protect your family, your Mob debt is cleared, Spilotro is protecting Marvin Krause and Rosalie Maxwell. Yet, Weakland's March 29, 1974, confession and subsequent testimonies were so fundamentally unreliable that nothing he said made sense or could be trusted. You be the judge of your own opinion, okay?

FRANKLY SPEAKING, PARDON ME

In 2019, I was no longer litigating my case in either state or Federal Court. Although both Courts denied the exculpatory and material issues I presented in both Courts, my conscience was clear not only that I personally knew, but also provided more than overwhelming evidence to prove I was totally innocent of the Hilda Krause murder/robbery. You know it is really easy to convict an innocent person and unfortunately once your convicted, it's almost impossible to get out of being incarcerated. Sad but true, wrongful convictions happen more times than you can believe. Purposeful or bad police investigations including but not limited to framing innocent persons. No question there are a lot of decent, honest, hardworking professional cops. On the other hand, like in my case, many cops have been known to fabricate evidence, lie and commit perjury on the stand (as they did with me) and are very good at it. They cut deals in return for untrue testimony, intimidate and threaten witnesses (Weakland's 1976-1977 trial testimony homicide detectives pressured him to incriminate both Rosalie and I), coerce confessions, false confessions, jailhouse lying snitches usually a cellmate, bad lawyering, biased judges. Judges should exclude confessions that are inconsistent with the physical evidence and obtained by questionable means. Yep! It's a mad, mad, mad world where some prosecutors have broken the criminal justice system by allowing or even encouraging flawed forensic testimony because it was molded to fit their theories of guilt.

What could be my next agenda? I'm on lifetime parole, report once a month to my assigned parole officer and provide them with my monthly report of not getting into trouble. My free time away from legal litigation was spent writing about the story of my life as only I could tell it. I have been employed at the Mob Museum (National Museum of Organized Crime and Law Enforcement) as a Guest Experienced Agent since April 2016. Oscar Goodman helped me obtain that position. Oscar is a class act, former mob Attorney with a good heart.

Don't recall the exact date, but while I was reporting to my parole officer, she informed me I was eligible to apply to the State of Nevada Board of Parole Commissioners an Application for Modification of Sentence NRS 176.033(2). This Application is designed for parolees currently being supervised by the Division of Parole and Probation for a sentence imposed by a Nevada Court. The Application allows a parolee who has served 10 or more years on parole to apply for a Modification of Parole if you were disciplinary free from violating any conditions of your parole. I had more than 14 years of being disciplinary free. To get off lifetime parole would be a blessing. Lucky me, I had a very nice female parole officer who sponsored me through this process. Parole officers carry a lot of weight to help a person get a possible reduction in their sentence. I talked to my special friend, Jonathan Kirshbaum, who helped me prepare this application. If my application is accepted, the Parole Board will forward it to the Chief of the Division of Parole and Probation requesting a recommendation. If I get a favorable recommendation from the Chief of the Division, a hearing will be scheduled by the Board in Compliance with NRS 213.130. If a Modification of Sentence is recommended by the Board, a petition will be sent to the Court of original jurisdiction where that Court will determine if my original sentence will be modified. Upon reading this statute, I was under the impression my application for Modification of Sentence would be decided by a State District Court Judge. I had nothing to lose and everything to gain to be actually free from my lifetime supervision.

PARDON ME

There are some dates in your life you never forget; July 1, 2019 is one of them. Working at my post (The Podium) that day my cell phone rang a few times which I ignored due to job policy. Later during my lunch break, I looked to see who called me. Two of the phone numbers I did not recognize who it was, however, one call was from Justice Michael Cherry whom I had personally known a long time. A great guy. I called the number back but was unable to get through. Recalled a couple of more times to no avail. Hmm! Maybe he left me a voicemail. I called my voicemail and received two messages that confused me and really threw me for a loop. NAW! I must be hearing the wrong thing I'm listening. One message is to call attorney Kristina Wildeveld's law office. I have very bad hearing and wear hearing aids, so I'm not sure if I'm hearing right when someone either talks to me or leaves a message. Okay, first off why should I call this attorney Kristina Wildeveld? I called and her office wanted to know when it could be possible for me to come to the office and set up a date for representation. Huh! Representation for what? I'm through doing legal work; makes no sense to me. Maybe I'm not hearing this right. The next message on my voicemail is from "Cia", who works for Justice Abbi Silver and left message to call her chambers. Wait a minute, what is going on? I needed to call my friend Jonathan Kirschbaum to let him help me to try and figure this out. He is an exceptional friend who has gone out of his way many times to help me adjust to this new world that is strange to me. I called and he said to come over to his office at the Federal Public Defenders Office. When I told Johnathan that Justice Michael Cherry called me; that attorney Kristina Wildeveld's law office called me about representation and that Justice Abbi Silver's office asked me to call her, Jonathan instantly told me, "you're going to the Pardons Board." What! No! Not more than a second that he told me this, my phone rang, and it was from Justice Abbi Silver's same person who had called me earlier. I hoped I spelled her name right. In my excitement I believe Cia told me to contact Kristina Wildeveld and that Justice Silver is placing me on the Pardon's Board. Hard for me to recall the exact words as I couldn't believe what had just happened to my life.

I called Kristina's law office; made an appointment to see her. I brought my wife Betty with me to help me with my hearing problem as Kristina soon found out. Upon meeting Kristina, it didn't take me long to sense this woman lawyer was a powerhouse. A force of shear strength with a great friendly smile and very attractive and elegant. I was very comfortable speaking with her. So was my wife. She told us that Justice Abbi Silver called her and asked a favor of her if she would represent me at the Pardons Board. She worked hard in preparing my Pardon Board package to be submitted to the members of the Board. I was on the schedule for November 6, 2019.

Wait a second here. I thought my application for modification of sentence was strictly to get myself off a lifetime parole/supervision. But this Pardon's Board issues was a whole new ball game. A new Nevada Law Assembly Bill #267, in part allowed a male or female who was out of custody and wrongfully convicted to seek a pardon on the grounds that he or she was actually innocent and also receive compensation. Justice Silver had given me a new lease on life by sponsoring me before the Pardons Board. An opportunity to present evidence before the Pardons Board.

FEDERAL YOUNG GUNS UNCOVER TYPE OF KILLER

THAT KILLED HILDA KRAUSE

Before you read what the Pardons Board decided, I'm going to take you back a few years, when to my delight, the 9th Circuit Court of Appeals issued an ORDER on November 16, 2016, appointing the Federal Public Defenders Office to represent me in my case in Federal Court. Yep! I had two "Young Guns" assigned to my case. JOHNATHAN M. KIRSHBAUM AND JEREMY BARON, and a very hard-working paralegal TAMMY SMITH. Without a doubt, God is watching out for and taking good care of me. All three of them became special friends in my life. And each one had a special gift of legal knowledge. My case was a monstrous task for them to undertake where they had 40 years of legal proceedings to digest, review, research and prepare spending I believe more than a thousand hours of getting my case ready to launch. They did a great job.

What they recognized and put together was something no other attorneys did in my 40 years battle with the State. What you are about to learn now as well as later is going to amaze you. I was blessed with young brilliant minds that had they been my trial attorneys, they would have totally shocked the Judge and jurors with their presentation. It would have led me to being acquitted of the Krause murder/robbery. Unfortunately, for me, this issue was never argued on my behalf in State Court.

Jonathan and Jeremy were well aware I was still litigating my DNA Petition in State Court before the Honorable Abbi Silver, had read some of her written decisions and determinations and they echoed what she had believed and ruled on my DNA case such as I recently stated.

DECISION AND ORDER GRANTING DNA TESTING

OCTOBER 25, 2011

"This Court echoes Justice Springer's concerns 'over an **absence** of physical evidence tying LaPena to the crime. The only evidence on record implicating LaPena is the testimony of Weakland', a notorious perjurer and murderer".

"…based on the facts of this case the Court believes, pursuant to NRS 176.0918, that a reasonable probability exists that the Defendant would **not** have been convicted if exculpatory results had been attained through a Genetic Marker Analysis. P.12, ll.7-10.

JANAURY 21, 2014 JUDGE ABBI SILVER'S OPINON OF

WEAKLAND'S TESTIMONY

"…It's clear as a bell that the physical evidence does not match what Weakland said, just doesn't, okay so something is awry here." P. 8, ll.10-13

Going through my court files they really studied Pathologist Dr. Clarke's autopsy examination and Court testimony of his determination as to what specific injuries caused Hilda Krause's death. This really piqued their interest. They went over and over and over Dr. Clarke's testimony and autopsy report until they were absolutely sure they solved what type of person it was who actually murdered Hilda Krause and it wasn't Weakland. In do so, they also centered their attention to LaMond Mills, 1989, trial cross-examination of Weakland, which you have already read and David Schiecks' October 17, 1995, examination of Gerald Weakland's testimony on not only how he claimed he murdered Hilda Krause but the manner in which he physically demonstrated the way he used the knife to murder Hilda Krause. Since I was present both times when Weakland demonstrated this, Jonathan and Jeremy asked me to show them Weakland's demonstration. That cemented it for them. They told me it was very difficult for them to believe none of my trial attorneys or Schieck did not see what they saw so easily. This evidence was sticking way out in the open. How could they have missed it!

You are finally going to read, what did they discover? The last clue of who the real killer is. Here is what they submitted before the 9th Circuit Court of Appeals and the Supreme Court of the United States, even though I had not raised this type of evidence in the manner it should have been done (in State Court) due to attorney negligence. United States Supreme Court refused to hear my case.

THE REAL KILLER OF HILDA KRAUSE

These two Young Guns were able to clearly see and decipher what Dr. James Clarke was actually saying based upon his expertise as a pathologist as to the precise cause of Hilda Krause's death results in her being repeatedly stabbed numerous times in the **deeper** portion on the "**Right-Side**" of her neck, and **Shallower** on the "**Left-Side**" of her neck. They were brought into my life for a reason. They became more than aware "as it was clear as a bell" that standing alone by Dr. Clarke's testimony, there was enough evidence for them to prove the real killer of Hilda Krause was "**LEFT-HANDED.**" Weakland is "**RIGHT-HANDED.**"

This only took 45 years for someone to figure it out and solve the type of person who was the real killer of Hilda Krause. I will echo the words of former Chief Justice Gunderson who spoke on my behalf at my 2003 pardons Board hearing. "After reviewing the case, 'I have become even more convinced than ever before that Frank LaPena should have never been charged'".

I'm going to give you a spin on basically what they wrote on this issue before the Supreme Court of the United States:

> *A conviction is unconstitutional if it is not supported by legally sufficient evidence…A state-court decision rejecting a sufficiency challenge may only be overturned on federal habeas review if the state decision was 'objectively' reasonable"*

> *This is one of the rare situations where a habeas petitioner can overcome the highly deferential legal insufficiency standard. No rational juror could conclude that Weakland actually committed the murder. It is simple. His account does not match up at all with the physical evidence. It boils down to one question: either believe the science or believe Weakland's story. Given this choice, there is only one rational conclusion: The science provides the truth of what happened and Weakland had no idea how Hilda Krause was actually murdered."*

> *Weakland's story of the murder is nothing like the coroner's account. Weakland denied strangling Hilda Krause or stabbing her in the neck; according to him, he only slit her throat. But it was the stabbing through the neck that would cause the most damage. There is only one rational way to explain this discrepancy. Weakland did not have first-hand knowledge of how Hilda Krause died."*

> *While Weakland said he slit Hilda Krause's throat, and while her throat was indeed slit, even this part of Weakland's testimony does not match up with the physical evidence. Weakland claimed he straddled Hilda from behind, lifter up her head, and cut her throat **from 'left to right'**. However, the coroner testified the **opposite was true.** He testified the 'neck wound extended roughly horizontally **'from right to left <u>across the neck'</u>**. The physical evidence showed why the coroner would say this. The cut was **much deeper** on the right side than on the **left**. Logically, the cut would be deeper on the side of the **initial incision.** Extra force would be necessary for the initial perforation of the skin. If the killer inflicted the cut from **left to right** (as Weakland testified), it would be physically difficult to make the cut deeper on the right side than on the left. Similarly, the **shallowness** of the cut on the left is more consistent with it being the terminus of the*

cut, rather than the location where the cut began.

*Put simply, Hilda's Throat was not cut in the manner Weakland described. It was cut in the opposite direction. This indicated the killer was left-handed or was standing in a different position than the one described by Weakland. At the very least, it showed that Weakland did not know **how** Hilda's throat was actually cut.*

Nothing that Weakland said about the murder was backed up by the physical evidence. To be sure. It is the responsibility of the jury not the court to decide what conclusions should be drawn from evidence admitted at trial. The science only pointed to one rational conclusion -Weakland did not know how Hilda was murdered. There was no blood on him. He could not be the killer.

*This is a bedeviling case. On the surface, it seems preposterous to suggest someone who was present at the crime scene and admitted to the murder was not actually the murderer. But something does not add up. It never has. There is a reason why this case has had so many twists and turns over its 40-year history. There is a blackhole at the center of it. It is not just   that Weakland is (as the Respondents have described) the 'iconic incredible witness.' **It is that he falsely confessed to a murder he did not commit.** It is maddening-we can never know why be sustained.*

In sum, the physical evidence can't be lying. Weakland can't be the killer. The evidence was legally insufficient to establish this element of first-degree murder. The Petition for a writ of certiorari should be granted.

(Emphasis added)

As you can see what my young guns Jonathan and Jeremy were able to ascertain just from reading pathologist Dr. James Clarke's testimony at both my jury trials was truly compelling evidence of actual innocence. What I found November 4, 2019, **two days before** my Pardons Board Hearing was **even more compelling evidence of actual innocence.** The Autopsy Examination Report, that you are going to read, **supported** everything Jonathan and Jeremy said, argued and submitted on my behalf in federal court.   It also proved overwhelmingly the State of Nevada framed me for the Krause Murder. I will include excerpts the Autopsy Examination Report and additional argument on this issue for your review of actual innocence.

ACTUAL INNOCENCE

There has been **two** Autopsy Reports submitted in this case. The **first** one to my knowledge was titled CERTIFICATE OF DEATH, where pathologist Dr. James Clarke medically determined at #(c) cause of death was from Homicidal traumatic injuries, "incised cutting and stab wound, neck", cited above which you already read. The **second** Autopsy Report by Pathologist James Clarke is titled in parts as POSTMORTEM EXAMINATION; EXTERNAL EXAMINATION; INTERNAL EXAMINATION; ORGANS; ORGANS OF NECK; SUMMARY AND COMMENT AND FINAL DIAGNOSIS, that are relevant and material to my herein other issues of Actual innocence.

Reverting back to what I previously cited when Weakland testified on May 9, 1989, he slit Hilda Krause's throat one time from "Left to Right". That testimony was highly relevant, material and right to the point exonerating me of the Hilda Krause murder and known by both the unethical prosecutors and cops I was being wrongfully prosecuted.

I already wrote what I thought of Counsel Mills failure to not see what both Jonathan and Jeremy easily saw that neither Harry Reid nor LaMond Mills "did not see." Yeah! Right and Mickey Mouse is a Cat!

At my DNA hearings, the DNA impeached Weakland's testimonies on how he claimed he murdered Hilda Krause. However, the DNA did not show, as this Autopsy Examination Report does, in more specific detail WHO the type of individual it was who actually murdered Hilda Krause.

Pathologist Doctor James Clarke's January 14, 1974, Postmortem Examination Report of Hilda Krause (APPENDIX 17), at Page 1, Paragraph 1, states:

> THERE IS A DEEP **INCISE** CUTTING AND STAB WOUND OF THE LOWER NECK EXENDING TRANSVERSELY **FROM** THE 'RIGHT' LATERAL NECK AREA **'AROUND'** TO THE **'LEFT'** LATERAL **'NECK AREA'**. THE **'DEEPEST AND LENGTHIEST'** PORTIONS OF THE **WOUND ARE UPON THE 'RIGHT'**. THE WOUND MEASURES 13 CM IN LENGTH. IT GAPES PARTICULARILY OVER THE **'RIGHT' NECK** AND MEASURES UP TO 2 CM IN WIDTH. ON **THE 'LEFT'** THE WOUND IS **'SHALLOW'** EXPOSING THE NECK MUSCLES AND EXGERNAL JUGLAR VEIN WHICH IS SEVERED.

ON THE **'RIGHT'**, **PARTICULARLY ON** THE **RIGHT** LATERAL PORTION, THE **WOUND BECOMES 'VERY DEEP'** AND IS ASSOCIAGTED WITH **ONE OR MORE** 'DEEP STAAB WOUNDS TO THE RIGHT' LATERAL **'NECK'** DESCRIBED MORE FULLY BELOW."

Pathologist Doctor Clarke's Examination Report at Page 2, Paragraph 3 states:

ORGANS OF THE NECK:..........IT IS MORE **'SUPERFICAL ON THE 'LEFT' AND IN THE 'MIDLINE'.** ON THE <u>RIGHT</u> THERE ARE ONE OR MORE STAB **WOUNDS** EXTENDING "**VERY DEEPLY"** INTO THE NECK.........THERE IS A COMPLETE SEVERANCE OF THE VERTEBRAL **ARTERY ON THE RIGHT.** The common carotid artery is lacerated, and the lumen is exposed to the surface but is **NOT COMPLETELY SEVERED."**

(Emphasis added)

Superficial just means that the cuts are **not deep enough to cut an "ARTERY"** and so, **"not life threatening".** They are cuts that make you feel pain **"but won't kill you".** Yahoo answers.

With respect to Doctor James Clarke's 1977 and 1989, Court testimonies and January 14, 1974, Autopsy Examination Report at Page 1, Paragraph 3, Page 2, Paragraph 8 of Hilda Krause, the conclusion makes clear that cause of death was due to the severed arteries on the **right side** of Hilda Krause's neck. On the **Left Side** the cut was **Superficial** to the **left** and **Midline** of her neck and **did not** sever her **arteries** being **shallow.**

Furthermore, this Autopsy Examination Report of January 14, 1974, reveals Hilda Krause was not murdered by right-handed Gerald Weakland, she was murdered by a Left-Handed killer, most likely the **Unknown Male Strangler** whose DNA was present all over the electrical cord found around Hilda's neck that was used to strangle her and Gerald Weakland's **DNA** was excluded as being on that electrical cord, during my Genetic Marker Petition before the Honorable Justice Abbi Silver.

You will be the judge and I hope you agree with me. Based on Gerald Weakland's

1989, trial testimony he cut Hilda Krause's throat one time from "left to right" with great force, then the "**DEEPEST** and **LENGTHIEST**" portions of the knife would have been **very deep** to the **left** of Hilda Krause's throat, and **Superficial** to the **right**.

Hilda Krause was not murdered by Gerald Weakland slicing her throat period. It never happened. Pathologist James Clarke's January 14, 1974 Autopsy Examination Report at Page 1, Paragraph 3, Page 2, Paragraph 8, totally and completely exonerates me of the Hilda Krause Murder.

PARDON ME ONCE MORE

On November 4, 2019**,** little did I know what God had in store for me. I believe he decided it was time for me to end this case once and for all by directing me to the one specific medical document that supported my theory for over 40 years that I never had anything to do with the Hilda Krause murder. I was in my "man-cave" looking for a newspaper article. My angel Cat, Sheba, was sitting on my lap helping me when I came upon an Autopsy Examination Report. I was stunned when I read it. It didn't take me a New York Minute to figure out who was the type of person who really murdered Hilda Krause. It was so Black and White you couldn't miss it.

Knowing this specific autopsy report was at one time in the possession of my trial attorneys, my disgust for them hit a new level of low and more so for Harmon and his nefarious gang of unethical bad cops who also had known about this particular autopsy report for over 40 years. Know what? Every time the news medica and prosecutors referred to me as the "mastermind" behind the Krause Murder, "My Blood Would Boil" knowing these POS knew I never had anything to do with the murder.

Emotionally trying to get my head on straight before the November 6, 2019 hearing, I had met with my friend Jonathan Kirshbaum who wanted to appear before the Board on my behalf. He wanted to make arrangements for the both of us to fly to Carson City, Nevada. For some time, I had not given him an answer about flying up there. Jonathan was unaware of my fear of flying. At one time it didn't bother me, but it did now. It was my wife Betty who eventually told Jonathan that. Well, they finally convinced me it was as short ride, and I could watch a movie on Jonathan's cell phone to distract my time in the air. What a great guy and friend Jonathan is. He made arrangements at a nice hotel, good room and terrific dinner along with my friend James Allen and his pastor.

I won't deny I had become somewhat nervous, even more so, when in 2003 I received clemency from the Pardon's Board reducing my life sentence. Why? It was a Pardon to restore my civil right. That's huge from my present position. All of this because of Justice Abbi Silver. She didn't have to do this, but she did. "Thank God for Abbi Silver".

As I sat in my seat listening to all the favorable testimony and statements being presented on my behalf as best, I could hear it due to my hearing loss, I'm thinking, "am I hearing right?" "Is this real?" 45 years of torture was now being exposed on my behalf. I started to get emotional and when asked to speak, I was almost at a loss for words, so my speech was short. Yes! It was a moment in my life I shall never forget.

During my November 6, 2019, Pardon's Board Hearing (APPENDIX 18), evidence was presented by Justice Abbi Silver that Gerald Weakland was a "Liar", when she stated in reference to me that the "DNA pretty much exculpated him, which is a 'whole new story,'" at Page 139, ll. 20-21…"All the DNA showed exactly the opposite of what Weakland testified to, especially how the killing went down", at Page 140, ll. 10-12…"There was a small amount of testimony by the coroner supporting that Weakland lied, but unfortunately for Mr. La Pena there was such ineffectiveness of counsel, which can be seen,…," at Page 140, ll. 17-21…"It's a tortured history, in 30 years, I've never seen a case like this, and that's why I put this on"… "the DNA basically contradicts everything that Weakland, who got a five year sentence who actually slit a woman's throat, said," at Page 142, ll. 1-7. Without a doubt, everything Justice Abbi Silver determined exculpated me. I hope you agree.

Also, Chief Justice Mark Gibbons, I believe in accordance with Justice Abbi Silver, went on record and stated: "I might say I was here. I think the only one on this Board that was here in 2003, I do remember this, and it was a 'compelling case for actual innocence' and fortunately, the right thing was done in the law. So, I appreciate Justice Silver everything she did as well on that". P. 164, ll. 1-7.

I believe Chief Justice Gibbon's reasoning for saying it was a compelling case of actual innocence came from hearing former Chief Justice Gunderson's testimony about how Chief Deputy District Attorney Addelair Guy told him about the three statements Weakland made as to who he claimed hired him to kill Hilda Krause, first naming Marvin Krause, her husband.

That I was not the "first" or "second" person Weakland told law enforcement authorities who hired him to kill Hilda Krause. I was the "third" person Weakland named which the cops immediately accepted, after refusing to charge the other two (suspects) for the contract murder.

Chief Justice Mark Gibbons for saying it was a compelling case for actual innocence may possibly have been based on his concern, "WHY"? were the other two persons not charged for the Hilda Krause murder? That based upon this evidence from Addelair Guy and Gunderson who possess impeccable credibility, I had no involvement with the Hilda Krause crime, and was actually innocent.

Yes, without a doubt at my Pardons Board Hearing Justice Abbi Silver was incredible in presenting her reason why she wanted to place me on the Pardons Board; Counsel Kristina Wildeveld was outstanding in her presentation before the Board and my friends Jonathan Kirschbaum was brilliant and James Allen short but powerful…and Chief Justice Mark Gibbons was amazing; I had a case of compelling actual innocence. On November 6, 2019, I was Pardoned on the grounds I was "actually innocent", but on a different issue than the "left-handed" killer, whom I believe the Board was not aware of since it was never brought to their attention by my trial attorneys.

As I'm sure you know life can be stranger than fiction. I don't believe Justice Abbi Silver knew when she placed me on the Pardons Board that she had any indication by doing so, she actually helped me find the one most important piece of medical document (January 14, 1974, Autopsy Examination Report) proving my innocence and that the State knew Weakland was not the real killer of Hilda Krause. Yes, God has blessed me with Angels in my life.

Alright now that we have established Hilda Krause was murdered by a "Left-Handed" killer, let's find out who may have ordered and killed Hilda Krause.

Two authors, William P. Roemer, Jr., and Dennis Griffin each wrote a book on the life of Anthony Tony "The Ant" Spilotro about how powerful and deadly Tony Spilotro was. You may find it quite interesting how this connects to my life story relating to the Hilda Krause murder. You read the first part of my doing a favor for Spilotro while in the County Jail. This one is my take on who may have been the real killer. Each book piqued my interest.

I have always maintained this was a **"Who Done It"** case at the top level because of the overwhelming evidence proved Weakland did not murder Hilda Krause.

You already read about Charlie the Knife when Avants testified at my 1974 preliminary hearing regarding his questioning of Rosalie Maxwell cited in Quite a Harry Situation. Here is my take on Spilotro, Charlie the Knife and Marvin Krause.

Although Marvin Krause was backed by Spilotro who, according to Greg Williams, was most likely instructed to protect Marvin Krause not only to be charged for the Hilda Krause murder, but also, (in my opinion) the skim money from the slot machines at Caesars Palace for the Chicago Outfit… It's well known that the other side of Mob Law, "You don't steal money from them" especially from Spilotro. I'm going to throw out some unanswered questions for you to review and make your own judgment.

Did Marvin Krause hire Charlie the Knife to murder Hilda Krause or did Spilotro decide to teach Marvin Krause a lesson by hiring an outside hit man to kill Hilda Krause, as a message to Marvin Krause, for stealing mob money by gambling it away?

These are viable theories- here's why:

- Marvin Krause was a compulsive gambler who asked his wife not to leave him as he had gambled away all his own money.

- Applying plain common sense, it's easy to figure out Marvin Krause more than likely gambled away MOB MONEY:

- You steal from the Mob either you or your family dies.

- Case in Point: On December 3, 1958, BESS and GUS GREENBAUM both had their "throats slashed". Greenbaum managed numerous Las Vegas Casinos until the "Mob" caught him skimming money to finance his drug habit and it was the Chicago Outfit who discovered Greenbaum's embezzlement. This Mob hit was never solved.

- Rosalie Maxwell testified at my 1995 evidentiary hearing before the Honorable Gene Porter, Marvin Krause was a "heavy gambler".

- Was Hilda Krause murdered by the Mob sending a message to Marvin Krause once you get your estate money (Hilda's) you're to pay back with interest what you get from her estate to us. Remember her throat was slashed.

In the book, THE ENFORCER, Spilotro, The Chicago Mob's Man over Las Vegas, by William F. Roemer, Jr. Roemer categorizes Spilotro power. He had a nice home, everything money could buy. He was coveted by dozens of show girls in the Sin Capital. With the snap of his fingers, he could have the car of his associate 'blown up'. "the throats of anybody who got in his way slashed". Just like Hilda Krause's throat was slashed. Interesting question don't you think?

See, Dennis Griffin's, *The Battle for Las Vegas*, at P.52. According to Griffin's take on Tony Spilotro, "It wasn't wise to think you could simply ignore Tony and go about your business without his finding out about it. He knew everything that went on within the criminal element. "No one did anything from contract killings" to burglaries, robberies, fencing stolen property or loansharking, 'without his approval'…and the sanctions for violating Tony's procedures could be much more severe than those imposed by a governmental licensing agency."

Therefore, as the most prominent street level criminal in Las Vegas, it is hard to believe Tony Spilotro would allow anyone to conduct a flagrant "contract murder" and robbery especially involving a high-ranking Casino executive "Without His Knowledge" and "approval." Whoever planned and murdered Caesars Palace Casino executive Hilda Krause would have needed Tony Spilotro's approval because he knew everything that went on within the Las Vegas criminal element.

This according to Dennis Griffin would clearly indicate Tony Spilotro **"knew"** the **"real killer"** of Hilda Krause (and it wasn't Weakland). Therefore, according to Griffin whoever murdered Hilda Krause would have needed Tony Spilotro's "approval". And, with Spilotro's approval then "**It was a Mob Hit**".

CHARLIE THE KNIFE

Why was Marvin Krause sitting in the Caesar's Palace coffee shop with a known hit man just "three months prior" to his wife's murder?

Why were the Detectives investigating Marvin Krause to begin with **before** his wife's murder?

You have a Mob hit man whose specialty is using a knife on his victims and you recall as you earlier read Hilda Krause was murdered by a knife. No doubt in my mind and possibly yours, Avants knew a lot more about Charlie the Knife and Marvin Krause socializing with each other than he let anybody know about.

Was Charlie the Knife the "Unknown Male Strangler" who also stabbed Hilda Krause numerous times in her neck from **right** to **left** and was Charlie the Knife "Left-Handed"? I don't know but it's an interesting theory. What do you think?

So, the question here is, did Marvin Krause hire Charlie the Knife to kill his wife so he could obtain all of her money or did Spilotro hire Charlie the Knife to murder Hilda Krause so Marvin Krause could pay back the skim mob money he lost? More unanswered questions.

Two people connected to the murder of Hilda Krause know who the real killer of Hilda Krause is, Mel Harmon and Tony Spilotro.

There is one thing I know and so do you now, prosecutor Mel Harmon has always known the identity of the Second Assailant; Unknown Male Strangler and left-handed killer who existed and physically participated in the murder of Hilda Krause and Tony Spilotro also knows the identity of the real killer of Hilda Krause as whoever murdered Hilda Krause would have needed Tony Spilotro's approval.

What I had in my hands, ladies and gentlemen, I had looked for, for over forty years. I've had many legal issues over the years that in my opinion showed very strong evidence of actual innocence that went before some judges and justices who exercised a deaf ear. To me, this is the granddaddy of all issues of innocence.

The DNA impeached Weakland's testimony on HOW he claimed he murdered Hilda Krause, but this document tells you WHO murdered Hilda Krause.

This document contains and supports the rankest form of governmental corruption by the State of Nevada of over 45 years. The worst to ever occur in the entire history of the State of Nevada. For 45 years, I've been in a battle of Good vs. Evil, Evil being the State of Nevada.

When I think back 45 years ago to every year, month, week, day, hour, minute and second, that I unlawfully spent in a jail, prison, every time I was on display in a courtroom, listening to these criminals with badges trying to murder me in any way that they could, my blood would just boil. The loss of my freedom, liberty, job, home, family, friends, my innocent pets, the nightmares do not stop. You can leave the prison, but the prison doesn't leave you. They stole my life from me but couldn't steal my heart or my character.

Like my book states this is the "Biggest Mob Murder Cover-Up by the State of Nevada in its History."

Like Weakland, a psychopath with an antisocial personality disorder, I believe Mel Harmon and his nefarious Keystone Cops are of the same cloth. Maybe one day they can all hold hands together in hell with their shiny pitchforks but being a nice guy up above I would probably send down some ice water for them.

For 45 years of fighting a corrupt legal system finally came to a halt when the 2019, Pardons Board members recognized the injustice that I had endured for all those years and Pardoned me on the grounds I was innocent. A great day for justice.

In conclusion, after being arrested on April 23, 1974, on June 30, 2021, during a court hearing before District Court Judge Gloria Sturman, I was granted a "Certificate of Innocence," along with a verbal apology from the state of Nevada for my wrongful conviction.

Do you think the Clark County District Attorney's Office, Prosecutor Harmon, and the cops who framed me would ever apologize to me for the crimes they committed against me? Seriously? Really? Yeah! Right! And Donald Duck is a horse. Forgetaboutit!

MY FINAL VERDICT

"NOT GUILTY"

CHOW!

ARTIST: RICHARD HINGER

. . . standing over her lifeless body, ligature and bloody knife in hand, the killer is pleased with his work, and hopes the Mob will be as well! This picture is a big clue to who the real killer is. What do you see?

FRANK'S PHOTO ALBUM

FRANK HOLDING DOG-BJ WITH HIS MOTHER, SISTER, & NEPHEW-SCOTT

Young Frank

Frank with his sister-Candy,
& nephew-Scott

My beautiful mother, Katherine.

Bookie Joint where I grew up, and where the cops would hang out, making bets.

Frank's nephew, Scott. He was a Navy Seal Special Forces Black Ops on leave visiting me on my 50th Birthday. He's a real war hero!!

FOOTBALL-AUGIE LIO SPORTS WRITER TOOK PICTURES OF FRANK.
ON HOME TURF, FRANK COULD PUNT A FOOTBALL 60 YARDS IN THE AIR.
HE PLAYED ON VARSITY AS A FRESHMAN.
HE COULD KICK THE FOOTBALL FURTHER THAN MOST NFL PUNTERS.

Painting of
Rosalie Maxwell

Wayne Newton visiting
Frank on his 50th Birthday

MY GORGEOUS WIFE BETTY

My best friend Tommy & I

Tommy-my best friend, Betty-my wife, and Annie-Tommy's wife.

JUNE 30, 2021,

The court hearing before District Court Judge Gloria Sturman, where Frank was granted a "Certificate of Innocence," and a verbal apology from the state of Nevada for his wrongful conviction.

PICTURED FROM LEFT TO RIGHT
JONATHAN ULLMAN (PRESIDENT & CEO OF THE MOB
MUSEUM), FRANK, BETTY, CASSONDRA,
& MICHAEL DIVICINO.

MICHAEL DIVICINO & FRANK

PICTURED FROM LEFT TO RIGHT
CASSONDRA, FRANK, BETTY, & MICHAEL DIVICINO.

MY ANGELS

FRECKLES   STAR   SOLOMAN

SHEBA   TROOPER & SAMSON   HOPE

JONATHAN KIRSHBAUM, FRANK, & KRISTINA WILDEVELD

KRISTINA WILDEVELD (FRONT LEFT), CASSONDRA (MIDDLE
LEFT), BETTY (BACK LEFT), HUNTER (BACK RIGHT), FRANK
(MIDDLE RIGHT), LISA RASMUSSEN (FRONT RIGHT)

FRANK

&

OSCAR GOODMAN

PICTURED FROM LEFT TO RIGHT

HARRISON NORD, FRANK, OSCAR GOODMAN,
CASSONDRA KEVEN, & HUNTER PEARCE

ASK THE JUDGE!
Nevada Supreme Court Justice Abbi Silver

By: Sarah Morninger

MYVEGAS Magazine had the chance to speak with Supreme Court Justice Abbi Silver. Judge Silver is the only judge in the history of Nevada to have presided at EVERY level of Nevada's court system and we asked her these 6 questions:

Q The Nevada Supreme Court is now, and for the first time, a female majority. How has the legal profession changed over the last 30 years with females in the profession?

A When I first started as a young attorney in 1989, I was one of only five female prosecutors at the Clark County District Attorney's Office. When I walked into the courtroom back then, the opposing male attorneys would ask me if I was the court reporter. They couldn't believe it when I told them that I was the prosecutor assigned to the criminal case. Their underestimating me as an opponent was my greatest weapon. Thankfully, women are treated much better today in our profession. I really enjoy my male colleagues on the bench—who treat me with dignity and respect. As females within the profession of law, we have truly come a long way.

Q What initially inspired you to pursue law?

A I was very inspired by Susan Dey from LA LAW. She was the epitome of a polished, passionate female trial attorney. Actually, I wanted to become a lawyer from the time I started high school. I couldn't stand to look at blood, so becoming a doctor like my father was not in the cards for me. However, getting paid to talk seemed like a dream come true for a teenaged chatter-box like me.

Q Being a well-seasoned judicial leader with over 30 years of experience, did you have a mentor throughout your rise in the legal ranks?

A Yes, I met Judge Nancy Oesterle (when she was a prosecutor) during the time that I was an undergraduate student at UNLV. I was fascinated when she spoke to our class. After returning from law school years

later, I became a prosecutor with her at the Clark County District Attorney's Office and she helped me every step of the way. She even helped me write my first closing argument in a rape case.

Q What does a typical day in your chambers look like?

A It would probably seem very boring to most people. After getting a cup of coffee, I read and write at my desk or my standing desk for a good eight hours. But, I really enjoy reading. After years of sitting on the bench inside of the courtroom and watching attorneys pick a jury or fight with one another, I am perfectly happy just reading by myself in my quiet chambers.

Q As a Nevada Supreme Court Justice, how do you make changes or get involved with the community?

A I am involved with the National Charity League, so I volunteer with teens at various non-profit organizations like Opportunity Village, the Salvation Army, Make-A-Wish and many others. And, being a member of the Nevada Supreme Court with my fellow colleagues allows me to shape Nevada's jurisprudence. I really enjoy that part of my job the best.

Q What advice would you give to someone aspiring to be a judicial leader or attorney?

A Never listen to the haters. If I listened to those individuals who put me down or gossiped about me based on my appearance or because of my gender, I wouldn't be where I am today. Believe in yourself and never let go of your dreams. You can do anything you set your mind to.

Supreme Court Of Nevada
408 E Clark Ave, Las Vegas, NV 1 702.486.9300
nvcourts.gov/supreme

Evidence
and
Files
Obtained

ROBBERY/HOMICIDE INVESTIGATION
....
Subject

Division Reporting......DETECTIVE................................ Division of Occurrence......DETECTIVE..............

Date and Time Occurred......JANUARY 14, 1974............... Location of Occurrence......COUNTRY CLUB ESTATES
LAS VEGAS, NEVADA

DETAILS:

VICTIM:	HILDA STOUT KRAUSE	
SUSPECT:	JERRY WEAKLAND	
	ID# 144537	

DETAILS:

On Monday, February 25, 1974 Detectives LYONS and LEE proceeded to
the I.D. Lab garage in order to physically check GAIL WEAKLAND's
1973 Chevrolet Monte Carlo bearing Nevada license CK3254. It
should be noted that this vehicle was impounded by Detective LYONS
and LEE on Thursday, February 21, 1974. The interior of the vehicle
was not examined at that time, due to the fact that I.D. Lab personnel
did not have an opportunity to examine it for possible physical
evidence; however, at that time, two rips were observed on the head-
liner of the rear seat, passenger's side.

Upon arrival at the I.D. garage on February 25, 1974, DETECTIVES
LYONS and LEE, with the use of a tape measure, physically measured
the distance between the previously described tears in the head-
liner. These measurements were as follows: 20 3/4 inches apart.
Also observed at this time, that this vehicle had four UNI-ROYAL
steel belted tires and one in the trunk.

Detectives LYONS and LEE then proceeded back to the victim's residence
2995 Pinehurst, Country Club Estates, and re-interviewed MARVIN KRAUSE.
Mr. KRAUSE permitted these detectives to re-enter the premises
and they proceeded to the guest bedroom, located on the second
floor. It should be noted that a Zenith color portable television
set, identical to the one taken the morning of the Robbery/Murder
was permanently mounted in the wall. Measurements were taken of the
case of this television set and the measurements indicated that the
cabinet measurements from left front corner to the right front
corner were exactly 20 3/4 inches.

Date and Time of This Report......3/13/74.................. Officer......R. LYONS............... Serial......P59..........

Approved... Officer......C. LEE.................. Serial......P489..........

B. AVANTS   P33

SIGNATURE..

20.38

It should be noted that these measurements were taken from the top
of the television set. Another measurement was made on the front
of the television set from the top of the case to the bottom of
the case. This measurement was fifteen and one-quarter inches
(15 1/4"). It should be noted that the measurements taken by Detectives
LYONS and LEE of the tears in the head-liner of the Monte Carlo
that was impounded and the measurements of the television set remaining
at the KRAUSE residence were identical. The distance between the
tear marks in the head-liner of the Monte Carlo was twenty and three-
quarters inches (20 3/4 ") and the measurements between the front
of the Zenith portable television set from left to right, was also
twenty and three-quarters (20 3/4) inches.

While at the KRAUSE residence, MARVIN KRAUSE informed Detectives
LYONS and LEE that he had some additional information to give them.
That the one hundred thousand dollar ($100,000.00) bond that had
been missing, he had located in the Valley Bank, down town branch
Las Vegas, Nevada. He states that he found out where the bond was as
result of a dividend payment he had received. Mr. KRAUSE further
stated that yesterday, he realized that three other items had been
taken at the time of the robbery and when his wife was murdered. He
states that these three items are all men's wrist watches. He states
that these three wrist watches were on his night stand in the master
bedroom. He specifically described these watches as follows:
All three watches are square in design. On the face of each one of
the watches are four markings; these markings being at the locations
where the numbers 3, 6, 9 and 12 would normally be. There was no
normal lettering on the face of the watches. All three watches are
yellow metal. The approximate value per watch is thirty dollars ,
($30.00). The description of the watches, as follows:

1. Brown checkered gold band with buckle.

2. Gray plaid cloth band with buckle.

3. Blue and white pin-stripe cloth band with buckle.

MARVIN KRAUSE stated that one to two months prior to the robbery,
his cousin's son-in-law, TILDEN BENNETT, who lives in the suburbs
of Pittsburgh Pennsylvania had sent him the watches. Mr. KRAUSE
further informed Detectives LYONS and LEE that he would attempt to
ascertain TILDEN BENNETT's telephone number and address and would
contact us when he has it in order that the police could obtain
a further description of the watches, possibly a picture of them
and learn the origin of the watches.

According to information previously received from the suspect's
wife, GAIL WEAKLAND, was that JERRY WEAKLAND had access to the 1973
Monte Carlo and had, in fact, used this vehicle the night of January
13, 1974 and the early morning hours of January 14, 1974.

On March 6, 1974 Detective LYONS submitted an Affidavit in order to obtain a Search Warrant in front of District Court Judge WILLIAM COMPTON. This Affidavit outlined the results and probable cause to search records of the Central Telephone Company in reference to certain accounts and telephone numbers as follows:

1. GORDON WEAKLAND -- telephone number 452-1417.

2. LEO WEAKLAND -- telephone number 457-0783.

3. GAIL BOSTWICK, aka GAIL WEAKLAND -- telephone number 734-6975.

4. Telephone number 452-6962 -- believed to be the telephone number of FRANK LAPENA.

As result of this Affidavit- a Search Warrant was obtained on March 6, 1974 and signed by District Court Judge WILLIAM COMPTON.

Detective LYONS executed the Search Warrant on March 7, 1974 and directed it to NEIL BELLER, legal council for Central Telephone Company, located at 601 E. Fremont St. Las Vegas, Nevada. As a result of the execution of the Search Warrant, the following information was obtained from the telephone company.

That on January 10, 1974 a telephone call was placed from telephone number 452-6962 to Lake Havasu City, Arizona, AC 602, phone number 855-3021 at 1424 hours. The number 452-6962 telephone number is in the name of FRANK LAPENA. The telephone number 855-3021 is in the name of the Ramada Inn, Lake Havasu City, Arizona.

On January 11, 1974 a long distance telephone call was placed from telephone number 734-6975, this telephone number is in the name of GAIL WEAKLAND, Las Vegas, to Lake Havasu City, Arizona AC602, telephone number 855-4721 at 1606 hours. This telephone number, 855-4721 is in the name of SUSAN WAYMIRE of 3423 ElToro Drive, Lake Havasu City, Arizona.

That on January 14, 1974 a long distance call was placed from telephone number 452-6962, this number being in the name of FRANK LAPENA of Las Vegas Nevada to Lake Havasu City, Arizona AC 602, telephone number 855-4721 at 1608 hours. Telephone number 855-4721 being registered to SUSAN WAYMIRE.

That on January 18, 1974, a long distance telephone call was placed from telephone number 452-6962 Las Vegas Nevada to Lake Havasu City Arizona, AC 602, telephone number 855-4721 at 2126 hours. This number, 855-4721 is registered to previously mentioned SUSAN WAYMIRE.

Records were also obtained of GORDON WEAKLAND, telephone number
452-1417 and also records of LEO WEAKLAND, telephone number of
457-0783.

The return on the Search Warrant was made and signed with Justice
Court on March 12, 1974.

On February 27, 1974, Wednesday at 11:00 AM, Lt. B. AVANTS and
Detective C. LEE proceeded to 136 Greenbriar, the home of ROSALIE
MAXWELL. At this time ROSALIE was interviewed and in substance,
related the following: That same afternoon at 4:00 PM, she had an
appointment with OSCAR GOODMAN. She, at that time was going to
drop the one million dollar ($1,000,000.00) law suit she had filed
against SHERIFF RALPH LAMB. She states that when she and FRANK
LAPENA had first met OSCAR GOODMAN in his law office in regards to
the loss of her work card, GOODMAN informed her and FRANK LAPENA,
" I can get you off even if you committed the murder, as long as you
didn't pay for it, or hire to have it done with a check." She
further related that FRANK LAPENA is going through with his law
suit. LAPENA had advised her in confidence that he had missed making
one thousand dollars ($1,000.00) in the past week, pimping at the
Hacienda Hotel, because he was afraid that all the tricks that had
approached him were policemen trying to hit him up.

On March 6, 1974, Wednesday, Lt. AVANTS, Detective R. IRVING and
Detective C. LEE interviewed LOIS WEAKLAND aka SAM, the wife of LEO
WEAKLAND at her residence, 2600 Howard Drive, telephone number 457-0783.
In substance, LOIS WEAKLAND related the following:

Approximately one month prior to that date, her husband LEO had
found a gold colored watch on the dog's blankets, located outside
their residence at 2600 Howard Drive. LEO had told her that apparently
their dog, "BRANDY", had drug the watch out of a hole and subsequently
carried it to his blankets. LEO brought the man's gold watch into
the house and showed it to his wife, LOIS. She states that the next
thing she remembered about the watch is that LEO gave it to JERRY
WEAKLAND and told him he didn't want it around the house.

Further questioning of LOIS, concerning the identity and description
of the watch, revealed that she described the watch as square in
shape and having rows of diamonds on the front of it, that it was
gold and the band had markings. She was then shown a photograph
of four watches by Detective IRVING and Detective LEE. She, at that
time, positively identified a BAUME and MERCIER men's wrist watch,
square in design, containing two rows of diamonds, as being identical
to the watch that her husband, LEO, stated he found on the dog's
blanket. During this period of time, she had an occasion one evening
to over-hear JERRY talking to his brothers in the kitchen area of
their home. JERRY stated, "she was alive when I left.".

At the conclusion of this interview, LOIS stated that she would
contact Detective IRVING if she was able to obtain any more information
from her husband LEO pursuant to the watch. She also stated that
she would attempt to talk to JERRY and see if he would tell her
anything about the crime.

On March 6, 1974 at 1430 hours, Detective C. LEE and R. LYONS
interviewed DOVIE WEAKLAND, the former wife of JOHN WEAKLAND, JERRY's
brother. She could add nothing as far as information pertaining
to this case. She did state that all of the WEAKLAND brothers have
a tendancy for violance and that her ex-husband, JOHN, was, in her
opinion, a confirmed alcoholic.

In view of the information received from the telephone company by
Detective R. LYONS, Detectives LYONS and LEE proceeded back to Lake
Havasu City, Arizona on Thursday, March 7, 1974. These officers
arrived at Lake Havasu City, Arizona at approximately 2:00 PM same
date, at which time they conferred with Detective B. SCOTT and
Corporal DOUG STEELE of the Mohave County Sheriff's Office.

On March 7, 1974 at 3:00 PM we proceeded to the Justice of the Peace
Office, where we contacted Justice of the Peace EVERETT E. MILAK;
wherein Detective SCOTT obtained a Search Warrant for the home of
RICHARD and SUSAN WAYMIRE, located at 3423 EL Toro Drive, Lake Havasu
City, Arizona; wherein at 8:30 AM on March 8, 1974, these Detectives
LYONS and LEE along with Detective SCOTT and Corporal STEELE served
the Search Warrant on RICHARD and SUSAN WAYMIRE and searched the
premises for the items listed on the search warrant that had been
taken during the Robbery/Homicide on January 14, 1974; however,
none of the items were found.

Following the search of the WAYMIRE's residence, RICHARD WAYMIRE was
subsequently transported to Mohave County Sheriff's sub-station by
Detective SCOTT and Corporal STEELE. Once at the sub-station, WAYMIRE
was interviewed by Detective LYONS and LEE and Detective SCOTT.
It should be noted that this interview was recorded on a cassette
tape, which is in the process of being repaired and transcribed.
In substance, RICHARD WAYMIRE related the following:

During December 1973 he first became suspicious of his wife, SUSAN
being involved in a love afair. He states that he couldn't put his
finger on any one thing, but it was a matter of a lot of little
things adding up. In view of the fact that he thought his wife
was involved in a love afair, he got a hold of an electronics expert
and placed a recording device inside his air conditioning vent in
his home, which would enable him to record conversations in the
livingroom as well as his bedrooms during his absence. He stated
that he had heard numerous conversations and at one point, heard

his wife SUSAN say, "I love you". He didn't know whether this was
directed to a male or one of the dogs. He also ran into difficulty
every time the heat and cooling system would go off from the
thermostat, as it would blot out the recordings.

In view of the circumstances, as mentioned previously, he told his
wife that he wanted her to take a polygraph examination. During
the latter part of December, he drove his wife to Las Vegas Nevada
and had WALTER SHAY, an employee of CAREX Security run his wife
on a Polygraph. during this trip, while having dinner with a
friend by the name of LOU CARDINAL, in a restaurant, on which he
described as being off Paradise Road, south of Desert Inn, he met
JERRY WEAKLAND. It should be noted that WAYMIRE identified JERRY
WEAKLAND from a Clark County Sheriff's Office report I.D. photograph
#144537.

CARDINAL advised WAYMIRE could do detective work for him. WAYMIRE
was interested in having WEAKLAND come up to Lake Havasu City Arizona
and follow his wife in the hopes of seeing her with her lover. He
decided on this course of action because after the first Polygraph
Examination of his wife, he was told by the examiner, "there is
something there.".

Sometime during the middle part of January 1974 he received a telephone
call from JERRY WEAKLAND at his residence in Lake Havasu City
Arizona. He states that he went to the Zodiak Bar and met JERRY
WEAKLAND, who was with an attractive blonde at that time. They
held a short conversation; at which time WEAKLAND asked him for some
money. WAYMIRE states that he slipped WEAKLAND fifty dollars ($50.00).
He further stated that he is kind of embarrased to talk about the
money he gave WEAKLAND because that is the last time he ever talked
to him or saw him. WEAKLAND was supposed to contact him the following
day and didn't. It should be noted that WAYMIRE transported his
wife, SUSAN, back to Las Vegas on two other occasions during January
at which time she was also given two more Polygraph Examinations.

It appeared to Detective LYONS and LEE that subject WAYMIRE is
obsessed with the idea that his wife is having sex relations with
another man or men. It is the opinion of Detectives LYONS and LEE that
subject WAYMIRE is not involved, nor did WEAKLAND approach him in
regards to selling him a television, ring or watch. For full details
refer to the transcription of the cassette recording, recorded under
DR# 74-1881.

On Tuesday, March 12, 1974, BILL UNDERWOOD came to the Homicide
Headquarters; at which time he was interviewed by Lt. AVANTS and
Detective C. LEE. UNDERWOOD in substance related the following:
Several days prior to this interview FRANK LAPENA had informed him
that he was going to beat Lt. AVANTS up. He also related that JERRY
WEAKLAND, who worked for him as a pool attendant, on the date of
the homicide, did not show up for work for three days at the time of

the murder. When he finally did come back to work, WEAKLAND informed
him that he had been in Arizona on business.

BILL UNDERWOOD also advised that a day or so after we had questioned
JERRY WEAKLAND and ROBERT WEBB, that he was at the shopping center
near Paradise and Flamingo and he saw WEBB pulling up behind him.
They stopped in a parking lot and WEBB asked, "what do you know is
going on about the murder, if you will tell me what you know, then
I will tell you what I know." UNDERWOOD said that he answered to
WEBB that he didn't know anything about the murder what so ever and
didn't have anything to say; however UNDERWOOD said that he had a
feeling from this and from other things that were happening, that
WEBB was connected to the murder. One thing being that WEBB and
BOUTWILL were very close, but after the murder went down, and even
before we had questioned the suspects, that they kept themselves
separated. JERRY WEAKLAND, after he had been questioned by this
department and after returning to work, told BILL UNDERWOOD that
he told those "big bastards (referring to WEBB and BOUTWILL) to
stay away from me,"meaning that it would be trouble if they were
seen together.

On January 4, 1974, Detective LEE received a telephone call from
JERRY WEAKLAND. WEAKLAND related at that time that he wanted to
make a deal. On this date, at 4:00 PM, Detective LYONS and LEE
met with JERRY WEAKLAND at the home of his brother GORDON WEAKLAND
of 4404 E. Stewart. WEAKLAND spoke to Detective LYONS and LEE
inside the squad car parked at this location and at Hadland Park.
WEAKLAND made certain inquiries as to whether his former wife, GAIL,
was actually in the hospital and if she was, what was her condition.
He was also very inquisitive as to the whereabouts of GAIL's
daughter ANGIE. He states that he received information from his
source, that ANGIE was in Child Haven and that GAIL was in Southern
Nevada Memorial Hospital. He also states that his source informed
him that his finger prints and hair fibers did not match up to
anything at the crime scene. WEAKLAND at this point, stated that
his only concern, at this time, was ANGIE's well-being and that if
it would help her he would gladly accompany us down town and confess
to the murder and robbery; but would not name anyone else involved.

Detective LYONS and LEE informed WEAKLAND at this time that they
were not in any position to make deals, that a representative from
the District Attorney's Office would have to examine the information
and make a decision. WEAKLAND was further informed that in the
Detective's opinion, there would be no deal unless he named the co-
conspirators in the crime.

However, WEAKLAND was told by these detectives that we would take
a confession if he wished to give one. He stated that he wanted
to think it over, over night. He was then returned to his brother's
residence.

WEAKLAND was contacted the following day on the telephone; at which
time he stated he hadn't made up his mind, yet, but would let
Detectives LYONS and LEE know once he made a decision.

As of this date, March 13, 1974, he has not contacted the Homicide
Detail.

Investigation to be continued...

RL:CL:BA:bb

DETECTIVE R. LYONS
DETECTIVE C. LEE
DETECTIVE LT. B. AVANTS

Case No. __CV92-314-WMB(B)__   Date __May 7, 1992__

Title __James Allen Hydrick -vs- James Gomez, Director, et al__

DOCKET ENTRY

PRESENT:

HON. __Volney V. Brown, Jr. U.S. Magistrate__ JUDGE

__Ysela Benavides__   __N/A__
         Deputy Clerk   Court Reporter

ATTORNEYS PRESENT FOR PLAINTIFFS: **ATTORNEYS PRESENT FOR DEFENDANTS:**

N/A   N/A

PROCEEDINGS: (IN CHAMBERS)

This Order responds to several recent filings of the parties.

On March 26, 1992, the Clerk lodged a letter from petitioner, a copy of which had been served on respondent's counsel, noting that he had been stabbed while in custody, that he would later seek an extension of time within which to file a Traverse, and that he might be transferred to another prison. This document, being merely advisory, requires to ruling by the court.

On April 8, 1992, petitioner filed Notice of Failure of Respondents to serve Return and to Show Cause, seeking judgment on the pleadings, effectively default judgment. This motion is denied because, by Order filed February 21, 1992, respondent was given to and including March 25, 1992 in which to file his Return. The Return was filed on the latter date.

On April 22, 1992, the Clerk lodged an impertinent letter from the Nevada Attorney General, advising that the Nevada Department of Prisons reserves the right to disobey a federal court order. The author of this letter, Nevada Deputy Attorney General J. Marty Howard should read Article VI, Clause 2 of the Constitution of the United States, before his ignorance of its provisions gets him into serious trouble. He should read, also, Spain v. Mountanos, 690 F.2d 742 (9th Cir. 1982). Petitioner having nominated another jailhouse lawyer to assist him, Frank LaPenia is hereby ordered to serve in that capacity.

(CONTINUED ON PAGE TWO)

Initials of Deputy Clerk ___yb___

MINUTES FORM 11
CIVIL—GEN   D — M

EXHIBIT "B"

CIVIL MINUTES — GENERAL

Case No. __CV92-314-WMB(B)__   Date __May 7, 1992__

Title _____James Allen Hydrick -vs- James Gomez, Dorector, et al_____

DOCKET ENTRY

(PAGE TWO)

PRESENT:

    HON. __Volney V. Brown, Jr., U.S. Magistrate__ JUDGE

    __Ysela Benavides__   __N/A__
         Deputy Clerk   Court Reporter

ATTORNEYS PRESENT FOR PLAINTIFFS: ATTORNEYS PRESENT FOR DEFENDANTS:

    N/A   N/A

PROCEEDINGS: (PAGE TWO)

    Finally, on April 27, 1992, the Clerk lodged the request of petitioner
for an extension of time within which to file his Traverse. Good cause
having been shown, IT IS ORDERED that the Traverse shall be timely if
received by the Clerk for filing on or before June 5, 1992.

    cc: James Allen Hydrick
        Attorney General
        Micro

Initials of Deputy Clerk __yb__

MINUTES FORM 11
CIVIL—GEN   D — M

IN THE SUPREME COURT OF THE STATE OF NEVADA

FRANK RALPH LAPENA,

        Appellant,

        vs.

THE STATE OF NEVADA,

        Respondent.

No. 23839

FILED

NOV 24 1993

JANETTE M. BLOOM

BY _____

<u>ORDER OF REMAND</u>

This is a proper person appeal from an order of the district court denying appellant's petition for post-conviction relief.

On July 14, 1989, the district court convicted appellant, pursuant to a jury verdict, of one count of murder in the first degree and one count of robbery with use of a deadly weapon. The district court sentenced appellant to serve in the Nevada State Prison a term of life without the possibility of parole for murder, with concurrent terms of fifteen years for robbery and fifteen years for the use of a deadly weapon. This court dismissed appellant's direct appeal. LaPena v. State, Docket No. 20436 (Order Dismissing Appeal, June 27, 1991).

On June 3, 1992, appellant filed in the district court a petition for post-conviction relief. The state opposed the petition. On August 31, 1992, without appointing counsel or conducting an evidentiary hearing, the district court denied appellant's petition for post-conviction relief. This appeal followed.

In his petition for post-conviction relief, appellant claimed the following: (1) Gerald Weakland had a secret agreement with state law enforcement officials; (2) Weakland committed perjury when he gave moral transformation testimony; (3) confidential informant Costanza had information connecting Weakland and Marvin Krause to the murder of Hilda Krause; (4) the state illegally suppressed vital evidence which connected Marvin Krause with the murder; (5) Costanza had a secret

EXHIBIT "1-A"

agreement with state law enforcement officials; (6) state law enforcement officials committed perjury when they stated that they did not conceal evidence relating to Costanza; (7) appellant was denied his right to effective assistance of counsel; and (8) the reasonable doubt instruction which was given during the trial was constitutionally defective.

When a petition for post-conviction relief raises claims supported by specific factual allegations which, if true, would entitle the petitioner to relief, the petitioner is entitled to an evidentiary hearing unless those claims are repelled by the record. Hargrove v. State, 100 Nev. 498, 686 P.2d 222 (1984). Having reviewed the record on appeal, we conclude that appellant's petition for post-conviction relief raises claims supported by specific factual allegations which, if true, would entitle appellant to relief. Accordingly, we vacate the order of the district court denying appellant's petition for post-conviction relief, and we remand this matter to the district court with instructions that the district court conduct an evidentiary hearing.[1]

It is so ORDERED.

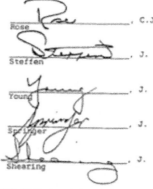

_____, C.J.
Rose

_____, J.
Steffen

_____, J.
Young

_____, J.
Springer

_____, J.
Shearing

---

[1]Although appellant has not been granted permission to file documents in this matter in proper person, see NRAP 46(b), we have received and considered appellant's proper person documents. We deny as moot appellant's motion to be released on personal recognizance pending appeal. We deny appellant's motion to file briefs and motion to amend the record on appeal.

2

cc: Hon. Thomas A. Foley, District Judge
Hon. Frankie Sue Del Papa, Attorney General
Hon. Rex Bell, District Attorney
Frank R. LaPena
Loretta Bowman, Clerk

CRIMINAL COURT MINUTES

82-C-059791-C   STATE OF NEVADA   vs LaPena, Frank R
                                              CONTINUED FROM PAGE: 012

08/08/95 09:00 AM 00 DEFT'S MOTION FOR SPECIFIC DISCOVERY OF
                        BRADY MATERIALS NOT PREVIOUSLY DISCLOSED

HEARD BY: GENE PORTER, Judge; Dept. 1

OFFICERS: PAULETTE TAYLOR, Court Clerk
          JANICE LISTON, Reporter/Recorder

PARTIES: STATE OF NEVADA   Y
          000398 Schwartz, David P.   Y

          001 D1 LaPena, Frank R   N
          000824 Schieck, David M.   Y

Mr. Schwartz advised he prepared a response but they have an evidentiary
hearing in October and he is not sure he needs to respond to the deft's
motion as he has counsel. Response FILED IN OPEN COURT. Argument by Mr.
Schieck and he is satisfied with the State's response. COURT ORDERED, motion
GRANTED.

NDP

...ought murder convictions to the Nevada Supreme Court and won new trials. A third trial request is pending.

A crime scene photograph shows the bedroom where Hilda Krause was attacked and had her throat slit. Her husband, Marvin, survived the 1974 robbery. He died in 1976 from a stroke.

Clark County officials remove Hilda Krause's body from her Las Vegas Country Club home.

MURDER WAS THE CASE

By Caren Benjamin
Review-Journal

Frank LaPena has spent most of the past 24 years in prison for a 1974 murder he maintains he had nothing to do with. He has been out on bail for more than a year, awaiting what he hopes will be a third trial.

Frank LaPena is something of a legend around the Clark County Courthouse, a relic from the Las Vegas era between mobsters and make-believe, between Bugsy Siegel and Bugs Bunny; the real Va Va Va Vegas when the cocktail waitresses at Caesars Palace were the most beautiful women in the world and no one ever dreamed of bringing a child into a casino.

These days the courthouse is one of the few familiar buildings left in a city LaPena says he barely recognizes, a land of pyramids, pirate ships and tract houses flowing over the once-barren desert like a stucco sea.

Still, one would guess he'd avoid the place rather than haunt its halls, shocking young lawyers as if he magically made flesh from volumes of legal documents, the sole free and surviving cast member in a melodrama from the days when every murder was front-page news.

"That's Frank LaPena?" a young prosecutor asks, passing him in the hall. "That guy made a lotta law."

LaPena has spent about 17 years in prison since he was arrested in 1974 on a murder charge. He's been out on bail for more than a year, awaiting what he hopes will be his third trial. Tanned and groomed, he looks more like a casino slot host than a man twice convicted of a capital crime.

When he was first released in June 1997, he could barely contain his excitement about a chance to finally work — as much as a jailhouse-trained barrister can — in the actual courthouse. He got a job as a de facto law clerk for Carmine Colucci, a friend and one of about a dozen attorneys who has worked on some stage of his case. LaPena filed motions on his own case and cases for friends he made in prison.

He had other big plans when he bailed out. He was going to drive a limousine, then maybe buy a fleet of his own. He had friends with business ventures

Please see LAPENA/11A

1 OPPS
   STEWART L. BELL
2 DISTRICT ATTORNEY
   Nevada Bar #000477
3 200 S. Third Street
   Las Vegas, Nevada 89155
4 (702) 455-4711
   Attorney for Plaintiff
5
                          DISTRICT COURT
6   CLARK COUNTY, NEVADA
7
8 THE STATE OF NEVADA,   )
9   Plaintiff,   )
)
10   -vs-   )   Case No.   C59791
)   Dept. No.   I
11 FRANK RALPH LAPENA,   )   Docket   J
   #0111655   )
12   )
)
13   Defendant(s).   )
14 _____)

15   OPPOSITION TO PETITION FOR

16   POST-CONVICTION RELIEF

17   DATE OF HEARING:
                TIME OF HEARING: 9:00 A.M.
18

19   COMES NOW, the State of Nevada, by STEWART L. BELL, District Attorney, through

20 MELVYN T. HARMON, Chief Deputy District Attorney, and files this Opposition to Petition for Post-

21 Conviction Relief.

22   This Opposition is made and based upon all the papers and pleadings on file herein, the attached

23 points and authorities in support hereof, and oral argument at the time of hearing, if deemed necessary

24 by this Honorable Court. Additionally, the State incorporates by this reference the facts and arguments

25 ///

26 ///

27 ///

28 ///

                                                                              CE31

302

Third, any evidence must be material before it must be disclosed. The test of materiality requires that there be a "reasonable probability that, had the evidence been disclosed to the defense, the result of the proceeding would have been different." Bagley, supra, at 3383. Here, all evidence in possession of the State was disclosed. Defendant has not pointed to any information that was withheld by the State that would have had a reasonable probability of changing the outcome of the trial.

Thus, Defendant is unable to meet any of the three prongs of Brady. The State, through its open file policy, went far beyond meeting the requirements of Brady. As such, his petition must be denied as to this issue.[4]

V.

THE STATE DID NOT VIOLATE A SPECIFIC ORDER TO PRODUCE THE IDENTITY AND WHEREABOUTS OF AN ALLEGED "SECOND ASSAILANT."[5]

Defendant claims that the State violated an order to produce information regarding the "second assailant" by failing to "exercise any due diligence to seek out the identity, address or whereabouts of this second assailant." However, the prosecution has no such duty. All information in possession of the State regarding this "second assailant" was disclosed. Defendant's petition must be denied as to this issue.

///

///

///

///

///

///

///

///

---

[4]Counsel in his brief acts as if either the State did not disclose the information, and thus violated Brady, or counsel did not find the material, and thus was ineffective. However, this convenient argument fails to appreciate an important point: if the evidence is neither exculpatory nor material then the State need not disclose it and counsel cannot be said to be ineffective in not finding it, as it cannot possibly prejudice Defendant.

[5]This issue is raised in Defendant's "Supplemental Post-Hearing Brief."

-18-

CONCLUSION

For the above reasons, including the reasons set forth in the State's original Opposition to Defendant's Petition for Post-Conviction Relief, the State respectfully requests this Honorable Court deny Defendant's instant petition, as the evidence produced at the evidentiary hearing has failed to provide the necessary support for his theories of conspiracy and governmental misconduct.

DATED this ___24th___ day of June, 1996.

Respectfully submitted,

STEWART L. BELL
DISTRICT ATTORNEY
Nevada Bar #000477

BY _____
MELVYN T. HARMON
Chief Deputy District Attorney
Nevada Bar #000862

RECEIPT OF COPY

RECEIPT OF A COPY of the above and foregoing OPPOSITION TO PETITION FOR POST-CONVICTION RELIEF is hereby acknowledged this ____ day of June, 1996.

DAVID M. SCHIECK, ESQ.

By _____ Att
302 E. Carson Ave., #918
Las Vegas, Nevada 89101

fopp\2g0003001\kjh

-19-

82-C-059791-C   STATE OF NEVADA   vs LaPena, Frank R
_____
CONTINUED FROM PAGE: 018

08/16/96   03:50 PM   00   MINUTE ORDER RE: DEFT'S PETITION FOR
                          POST-CONVICTION RELIEF

HEARD BY: GENE PORTER, Judge; Dept. 1

OFFICERS: PAULETTE TAYLOR, Court Clerk

PARTIES: NO PARTIES PRESENT

This Court, having conducted an evidentiary hearing pursuant to the November 23, 1993 Order of Remand from the Nevada Supreme Court, considered the written and oral arguments of counsel and taken the matter under advisement, hereby FINDS that the failure of defendant's trial counsel to utilize known exculpatory witnesses, and further failure to investigate, develop and present evidence which would have corroborated defendant's proposed testimony and discredited the State's feature witness, Gerald Weakland, was prejudicial to his defense and amounted to ineffective assistance of counsel. Sanborn v. State. 107 Nev. 399 (1991). This Court FURTHER FINDS that it need not reach the issue of whether counsel should have moved to recuse Judge Foley from the case, or whether his adjudication of the case was improper. Therefore, it is hereby ORDERED, Defendant's Petition for Post-Conviction Relief is GRANTED and his CONVICTION and SENTENCE are VACATED. Defendant's counsel to prepare appropriate findings and submit an order to the Court. FURTHER ORDERED, matter placed on calendar for trial setting.

NDP

9-26-96 9:00 AM TRIAL SETTING

CLERK'S NOTE: Notified Mr. Harmon's and Mr. Schieck's offices and placed a copy of this minute order in their respective attorney folders. pt

IN THE SUPREME COURT OF THE STATE OF NEVADA

FRANK LaPENA,	)	CASE NO. 35981
Appellant,	)	
	)	**FILED**
vs.	)	
THE STATE OF NEVADA,	)	JUN 27 2002
	)	JANETTE M. BLOOM
Respondent.	)	CLERK OF SUPREME COURT
	)	BY S. Young DEPUTY CLERK

APPELLANT'S AMENDED OPENING BRIEF

Appeal from the Eighth Judicial District Court
Clark County, Nevada
Honorable Donald M. Mosley

CARMINE J. COLUCCI, ESQ.
Colucci & Winkler, Ltd.
Nevada Bar #000681
629 South Sixth Street
Las Vegas, Nevada 89101
(702) 384-1274

STEWART L. BELL
Clark County District Attorney
Nevada Bar No. 000477
Clark County Court House
200 S. Third Street, Suite 701
Post Office Box 552212
Las Vegas, Nevada 89155-2211
(702) 455-4711

FRANKIE SUE DEL PAPA
Nevada Attorney General
Nevada Bar No. 000192
100 North Carson Street
Carson City, Nevada 89701-4717
(775) 684-1265

Counsel for Appellant

Counsel for Respondent

MAILED ON
6/11/02

AP. 107816

scheme. They were each given unbelievable and extremely lenient plea bargains in exchange for their testimony against LAPENA. Weakland is and was a convicted perjurer. Again this makes the Lynn Brady material even more important and its unlawful suppression so highly prejudicial.

At the September 20, 1999 evidentiary hearing on LAPENA'S pending motions and his Petition for Writ of Habeas Corpus (Post-Conviction), Lynn Brady testified she was subpoenaed by Deputy District Attorney Harmon to testify for the State at LAPENA'S 1974 preliminary hearing and at that time in 1974 she made the following disclosures to prosecutor Mel Harmon:

BY MR. COLUCCI:

Q. And did you have any conversations with Mr. Harmon, either prior to or after he subpoenaed you for the preliminary hearing?
A. Yes.
Q. Do you recall when you had your first conversation with Mr. Harmon?
A. It was when I went in, and I got so upset when I went in . . . and while I was in the hallway something occurred which upset me so much that I didn't have my mind on what I was saying to him. (Emphasis added)
(RT, 9/20/99, p. 15)

Q. How long did your conversation with Mr. Harmon last?
A. Because of my own fault it didn't last long as it possibly would have because I was furious about someone I saw in the hallway before I went into his office with him.

...

Q. And who did you see that made you furious?
A. I didn't know his name, I knew who he was, because he was the person that came into the office where I was working late at night with a key . . . and he had a gun to my head, taped me, gagged me, bound me, and was looking for some things in this office.
(RT, 9/20/99, p. 19)

Q. Who did you work for?
A. Dr. Zacks.
Q. Did you later learn the name of this person?

- 22 -

307

A. Mel Harmon told me what his name was.

Q. What was his name?

A. Bobby Webb.

Q. Did you have a conversation with Mr. Harmon regarding Bobby Webb?

A. I certainly did.

Q. When did that occur?

A. Right then, that first meeting.

Q. Prior to the preliminary hearing?

A. I said I had signed papers, that I would prosecute, if he was ever caught. And I didn't know what his name was, I only knew that he looked like, and why he was sitting in the hallway.

Q. Where you sure this was the man?

A. I knew it was because . . . . He was quite tall. He had a beard and mustache, ... He was a professional football player. . . .

Q. Were you ever called as a witness in a case against him?

A. Never. I was told that –

Q. Did you have a conversation with Mr. Harmon regarding what crimes this gentleman had committed against you?

A. Yes.

Q. And what was his response?

A. He said that it was the strongest witness they had against the person that had killed Mrs. Krause, and that it was better not to mention that at this particular time, that it had nothing to do with this situation.

Q. To your knowledge, was Mr. Webb ever prosecuted for the crimes he committed against you?

A. In so far as I know, no.

(RT, 9/20/99, pp. 19-21)

...

Q. Did you ever tell Frank about these interviews?

A. In 1998 I did, because I thought this time he's out, everything is going to be all right, and then I finally told him.

...

Q. Was this the first time that you told Mr. LaPena about this interview with Detective Lyons?

A. Yes.

(RT, 9/20/99, p. 24)

When Lynn Brady told Mel Harmon about the crimes that Webb had committed against her, Mr. Harmon had a constitutional duty to inform LAPENA and his counsel of this "oral" information. Mr. Harmon's failure for over 24 years to disclose this information to LAPENA

- 23 -

IN THE SUPREME COURT OF THE STATE OF NEVADA

FRANK R. LAPENA,
Appellant,
vs.
THE STATE OF NEVADA,
Respondent.

No. 35981

FILED

MAY 2 2 2003

JANETTE M. BLOOM
CLERK OF SUPREME COURT
BY _____
CHIEF DEPUTY CLERK

ORDER OF AFFIRMANCE

This is an appeal from an order of the district court denying a post-conviction petition for a writ of habeas corpus, a motion for a new trial based on newly discovered evidence, and a motion to dismiss the indictment.

In 1982, the district court convicted appellant Frank R. LaPena, pursuant to a jury verdict, of first degree murder and robbery with the use of a deadly weapon. On appeal, this court reversed LaPena's conviction and remanded his case.[1] LaPena was retried in 1989, and the district court again convicted LaPena, pursuant to a jury verdict, of first degree murder and robbery with the use of a deadly weapon. The district court sentenced LaPena to serve a term of life without the possibility of parole for the murder and a concurrent term of thirty years for the robbery with the use of a deadly weapon. This court dismissed LaPena's appeal from his judgment of conviction and sentence.[2]

---

[1]See LaPena v. State, 98 Nev. 135, 643 P.2d 244 (1982).

[2]See LaPena v. State, Docket No. 20436 (Order Dismissing Appeal, June 27, 1991).

EXHIBIT "I"

03-08646

On June 3, 1992, LaPena filed a petition for post-conviction relief in the district court. The petition was ultimately unsuccessful.[3]

On March 26, 1999, LaPena filed an untimely second post-conviction petition for a writ of habeas corpus in the district court. The district court conducted evidentiary hearings at which Lynn Brady, many of LaPena's trial counsel, and the prosecutors who tried LaPena's case testified. The district court denied LaPena's petition and motions. This appeal followed.

LaPena filed his petition approximately eight years after this court issued the remittitur from his direct appeal. Thus, LaPena's petition was untimely filed.[4] Moreover, LaPena's petition was successive because he had previously filed a petition for post-conviction relief.[5] LaPena's petition was procedurally barred absent a demonstration of good cause and prejudice.[6]

In an attempt to overcome the procedural defaults, LaPena claims that the State violated Brady v. Maryland[7] in failing to disclose the tape-recorded statement of Lynn Brady. LaPena also claims that he is factually innocent and raises four other claims: (1) ineffective assistance of counsel; (2) inadequate appellate review; (3) prosecutorial misconduct; and (4) district court error in denying LaPena's motion to dismiss the

---

[3]See State v. LaPena, 114 Nev. 1159, 968 P.2d 750 (1998).

[4]See NRS 34.726(1).

[5]See NRS 34.810(1)(b), (2).

[6]See NRS 34.726(1); NRS 34.810(1)(b), (3).

[7]373 U.S. 83 (1963).

inadequate indictment. We conclude that LaPena failed to overcome the procedural defaults.

LaPena claims that the State violated <u>Brady</u> in failing to disclose the tape-recorded statement of Lynn Brady, a friend of LaPena. LaPena claims that Brady's statement was favorable to the defense because it supports LaPena's theory at trial that the murder victim's husband, Mr. Krause, not LaPena, was the "mastermind" behind the crime. The statement also connects Mr. Krause and a State witness, Bobby Webb, to a prior criminal scheme where Mr. Krause hired Webb to commit crimes against Lynn Brady and her place of employment. LaPena claims that this part of the statement could have been used as impeachment material.

<u>Brady</u> requires a prosecutor to disclose evidence favorable to the defense when that evidence is material either to guilt or to punishment.[8] Evidence must also be disclosed if it provides grounds for the defense to impeach the credibility of a State witness or to bolster the defense case.[9] "[T]here are three components to a <u>Brady</u> violation: the evidence at issue is favorable to the accused; the evidence was withheld by the State, either intentionally or inadvertently; and prejudice ensued, i.e., the evidence was material."[10] When a <u>Brady</u> claim is raised in an untimely and/or successive post-conviction petition for a writ of habeas corpus, the petitioner has the burden of pleading and proving specific facts that demonstrate good cause and prejudice to overcome the procedural

---

[8]<u>See</u> <u>Mazzan v. Warden</u>, 116 Nev. 48, 66, 993 P.2d 25, 36 (2000).

[9]<u>See</u> <u>id</u>. at 67, 993 P.2d at 37.

[10]<u>Id.</u>

bars.[11] A showing of good cause and prejudice for failing to raise a <u>Brady</u> claim earlier parallels the last two of the three <u>Brady</u> components.[12] Cause can be shown by proving that the State withheld the evidence.[13] Prejudice can be shown by proving that the withheld evidence was material.[14]

In determining whether LaPena demonstrated good cause and prejudice to overcome the procedural defaults, we must first determine if Lynn Brady's statement would have been favorable to the defense. The part of the statement regarding Mr. Krause's plan to have himself robbed and his wife murdered would have corroborated the defense theory that LaPena did not plan the crimes. The alleged robbery by Webb at the instigation of Mr. Krause may have been used as impeachment material. Thus, these parts of Brady's statement were favorable to the defense.

Next, we must determine if Lynn Brady's statement was withheld by the State. The State claims that it did not withhold this evidence because the tape-recorded statement of Brady and other documents listing Brady's name, including a list of witnesses attached to the indictment, were contained in the evidence files that LaPena's counsel and LaPena himself searched through. The record, however, does not support the State's claim. At the evidentiary hearing, LaPena's counsel testified that when they looked through the files they did not discover

---

[11]<u>See</u> <u>id.</u>

[12]<u>See</u> <u>id.</u>

[13]<u>See</u> <u>id.</u>

[14]<u>See</u> <u>id.</u> at 66-67, 993 P.2d at 36-37.

SUPREME COURT
OF
NEVADA

(O) 1947A

4

Brady's statement. Moreover, the State initially claimed that Brady's tape-recorded statement did not exist because the State's attorney could not find it in the files; however, he eventually found it.

The State also claims that LaPena had knowledge of Brady because he was friends with her. Thus, the State asserts that pursuant to Steese v. State[15] it was not required to disclose Brady's statement because the defense could have discovered it with due diligence. We disagree.

Steese states that "Brady does not require the State to disclose evidence which is available to the defendant from other sources, including diligent investigation by the defense."[16] It is true that LaPena and his attorneys probably had knowledge of Lynn Brady and could have interviewed her as the State did; however, the defense cannot be expected to uncover a prior recorded statement of Brady that only the State possesses.[17] Access to a witness does not equate to access to her prior recorded statement.[18] Therefore, even diligent investigation by the defense would not necessarily have discovered the prior recorded statement of Lynn Brady.

Because the State failed to disclose favorable evidence to LaPena, we must next determine if this evidence was material.[19] We conclude that it was not.

---

[15]114 Nev. 479, 495, 960 P.2d 321, 331 (1998).

[16]Id.

[17]See Lay v. State, 116 Nev. 1185, 1200 n.3, 14 P.3d 1256, 1266 n.3 (2000).

[18]See id.

[19]See Mazzan, 116 Nev. at 66, 993 P.2d at 36.

times. Second, she made many negative references to LaPena such as that he was "intrigued with Mafiosi type of things" and that he may have been "ripping off cars" at the car lot he worked at. Third, LaPena's former counsel stated that they would not have called her as a witness because she was a "loose cannon." Fourth, the prosecutor in the case testified that he decided not to call her as a witness because she was not credible. Fifth, she never actually stated that LaPena did not plan the Krause murder and robbery; Brady simply speculated that Mr. Krause may have been behind it or that Rosalie Maxwell may have been behind it so she could get Mr. Krause's money for her and LaPena. This latter theory supports the State's theory at trial. Sixth, Webb's alleged robbery of Brady was not material because whether he would have been charged with a crime was too speculative. We conclude that LaPena failed to demonstrate a reasonable probability that Brady's statement would have changed the result of the trial. Thus, LaPena failed to demonstrate prejudice to overcome the procedural defaults with respect to this <u>Brady</u> claim.

LaPena also attempts to overcome the procedural defaults by making a claim of factual innocence. He claims that because Weakland's testimony regarding how Weakland killed Mrs. Krause does not coincide with the physical evidence contained in the autopsy report, Weakland could not have been the person who killed Mrs. Krause and therefore LaPena is innocent. We conclude that LaPena has failed to make a credible claim of factual innocence. LaPena essentially raised this claim in his first petition for post-conviction relief and motion to dismiss the indictment, which we considered and rejected.[20]   LaPena failed to demonstrate good cause and prejudice for raising this claim again.

Next, LaPena claims that his trial counsel were ineffective for failing to investigate and uncover Lynn Brady or her tape-recorded statement.   To establish ineffective assistance of counsel, LaPena must demonstrate that his counsel's actions fell below an objective standard of reasonableness and a reasonable probability that but for counsel's errors the result of the trial would have been different.[21]   Because LaPena's petition is untimely and successive, he must also demonstrate good cause and prejudice for failing to raise this claim earlier.

We conclude that LaPena can demonstrate cause for failing to raise this claim earlier because the existence of Lynn Brady's tape-recorded statement was not discovered until 1998 when she contacted LaPena; however, we conclude that LaPena cannot demonstrate prejudice. As stated previously, there is no reasonable probability that Lynn Brady's statement would have changed the result of the trial. Thus, the district court did not err in denying this claim.

Next, LaPena claims that this court was not able to conduct a fair and adequate review of his previous appeal regarding his first petition for post-conviction relief because this court "misunderstood certain facts in support of LaPena's claims, accepted summaries of testimony by the State's witnesses that did not exist in the record, applied 'old' facts against LaPena that have been repelled by 'new' exculpatory facts." We conclude that the district court did not err in denying this claim. LaPena failed to

---

[20]See LaPena, 114 Nev. at 1167, 968 P.2d at 755.

[21]See Strickland v. Washington, 466 U.S. 668 (1984).

demonstrate good cause and prejudice for failing to raise this claim earlier.

Next, LaPena claims that the State committed prosecutorial misconduct in violating <u>Brady</u> by failing to disclose Lynn Brady's statement and police reports, notes, memoranda, and district attorney reports regarding three statements made by Jerry Weakland. As stated previously, the State did not violate <u>Brady</u> by failing to disclose Lynn Brady's statement because the statement was not material. The State also did not violate <u>Brady</u> by failing to disclose evidence relating to statements made by Weakland because LaPena failed to demonstrate that this evidence existed. Moreover, it was known at trial that Weakland changed his testimony regarding who committed the crimes on three occasions. Therefore, the district court did not err in determining that LaPena failed to demonstrate good cause and prejudice to overcome the procedural defaults.

Next, LaPena claims that the district court erred in denying his motion to dismiss the inadequate indictment. LaPena claims that the indictment was inadequate because the State did not prove that Weakland murdered Mrs. Krause. We conclude that the district court did not err in denying this motion. LaPena previously filed a motion to dismiss the indictment in conjunction with his first petition for post-conviction relief. This court concluded that the district court's denial of that motion was proper. Thus, this claim is barred by the doctrine of the law of the case.[22]

Lastly, LaPena appeals from the district court's denial of his motion for a new trial based on newly discovered evidence. We conclude

---

[22]<u>See</u> <u>Hall v. State</u>, 91 Nev. 314, 535 P.2d 797 (1975).

that the district court did not err in denying this motion because it was filed more than two years after the verdict.[23]

Having reviewed the record on appeal, and for the reasons set forth above, we conclude that LaPena is not entitled to relief. Accordingly, we

ORDER the judgment of the district court AFFIRMED.

_____, C.J.
Agosti

_____, J.
Shearing

_____, J.
Becker

cc: Hon. Donald M. Mosley, District Judge
      Carmine J. Colucci & Associates
      Attorney General Brian Sandoval/Carson City
      Clark County District Attorney David J. Roger
      Clark County Clerk

---

[23]See NRS 176.515(3).

IN THE SUPREME COURT FOR THE STATE OF NEVADA

1

2

3

4

5

6 FRANK LAPENA,   )   Supreme Court Case No.: 35981
)
7   Appellant,   )   **FILED**
)
   vs.   )
8   )
   STATE OF NEVADA,   )
9   )   JUN 02 2003
                         Respondent.   )
10 _____)   JANETTE M. BLOOM
                                                    CLERK OF SUPREME COURT
                                                    DEPUTY CLERK

11 **MOTION TO ALLOW ORAL ARGUMENT BEFORE EN BANC COURT**

12   COMES NOW the Appellant, Frank LaPena, by and through his attorney, Carmine

13 J. Colucci, Esq., of the law firm of Carmine J. Colucci, Chtd., who moves this Court

14 pursuant to NRCP 34 for an Order allowing oral argument before the En Banc Court.

15   On May 22, 2003, the Order of Affirmance was filed affirming the decision of the

16 District Court denying LaPena's Post-Conviction Petition for Writ of Habeas Corpus, a

17 Motion for New Trial Based on Newly Discovered Evidence and a Motion to Dismiss

18 Indictment. The Order of Affirmance was signed by three Justices which constitutes less

19 than a majority of this Court.

20   Appellant herein hereby requests that the parties be given the opportunity to argue

21 each of the respective parties' position to the En Banc Court so that the Justices who were

22 not signatories to the order and those who were will have the opportunity to ask counsel

23 questions and to have the benefit of oral argument. Further, given the magnitude of this

24 case, its history, its impact on legal precedent and its constitutional issues, the entire Court

25 should consider the issues raised in this appeal.

26   Appellant is also requesting pursuant to NRAP 34(b) that each side be allowed a

27 minimum of thirty (30) minutes to argue its position. Appellant is making this request not

28 for purposes of delaying the resolution of this matter but in the belief that consideration by

the En Banc Court and oral argument will assist the Court in addressing the issues raised

EXHIBIT "J"

1 | under the Fifth, Sixth and Fourteenth Amendments to the United States Constitution and
2 | to afford Appellant due process of law thereunder.

3 | Further, the three Justice panel did not address the impact of the testimony of
4 | former Chief Justice Al Gunderson whose statement from the bench, while a member of
5 | this Court, which was stipulated to and entered into evidence. Additionally, Appellant in
6 | reading the Order of Affirmance, contends that the crucial testimony and prior recorded
7 | statement of suppressed witness Lynn Brady **was** relevant and material and should be
8 | considered by a jury which is the proper entity to consider its weight.

9 | Appellant contends that the language of the Order of Affirmance clearly shows that
10 | the components of ***Brady*** have been met. It is an inescapable fact that the recorded
11 | statement of Lynn Brady was not disclosed by the State. The three Justice panel found
12 | that the record did not support the State's claim that it did not withhold this evidence. (See
13 | p. 4, 5 of Order of Affirmance)

14 | More over, the State affirmatively claimed that the recorded statement did not exist.
15 | This goes beyond mere negligence and dangerously approaches intentionally withholding
16 | of evidence. In a later proceeding, the State produced the tape and transcript. The three
17 | Justice panel next concluded that the defense could not have been expected to uncover
18 | a prior recorded statement by Brady that only the State possessed. (See p. 5)

19 | The three Justice panel next posed the question; "Because the State ***failed*** to
20 | disclose ***favorable*** evidence to LaPena, we must determine if this evidence was material."
21 | (Emphasis added). (See p. 5) The use of the words "failed" and "favorable" require that
22 | LaPena's petition should have been granted or at the very least warrants reconsideration
23 | by the En Banc Court. Evidence must be disclosed if it provides grounds for the defense
24 | to attack the reliability, thoroughness and good faith of the police investigation, to impeach
25 | the credibility of the State's witnesses or the bolster the defense case against prosecutorial
26 | attacks. See ***Mazzen v. Warden***, 116 Nev. 48, 993 P.2d 25 (2000) Clearly those were the
27 | intended uses for Lynn Brady's testimony.

28 | At page 6 of the Order of Affirmance, the three Justice panel, in a vacuum assessed

- 2 -

the weight of Lynn Brady's testimony. That seems to be usurpation of the jury's function. Brady would have testified that Bobby Webb, a crucial state witness, committed several felonies of which she was the victim. She would have testified that she mentioned this to the prosecutor prior to the preliminary hearing but he told her to withhold this information since Webb was an important witness against LaPena, she would also have testified Webb was never charged with these crimes. The jury should have been allowed to consider this evidence in order to assess Webb's credibility, his possible motives for testifying against LaPena and the prosecutor's possible misconduct.

The trial defense attorney said that he would not have used Lynn Brady. This was purely hindsight. That is as speculative as trying to say LaPena would not have insisted that he would have demanded that she testify. Lynn Brady's testimony was "favorable" and was withheld. These are facts. Its weight was for a jury to decide at trial.

The United States Constitution guarantees under the Fifth, Sixth, and Fourteenth Amendments to the United States Constitution require that this matter, as well as the other issues raised and decided by the Order of Affirmance, be considered by the En Banc Court.

CONCLUSION

For the above stated reasons, LaPena seeks a reversal of his conviction or at the very least en banc consideration by this Court.

DATED this 30th day of May, 2003.

CARMINE J. COLUCCI, CHTD.

CARMINE J. COLUCCI, ESQ.
Nevada Bar No. 000881
629 South Sixth Street
Las Vegas, NV 89101
Attorney for Appellant

- 3 -

320

1 CARMINE J. COLUCCI, ESQ.
2 Nevada Bar No. 000881
   CARMINE J. COLUCCI, CHTD.
3 629 South Sixth Street
   Las Vegas, NV 89101
4 Attorney for Appellant

5   IN THE SUPREME COURT FOR THE STATE OF NEVADA

6

7

8 FRANK LAPENA,   )   Supreme Court Case No.: 35981
)
9   Appellant,   )
)
10 vs.   )
)
11 STATE OF NEVADA,   )
)
12   Respondent.   )

13   CERTIFICATE OF MAILING

14   I HEREBY CERTIFY that on the 30ᵗʰ day of May, 2003, I deposited in the United

15 States Mail at Las Vegas, Nevada, a true and correct copy of Appellants' *MOTION TO*

16 *ALLOW ORAL ARGUMENT BEFORE EN BANC COURT* enclosed in a sealed envelope

17 upon which first class postage has been fully prepaid, addressed to:

18   David Roger
19   CLARK COUNTY DISTRICT ATTORNEY
       Clark County Court House
20   200 South Third Street, Suite 701
       Post Office Box 552212
21   Las Vegas, NV 89155-2211

22   Frankie Sue Del Papa
       NEVADA ATTORNEY GENERAL
23   100 North Carson Street
       Carson City, Nevada 89701-4717
24   Attorneys for Respondent

25

26   _____
                                      An employee of
27   CARMINE J. COLUCCI, CHTD.

28

321

UNITED STATES COURT OF APPEALS

FOR THE NINTH CIRCUIT

FRANK RALPH LaPENA,	No. 15-16154
Petitioner - Appellant,	D.C. No. 2:00-cv-00960-RFB-NJK
	District of Nevada,
v.	Las Vegas
GEORGE GRIGAS and ADAM PAUL LAXALT,	ORDER
Respondents - Appellees.	

Before: M. SMITH and CHRISTEN, Circuit Judges.

The request for a certificate of appealability is granted with respect to the

following issues: (1) whether there was sufficient evidence to sustain appellant's

conviction for murder and robbery; (2) whether appellant is actually innocent

within the meaning of *Herrera v. Collins*, 506 U.S. 390, 417 (1993); (3) whether

trial counsel was ineffective; (4) whether appellant's constitutional rights were

violated because the state withheld exculpatory evidence before the grand jury; and

(5) whether the district court properly concluded that the following claim was

unexhausted: the trial court violated appellant's constitutional rights by

improperly restricting the cross-examination of Gerald Weakland. *See* 28 U.S.C.

§ 2253(c)(3); *see also* 9th Cir. R. 22-1(e).

322

CASE NO. ~~29339~~ C05~~7791~~

DEPT. NO. . ~~One~~ XV

IN THE Eighth ____ JUDICIAL DISTRICT COURT OF THE

STATE OF NEVADA IN AND FOR THE COUNTY OF Clark ____

6/21/11
9:00 AM

Frank LaPena ____ ,   )
)
                    Petitioner   )
)
            vs.   )
)
STATE OF NEVADA,   )
)
_____ Respondent   )

POSTCONVICTION PETITION
REQUESTING A GENETIC MARKER
ANALYSIS OF EVIDENCE WITHIN
THE POSSESSION OR CUSTODY
OF THE STATE OF NEVADA
(NRS 176.0918)

TO: THE CLERK OF THE COURT FOR Clark _____ COUNTY,
                                  (County Where Petitioner Was Convicted)
STATE OF NEVADA; THE ATTORNEY GENERAL OF THE STATE OF NEVADA,

AND; THE OFFICE OF THE DISTRICT ATTORNEY FOR THE STATE OF

NEVADA, COUNTY OF Clark _____
                      (County of District Attorney Where Petitioner Was Convicted)

1.   I, Frank LaPena _____ , am the Petitioner in this matter. This
         (Name of Petitioner / Convicted Inmate)
Petition requests this Court to issue an Order for a Genetic Marker Analysis of evidence

pursuant to NRS 176.0918.

2.   Petitioner is informed and believes, and on the basis of such belief, alleges in good

faith that the State of Nevada, or a political subdivision of the State of Nevada, has

possession and control evidence in the form of Genetic Marker Information relating to the

investigation or prosecution that resulted in Petitioner's Judgment of Conviction.

1

3.   The Petitioner was convicted of committing all of the following Category A or Category B felony / felonies:

200.380   Robbery
_____   _____   _____   _____
Crime's NRS   Title of Crime   Category A or B Date of Conviction

200.030   Murder
_____   _____   _____   _____
Crime's NRS   Title of Crime   Category A or B Date of Conviction

193.165   Use of Deadly Weapon
_____   _____   _____   _____
Crime's NRS   Title of Crime   Category A or B Date of Conviction

_____   _____   _____   _____
Crime's NRS   Title of Crime   Category A or B Date of Conviction

4.   (If applicable) The Petitioner was sentenced to death and the date set for the execution is N/A _____.
                    (Date of Execution if known)

5.   Pursuant to NRS 176.0918(3)(a), the following information identifies the specific evidence either known or believed by the Petitioner to be in the possession or custody of the State of Nevada that can be subject to Genetic Marker Analysis. (Set forth the identity of such evidence here)

At the crime scene, hairs were collected from the victim's right and left hands They were identified by the criminalist at trial as "item 13" and were placed in a paper bindle. Fingernail scrapings were taken during the autopsy of the victim.

2

324

6.   Pursuant to NRS 176.0918(3)(b), the following is the Petitioner's rationale as to why a reasonable possibility exists that the petitioner would not have been prosecuted or convicted if exculpatory results had been obtained through Genetic Marker Analysis of the evidence identified in paragraph 5. (Set forth your rationale here)

DNA evidence will provide proof as to the person who killed the victim. If DNA evidence shows that the killer was Marvin Krause, the husband of the victim rather than Gerald Weakland, that proof would exonerate the defendant, Frank LaPena

7.   Pursuant to NRS 176.0918(3)(c), the type of Genetic Marker Analysis the Petitioner is requesting to be conducted on the evidence identified in paragraph 5 is:

DNA analysis of the evidence using the most accurate and current method

3

8. [If applicable] Pursuant to NRS 176.0918(3)(d), the following are the results of all prior Genetic Marker Analysis performed on the evidence in the trial which resulted in the Petitioner's conviction. (Set forth all of such evidence here)

No testing was performed on the hairs or the fingernail scrapings.

9. (If applicable) Pursuant to NRS 176.0918(3)(e), the following is a statement of the Petitioner that the type of Genetic Marker Analysis the Petitioner is requesting was not available at the time of trial or, if it was available, that the failure to request Genetic Marker Analysis before the Petitioner was convicted was not a result of a strategic or tactical decision as part of the representation of the Petitioner at the trial. (Set forth the applicable facts here)

This case was originally tried in 1977. A retrial occurred in 1989. At the trial in 1989, Captain Jerry Keller testified that hair comparison was not reliable. DNA testing was not available at either time.

4

_____
_____
_____
_____
_____
_____
_____
_____

PRAYER FOR GRANTING OF PETITION

The petitioner respectfully requests that the Court, pursuant to NRS 176.0918,

grant the Petitioner's POSTCONVICTION PETITION REQUESTING A GENETIC

MARKER ANALYSIS OF EVIDENCE WITHIN THE POSSESSION OR CUSTODY OF

THE STATE OF NEVADA and the Petitioner requests this Court to issue an Order for a

Genetic Marker Analysis of evidence pursuant to NRS 176.0918 (9).

Dated this _10th_ day of _June 2011_

Frank La Pena
(Petitioner's Signature Here)

DECLARATION OF PETITIONER

I, Frank La Pena _____, declare and attest under penalty of perjury
(Name of Petitioner / Convicted Inmate)
of the laws of the State of Nevada that the information contained in this Petition does

not contain any material misrepresentation of fact and that I have a good faith basis for

relying on particular facts for the request.

Dated this _10th_ day of _June 2011_

Frank La Pena
(Petitioner's/Declarant's Signature here)

DOC 2083 (04/10)

5

1 MTN
   FRANK R. LaPENA
2 1632 N. Torrey Pines #103
   Las Vegas, Nv 89108
3
   Petitioner In Propria Persona
4

5   DISTRICT COURT

6   CLARK COUNTY, NEVADA

7

8 FRANK R. LaPENA,   )   Case No: C059791
)   Dept No: XV
9   Petitioner,   )
)
10 -vs-   )
)
11 STATE OF NEVADA,   )
)
12   Respondent.   )
)
13 ────────────────────────────)

14   NOTICE AND MOTION FOR SPECIFIC DNA BLOOD TESTING
         REGARDING BLOOD STAINS FOUND IN BOTH THE NORTH AND
15   SOUTHEAST BEDROOMS OF THE KRAUSE RESIDENCE LOCATED
                 AT 2995 PINEHURST LAS VEGAS, NEVADA
16

17   COMES NOW, the Petitioner Frank R. LaPena, in propria persona and

18 respectfully moves this Honorable Court for an Order granting Petitioner's

19 request to direct the State to conduct specific DNA blood tests on the victim's

20 clothing and blood stains found in both the North and Southeast bedrooms where

21 violent struggles both occurred.

22   This Motion is made and based upon the following grounds:

23   1.   On December 13, 2011, the State, via, Deputy District Attorney, Marc

24 Schifalacqua, informed the Court they were going to do some DNA Blood tests,

25 Petitioner believes from a blood vial containing Hilda Krause's blood.

26   2.   This Honorable Court then clarified, what needs testing is the

27 unknown blood or DNA that belongs to anyone other than the victim.   See,

28 Exhibit "1", attached hereto.

                              1

3. On April 10, 2012, Petitioner was attempting to find out what specific type of DNA was being tested by the State on the hairs and also wanted to know if the State conducted DNA blood testing on the blood stains or what appears to be blood stains in the Southeast bedroom and North bedroom to the best of his knowledge. Petitioner further believes the Court stated for him to file a motion for what Petitioner wanted to have tested re: blood tests and believes the Court said it would grant such motion.

This Motion is further made and based upon the pleadings, documents, exhibits and papers on file herein and any supplemental documents to be filed hereafter.

NOTICE OF MOTION

TO: THE STATE OF NEVADA, Respondent and

TO: STEVEN WOLFSON, DISTRICT ATTORNEY, its Counsel

PLEASE TAKE NOTICE that the undersigned will bring the foregoing Motion on for a hearing before this Honorable Court on the 5/8/12 day of April, 2012, at the hour of 9:00 a.m. or as soon as Petitioner can be heard in Department XV, at the Clark County Courthouse, Las Vegas, Nevada.

FACTS, ARGUMENT AND POINTS AND AUTHORITIES

When seeking justice, the justice system, without a doubt, is about finding out the truth. The search for truth in criminal trials demands nothing less in respecting this nations primal aversion to conviction of the innocent. Smith v. State, 894 P.2d 974, at 979 (Nev. 1995), C.J. Steffen and J. Shearing, concurring in part and dissenting in part.

DNA BLOOD STAINS & VIOLENT STRUGGLE IN BOTH NORTH & SOUTHEAST BEDROOMS

Unless otherwise stated, the EXHIBITS herein stated are from the State's August 25, 2011, SUPPLEMENTAL OPPOSITION as so argued by Petitioner.

//

//

2

MARVIN KRAUSE'S TESTIMONY

BY: MR. CARTER via MR. ECKER

Q.   Did you attempt to **struggle**?
A.   <u>No, I did not.</u>
Q   Did you attempt?
A.   No, sir.
Q.   <u>Were you very cooperative?</u>
A.   **Yes.**   See, Exhibit 4F, at P.162, Lns 1-7 (emphasis ...
     added)
....

BY: MR. CARTER via MR. ECKER

Q.   Did you **touch** her body
A.   No, sir, I did not.
Q.   Did you **bend** over her?
A.   No, I did not.
Q.   Was she **tied** at that time?
A.   I couldn't tell you. I **didn't** take that close
.... a look, that close of a look. See, Exhibit 4F, at P. 66, Lns 9-15
....

A.   I **didn't** stand over her, sir.   Exhibit 4F, at P. 66
....

Q.   What did you do after you called the police?
A.   I went downstairs **immediately** and stood in
     front of the doorway or garage and waited for the
     police.   Exhibit 4F, at P. 67, Lns 3-6
....

GERALD WEAKLAND'S TESTIMONY

BY: MR. MILLS

Q.   When you walked in there, she **didn't** "struggle
     or resist" you, did she?
A.   No.   See, Exhibit 4B, at P. 81, Lns 10-12
....

CHARLES LEE TESTIMONY

BY: MR. SCHWARTZ

Q.   Now, the second bedroom, which would be referred
     to as the southern or south bedroom, is that the second
     bedroom you entered?
A.   Yes.   See, Exhibit 4D, at P. 7, Lns 21-24
....

Q.   .... and it appeared to you that a **struggle** had occurred?
A.   Yes.
Q.   That would be the south bedroom?
A.   South bedroom.
Q.   The bedroom wherein Hilda Krause "was not"
     located?
A.   That's correct. Exhibit 4D, at P. 8, Lns 4-10

1	Q.	With regard to the south bedroom, ... did you make an observation regarding a lamp?
2	A.	Yes. The lamp was on the floor next to the bed.
3	Q.	Do you recall if you noticed any other items or articles in the south bedroom ... anything that would lead you to believe a struggle had
4		occurred?
5	A	Yes, the general atmosphere of the bedroom itself, bedding was messed up.
6	Q.	Did you observe any "stains" in that bedroom?
	A.	Yes, there were stains. Exhibit 4D, at P. 12, Lns 6-18

....

7   BY   MR. CARTER   CROSS-EXAMINATION

8 ... how many people were involved in the struggle or
   how violent it had been?

9 A. Well, there were more than one, that's for sure,
       two, three. Exhibit 4D, at P. 93, Lns 23-25; P. 94, Ln 1

10 ....

11 JERRY RAY KELLER'S TESTIMONY

12 BY   MR. SCHWARTZ

13 A. In the southeast bedroom the bed covers were
        laid back. A lamp was knocked off and on the floor there
14   was some signs of what appeared to be a struggle. Exhibit 3B,
        at P. 61   And, Keller also determined there was evidence of a
15   struggle that occurred in the North bedroom where Hilda Krause
        was killed.   State's Supplemental Opposition, at P. 9, Lns 8-11
16

17 Based upon the foregoing Petitioner respectfully requests DNA Blood

18 testing upon the following recovered evidence in both the North and Southeast

19 Bedrooms containing evidentiary significance and value that can be probative

20 in determining whether Hilda Krause was engaged in a violent life or death

21 struggle with someone whom she pulled hairs from, where, as here, the results of DNA

22 tests help police and prosecutors identify a suspect or suspects as well as

23 exclude someone who is innocent.

24 DNA TESTING IN THE SOUTHEAST BEDROOM

25	PKG #3 ITEM #8	One piece of green cord recovered from floor.
26	PKG #3 ITEM #9	One Westinghouse light bulb removed from lamp with stain that appeared to be blood.
27	PKG #4 ITEM #10	One vial containing sample of blanket with blood stain from the bed.
28	PKG #7 ITEM #18	Sample of substance recovered from lamp basin that appears to be a blood stain.

4

PKG #7	ITEM #19	One piece of bed sheet from lower porion west side of bed containing blood, Refer, Exhibit 3B, at P. 123, Lns 7-1
PKG #7	ITEM #20	One piece of Green Blanket recovered from floor on West side of bed containing blood.

DNA TESTING IN THE NORTH BEDROOM

EXHIBIT 2

PKG #1	ITEM #1	One yellow throw rug, recovered from door way of North bedroom containing blood stain.
PKG #1	ITEM #6	Two pieces of electrical cord, near right side of body of Hilda Krause (Marvin Krause testified he untied himself in the other bedroom, yet police found the two electrical cords in the North bedroom where) If his DNA Blood is found to be on either of the two electrical cords powerful inferences can be shown they engaged in a violent struggle with each other.
PKG #5	ITEM #11	Sample of carpet recovered near victim's waist that appears to be blood.
PKG #5	ITEM #12	Sample of carpet that appears to be blood.
PKG #5	ITEM #16	Substance recovered from lower drawer handle of nightstand stand that appears to be blood.

OTHER DNA BLOOD THAT MAY BELONG TO SOMEONE ELSE
OTHER THAN HILDA KRAUSE MAY BE FOUND ON HER CLOTHING
OR SCARF DR. JAMES CLARKE FOUND AROUND HER NECK

See Exhibit "2", attached hereto;

PKG #2	ITEM #3	One pajama house coat.
	ITEM #4	One pajama top
	ITEM #5	One pair of pajama pants.

CONCLUSION

Based upon the foregoing arguments, Petitioner respectfully requests this Honorable Court to grant his above requested DNA Blood testing.

Dated this _17th_ day of April, 2012.

Respectfully Submitted,

Frank R. LaPena
FRANK R. LaPENA
1632 N. Torrey Pines Unit 103
Las Vegas, NV 89108

Petitioner In Propria Persona

5

I HEREBY CERTIFY that on April 17, 2012, I deposited in the United States Mail at Las Vegas, Nevada, a true and correct copy of the foregoing document of NOTICE AND MOTION FOR SPECIFIC DNA BLOOD TESTING REGARDING BLOOD STAINS FOUND IN BOTH THE NORTH AND SOUTHEAST BEDROOMS OF THE KRAUSE RESIDENCE ETC ETC, enclosed in a sealed envelope upon which first class postage has been fully prepaid, addressed to:

STEVEN WOLFSON, DISTRICT ATTORNEY
200 Lewis Avenue, 3rd Floor
Las Vegas, NV 89155

BY: *Frank R. LaPena*
FRANK R. LaPENA
1632 N. Torrey Pines #103
Las Vegas, NV 89108

Petitioner In Propria Persona

6

Clark County Sheriff's Department
PROPERTY REPORT

Evidence [XX]   Found Property [ ]   Lost Property [ ]   Dc   DR NO. __74-1881__

Incident AUTOPSY	Location BUNKER BROTHERS	Date 1-14-74
Victim HILDA KRAUSE	Address	Phone
Suspect #1	Arrested	Charge	ID No.
Suspect #2	Arrested	Charge	ID No.
Recovered by W. LEAVER #759	Address LVMPD CRIME LAB	Phone 386-3471
Hold for Prosecution XX	Proof of ownership	Registration check
Safe Custody	Release to Owner
Owner notified	By	Date	Via
List connecting Reports MORGUE REPORT

Details or circumstances - itemize, describe & give value of each item:

ON 1-14-74, AT APPROXIMATELY 1530 HOURS, DET. W. BEEN AND THE EXAMINING
OFFICER RECOVERED THE BELOW LISTED ITEMS AT THE ABOVE LISTED LOCATION:

PKG. #1

    ITEM #1 - ONE VIAL OF BLOOD

    ITEM #2 - ONE VIAL OF BLOOD

PKG. #2

    ITEM #3 - ONE PAJAMA HOUSE COAT

    ITEM #4 - ONE PAJAMA TOP

    ITEM #5 - ONE PAIR OF PAJAMA PANTS

THE ABOVE ITEMS WERE BOOKED INTO EVIDENCE UNDER DR #74-1881.

NO. ISSUED NT
DISTR. R3
INDEX
STATS
FILE

DATE AND TIME TYPED - DIVISION - CLERK

Approved By _____ Officer(s) _____ #759   Div. T.S.   Date 1-14-7
S-71

EXHIBIT "2"

CC'D:
District Attorney
Attorney General
Christopher
Oram

th 1/22/15

IN THE SUPREME COURT OF THE STATE OF NEVADA

C059791

IN THE MATTER OF THE
ASSIGNMENT OF Court of Appeals
Judge Abbi Silver to the District Court.

No. 15-0001

FILED

JAN 22 2015

TRACIE K. LINDEMAN
CLERK OF SUPREME COURT
BY
CHIEF DEPUTY CLERK

ADMINISTRATIVE ORDER OF ASSIGNMENT

WHEREAS, the Honorable ABBI SILVER, a Judge on the Court of Appeals, presided as a District Court Judge over the matter of *Frank LaPena v The State of Nevada*, Case Number C059791, now pending in the Eighth Judicial District,

WHEREAS, the proceedings in the case are nearing conclusion and judicial economy warrants completion of the case by the Honorable ABBI SILVER,

WHEREAS, Article 6, Section 3A(4) of the Nevada Constitution permits the assignment of judges of the Court of Appeals to supplemental service as District Court Judges, where needed, now therefore;

IT IS HEREBY ORDERED that the Honorable ABBI SILVER, a Judge of the Court of Appeals, is assigned to hear any and all matters in *Frank LaPena v The State of Nevada*, Case Number C059791. now pending in the Eighth Judicial District Court and she shall have authority

335

to sign any orders arising out of this assignment. The Eighth Judicial District Court shall notify the parties of the assignment and provide Judge ABBI SILVER with any assistance as requested.

DATED this 22nd day of January, 2015.

_____, C.J.

cc: Hon. Abbi Silver
Hon. David Barker
Eighth District Court Clerk

1 _____, ESQ.
2 Nevada State Bar #004349
   520 S. Fourth Street, 2nd Floor
3 Las Vegas, Nevada 89101
   ( )
4
   Attorney for Defendant
5 FRANK LAPENA

6   DISTRICT COURT
                 CLARK COUNTY, NEVADA
7   * * * * *

8
   THE STATE OF NEVADA,   CASE NO.   C059791
9   DEPT. NO.   XV
            Plaintiff,
10
11 vs.
12
   FRANK LAPENA,
13
            Defendant.
14
   ENDORSEMENT OF DEFENDANT'S
15 SUPPLEMENTAL MOTION FOR NEW TRIAL BASED UPON NEWLY DISCOVERED
   DNA PHYSICAL EVIDENCE AND MOTION FOR CLARIFICATION OF DNA
   TESTING
16
       COMES NOW, _____, ESQ., attorney for defendant, FRANK
17
   LAPENA, and hereby submits this Endorsement of Defendant's Supplemental Motion for New
18
   Trial Based upon Newly Discovered DNA Physical Evidence (attached as Exhibit A) and Motion
19
   for Clarification of DNA Testing.
20
       DATED this ⤺ day of May, 2014.
21
                                        Respectfully submitted by:
22
23   _____
24   Nevada Bar
                                        520 S. Fourth Street,
25   Las Vegas, Nevada, 89101

26   Attorney for Defendant
                                        FRANK LAPENA
27
28

337

1   This motion is made and based upon, papers and pleadings, points and authorities and the

2 Affidavit of   Esq., attached hereto.

3   DATED this ⊆ day of May, 2014.

4   Respectfully submitted by:

5

6   , ESQ.

7   Nevada Bar No.

8   Las Vegas, Nevada 89101

9   ( )

10   Attorney for Defendant
                         FRANK LAPENA

11   **NOTICE OF MOTION**

12   PLEASE TAKE NOTICE that the undersigned will bring the above and foregoing

13 **ENDORSEMENT OF DEFENDANT'S SUPPLEMENTAL MOTION FOR NEW TRIAL**

14 **BASED UPON NEWLY DISCOVERED DNA PHYSICAL EVIDENCE AND MOTION**

15 **FOR CLARIFICATION OF DNA TESTING** on for hearing before the above-entitled Court on

16 the _3_ day of _September_ 2015, at _11_:00 o'clock _a_ .m. of said day, or as soon

17 thereafter as counsel can be heard in District Court, Department No. XV.

18   DATED this _5_ day of May, 2014.   Respectfully submitted by:

19

20   ESQ.

                     Nevada Bar No. 004349

21   Las Vegas, Nevada 89101

22   ( )

23   Attorney for Defendant
                         FRANK LAPENA

24

25

26

27

28

LAS VEGAS, NEVADA 89101
TEL. ····· | FAX. 702.974-0623

POINTS AND AUTHORITIES

In the instant case, the undersigned is endorsing Mr. LaPena's Supplemental Motion for New Trial Based upon Newly Discovered DNA Physical Evidence (attached as Exhibit A).

Moreover, the undersigned places this motion on the Court's calendar for the purposes of clarifying the DNA testing. Mr. Lapena is awaiting the final examination of the hairs for the DNA results regarding all seven hairs.

On April 24, 2012, the metropolitan police department issued a forensic laboratory result of examination. In the report, attached as Exhibit 1 of the Supplemental Motion for New Trial, there appear to be four hairs located in the victim's right hand. Additionally, the report provides evidence of three light brown hairs in the victim's left hand. Yet, the FBI laboratory examination dated February 14, 2014 only appears to have tested three hairs; Q5.1.1 is a hair from the victim's right hand. Q5.2.1 is a hair from the victim's right hand. Q6.2.1 is a hair from the victim's left hand. On March 26, 2015, counsel for Mr. LaPena specifically stated the defense's belief that the testing was not completed.

As of the filing of this motion, at least four hairs are untested or unaccounted for. Therefore, Mr. LaPena would respectfully request that this Court inquire of the State the result of the testing of those four hairs.

DATED this $\underline{5}$ day of May, 2014.

Respectfully submitted:

_____, ESQ.

Nevada State Bar

Las Vegas, Nevada 89101

Attorney for Defendant
FRANK LAPENA

3

1   **CERTIFICATE OF SERVICE**

2   I hereby certify that on the ⩽ day of May, 2014, I served a true and correct copy of the

3 foregoing document entitled **ENDORSEMENT OF DEFENDANT'S SUPPLEMENTAL**

4 **MOTION FOR NEW TRIAL BASED UPON NEWLY DISCOVERED DNA PHYSICAL**

5 **EVIDENCE AND MOTION FOR CLARIFICATION OF DNA TESTING** to the Clark

6 County District Attorney's Office by sending a copy via electronic mail to:

7

8 CLARK COUNTY DISTRICT ATTORNEY
Colleen.Baharav@clarkcountyda.com

9 pdmotions@clarkcountyda.com

10

11   BY:

12

13   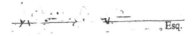, Esq.

14

15

16

17

18

19

20

21

22

23

24

25

26

27

28

               4

EXHIBIT A

1   MTN

2

3   **DISTRICT COURT**

4   **CLARK COUNTY, NEVADA**

5   * * * * *

6   THE STATE OF NEVADA,   CASE NO.   C059791

                               DEPT. NO.   XV

7   Plaintiff,

8   vs.

9

10 FRANK LAPENA,

11   Defendant.

12   **SUPPLEMENTAL MOTION FOR NEW TRIAL BASED UPON NEWLY DISCOVERED DNA PHYSICAL EVIDENCE**

13   COMES NOW, the Defendant, FRANK LAPENA and respectfully moves this Honorable

14 Court for a new trial based upon newly discovered DNA physical evidence pursuant to Nevada's

15 Genetic Marker Analysis Statute NRS 176.0918, subsection 1, 7(a) and 10(a), and NRS 176.515.

16   This Motion is further made and based upon all pleadings and papers on file herein, DNA

17 Results and Conclusions of October 29, 2013 and March 25, 2014, the attached Exhibits in the

18 case at bar, as well as any oral arguments of counsel at the time of hearing.

19

20

21

22

23

24

25

26

27

28

FACTS, ARGUMENT AND POINTS AND AUTHORITIES

Nevada's Genetic Marker Analysis Statute NRS 176.0918, specifically

states, in subsection 1, 7(a) and 10(a):

7(a) The Court shall order a genetic marker analysis after considering the information contained in the petition to subsection 3 and any ...

10(a) If the results of a genetic marker analysis performed pursuant to this section are favorable to the petitioner, 7(a). The Petitioner may bring a motion for a new trial based on the ground of newly discovered evidence pursuant to NRS 176.515.

I.
DNA PETITIONS HAVE BEEN GRANTED TO DEFENDANT'S WHEN THE DNA EVIDENCE HAS SHOWN SOMEONE ELSE OTHER THAN THE PERSON THE PROSECUTION SAID, DID THE KILLING WHICH IN THIS CASE AT BAR, WOULD BE THE "UNKNOWN MALE" WHO STRANGLED HILDA KRAUSE WITH AN ELECTRICAL CORD.

LAPENA submits during the January 21, 2014, Court proceedings this Honorable court

addressed in part Gerald Meakland's DNA blood evidence, two pieces of electrical cord found

next to the body of Hilda Krause, and a piece of green electrical cord (CK7A) that came back

negative to Weakland, but positive to DNA, unknown male.

As set forth herein, LAPENA states this Honorable Court made the following

observations after the court went over a multitude of transcripts frrm LAPENA'S

first, second and even post-conviction relief, as the court was also preparing to gear

up for DNA criminalist Craig King, where the Court stated as follows:

<u>January 21, 2014</u>

THE COURT: "And, I'm gunna go over that; however, ...,
It's the courts position that based on the blood
Evidence the petition will be denied because
There's nothing in the blood DNA would
Exculpate him";   P. 4, Lns. 5-12

THE COURT: "And what was presented to the jury at the time,
The jury was presented by Lamond Mills, by defense,
That there were the <u>ligature marks</u>, okay. ....
They had Clarks, Dr. Clark's testimony that <u>clearly</u>
She was strangled before she was sliced by Gerald
Weakland." P. 6, Lns. 6-12   emphasis added

"Now, Gerald Weakland tells the jury in the second
Trial the <u>he never strangled her</u>. There was no struggle,..."

2

P. 6, Lns. 13-15 emphasis added

" He testified never strangled her, no struggle."
P. 6, Lns 23-24

THE COURT: "However,-- and you can see there's two cords.
Like how'd she get – the tie didn't untie itself
Okay. Clearly something happened." P.8 Lns 17-19

THE COURT: "Item six. Two pieces of electrical cord, which I showed
You next to the body. What does that come back?
It comes back DNA one in 78 million to Hilda Krause."
P. 13, Lns. 6-9

THE COURT: "The DNA as the court sees it, and I went over it,
They wore gloves, nothing – Weakland's excluded,
Boswell's in the car, Hilda's dead and we have her DNA."
P. 17, Lns. 8-11;

" I'm gonna start writing a petition denying it on the DNA
Portions as far as the blood evidence." P.17, Lns. 19-21;

.... "What – the only thing that's gonna change this case is how
The hairs come out a the FBI because that's going to show
A struggle and it's going to then go against everything
weakland testified to over and over and over.
"If it's the unknown male, I don't even think I need to go dig
up the body." P. 18, Lns 16-17 (emphasis added).

LAPENA submits on February 20 , 2014, this Honorable Court held a evidentiary hearing

inter alia regarding the three electrical cords found at the Krause crime scene on January 14, 1974,

where the following occurred between the court, Defense Counsel and criminalist Craig King, as

follows:

EXAMINATION

BY THE COURT:
Q. "Okay. Next is the Item 6: Two pieces of electrical cord near the
Right side of – of the body of Hilda Krause.
And is that depicted in 5, page 5 of court's 10?

A. Yes, it is.
Q. Okay. Tell us what you did and your results.
A. Again, I examined it and there were apparent stains present.
P. 75, Lns. 18-25, P. 76, Ln. 1

....

3

1	Q.	Hilda Krause's DNA?	
	A.	Yes.	
2	Q.	THE COURT:	All right. And, Defense, do you have Some questions on that?
3		MR.	Yes, Your Honor.
		THE COURT:	Go ahead" P. 76, Lns. 9-14
4			

EXAMINATION

BY MR.

6	Q.	Mr. King, is that two cords, or is that one?
	A.	It was two pieces.
7	Q.	And when you say it was two pieces, you mean it And appears to be two separate pieces of cords?
8	A.	Yes.
	Q.	Is that right?
9	A.	Yes.
	Q.	Are you familiar with DNA fingerprinting? P. 76, Lns. 16-25
10	A.	It's an old term that they used to use for–for DNA profile, yes.
11	Q.	And you tested this for some type of touch DNA?
	A.	No. I tested this for the blood.
12	Q.	So you have never tested these cords for touch DNA?
	A.	I did not. The stains were kind of spread across
13		Most of the cord in different areas. So any touch might have Been overwhelmed by the -- by the DNA of the blood present.
14	Q.	But it could be there?
	A.	It could be, yes.
15	Q.	If I was to tell you there is some indication that this lady was strangled, and these cords were found near the body, that would
16		Lead you to determine, wouldn't it, that it's possible somebody Was handling that. Emphasis added
17	A.	Yes.
	Q.	And when people handle objects do you want to look for touch
18		DNA?
	A.	Yes.
19	Q.	Okay. Now, obviously, you didn't know all the facts about this case when you were looking at this individual?
20	A.	Correct.
	Q.	So you were looking at the – at what appeared to be
21		Apparent blood stains?
	A.	Yes.
22	Q.	Now that I've told you that, would you agree that it? P. 77, Lns. 1-25
23	A.	It's possible, yes

24	THE COURT:	Can you do it now?
	THE WITNESS:	I can go back and try–
25	THE COURT:	Let's order it.
	MR. :	Can we have it?
26	THE COURT:	Yeah we need to order that because That's definitely part of his defense. And I understand
27		Where you're coming from with that, because if he gets– Well that could solve the whole case right there, to be
28		honest. You could solve the whole case if you got–

4

1 If you have an unknown male on that as touch DNA, I
   Could probably grant this petition just almost on that
2 Alone." P. 78, Lns. 1-12

3 BY THE COURT:

4   Q.   "Well I want to follow up what she's talking about
             Because if – if – excuse me, cord was used, as Mr. Lapena
5   Suggest in his Defense , but also there is evidence of.
             Strangulation of the victim. Hilda Krause, would the neck.
6   You know if the neck is touching the cord, hilda krause's neck,
             you and then the person who's strangling her P. 96, Lns. 18-25
7   Is touching the cords there's going to be two different DNA'S
             On there right? (Emphasis added)
8   A.   Potentially yes. P.97, Lns. 1-3
       COURT: Mr. Lapena has proffered that it's the cord because they're
9   By the body, and there's nothing else that could have strangled
             her 'maybe' P. 97, Lns. 10-12

10 Based upon the foregoing LAPENA alleges and avers "maybe" has now proven to be,

11 without a doubt, "positively" for this Honorable Court's review as to lab Item 1.1, 1.2 and Lab

12 item 1.3 as set forth below.

13   II.
14 **CRAIG KINGS MARCH 25, 2014, TOUCH DNA RESULTS AND CONCLUSIONS**
    SOLVES THE WHOLE CASE FOR DEFENDANT FRANK LAPENA

15 LaPENA respectfully contends during these Court proceedings cited herein, this

16 Honorable Court noted and held when addressing Criminalist Craig King's retesting of the

17 electrical cords "you could solve the whole case if you got unknown male on that as touch DNA."

18 Refer, February 20, 2014, p. 78, lns. 11-13.

19 Based on the foregoing, that is precisely what Craig King accomplished. Craig King's

20 March 25, 2014, touch DNA results and conclusions in fact, conclusively solved this whole case

21 in favor of Defendant, FRANK LAPENA, where King found and obtained "unknown male DNA"

22 on the electrical cord used by the strangler who wanted Hilda Krause dead.

23 LaPENA alleges and avers the Court was without a doubt clearly correct as where the

24 victim's neck is touching the cord while being strangled and the person who is strangling her is

25 touching the cord, there's going to be "two different DNA's on the cord that was used to strangle

26 Hilda Krause, and, that is precisely what Criminalist Craig King obtained during his retesting as

27 depicted in his March 25, 2014, touch DNA Results and Conclusions as argued below:

28

                                        5

1. According to LVMPD Forensic Scientist Craig King per his March 25, 2014 DNA Report and conclusions as to lab item 1.1 he obtained a touch DNA profile From the swabbing of the " plug and receptacle ends" of the electrical cord (lab item (1.1) that was consistent with a mixture of at least "two individuals" ; meaning two different DNA'S on the cord;

    Craig Kings touch DNA results further reveals the major touch DNA profile is consistent with Hilda Krause (CK2A). The other touch DNA showed a " Male Contributor" and by Kings own Touch DNA Results and conclusions the "Male Contributor is and unknown male".

    Further since Craig King identified lap item 1.1 as the electrical cord that contained 'stains that were kind of spread across most of the cord' in different areas the electrical cord that was used to viciously and brutally strangle Hilda Krause said cord contains an 'unknown males touch DNA', that has excluded Gerald Weakland as a contributor to that cord.

LAB ITEM 1.2

2. According to LVMPD Forensic Scientist Craig King per his March 25, 2014 touch DNA results and conclusions as to lab item 1.2, Mr. King obtained a partial touch DNA profile from the swabbing of the " cut ends" of the electrical cord (lab item (1.2) that was consistent with a mixture of " two individuals"; meaning two different DNA'S on the cord;
    Craig Kings partile major touch DNA profile was consistent with Hilda Krause (CK2A). The other touch DNA profile of the " cut ends" of the electrical cord revealed a minor contributor. A reasonable mind can easily conclude the two individual touch DNA mixtures contains a " female and male" DNA mixture;

    Furthermore, since Craig King identified (Lab Item 1.1& 1.2) as the electrical cord that contained stains that were kind of spread across most of the cord in different areas, the electrical cord that was used to savagely and brutally strangle Hilda Krause, said cord, contains an " unknown males touch DNA" on the cut end of the cord, aka, minor contributor, again excluding Gerald Weakland as a contributor to that cord;

LAB ITEM 1.3

3. According to LVMPD Scientist Craig King, per his March 25, 2014, Touch DNA Results and conclusions as to Lab Item 1.3, Mr. King obtained from the swabbing of the "middle" of the electrical cord Lab Item 1.3, a touch DNA mixture of at least two different individuals, meaning two different DNA'S on the cord;

    Craig King's touch DNA results and conclusions revealed the major touch DNA profile of the "middle" of the electrical lab item 1.3, was consistent with that of Hilda Krause's touch DNA (CK2A). A reasonable mind can easily conclude that the two different individual's touch DNA mixtures contain a " Female aka Hilda Krause and "unknown male's touch DNA" aka minor contributor, in the middle of the electrical cord, once again excluding Gerald Weakland as a contributor to that cord.

6

As set forth herein, LAPENA strongly contends Craig King's Touch DNA results and conclusions of March 25, 2014, conclusively state: the "plug and receptable ends", the "cut ends" and "middle" of the electrical cord are all consistent with a mixture of two different individuals containing two different DNA's on the cord, with the major touch DNA being Hilda Krause, and King also obtained "Unknown Male Touch DNA" on the "plug and receptable ends" the "cut ends" and "middle" of the electrical cord that contained stains kind of spread across most of the specific cord use by the "Unknown Male" strangler who strangled Hilda Krause.

Without, a doubt, Craig Kings retesting on touch DNA excluded Weakland's DNA on Lab Item 1.1 Lab Item 1.2 and Lab Item 1.3 regarding the mixture of two different individuals having two different DNA'S on the cord, with one DNA being a unknown male.

LaPENA infer's that a reasonable mind can conclude via touch DNA that the strangler's blood DNA was also on the electrical cord mixed along with Hilda Krause's blood DNA, as evidence in this case showed only two people at the crime scene had "blood splatters" from their injuries, both Marvin and Hilda Krause and, Craig King testified he obtained stains (blood stains) that were spread across most of the cord in different areas.

Furthermore, having obtained two different mixtures of DNA from two difference individual's DNA on the electrical cord used by the male stranger who wanted Hilda Krause dead, is exculpatory, material and favorable exonerating DNA evidence LaPENA never hired Gerald Weakland to kill Hilda Krause, and, also, said DNA evidence has conclusively proven Hilda Krause was not killed by a lone assailant, but also, by an unknown male who committed the crime of strangulation.

As this Honorable Court also previously held: "If it's not them and it's unknown, then the petition's gonna be granted" "What if - - what it was male and it's not Weakland though. That's all I need for petition granted."

Whether, unknown hairs or unknown male touch DNA on the electrical cord, makes no difference in this case, as it clearly supports LaPENA's defense, because both situations directly relate one with the other and deal with the fact Hilda Krause was struggling with her strangler and fighting for her life while she was being brutally strangled that DNA science has now proven

7

1 contains two different DNA's on the cord, hers and the stranglers. And, these facts are irrefutable.

2   LaPENA alleges and avers for the very first time in the agonizing long history of this case

3 we now have irrefutable physical DNA evidence Hilda Krause was in fact strangled with an

4 electrical cord by an "Unknown Male Strangler" whose touch DNA is still present on the specific

5 electrical cord used to strangle her that contains stains that were kind of spread across most of the

6 cord in different areas.

7 BY THE COURT: "Because one of the things that were looking at is both
        Marvin Krause, the husband of Hilda and Boswell, P.98, Lns 24-25

8   Weakland, all three – there's only four people there, one
        Person is dead."   P.99, Lns. 1-2

9   " so we don't have his DNA or anything to compare it with
        Without examining a body. We don't want to do that,

10   Obviously, because we can make eliminations based on Hilda,
        We have. We have Weakland's. Boutwell wasn't there during the

11   murder, it's uncontested on that.
        So the only person that's left unidentified is Mr. Krause.

12   P. 99, Lns. 12-18 emphasis added

13 BY THE COURT: " Item 8 has an apparent cord of an, – its item 8,

14   One green piece of cord with plastic cord
        Recovered from the floor, is that what were talking about?

15   A.   That's one of them, yes.

16   Q.   Okay.
        A.   Yeah, it's package 3, item 8, green card.

17   Q.   You've already excluded Weakland as a contributor to
           That?

18   A.   That's correct. P. 101, Lns. 4-12

19   By way of elimination, Lapena submits some irrefutable facts in his Supplemental Petition

20 that can just about pinpoint who the strangler is or probably is;

21

22 IRREFUTABLE FACT #1

23 On January 14,1974, someone in the Krause residence on that day strangled
Hilda Krause with an electrical cord

24 IRREFUTABLE FACT #2

25 Pathologist Dr. James Clark Determined Hilda Krause was Strangled by a cord or rope

26 causing her to suffer a ligature groove mark all across her neck;

27 IRREFUTABLE FACT #3

28 No evidence has been produced in this case that Hilda Krause strangled herself;

8

IRREFUTABLE FACT #4

On January 14, 1974 only four people are known to have been present at the Krause crime scene residence at 2995 Pinehurst, Las Vegas, NV;

IRREFUTABLE FACT #5

The four people known to have been present at the Krause crime scene at 2995 pinehurst, Las Vegas, NV on January 14 1974, were Hilda Krause, Marvin Krause, Gerald Weakland and Thomas Boutwell, and whoever strangled Hilda Krause with an electrical cord, was a male;

IRREFUTABLE FACT #6

Based upon criminalist Craig King's February 20, 2014 testimony, Gerald Weakland was excluded as a contributor to (CK2A) green electrical cord and, King's March 25, 2014, Touch DNA Results and conclusions shows again Weakland being excluded as a contributor to Lab Item 1.1, Lab Item 1.2 and Lab Item 1.3;

IRREFUTABLE FACT #7

DNA Evidence for the first time in over 41 years has proven Hilda Krause was in fact, strangled by an electrical cord;

IRREFUTABLE FACT #8

Lab Item 1.1, Lab Item 1.2 and Lab Item 1.3 contains mixture of two individuals having two different DNA'S on the cord, with one male's touch DNA belonging to the Strangler;

IRREFUTABLE FACT #9

DNA Evidence proved for the first time in 41 years it was a male who committed the crime of strangulation upon Hilda Krause;

IRREFUTABLE FACT #10

The unknown male is neither Gerald Weakland nor Thomas Boutwell, leaving only one other male person present in the Krause residence who used an electrical cord to strangle Hilda Krause, and Marvin Krause has not been excluded by DNA Evidence as the strangler of Hilda Krause that contains two different DNA'S on that cord.

IRREFUTABLE FACT #11

On January 14, 1974, Hilda Krause "was still alive" when Gerald Weakland left the crime scene. See, Defendant's Exhibit 4, attached hereto, aka, State's August 25, 2011, Supplemental Opposition, Exhibit 1, Police Reports and Coroner's Report's dated, March 13, 1974, where on March 6, 1974, Lt. Avants, Detectives R. Orving and C. Lee, interviewed Lois Weakland (aka Sam), the wife of Leo Weakland, and she told Avants, Orving, and Lee, she had an occasion one evening to over hear Jerry tal5king to his brothers in the kitchen area of their home, Jerry stated, **"she was still alive when I left"**.

LaPENA submits the State's own investigative evidence, State's Exhibit 1, raised the

DNA questions, "How could Gerald Weakland have killed Hilda Krause if she **"was still alive**

1 **when he left".** If Hilda Krause was still alive, that means "she was not dead at the time Weakland
2 and Boutwell left the Krause residence," leaving only Marvin Krause as the sole male left, when
3 Weakland and Boutwell departed the crime scene on January 14, 1974. So who then really killed
4 Hilda Krause? This material and highly exculpatory statement by Gerald Weakland also raises the
5 DNA question that the knife handle and wood chip, that was not retested by Craig King, despite
6 orders to do so by this Honorable Court, would probably identify by Nuclear DNA testing, by an
7 independent lab, the identity of the "unknown male" who stabbed Hilda Krause multiple times
8 after "Weakland left Hilda Krause alive" as he departed the crime scene.

9   LaPENA would respectfully request, both the knife handle and wood chip be preserved for
10 future DNA testing, in the event LaPENA is granted a new trial based upon his DNA Petition.

11   Furthermore, DNA has 100% proven LaPENA was convicted on the word of a notorious
12 liar and police frame-up who knew Weakland's murder confession on March 28, 1974, and trial
13 testimony was blatantly false.

14
        III.
15 **DNA EVIDENCE CONCLUSIVELY CONFIRMED FOR THE FIRST TIME IN OVER 41
YEARS HILDA KRAUSE WAS PHYSICALLY ATTACKED BY TWO DIFFERENT
16 MALES AT THE CRIME SCENE ON JANUARY 14, 1979**

17   LaPENA alleges and avers DNA evidence has conclusively confirmed for the first time in
18 over 41 years there was two different DNA's on the cord used to strangle Hilda Krause
19 confirming Hilda Krause was physically attacked by two different males at the crime scene on
20 January 14, 1974, exonerating Frank LaPena in the case at bar.

21   LaPENA, additionally alleges and avers, the new DNA evidence has now been positively
22 proven by physical DNA evidence that LaPENA's prior 1995 argument and issue he believed
23 another male person also attacked Hilda Krause, is now an established irrefutable fact that clearly
24 undermines Gerald Weakland's March 1974, murder statement/confession and prior court
25 testimony in 1974, 1977, 1989 and 1995, and, is contrary to the 1989, jury verdict on conflicting
26 evidence. See, State v. Busher, 81 Nev. 587, 407 P.2d 715 (1965) (Nevada has empowered the
27 trial court in a criminal case where the evidence of guilt is conflicting, to independently evaluate
28 the evidence and order another trial if it does not agree with the jury's conclusion that the

X

1 defendant has been proven guilty beyond a reasonable doubt). See also, Evans v. State, 112 Nev.

2 1172, 926 P.2d 265 (1996) and NRS 176.0918, subsection 1, 7(a) and 10(a).

3 ### CONCLUSION

4 For the reason herein above set forth, LAPENA alleges and avers, LVMPD Scientist,

5 Craig Kings March 25 , 2014, Touch DNA Results and Conclusions as to Lab Item 1.1, Lab Item

6 1.2, and Lab Item 1.3, has in fact solved this whole case in favor of Defendant FRANK LAPENA,

7 as King found and obtained "Unknown Male DNA" on the electrical cord used by the strangler

8 who wanted Hilda Krause dead.

9 LAPENA respectfully submits that this exculpatory and material DNA evidence is newly

10 discovered to LAPENA'S defense, such that it could not with reasonable diligence have been

11 discovered and produced at his 1989, trial. That a reasonable probability exists had this DNA

12 evidence been produced at this 1989, trial, the results of these proceedings would have been

13 different.

14 Based on the above and foregoing, LaPena respectfully moves this Honorable Court for an

15 Order granting the Genetic Marker Analysis Petition.

16

17

18

19

20

21

22

23

24

25

26

27

28

11

351

EXHIBIT 1

Las Vegas Metropolitan Police Department Forensic Laboratory Report of Examination Biology/DNA Detail		Distribution Date: APR 24 2012
Subject(s):	Frank LaPena (suspect) Hilda Krause (victim)	Case: 74-1881
		Agency: LVMPD
		Incident: Homicide
		Requester: D. Culver/ C. Brown DDA

The Biology/DNA Detail of the Las Vegas Metropolitan Police Department Forensic Laboratory examined evidence in this case and reports the following results:

Impound Pkg#	Impound Item#	Lab Pkg #	Description		Results
534-5	13	CK1	A)	Hairs from victim's right hand	
			1)	Light brown/blonde hair	• No DNA profile obtained
			2)	Dark hair	• No DNA profile obtained
			3)	Light brown/blonde hair	• No DNA profile obtained
			4)	Light brown/blonde hair	• No DNA profile obtained
	14		B)	Hairs from victim's left hand	
			1)	Light brown hair	• Not suitable for STR DNA typing
			2)	Light brown hair	• Not suitable for STR DNA typing
			3)	Light brown hair	• No DNA profile obtained
	11,12, 15,16		---	Carpet samples, doorway substance, and drawer handle substance	• Not examined
759-1	1	CK2	A)	Reference blood (w/preservative) - Hilda Krause	• Full female profile
	2		B)	Reference blood (w/o preservative) - Hilda Krause	• No DNA profile obtained

CONCLUSIONS

Items CK1A1, CK1A2, CK1A3, CK1A4, CK1B3, CK2A, and CK2B were subjected to PCR amplification at the following STR genetic loci: D8S1179, D21S11, D7S820, CSF1PO, D3S1358, TH01, D13S317, D16S539, D2S1338, D19S433, vWA, TPOX, D18S51, D5S818, and FGA. The sex-determining Amelogenin locus was also examined.

DNA profiles were not obtained from the hairs (CK1A1, CK1A2, CK1A3, CK1A4, and CK1B3).

A reference DNA profile was obtained from the blood sample from Hilda Krause (CK2A).

Las Vegas Metropolitan Police Department Forensic Laboratory (Supplemental 3) Report of Examination Biology/DNA Forensic Casework	Distribution Date:	April 10, 2014
	Agency:	LVMPD
	Primary Case #:	74-1881
	Incident:	Homicide
	Requester:	David M Culver
	Location:	Robbery/Homicide Bureau
	Lab Case #:	13-05472
Subject(s):	Frank LAPENA (Suspect) Hilda KRAUSE (Victim)	

The following evidence was examined and results are reported below.

Lab Item #	Impound Pkg #	Impound Item #	Description	Summary
Item 1 Item 1.1	000534 - 2	6	Electrical cord** - Swabbing of plug & receptacle ends of electrical cord	• Negative presumptive blood test(s) • Mixture profile
Item 1.2			- Swabbing of the cut ends of the electrical cord	• Positive presumptive blood test(s) • Partial mixture profile
Item 1.3			- Swabbing of the middle of the electrical cord	• Positive presumptive blood test(s) • Mixture profile

*Refer to the original report by C. King dated April 13, 2012 for related information.
**This item was reexamined; see report dated October 29, 2013 for previous analysis results from C. King, P#9971.

Results and Conclusions:

Item 1.1, Item 1.2, and Item 1.3 were subjected to PCR amplification at the following STR genetic loci: D8S1179, D21S11, D7S820, CSF1PO, D3S1358, TH01, D13S317, D16S539, D2S1338, D19S433, vWA, TPOX, D18S51, D5S818, and FGA. The sex-determining Amelogenin locus was also examined.

Lab Item 1.1
The DNA profile obtained from the swabbing of the plug and receptacle ends of the electrical cord (Item 1.1) is consistent with a mixture of at least two individuals. The major DNA profile is consistent with Hilda Krause (CK2A*). The estimated frequency of the major DNA profile among unrelated individuals in the general population is rarer than 1 in 700 billion (identity assumed). Although there are indications of a male contributor below the interpretation threshold, sufficient data was not obtained for comparison. No further conclusions can be made regarding the minor contributor(s).

Lab Item 1.2
The partial DNA profile obtained from the swabbing of the cut ends of the electrical cord (Item 1.2) is consistent with a mixture of at least two individuals. The partial major DNA profile is consistent with Hilda Krause (CK2A*). The estimated frequency of the partial major DNA profile among unrelated individuals in the general population is rarer than 1 in 700 billion (identity assumed). No conclusions can be made regarding the minor contributor(s).

Lab Item 1.3
The DNA profile obtained from the swabbing of the middle of the electrical cord (Item 1.3) is consistent with a mixture of at least two individuals. The major DNA profile is consistent with Hilda Krause (CK2A*). The estimated frequency of the major DNA profile among unrelated individuals in the general population is rarer than 1 in 700 billion (identity assumed). No conclusions can be made regarding the minor contributor(s).

The evidence is returned to secure storage.

Craig W King, #9971   03/25/2014
Forensic Scientist II

- END OF REPORT -

March 20, 2001

Hey Frank:

I got your letter after I had already responded to Father Dave. So much time
passed, I had about given up on a response to my original letter.

Man, your case just continues to amaze me; every time I think I've seen it all
here comes a new twist! The average person couldn't begin to fathom the abuses
cops and prosecutors are allowed to get away with.

I know how important this is, so I'm going to be perfectly candid: I'm not sure,
anymore, how much my info. can help your court battle, simply because you already
have everything imaginable in front of the courts. Some of the issues that I
thought would be news to you are already in your appeals. For example: I know a
former prosecutor who is now in private practice. Privately he has made statements concerning the injustice in your case, but it's nothing compared to the
way you have Mel Harmon and Det. Lyons nailed for tampering with evidence. I
also didn't know you had already made the personal connection between Marvin
Krause and G.W.

Let me give you some of what I know and believe to be relevant: I got out of
prison the first time in 1973 and was rousted but not arrested after the Krause
incident. Initially, the cops seemed to think the perpetrators were Black and
that I might be able to point them in the right direction or find out something
for them.

In late "74" or early "75" I met G.W. in the old Clark County Jail. He was the
tank boss in the 62-man tank. However, it wasn't until I came back to jail again
that things began to get interesting. G.W. had moved upstairs (I believe 4-F).
He was also the tank boss up there. Some months prior to my return there had
been a big fight in 4-F, and G.W. decreed that no more Blacks were allowed up
there. Myself and some more guys took offense to that and had Tucker move a
bunch of us up there.

During my stay on 4-F, G.W. went out of his way to try to convince me that he
wasn't a racist or an informant. He told me that the Krause incident was an
inside move put together by Marvin Krause and that you had nothing to do with
it and would be acquitted and compensated for your "inconvenience." His spiel
was that it was all a strategically arranged situation with you all going thru
the motions to derail any future chances of the state making a case against M.K.
I wasn't the only one present at some of these sessions in which G.W. tried to
make the point that he wasn't a snitch and everything was being orchestrated to
protect M.K. The only question is whether anybody else will step up. You know
how that goes, Frank. People know things and don't have a problem repeating
what they know, but when a court stenographer enters the picture everybody starts
getting nervous.

G.W. found out I was arranging my bail through Dale Phiefer (Burton's Bail
Bonds) and he stated he knew Dale. When I got out I mentioned this to Dale.
I was told in no uncertain terms that if G.W. said anything _else_ about M.K.
or Rosalie he would be dealt with, and if I ever saw G.W. again I was to relay that to him. Supposedly, Spilotro, Fat Herbie Blitzstein, and the "Hole
in the Wall" mob was backing M.K. Of course, in those days everybody claimed
to be backed by Spilotro.

354

In 1983 you and I both got out of prison. My release was a little less conventional than yours :). (Ironically, we were both taken back into custody in 1989). While I was on my "vacation" in L.A., I hooked up with a crew of guys from the Carson and Compton area. Most of these guys were prominent players in the escort/ prostitution game. Some of them were operating in Vegas in the late 60's and 70's.

I don't know if you are aware of it or not but G.W. tried his hand at hustling as a pimp prior to the Krause incident. A very heavy-handed operator he turned out to be- a gorilla pimp. He clashed with some of this Carson&Compton mob over a couple of hookers who G.W. was putting pressure on. This situation escalated and at least one of the women got seriously hurt- real sadistic brutal stuff. Deja Vu in the late 80's, a young prostitute associated with this same crew got contacted by a "trick" who had read her sex add in the <u>Hollywood</u> <u>Free</u> <u>Press</u>, an underground newspaper. To make a long story short, this trick was a sicko and he committed murder and mayhem against this woman.

I was with some of the Carson&Compton crew within days of this incident and guess what they compared the carnage to? Acts committed by G.W. back in the days- and not just in the one incident where they were beefing with him. I believe your boy is into cereal, and I'm not talking about Captain Crunch.

I pointed some of the things I know about your case out to Oscar G., who as you know represented Rosalie at one point and who I hired after my capture in 1989. Oscar expressed to me that he was well aware of how royally you had got screwed around and claimed that one of his regrets was that he hadn't stayed on that case and crushed Mel Harmon and G.W. He suggested to me that the way to win the case was to put M.H. and the entire snitch system on trial and the one sure way to do that is to make the connection between G.W. and Captain Crunch.

In 1998, I began to take a nonfiction bookwriter's course. I wanted to write about what I call "Ninja Rats." Ninja Rats is the term I use for these guys who prosecutors and cops allow to get away with everything under the sun simply because they are willing to point the finger at the next man. As I listed the most egregious examples of these occurrences, your case was high up on the list. I got Oscar G. involved in this project and he promised to do the introduction. He also promised me a boatload of ammunition from his files with which I could use to go after M.H. One of the cases he directed me to was the Haupt case. You probably remember that Haupt was the guy from Cali that got railroaded for the molestation and I believe killing of a child. Anyway, M.H. committed high crimes in the Haupt matter.

Unfortunately, since O.G. has thrown his hat in the political arena he isn't as cooperative. However, I'm still after him. Even if I can't get him to go as hard at his new found prosecutor buddies, I'm still holding him to the intro to the book and comments as to the injustices in the Krause case.

Frank, I must ask you to keep what I'm telling you close to your chest, because a lot of what I know involves "street" people and you know how fast they can abandon ship. Even the former prosecutor, I mentioned earlier, had diarrhea of the mouth as long as O.G. was encouraging, is a little more tentative. I'm walking a tightrope as I try to get this manuscript prepared without spooking the supporting cast.

I'm not going to sit here and say I can get anybody from the Carson&Compton crew to come to court, but what I do believe can happen is enough info. can be gathered to put a spotlight on G.W. linking him to Captain Crunch which would put a tremendous amount of pressure on the DA's office to do the right thing.

Also, if you succeed in getting a new trial, I'm more than glad to testify about what went on in 4-F, and I will try to encourage others to step up and repeat what G.W. and Boutwell were saying.

By the way, why was the State so generous with Boutwell when G.W. was already talking? Whatever happened with Joesph Costanza?

I'm not sure who Mazzan is, although the name sounds familiar. Was he a victim of the Paul Goldman and Mel Harmon buzzsaw?

Frank, was Paul Goldman the Judge at any of your trials?

I'm guessing that the Coop you are talking about is Cecil "Kelly" Cooper? Which-ever one he is, tell him I look forward to hearing from him. I need all the feedback I can get from that end.

This Virginia transfer has to do with politics, payback for the vacation, and an attempt to isolate me. I did a Fox TV show in 1994 and the sh-- hit the fan! Too bad I didn't start talking about G.W. and Captain Crunch, on the air.

I would like to get you a copy of the overview and first chapter of my manuscript. it is entitled: Tank Boss. Would you like to see it? I think it can benefit you, because we can get things out in the open that aren't likely to be allowed in court. Also, in the event you ever decide to tell your story, the publica-tion of Tank Boss will greatly facilitate your endeavor.

I have some more things that I would like to discuss with you, but I will wait until I hear from you before going into them.

Take care of yourself and get back with me at your earliest convenience.

JAMES Y. CLARKE, M.D., F.C.A.P.
540 EAST SAHARA
LAS VEGAS, NEVADA 89105

CLINICAL PATHOLOGY
PATHOLOGICAL ANATOMY

NAME: KRAUSE, HILDA   NUMBER: MEA 107-74

POSTMORTEM EXAMINATION

THE AUTOPSY WAS PERFORMED AT BUNKER BROTHERS MORTUARY, JANUARY 14, 1974, LAS VEGAS, NEVADA.

EXTERNAL EXAMINATION

THE BODY IS THAT OF A WELL DEVELOPED, WELL NOURISHED ELDERLY WHITE FEMALE MEASURING 64 INCHES IN LENGTH AND WEIGHING AN ESTIMATED 116 POUNDS.

THERE IS A DEEP INCISED, CUTTING AND STAB WOUND OF THE LOWER NECK EX-TENDING TRANSVERSELY FROM THE RIGHT LATERAL NECK AREA AROUND TO THE LEFT LATERAL NECK AREA. THE DEEPEST AND LENGTHIEST PORTIONS OF THE WOUND ARE UPON THE RIGHT. THE WOUND MEASURES 13 CM IN LENGTH. IT GAPES PARTICULARLY OVER THE RIGHT NECK AND MEASURES UP TO 2 CM IN WIDTH. ON THE LEFT THE WOUND IS SWALLOW EXPOSING THE NECK MUSCLES AND EXTERNAL JUGULAR VEIN WHICH IS SEVERED. ON THE RIGHT, PARTICULARLY ON THE RIGHT LATERAL PORTION, THE WOUND BECOMES VERY DEEP, AND IS ASSOCIATED WITH ONE OR MORE DEEP STAB WOUNDS TO THE RIGHT LATERAL NECK DESCRIBED MORE FULLY BELOW.

HIGHER UP ON THE NECK IS A DEEP LIGATURE GROOVE ENCIRCLING THE NECK FROM THE RIGHT POSTERIOR MID NECK TO THE POSTERIOR PORTION OF THE NECK ON THE LEFT. THE LIGATURE GROOVE MEASURES 20 CM IN LENGTH AND LESS THAN A CM IN WIDTH IN ITS WIDER PORTIONS ON THE FRONT PART OF THE NECK WHERE THE GROOVE IS DEEPEST.

A SIMILAR APPEARING GROOVE EXTENDS LATERALLY FROM THE LEFT PORTION OF THE MOUTH INTO THE CHEEK. THIS WOUND APPEAR TO BE THE REMAINS OF A GAG LIGATURE.

ASIDE FROM THESE THE SKIN SURFACES SHOW NO EVIDENCE OF RECENT TRAUMATIC INJURIES. THE ANUS AND EXTERNAL GENITALIA ARE NORMAL IN APPEARANCE.

INTERNAL EXAMINATION

BODY CAVITIES

PERITONEAL CAVITY: THE PERITONEAL CAVITY CONTAINS NO FLUID. THE PERITONEAL SURFACES ARE SMOOTH.

PLEURAL CAVITIES: THE PLEURAL CAVITIES CONTAIN NO FLUID. THE PLEURAL SURFACES ARE SMOOTH.

PERICARDIAL SAC: THE PERICARDIAL SAC CONTAINS A SMALL AMOUNT OF CLEAR YELLOW SEROUS FLUID. THE PERICARDIAL SURFACES ARE SMOOTH.

357

KRAUSE, HILDA
POSTMORTEM EXAMINATION
PAGE -2-

BODY ORGANS

HEART: THE HEART WEIGHS APPX 260 GRAMS. THE EPICARDIUM IS
SMOOTH AND THE MYOCARDIUM IS A HOMOGENEOUS REDDISH BROWN. THE
ENDOCARDIUM IS SMOOTH AND THE VALVES SHOW NO DEFORMITIES. THE
CORONARY ARTERIES ARE WIDELY PATENT AND SHOW BUT SLIGHT EVIDENCE
OF ATHEROSCLEROSIS.

LUNGS: THE RIGHT LUNG WEIGHS APPX 340 GRAMS. CREPITATION IS NOT
DIMINISHED. ON SECTION THE LUNG SHOWS A MOTTLED PINKISH GRAY SUR-
FACE AND NO FLUID EXUDES. THE BRONCHI AND VESSELS SHOW NOTHING
OF NOTE. THE LEFT LUNG WEIGHS APPX 320 GRAMS AND IS SIMILAR IN
APPEARANCE.

LIVER: THE LIVER WEIGHS APPX 1600 GRAMS. THE CAPSULE IS SMOOTH.
ON SECTION THE PARENCHYMA IS A HOMOGENEOUS BROWN.

SPLEEN: THE SPLEEN WEIGHS APPX 140 GRAMS. THE CAPSULE IS TENSE.
ON SECTION THE PULP IS A DARK PLUM RED AND THE FOLLICLES ARE IN-
CONSPICIOUS.

GASTROINTESTINAL TRACT: THE ESOPHAGUS, STOMACH AND DUODENUM SHOW
NOTHING OF NOTE. THE REMAINDER OF THE SMALL AND LARGE BOWEL ARE
NORMAL IN APPEARANCE.

GENITOURINARY SYSTEM: THE RIGHT KIDNEY WEIGHS APPX 140 GRAMS.
THE CAPSULE STRIPS WITH EASE LEAVING A SMOOTH SURFACE. ON SECTION
THE CORTEX IS NOT THINNED AND THE CORTICAL MARKINGS ARE NORMAL.
THE PELVIS AND URETER SHOWING NOTHING OF NOTE. THE LEFT KIDNEY
WEIGHS APPX 140 GRAMS AND IS SIMILAR IN APPEARANCE. THE BLADDER
CONTAINS A SMALL AMOUNT OF CLEAR URINE AND THE MUCOSAL SURFACE IS
SMOOTH AND WHITE.

THE UTERUS, OVARIES AND FALLOPIAN TUBES SHOW SOME ATROPHIC CHANGES.
THE VAGINA SHOWS NOTHING OF NOTE.

ORGANS OF NECK: THE EXTERNAL APPEARANCE OF THE INCISED, CUTTING AND
STAB WOUND IS DESCRIBED ABOVE. IT IS MORE SUPERFICIAL ON THE LEFT
AND IN THE MIDLINE. ON THE RIGHT THERE ARE ONE OR MORE STAB WOUNDS
EXTENDING VERY DEEPLY INTO THE NECK. THESE STAB WOUNDS EXTEND DOWN
TO THE LATERAL PROCESSES OF THE CERVICAL VERTEBRAE WITH A FRACTURE
OF ONE LATERAL PROCESS. THERE IS A COMPLETE SEVERANCE OF THE VERTE-
BRAL ARTERY ON THE RIGHT. THE COMMON CAROTID ARTERY IS LACERATED
AND THE LUMEN IS EXPOSED TO THE SURFACE BUT IS NOT COMPLETELY SEVERED.

THE THYROID IS QUITE LARGE AND HAS A SOMEWHAT NODULAR APPEARANCE ON
SECTION WITH A FIRM CONSISTENCY.

HEAD: THE SCALP IS NORMAL IN APPEARANCE. THE SKULL SHOWS NO EVIDENCE OF FRACTURE. THE LINING OF THE DURA IS SMOOTH. THE CONVOLUTIONS AND SULCI OF THE CEREBRUM ARE OF NORMAL WIDTH. MULTIPLE SECTIONS OF THE CEREBRUM, CEREBELLUM, BRAIN STEM AND UPPER CERVICAL SPINAL CORD SHOW NO GROSSLY EVIDENT CHANGES.

SIGNIFICANT MICROSCOPIC FINDINGS

LUNGS: THE ALVEOLAR STRUCTURE IS NORMAL IN APPEARANCE WITH SOME EMPHYSEMATOUS CHANGES. NO FLUID IS PRESENT.

HEART: THE MUSCLE FIBERS OF THE MYOCARDIUM ARE WELL PRESERVED.

LIVER: THE HEPATIC CORD CELLS SHOW NO DEGENERATIVE CHANGES.

THYROID: THE THYROID ACINI ARE RELATIVELY SMALL BUT THE COLLOID CONTENT IS NORMAL. IN QUITE LARGE AREAS THE ACINI ARE REPLACED BY VASCULAR FIBROUS TISSUE WITH NUMEROUS LYMPHOID FOLLICLES SCATTERED ABOUT.

KIDNEYS: THE GLOMERULI AND TUBULES SHOW NOTHING OF NOTE.

SUMMARY AND COMMENT

DEATH WAS HOMICIDAL AND DIRECTLY DUE TO MASSIVE EXTERNAL HEMORRHAGE FROM THE SEVERED VERTEBRAL ARTERY AND PARTIALLY SEVERED COMMON CAROTID ARTERY. THE VASCULAR TRAUMA RESULTED FROM THE INCISED CUTTING AND STAB WOUND OF THE NECK DESCRIBED ABOVE. THERE APPARENTLY WAS AN ATTEMPT AT STRANGULATION BY LIGATURE PRESUMABLY PRIOR TO THE THROAT CUTTING. LOSS OF CONSCIOUSNESS WOULD HAVE BEEN IMMEDIATE AND DEATH WOULD HAVE RESULTED IN A VERY SHORT INTERVAL FOLLOWING THE INCURRING OF THE NECK WOUNDS.

THE COMPLETE AUTOPSY SHOWS NO EVIDENCE OF OTHER SIGNIFICANT DISEASE PROCESSES WHICH COULD HAVE CONTRIBUTED TO DEATH.

FINAL DIAGNOSIS

IMMEDIATE CAUSE OF DEATH: MASSIVE EXTERNAL HEMORRHAGE.

DUE TO: SEVERANCE OF RIGHT VERTEBRAL ARTERY AND LACERATION OF THE RIGHT COMMON CAROTID ARTERY.

DUE TO: HOMICIDAL TRAUMATIC INJURIES - INCISED CUTTING AND STAB WOUNDS OF NECK.

ASSOCIATED CONDITIONS: LIGATURE STRANGULATION.
CHRONIC THYROIDITIS (HASHIMOTO'S STRUMA).

JAMES Y. CLARKE, M.D.
CHIEF MEDICAL EXAMINER
CLARK COUNTY, NEVADA

RK

NEVADA BOARD OF PARDONS

-oOo-

MEETING AND PUBLIC HEARING

9:00 a.m., Wednesday
November 6, 2019

Supreme Court Building
201 South Carson Street
2nd Floor
Carson City, Nevada

VIDEOCONFERENCED TO:

Nevada Supreme Court
408 East Clark Avenue
Las Vegas, Nevada

Reported by: DEBRA J. BARTGIS, CCR #56

SILVER STATE COURT REPORTERS, LLC   (775) 329-6323

BOARD MEMBERS PRESENT

STEVE SISOLAK
Governor, Chairman

AARON D. FORD
Attorney General, Member

MARK GIBBONS
Chief Justice, Member

KRISTINA PICKERING
Justice, Member

JAMES W. HARDESTY
Justice, Member

RONALD PARRAGUIRRE
Justice, Member

LIDIA STIGLICH
Justice, Member

ELISSA F. CADISH
Justice, Member

ABBI SILVER
Justice, Member

APPEARANCES

DENISE DAVIS
Executive Secretary

HAROLD WICKHAM
Acting Director
Department Corrections

CHRIS DeRICCO
Chairman
Nevada Parole Board

SHANNON MOYLE
Chief
Offender Management Division
Dpartment of Corrections

ANNE CARPENTER
Acting Chief
Parole and Probation Department

ROSALIE BORDELOVE
Deputy Attorney General

SILVER STATE COURT REPORTERS, LLC   (775) 329-6323

X

ATTORNEYS PRESENT

PAUL WOLFE
Attorney
432 Court Street
Reno, Nevada 89501

KRISTINA WILDEVELD
Attorney at Law
CAITLYN McAMIS
Attorney at La
615 Souoth 6th Street
Las Vegas, Nevada 89101

COLLENE McCARTY
Attorney at Law
3960 Howard Hughes Parkway
Las Vegas, Nevada 89109

INDEX

INDEX
(Continued)

1	CARSON CITY AND LAS VEGAS, NEVADA
2	WEDNESDAY, NOVEMBER 6, 2019
3	9:00 a.m.
4	-oOo-
5	AGENDA ITEM IV(TT)
6	FRANK LaPENA
7	-oOo-
8	GOVERNOR SISOLAK: The next one I've
9	got is -- or did I have somebody else that has to
10	catch a plane? Mr. LaPena?
11	MS. DAVIS: Yes, Mr. LaPena.
12	GOVERNOR SISOLAK: Mr. LaPena, (tt).
13	JUSTICE SILVER: Maybe I can ask if
14	there are any questions.
15	I had this case for five years, and I
16	wrote -- it took me five years to write the order
17	in this case, going through 50 years of procedural
18	history, so I didn't know -- I'm the one that put
19	this on the agenda based on my being constrained
20	not to grant him a new trial after DNA pretty much
21	exculpated him, which is a whole other story.
22	(CROSS-TALK)
23	JUSTICE CADISH: Well, perhaps you can
24	explain what the DNA showed that exculpated him,
25	but yet he wasn't --

```
1                    JUSTICE SILVER:  Here's the deal --

2                    JUSTICE CADISH:  -- found actually

3       innocent.

4                    JUSTICE SILVER:  -- yes, he never was

5       there.  The killer, Weakland --

6                    JUSTICE CADISH:  Right.  He wasn't at

7       the scene.

8                    JUSTICE SILVER:  Right, he wasn't at

9       the scene.

10                   So basically all the DNA showed exactly

11      the opposite of what Weakland testified to,

12      especially how the killing went down.  So the query

13      I had on the novel issue was, if a witness, the

14      only witness in the case, is shown to have

15      completely lied about how the crime occurred,

16      could the District Court grant him a new trial?

17                   There was a very small amount of

18      testimony by the coroner supporting exactly

19      that, that Weakland lied, but unfortunately for

20      Mr. LaPena there was such ineffectiveness of

21      counsel, which can be seen, that the co-defendant

22      was completely acquitted.

23                   And as you know, in at least one of

24      his many reversals, three Justices of the Supreme

25      Court, not even the Justice that wrote in on this,
```

1   which was Gunderson, Springer actually wrote a

2   scathing dissent saying that it was ineffective

3   assistance of counsel. It was 4 to 3 on that.

4   Judge Porter had originally, in 1995,

5   granted the ineffective assistance of counsel, and

6   it was reversed by the Supreme Court, and he went

7   to trial the second time.

8   Offered by the District Attorney murder

9   in the second degree, credit time served. He

10 refused that, as he stated to Dr. Pagline - which

11 I read here confirming what I'm saying - and he

12 ended up going to a second trial, and -- or I'm

13 sorry. It wasn't a second trial. By then he had

14 to serve the rest of that second trial sentence.

15 And that's what happened there.

16   I was constrained on the novel issue

17 and because, unfortunately, I had to find that it

18 was cumulative to what the coroner testified to,

19 but was, quite frankly, never highlighted by

20 counsel, despite the -- and by the way, I read all

21 the cross-examination, I read the trials in both

22 cases, and never was there even cross about the

23 fact that Weakland was convicted of perjury after

24 the first trial where Weakland said Mr. LaPena

25 didn't do it.

1   It's a tortured history, in 30 years

2 I've never seen a case like this, and that's why

3 I put this on.

4   But I can ask specific -- the DNA

5 basically contradicts everything that Weakland,

6 who got a five-year sentence, who actually slit

7 the woman's throat, said.

8   I don't know if that makes sense.

9   GOVERNOR SISOLAK: Okay.

10 Miss Wildeveld, did you want to --

11   MS. WILDEVELD: Thank you, Governor

12 Sisolak, Attorney General Ford, Chief Justice

13 Gibbons, Members of the Supreme Court.

14   Thank you, Justice Silver, for giving

15 an overview of Mr. LaPena's case.

16   My name Kristina Wildeveld, and I'm

17 here on behalf of Frank LaPena.

18   As Justice Silver had indicated, I

19 think I could even go so far as to say in Justice

20 Silver's opinion that she had written, it was a

21 very lengthy opinion which I attached to my

22 petition, and it was a very, very large petition

23 that we submitted, and I thank you all for going

24 through the history of Mr. LaPena's case, because

25 it is a sordid history, and a very interesting one,

1   and an academic one, so to speak.

2   I think that Justice Silver would have,

3   if she could have, if the issues were before her

4   as a Judge, if the attorneys representing

5   Mr. LaPena at the time had put the issues before

6   her, would have been able to say, even declare,

7   that Mr. LaPena was actually innocent, if those

8   issues were before her.

9   But Mr. LaPena was originally sentenced

10   to life without the possibility of parole, and she

11   went through the history so I don't want to belabor

12   that point.

13   But on October 25th, 2011 he was

14   released from custody -- after appearing before

15   this Board in February -- December of 2003, he

16   was released from custody in February of 2005.

17   On October 25th, 2011 the Nevada

18   Supreme Court granted Frank's post-conviction

19   petition, noting that Frank's conviction resulted

20   almost exclusively - as Justice Silver indicated -

21   from Weakland's testimony alone, the veracity of

22   which has consistently been called into question

23   and recanted.

24   And as a result of the Court's granting

25   of the petition, the DNA testing was done and was

1   performed for the first time in Frank's case ever.

2   And from 2011 to 2015 DNA blood and

3   hair evidence was ordered by the Court, and two

4   evidentiary hearings were held.

5   And it's become clear, since all of

6   that has been done, that Frank LaPena served 25

7   years in prison, and much of his life, tied to

8   a murder he did not play a role in or commit.

9   Frank is now 81 years old. During

10   his total of 25 years of incarceration and his

11   sporadic bouts of freedom, Frank has not only

12   completely been discipline-free, but he has also

13   been a model citizen, and even gone out of his

14   way performing heroic acts of saving more than

15   one human life, including one prison guard.

16   He has always maintained his innocence,

17   and it is my honor and privilege to stand before

18   this Board, after all of these years, and to humbly

19   request on his behalf, at the very least, the grant

20   of a pardon at this time, or any other act of grace

21   that this Board may deem appropriate.

22   In doing so, I want to point out that

23   this is not Frank's first time before this Board.

24   He was before the Board in 2003. And in 2003,

25   when his life without the possibility of parole

1   was granted, he was granted clemency, and he was

2   released two years later, Justice Gunderson

3   appeared before this Board. And it was a very

4   unusual step for a former Supreme Court Justice

5   to appear before a Pardons Board and advocate on

6   another person's behalf.

7   And although you all had the 2003

8   transcript in your packet, I do want to highlight

9   some of those, some of the words that Justice

10 Gunderson said.

11   He said: Personally, I have the

12 conviction that they made a wrong call in charging

13 Mr. LaPena, and I say that from the bottom of my

14 heart. I say it on the basis of my study of many,

15 many records, but I really don't think that he

16 has all the - I'm sorry - the knowledge that

17 Justice Batjer and I had when we filed the first

18 dissent in this case in the first opinion, which

19 was presented by Justice Zenoff.

20   Justice and I crafted the dissent.

21 Justice Cameron Batjer undertook to study it, he

22 took a long time studying it, and we all know, or

23 at least all of us who have served on the Court or

24 around the Court, as Justice Rose and I did, that

25 Cameron Batjer is, certainly was by no means a

1   bleeding heart liberal.

2   And he studied my opinion, my draft

3   opinion for a long time, and he came back to me,

4   having studied it and Justice Zenoff's proposed

5   opinion, and he said I agree with you. You're

6   right on.

7   And he went on to say, I don't know if

8   any of you looked at that opinion. Justice Rose

9   probably has since he wrote a later opinion. But

10   if you were to take the opinion, you would see that

11   I took up every point of Justice Zenoff's opinion,

12   and Justice Batjer said I think I hit every

13   baseline of his opinion and demonstrated that there

14   was no sufficient evidence under any legal standard

15   to charge Frank LaPena with the murder of Hilda

16   Krause.

17   I have looked through I think most all

18   of the opinions, I have gone back over them, and I

19   have become even more convinced than ever before

20   that Frank LaPena should have never been charged.

21   But I want to tell you, after I wrote

22   my first opinion, Judge Guy came to see me. He had

23   not been a Judge at that time that Frank LaPena was

24   charged; he had been a Chief Deputy, Chief Criminal

25   Deputy Attorney in the Clark County District

1   Attorney's Office, and he said I agree with you

2   entirely.

3   And then he went on to describe all the

4   clothes that Chief Deputy District Attorney Adler

5   Guy was wearing when he came to talk to Justice

6   Gunderson.

7   He talked about his infantry wear, the

8   badge that he was wearing, and he said that he was

9   manifestly distressed by what was happening in this

10   case, and he told him what happened, and how Frank

11   LaPena came to be charged; how Weakland was buying

12   his way out of the charge, and he kept changing his

13   story again and again and again between the

14   District Attorney's Office and the Police

15   Department, until finally it was a story that

16   would be bought, and they came to what he called

17   the Rube Goldberg cartoon, and Frank LaPena came

18   to be caught up in a murder charge.

19   And then Justice Rose made a

20   conclusion, which you all have before you, and

21   Justice Gunderson concluded that an injustice

22   has been one of the things that this Board, this

23   Pardons Board, has always been willing to focus on

24   where there has been an imposition on a defendant

25   and an abuse of process.

SILVER STATE COURT REPORTERS dbartgis@nvbell.net

1   And he said, I've never been more

2   sincere about anything in my entire life than the

3   fact that I believe that Batjer, Cameron Batjer and

4   I were right in our analysis of what the quality of

5   evidence was against Frank LaPena, or the lack of

6   it, so to speak.

7   And today we're before you. I am

8   standing before you with Frank LaPena. And as

9   Justice Gunderson pointed out when he appeared

10   before this Board, and after his discussion with

11   former Justice Rose, he was convinced that Frank

12   had nothing to do with the murder of Hilda Krause,

13   yet to date Frank LaPena was not only charged, he

14   was convicted, imprisoned, and has served and

15   suffered, and continues to suffer, the collateral

16   consequences of his murder conviction.

17   Frank is 81 years old, and continues to

18   be an upstanding member of society, and has never

19   had any negative contact with the law since that

20   time.

21   Because of his status as an ex-felon

22   Frank has continuously struggled to find a job,

23   and the only people who have been willing to hire

24   Frank are those people who he tells his story to

25   or knows about his story.

1   Frank LaPena is asking for a full,

2   unconditional pardon. And I think in our petition

3   we asked that -- or Frank has said in his

4   application that he doesn't require the right to

5   bears arms. I see no reason for Frank not to have

6   the right to bear arms.

7   But despite having been tried and

8   retried, and having served at least 25 years of his

9   life in the Nevada Department of Corrections, he

10   has always maintained his innocence for the crimes

11   for which he has been charged and convicted.

12   People in all levels of the community

13   and all levels of law enforcement and all sides of

14   the law also believe in Frank LaPena. He deserves

15   a pardon at this point in his life, as he has never

16   asked for one before.

17   He has lived an honorable and

18   crime-free life, he is 81 years old, and he would

19   like to be able to travel freely and live out the

20   rest of his life without permission. At this time

21   we ask for that grant.

22   I do want to address the psych report,

23   that there was a negative comment in there in 2003

24   from the prison psychiatrist. Following that, when

25   the doctor saw him in the prison, Dr. Pagline went

1   and interviewed Frank again privately, and

2   Dr. Pagline found that there was no psychological

3   issues or mental health issues with Frank.

4   And I submitted Dr. Pagline's report,

5   I supplemented his petition with Dr. Pagline's

6   report. So I hope you've all had the opportunity

7   to review that as well, finding that Frank does

8   not in fact have any antisocial personality

9   disorders or suffer from anything. And I think

10   that also speaks to the time that he served in

11   prison and the time that he has been out in

12   society, where he has never had any kind of

13   negative interaction with anybody.

14   And he has proven himself, both in

15   and out of prison, that he can function in the

16   community as a productive citizen.

17   And we humbly ask you to pardon him

18   at this time.

19   GOVERNOR SISOLAK: Thank you.

20   Does anybody have any questions for

21   Miss Wildeveld?

22   (No Response)

23   GOVERNOR SISOLAK: No? Okay.

24   Did your client want to make a

25   statement?

1   MS. WILDEVELD: I'm sorry?

2   GOVERNOR SISOLAK: Did your client want

3   to make a statement?

4   MS. WILDEVELD: He does, Your Honor.

5   Thank you.

6   Frank?

7   He has a hard time hearing.

8   MR. LaPENA: Excuse me. The VA gave

9   me some hearing aids, and I still can't hear that

10   well.

11   It's an honor to be before this Board.

12   I appreciate any relief that you would grant me.

13   Chief Justice Gibbons, in 2003 you

14   made the move to give me clemency. I respected

15   that, and I felt that you had trust that I would

16   be a good citizen when I was out, and I've done

17   everything I possibly can to respect you and have

18   your trust in doing that.

19   Justice Silver, thank you from the

20   bottom of my heart.

21   GOVERNOR SISOLAK: Thank you.

22   Do we have anyone wishing to speak in

23   Carson City in support of this applicant?

24   Come forward, please.

25   MR. KIRSHBAUM: Good morning,

1   Governor Sisolak, Attorney General Ford, Chief

2   Justice Gibbons, and the remainder of the Nevada

3   Supreme Court Justices.

4   My name is Jonathan Kirshbaum. I'm an

5   Assistant Federal Public Defender, and the Chief of

6   our Non-Capital Habeas Unit.

7   I've known Frank to over four years

8   now, dating back to when my office was appointed to

9   represent him on his habeas appeal before the Ninth

10   Circuit. That case is over, but Frank and I have

11   remained in contact.

12   In fact, I'm happy to call Frank LaPena

13   my friend. I know I may look young, but I've been

14   an attorney for a long time, almost 25 years now,

15   and I never would have imagined calling one of my

16   clients friends. But it is true, Frank is my

17   friend, and it is a reflection of the person who

18   he is. He is a wonderful human being.

19   And in the four years that I've known

20   him, I have gotten a chance to know Frank quite

21   well. I had the true pleasure of attending Frank's

22   80th birthday party at his house last year, and I

23   actually brought one of my daughters with me.

24   Frank's house was packed with friends and family,

25   all celebrating someone who they cared deeply

1   about.

2   It was a wonderful experience. And I

3   just hope that when I turn 80, if I am so lucky to

4   make it that far, I have as many people who care

5   about me as there are who care about Frank.

6   But it isn't any wonder why there are

7   so many people who feel that way about Frank. All

8   of my experiences with Frank have led me to believe

9   that I don't know anyone more worthy of grace than

10   Frank LaPena.

11   Frank is a truly exceptional person.

12   He exudes positive energy in his zest for life.

13   People are drawn to him because he is warm and

14   funny and kind.

15   I've seen how lovingly he treats his

16   wife Betty, his two pets, Sampson his dog and Sheba

17   his cat, and the rest of his family and friends,

18   including his brother-in-law and best friend who

19   is now deceased, Tommy, who I know is looking down

20   from above with his one good beautiful eye.

21   I've also had the benefit of seeing him

22   in action at his job at the Mob Museum. It's

23   enthralling. His enthusiasm for what he does is

24   inspiring. People are captivated by his

25   storytelling, and just love to be around him.

```
 1              I've read the glowing reviews he
 2    receives both from his employer as well as from
 3    the visitors.  The Mob Museum has welcomed him in
 4    as a member of their family, all thanks to Oscar
 5    Goodman, who connected him to the Mob Museum.  And
 6    it is easy to see that his joyfulness makes an
 7    impact on people's lives.
 8              The best way to see Frank as a person
 9    is to look at how he lives his life.  Both when he
10    was inside prison, and the many years now that he
11    has been out, he stays out of trouble completely.
12    No disciplinary incidents in over 20 years while
13    in prison.  That is remarkable.  No issues once
14    released; just as remarkable.
15              Frank follows the rules of society.
16    He wants to play a role in bettering the lives
17    around him, that is all he cares to do, everybody
18    who knows him knows that is true.
19              But there is another aspect of his life
20    that is exceptional, and that's his criminal case.
21    I spent hours and hours diving deep into his case,
22    just like Justice Silver did.  It was fascinating.
23    It was a case that grabbed headlines for years.
24    The number of astounding twists and turns, as well
25    as the colorful and famous participants, including
```

1   Oscar Goodman and Harry Reid, both who represented
2   Frank at different times, made the case cinematic,
3   and in fact quite legendary in Nevada.
4   But my personal opinion, after reading
5   thousands and thousands of documents in this case,
6   is that it is exceptional because there are just so
7   many unanswered questions.
8   And I was not the only one to hold that
9   opinion. These questions date all the way back to
10 the Nevada Supreme Court's first of its many
11 opinions in this case back in 1976.
12   In a petition that Oscar Goodman filed
13 after the preliminary hearing -- and as an aside,
14 Oscar Goodman loves to describe the preliminary
15 hearing as the longest one in Nevada history. Now
16 personally, I don't know that's true, I don't know
17 if you can even verify that, but it's part of the
18 legend of this case.
19   And in the appeal in that petition -
20 and this has been talked about already - two
21 Justices drafted a lengthy dissent explaining the
22 reasons why there wasn't even sufficient probable
23 cause in Frank's case. As was stated in that
24 dissent about the evidence, nothing plus nothing
25 plus nothing is nothing.

SILVER STATE COURT REPORTERS dbartgis@nvbell.net

1   And one significant part of that

2 dissent was its take-down of the State's farfetched

3 theory connecting Frank to the case. From its

4 inception, that theory never made one ounce of

5 sense.

6   But the questions and the exceptional

7 aspects of this case did not end there. There was

8 Weakland's recantations, done under great danger

9 to Weakland, at both Frank and Rosalie's separate

10 trials, Rosalie's acquittal - Rosalie was the

11 co-defendant - the Nevada Supreme Court's reversal

12 of Frank's first conviction, the promises made

13 to Weakland to get him to un-recant, which put

14 Weakland, the murderer, back on the street, the

15 years and years the defense spent in an

16 unsuccessful attempt to get a crucial witness to

17 appear at the second trial, a witness who seemed

18 to have an important knowledge about what may have

19 really happened here.

20   Then there was the grant of

21 post-conviction relief in the District Court, but

22 followed by the Nevada Supreme Court reversing

23 that grant. But even that decision was over a

24 dissenting Justice who stated that Frank's

25 conviction is subject to so many questions and

1   weaknesses that it would be burdensome to recount

2   them in this dissenting opinion.

3   And the exceptional twists and turns

4   did not even end when the State Court case was

5   over. In a moment unprecedented in Nevada history

6   - and Miss Wildeveld read that statement here - a

7   former Chief Justice of the Nevada Supreme Court

8   made a public statement on Frank's behalf,

9   indicating that he had evidence that Frank was

10 merely a patsy, and stuck smack-dab in the middle

11 of all this was Weakland, who one Judge has

12 described as the notorious perjurer.

13   He was the one who linked Frank to this

14 case. And his role here is the craziest of them

15 all, and Justice Silver did a really good job of

16 describing this. While he admitted to the murder,

17 his testimony about how that murder happened

18 doesn't match the evidence of the crime scene

19 in almost every conceivable way. It's as if he

20 had no personal knowledge of how the murder

21 actually happened. It's truly confounding.

22   Now my office went in hoping for

23 answers, probably naively as it was 40 years

24 after the crime, but all we could do was come

25 up with more and more intractable questions.

1   But I'm not here to necessarily to

2   talk about the guilt or innocence, that's not

3   why I brought all this up. We were just lawyers

4   working on this case, so all of these questions,

5   they weighed on us, but I could only imagine how

6   much they weighed on Frank.

7   He had to experience this case, this

8   crazy criminal case for 40 years, experiencing

9   all of its twists and turns, and shouldering the

10   weight of all of these intractable questions, yet

11   through all of it Frank persevered.

12   He had years and years of hard time,

13   and he came out the other end still standing as

14   a carrying and giving individual. Those

15   experiences did not make him cynical or lead him

16   to carry ill-feelings towards anyone. To the

17   contrary, I have never met a more positive person

18   than Frank. When he faces adversity, he refuses

19   to buckle. He always looks at the bright side.

20   It happens every single time. He simply never

21   gives up hope. He never stopped believing that

22   if you do right, good things will happen.

23   We saw it throughout his case. He

24   was released from custody multiple times after

25   favorable court decisions, and each time he was

SILVER STATE COURT REPORTERS dbartgis@nvbell.net

1   ordered back to custody, he immediately and

2   voluntarily returned.

3   He also turned down a deal, which was

4   mentioned before, for time served after his first

5   conviction was vacated, because he trusted that the

6   system will do him justice. He has always believed

7   in himself and our criminal justice system. He's

8   always just wanted to do the right thing.

9   His positivity and enthusiasm for life

10   is infectious. It is a true sign of who he is. He

11   is an exceptional individual, and he is worthy of

12   grace.

13   Thank you.

14   GOVERNOR SISOLAK: Thank you.

15   Anyone else in Carson City wishing to

16   speak on behalf of this application?

17   Okay. I'm going to make a statement

18   here. I already got started, normally this would

19   be limited to three minutes, and you're going way

20   over the three minutes, so if we could try to keep

21   it concise I would appreciate it. We've got a

22   lengthy agenda.

23   MR. KIRSHBAUM: I'm sorry, Your Honor.

24   GOVERNOR SISOLAK: No problem.

25   MR. ALLEN: Good morning again, Your

1   Honorable Board, Governor Sisolak.

2   My name is James Allen.

3   And I'm sorry, to the Justices, Chief

4   Justice, and Attorney General Ford, I'm here for

5   Frank because Frank made an impression on me. As

6   I said earlier, I'm a former death row inmate.

7   Frank was the Senior Law Clerk at Nevada State

8   Prison, and he was the only one allowed to come

9   up to the condemned man's unit.

10   When he would come up there, I didn't

11 want to see him. I didn't want to hear nothing he

12 had to tell me. These people are going to execute

13 me. I took a person's life. But Frank had the

14 patience to stand in front of my cell door, and

15 no matter how much grief I gave him, he stood

16 there: I'm going to bring you law books, you got

17 to learn what happened to you, you're not going to

18 be ignorant, you're going to learn the law, and

19 you're going to learn Nevada's law, how they came

20 to this decision about your life.

21   Me and Frank developed a bond. When I

22 was released off of death row, Frank was one of the

23 guys to meet me on the yard. He took me in; he got

24 me my first job. I ran books up and down the

25 prison yard, law books, $10 an hour -- I mean $10 a

1   month, I'm sorry. $10 an hour; imagine that.

2   But anyway, I owe so much of the person

3   who I am today because of Frank.

4   When I was released in 2008, Frank

5   stepped up, got me a job at the Mob Museum; not in

6   2008, because the Museum has only been open seven,

7   eight years. But Frank was instrumental in getting

8   me in at the Mob Museum, and now we both are one of

9   the main staples, because one of the chairs from

10   the chamber is at the museum, and guess who gets to

11   tell that story? I do. All because of Frank.

12   And when Mr. Oscar Goodman come in, and

13   the other dignitaries - you know, I think you've

14   even been there, Mr. Sisolak, Governor Sisolak -

15   but I say all this to say that Frank is deserving

16   of a pardon.

17   I'm on a lifetime supervision of

18   parole, and if I was in front of this Board I would

19   want someone to come up and speak on my character,

20   my good traits about me, my personality.

21   Frank is a good man, and he deserves

22   to have a life of freedom to travel.

23   The guy that you were speaking on,

24   Jerry Weakland, I saw this man stand in front of a

25   group of Aryan Warriors at Nevada State Prison and

1 told them, you're not going to kill him. And

2 everybody hated Jerry Weakland from what he did to

3 Frank. But Frank stood there and said: No, you're

4 not going to stab him. You're not going to kill

5 this man.

6

7 And that's why Jerry Weakland gets to

8 walk around today, because Nevada State Prison

9 wasn't no joke in the late 70's early 80's. If

10 they wanted to take you out, you're going to be

11 taken out.

12 The only reason they were going to do

13 that for Frank, because Frank did their law work.

14 He did everybody's law work, he helped them out,

15 he showed them how to get their sentences reduced,

16 you know, how to get to the Pardons Board, how to

17 approach the Parole Board; he just took patience

18 and did that for us.

19 When I stood in front of somebody and

20 said, you know, the person that testified against

21 me and put me on death row, maybe not at that time,

22 maybe not at that time - I was a young, ignorant

23 fool - but Frank, still a young man at that time,

24 wouldn't let nobody do anything to that man.

25 And he deserves this pardon today.

Thank you, guys.

```
1              GOVERNOR SISOLAK:  Thank you very much.
2              Anyone else in Carson City wishing to
3     testify on behalf of this applicant?
4              (No Response)
5              GOVERNOR SISOLAK:  Seeing no one, do we
6     have anyone in Las Vegas to testify on behalf of
7     this applicant?
8              MS. HEDRICK:  Governor, no one is
9     coming forward.
10             GOVERNOR SISOLAK:  Okay.  Anyone in
11    Carson City in opposition to this applicant?
12             (No Response)
13             GOVERNOR SISOLAK:  Seeing no one,
14    anyone in Las Vegas in opposition to this
15    applicant?
16             (No Response)
17             MS. HEDRICK:  You may proceed,
18    Governor.
19             GOVERNOR SISOLAK:  Thank you.
20             I will turn it over to the Board.
21             CHIEF JUSTICE GIBBONS:  Governor, can
22    I make a comment about this?
23             GOVERNOR SISOLAK:  Please.
24             CHIEF JUSTICE GIBBONS:  Thank you,
25    Mr. LaPena for your comments.
```

SILVER STATE COURT REPORTERS dbartgis@nvbell.net

1   I might say I was here, I think the

2   only one on this Board that was here in 2003. I

3   do remember this, and it was a compelling case for

4   actual innocence, and fortunately, the right thing

5   was done in the law.

6   So I appreciate Justice Silver,

7   everything she did as well on that.

8   So Justice Silver, did you want to make

9   the motion or let me --

10   JUSTICE SILVER: Yes. I'll make the

11   motion.

12   CHIEF JUSTICE GIBBONS: Okay.

13   JUSTICE STIGLICH: You have to make the

14   motion.

15   JUSTICE SILVER: For the

16   recommendation, which is the unconditional pardon

17   without the right to bear arms.

18   GOVERNOR SISOLAK: Okay.

19   JUSTICE PARRAGUIRRE: I'll second.

20   GOVERNOR SISOLAK: I've got a question

21   about that.

22   The application was for a pardon

23   without the right, but then you make the case,

24   Miss Wildeveld, that let's throw that in, too. I

25   don't know, you're asking for something that he

1   didn't ask for, so.

2   MR. LaPENA: Right, Governor

3   (inaudible).

4   JUSTICE HARDESTY: You need the mike.

5   MR. LaPENA: No, I didn't see any

6   reason to bear arms any longer. I did it in the

7   Military. I've never, when I got out, I never

8   purchased a weapon, I never went anywhere to shoot

9   another weapon, and weapons get you in trouble. So

10   I don't really need one, Your Honor.

11   GOVERNOR SISOLAK: Okay. Thank you

12   very much.

13   (CROSS-TALK)

14   MR. LaPENA: I'm fine with out one.

15   GOVERNOR SISOLAK: I appreciate it.

16   Okay. Thank you.

17   We have a motion on the floor and a

18   second.

19   Is there any discussion on that motion?

20   (No Response)

21   GOVERNOR SISOLAK: Seeing none, do you

22   want to take a role call?

23

24   MS. DAVIS:

25   JUSTICE SILVER: YES

1	MS. DAVIS:	
2	JUSTICE CADISH:	YES
3	JUSTICE STIGLICH:	YES
4	JUSTICE PARRAGUIRRE:	YES
5	JUSTICE HARDESTY:	YES
6	JUSTICE PICKERING:	YES
7	CHIEF JUSTICE GIBBONS:	YES
8	ATTORNEY GENERAL FORD:	YES
9	GOVERNOR SISOLAK:	YES

10

11   MS. DAVIS: Motion passes.

12   GOVERNOR SISOLAK: Congratulations. I

13   hope you catch your plane.

14   MR. LaPENA: Thank you.

15   GOVERNOR SISOLAK: Thank you.

16   (12:12 p.m.)

17   -oOo-

18

19

20

21

22

23

24

25

SILVER STATE COURT REPORTERS dbartgis@nvbell.net

```
STATE OF NEVADA,        )
                        )        ss.
COUNTY OF WASHOE.       )
```

I, DEBRA J. BARTGIS, Certified Court Reporter #56, do hereby certify:

That onWednesday, November 6, 2019 at 9:00 a.m. thereof, at the Supreme Court Building, 201 South Carson Street, 2nd Floor, Carson City, Nevada, I was present and took stenotype notes of the Meeting held before the NEVADA BOARD OF PARDONS in the within-entitled matters, and thereafter transcribed the same as herein appears;

That the foregoing transcript is a full, true and correct transcription of my stenotype notes of said Meeting.

DATED: At Sparks, Nevada, this 22nd day of November 2019.

/ss Debra J. Bartgis
_____
Debra J. Bartgis, CCR #56

APPENDIX

THE END

Made in the USA
Las Vegas, NV
01 November 2022

58598560R00227